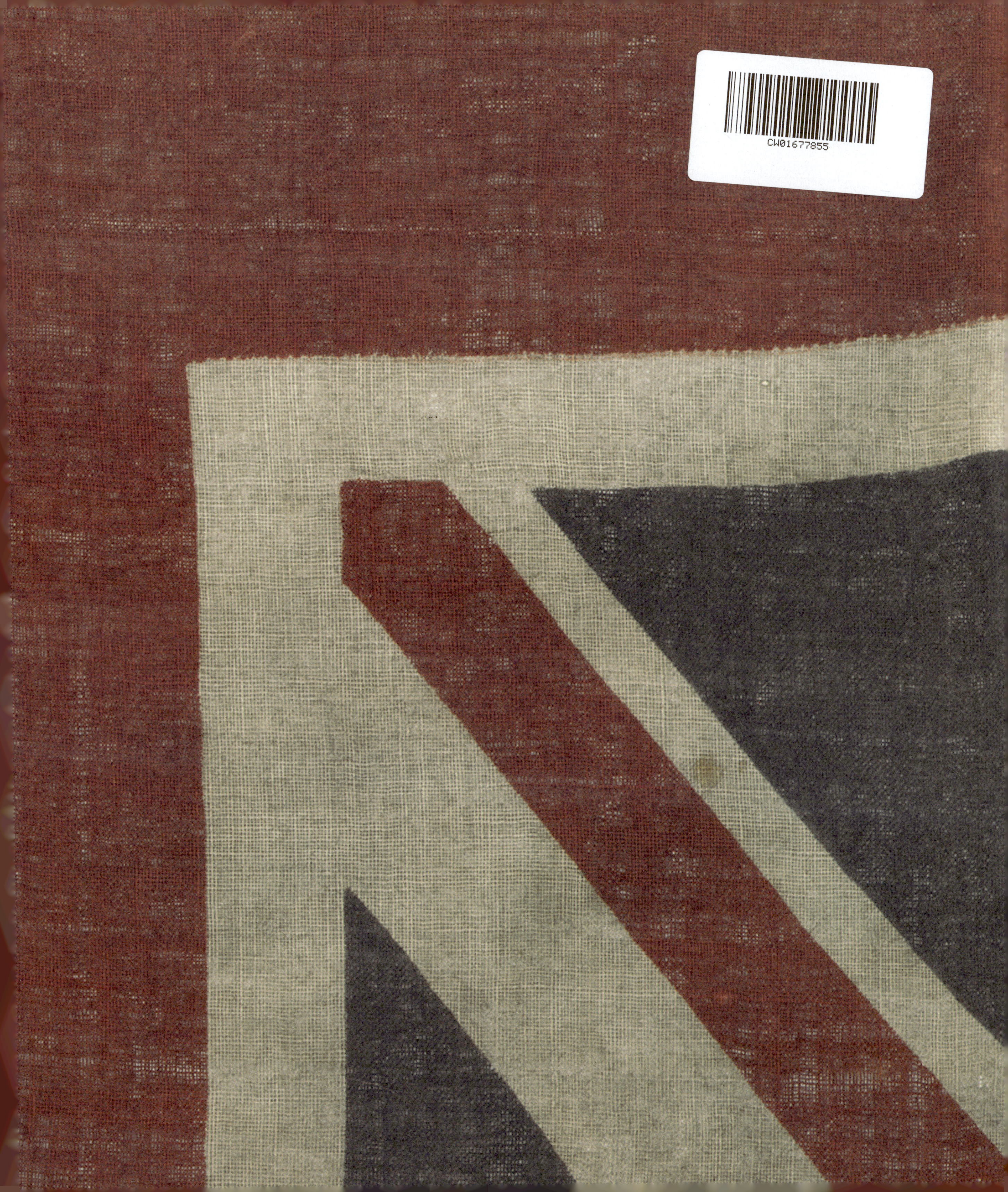

Peter Blake

one man show

Peter Blake

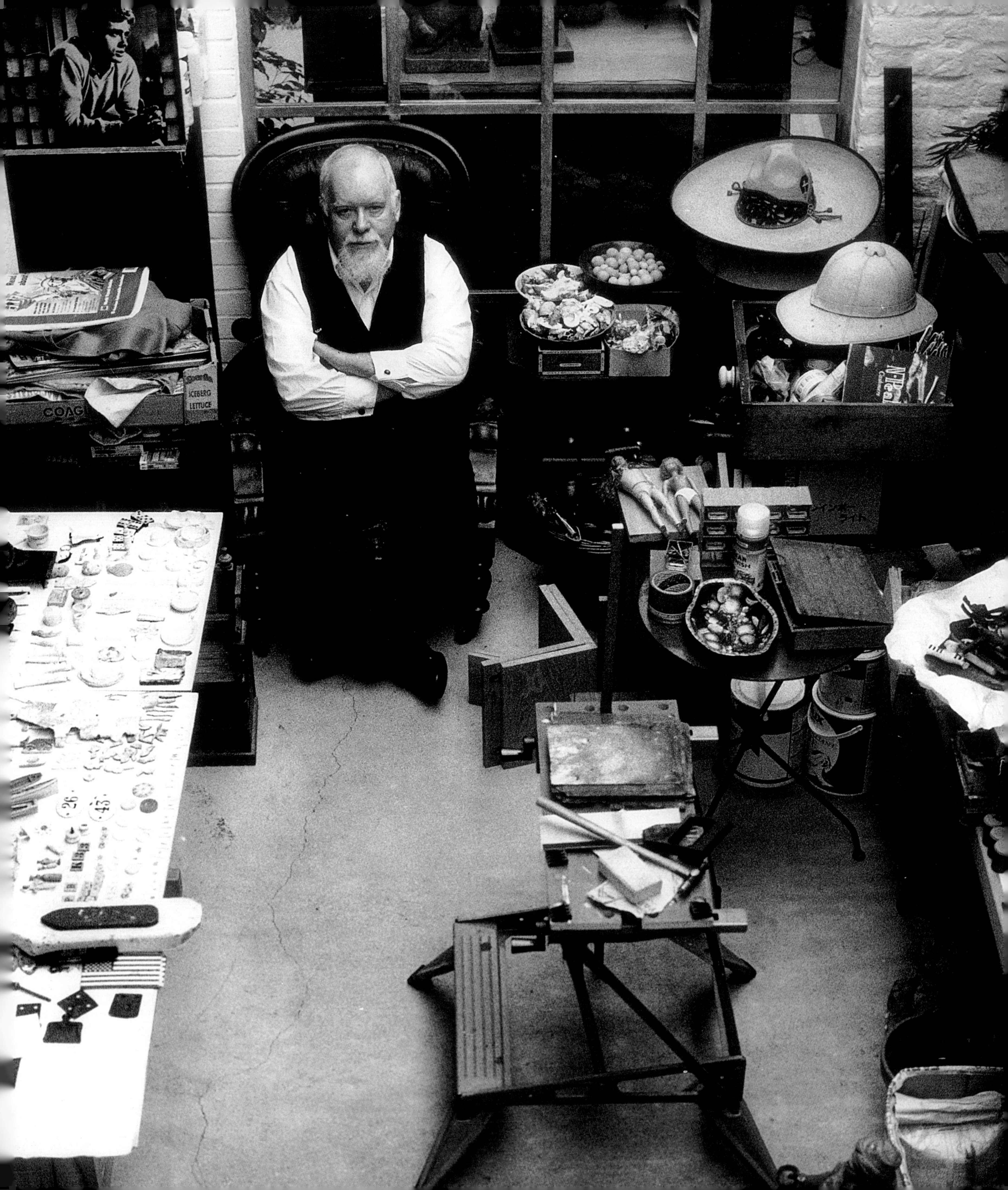
ICEBERG
LETTUCE
COAG
26
43

Peter Blake
one man show

Marco Livingstone

Lund Humphries

First published in 2009 by Lund Humphries

Lund Humphries
Wey Court East
Union Road
Farnham
Surrey GU9 7PT

and

Suite 420
101 Cherry Street
Burlington
VT 05401-4405
USA
www.lundhumphries.com
Lund Humphries is part of Ashgate Publishing

British Library Cataloguing-in-Publication Data
A catalogue record for this book is available from the British Library

ISBN: 978-0-85331-980-1 (hardback)
ISBN: 978-1-84822-015-7 (paperback)
ISBN: 978-1-84822-039-3 (special edition)

Library of Congress Control Number: 2008932973

Designed by Herman Lelie and Stefania Bonelli
Set in Scala and Helvetica Neue Condensed
Edited by Howard Watson
Origination by MRM Graphics Ltd Winslow Bucks
Printed in Thailand

Jacket: *Marcel Duchamp's World Tour: The Tarzan Family*, 1995–2005
Frontispiece: Peter Blake in his studio, photographed by Mary McCartney
Collages, Peter Blake, 2008: pp 18–19, 48–9, 84–5, 136–7, 152–3, 182–3, 218–9

Contents

This book, first discussed with Peter Blake 19 years ago, is dedicated
to Stephen Stuart-Smith, my partner of 19 years,
and to my nephew, Stephen Huws, on his 19th birthday

Acknowledgements

Since first writing about Peter Blake's work in the context of a review of his stunning Tate Gallery retrospective of 1983 I have had many occasions for commenting on different aspects and periods of his work, sometimes in the catalogues of solo exhibitions and often, too, as part of a broader examination of Pop Art, in which he has played such a leading role. Peter and I first discussed the possibility of my writing a monograph on his work immediately after the publication of my book *Pop Art: A Continuing History* in 1990. It has taken nearly two decades to find the right publisher and circumstances with which to bring this finally to fruition. Given the long gestation period of many of Blake's celebrated paintings, and his habit of reconsidering and reworking them over years and even decades, it feels oddly appropriate that this book should also have taken longer to bring to the public than any other I have written. This long passage of time has also given me the opportunity to interweave fragments of some of my previously published texts on him into a new narrative, not so much as a compendium of my writing on him as a summation of my thoughts on his multifaceted art over the period of 25 years that I have been most closely examining it. During this time I have spoken at regular intervals to the artist, written about developments as they happened and formed a perspective on more than half a century of intense productivity and inventiveness.

Blake had long put off having a major monograph published on his work out of feelings that the right time for it had not yet come and that his art was still in transition. Happily he has now decided, in his mid-seventies, to give his enthusiastic support to just such a publication, knowing that both the ideas and the paint continue to flow in as lively and committed a fashion as ever. Having amusingly declared himself first to have retired from the fray at the age of 65 and to have now entered his 'late period', he can afford himself the satisfaction of looking back on his own evolution as an artist, knowing that there is much more still to come.

To Peter and to his wife Chrissy, who has also been as tireless in her support of this publication as of the artist's many other activities, I would like to express my warm appreciation. The respect and affection with which I hold the artist and his work should be self-evident from the text that follows. Leslie Waddington and his staff, particularly Louise Shorr, have greatly facilitated my research and the very existence of this book. My thanks, too, to all at Lund Humphries: to its chairman, Nigel Farrow, and commissioning editor, Lucy Myers, for their enthusiasm in taking this on, and to its head of editorial and production, Miranda Harrison, for seeing it through. The editing process has been unusually painless thanks to Lucy's very helpful initial comments and to Howard Watson's close scrutiny and tactful editing. For their roles in carrying out the picture research, we are all greatly indebted to Alex Hitchins and Emma Brown, as we are to Joan Dearnley in compiling the index. Herman Lelie and his partner Stefania Bonelli, with whom I had the pleasure of working on a previous Lund Humphries book, the monograph on Patrick Caulfield published in 2005, have again brought a clarity and clean simplicity to their design of this volume; their appreciation of the precise visual qualities of Blake's art and their attentiveness to the marriage of text and image make this book a joy to read and experience.

A great amount of information about Blake's early life, through to his arrival at the Royal College of Art at the age of 21 in 1953, is recounted by the artist in some 20 hours of interviews with Linda Sandino for the Artists' Lives series of oral histories being gathered together for the British Library Sound Archive. Though he was coming up to his 71st birthday when these conversations began on 22 April 2003, his candid memories even of his early childhood remained as astonishingly clear and detailed as the facial features in his mature paintings. All this will be of great value to future biographers and social historians alike. The present volume, in concentrating on Blake's art rather than on his life, will touch on these circumstances as and when such facts substantially help to illuminate the art.

As always, a special word of gratitude to Stephen Stuart-Smith for his forbearance in listening to me talk incessantly about the book while I was working on it, and for carrying some of the weight of the anxiety that always accompanies me when I embark on a new piece of writing. Since he shares my love of Peter's work and my fondness for Peter himself, I knew that I could count on him to bolster my enthusiasm when writing about one of Britain's most deservedly popular artists.

1 **Locker** (open), 1959

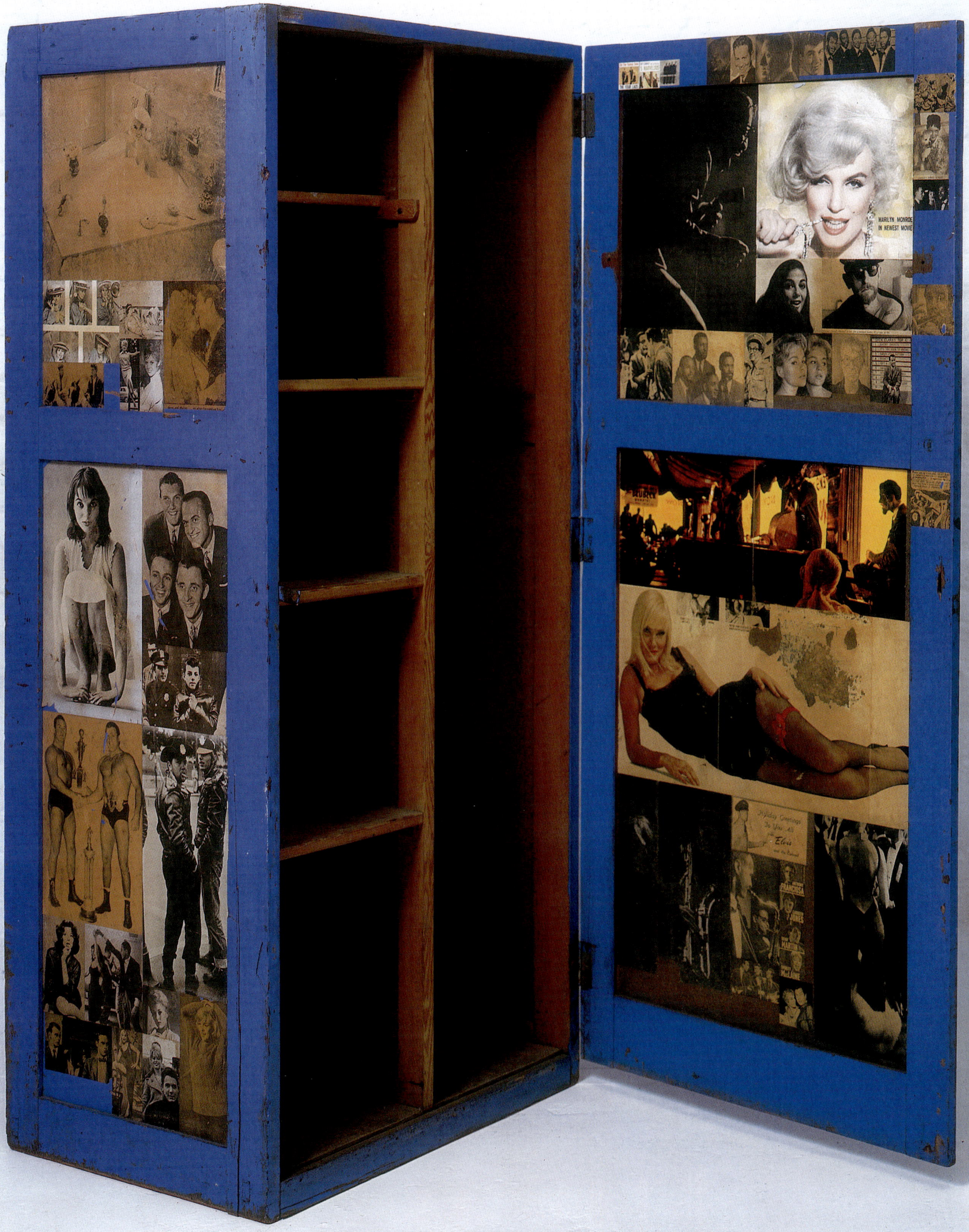
MARILYN MONROE
IN NEWEST MOVIE

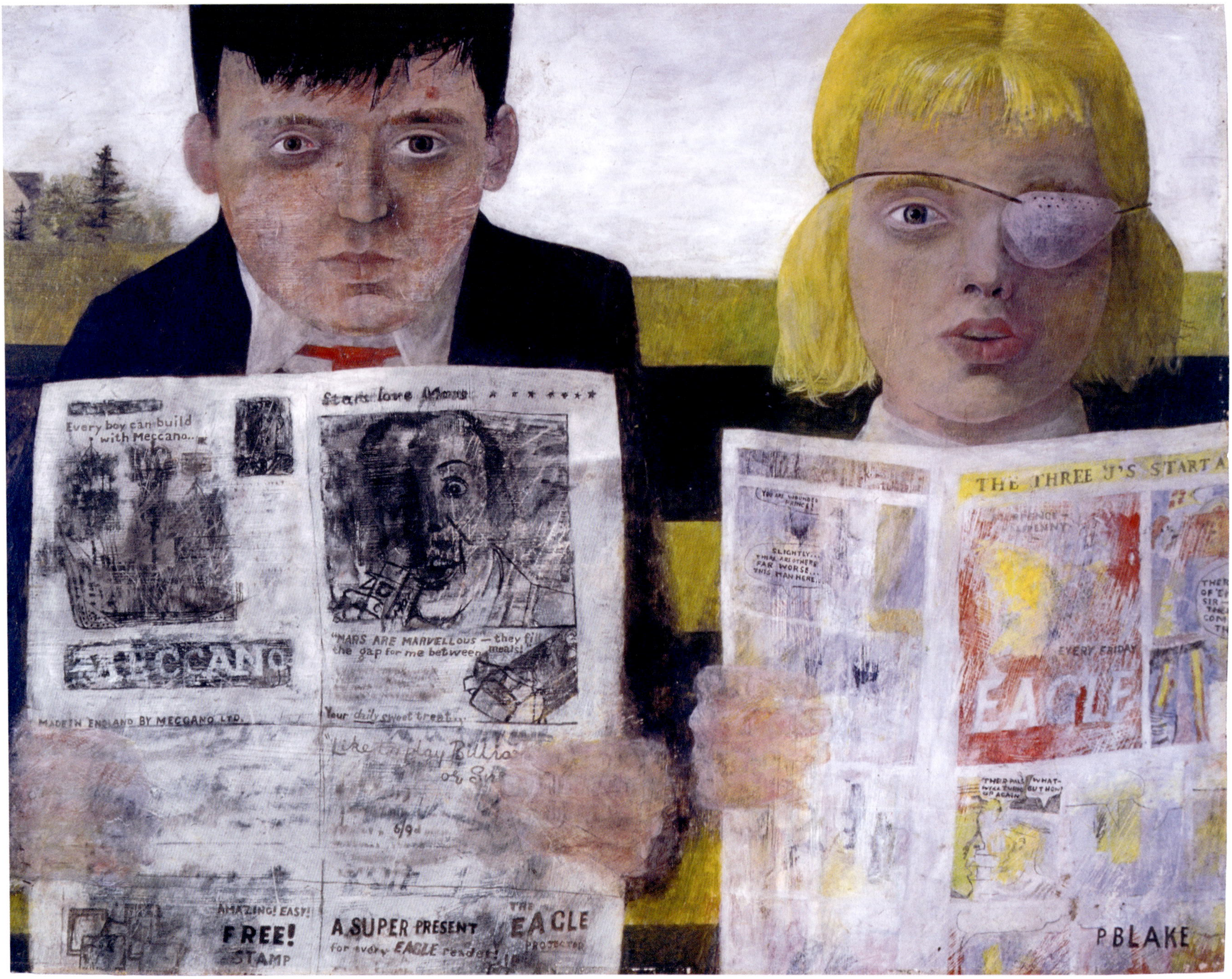

2 **Children Reading Comics**, 1954

Introduction

Born on 25 June 1932 into a working-class family in Dartford, Kent, on the south-eastern fringes of London, Blake developed an early taste for many kinds of popular entertainments including the cinema, the circus, wrestling matches, jazz and popular music. All of these passions found their way naturally into his art by the time he was in his early twenties as a postgraduate student at the Royal College of Art in London between 1953 and 1956. During the same years that older artists such as the Scottish sculptor Eduardo Paolozzi (born 1924) and the English painter Richard Hamilton (born 1922) were laying the theoretical basis for Pop Art through their participation in the Independent Group, a collection of radical artists, architects and critics who met at the Institute of Contemporary Artists in London, Blake was creating his first proto-Pop pictures as a direct, unpretentious and sincere response to his immersion in popular culture. Some of the earliest of these, such as *Children Reading Comics* (1954, Plate 2), in which he depicted himself as a boy with his younger sister, were explicitly autobiographical. These established a precedent for celebrated later works such as *Self-Portrait with Badges* (1961, Plate 40), in which he displays himself festooned with metal badges and clutching an Elvis Presley fan club magazine.

In his paintings of imaginary circus performers (such as 1955's *Loelia, World's Most Tattooed Lady*, Plate 21) or invented wrestlers (beginning with *Baron Adolf Kaiser* in 1961–3, Plate 81), Blake positioned himself in the role of the admiring fan. He stated this even more obviously in his first full-blown Pop pictures from 1959, in which photographic images – either of movie stars such as Kim Novak and Tuesday Weld (Plate 47) or of popular musicians including Frank Sinatra and the Everly Brothers (Plate 3) – were glued onto hardboard panels that were brightly decorated in primary colours to resemble fragments of doors and walls. The notions of the celebrity icon and of the passionate fan, each needing the other for sustenance, first emerged as important themes in Blake's work at that time.

Blake's art is firmly grounded in the working-class existence that he led as a child and teenager, and in his academic training in disciplines including life drawing and lettering. The artist's early family life and his art-school education at Gravesend School of Art provide a touchstone for an understanding of his later development and of the nostalgic impulses at work in much of his mature art. The yearning for the innocence of childhood that gives much of Blake's work a bittersweet quality is already apparent in paintings of the early to mid-1950s depicting children reading comics or going to the Saturday matinee at the cinema; his choice even of *Adam and Eve* (Plate 12) as a subject for a small painting in about 1954–5 provides evidence of this desire to return to a state of grace. Likewise, the various figurative traditions from which Blake drew sustenance in his earliest work – naturalistic and academic approaches ranging from fifteenth- and sixteenth-century Flemish and German portraiture through to nineteenth-century British and Continental precursors – have provided a constant reference point to which he has continued to return from his forays into more experimental areas.

While studying at the Royal College, Blake concerned himself with popular entertainments as both the subject matter and the source of formal solutions for his paintings. The cinema, the circus, the funfair, wrestling and popular music, previously largely neglected or derided as beneath the dignity of the fine artist, were appreciated as forms of creative expression in their own right, to be honoured for the glimpses they offer into mass culture. The very notion of presenting his own art in the guise of entertainment was a radical and iconoclastic one in its affront to the earnest seriousness and high moral tone characteristic not only of academic traditions but also of much avant-garde art of the twentieth century. Allying himself with journeymen decorators, sign painters, commercial artists and self-taught naive painters, Blake bravely and democratically declared himself as an artist of the people rather than as one who wished to address only his fellow painters or a cultural elite. He did so not only through his choice of subjects, but also by apparently submerging his own artistic identity into that of existing styles from outside fine art traditions, presenting his paintings as if they were objects he had found ready-made in a timeworn condition.

The directness with which Blake gave expression to his enthusiasms for mass culture during the 1950s – independently of the investigations of other British, American and European artists into similar areas – brought him to the forefront of the Pop Art movement before it had even been named. As soon as news filtered back to Britain in the late 1950s of the incursions into popular culture by American artists – as exemplified by the flags and targets of Jasper Johns, the 'combines' of Robert Rauschenberg and Larry Rivers's paintings based on found imagery and such banal artefacts as playing cards or restaurant menus – Blake was poised to act on his understanding of the radical implications of this new work.

The cheeky aside to Johns represented by *The First Real Target?* (1961, Plate 59), delivered in a spirit of both homage and challenge, provides evidence of the role allotted to humour in Blake's art but hints also at the importance attached by him and other artists to the question of influence and historical precedence. While much attention has rightly been given to the discussions of the Independent Group in London during the 1950s in creating an intellectual atmosphere in which Pop Art could flourish, and to the work produced by Hamilton and Paolozzi in relation to their membership of that group, Blake's early and sustained exploration of his own brand of Pop Art has often failed to be given

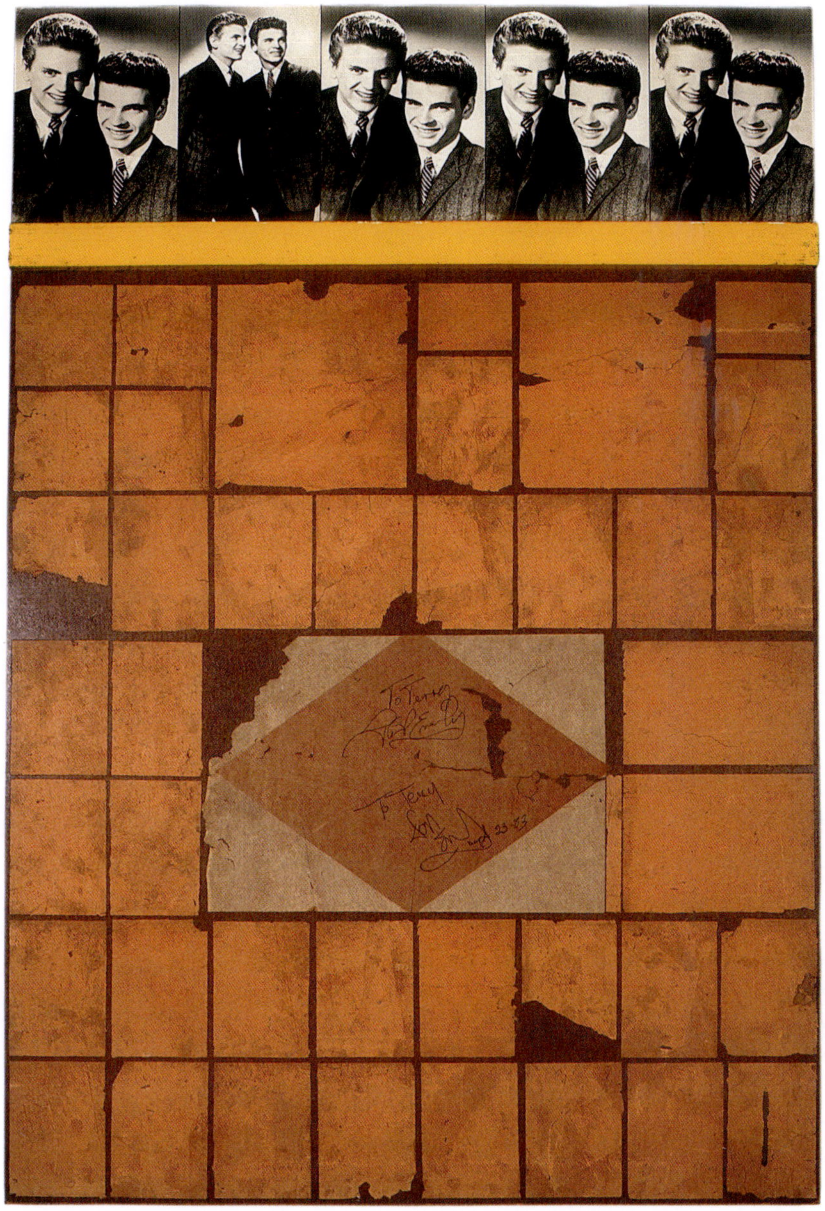

3 **Everly Wall**, 1959

due credit. The fruitful dialogue that he established both with contemporaries such as Richard Smith and Joe Tilson and with younger artists including David Hockney, Derek Boshier, Peter Phillips, Patrick Caulfield, Pauline Boty and his future wife Jann Haworth also made him a singularly influential figure within British Pop.

Momentarily setting aside the manual dexterity on which he had worked so assiduously, Blake gave vent instead to the magpie-like collecting instincts and insatiable curiosity for the artefacts of popular culture which were already at work when he travelled through Europe in 1956–7 on a Leverhulme Research Award to study popular art. His solution, in works such as *The Fine Art Bit* (Plate 37), *Everly Wall* (Plate 3) and *Girlie Door* (Plate 44)

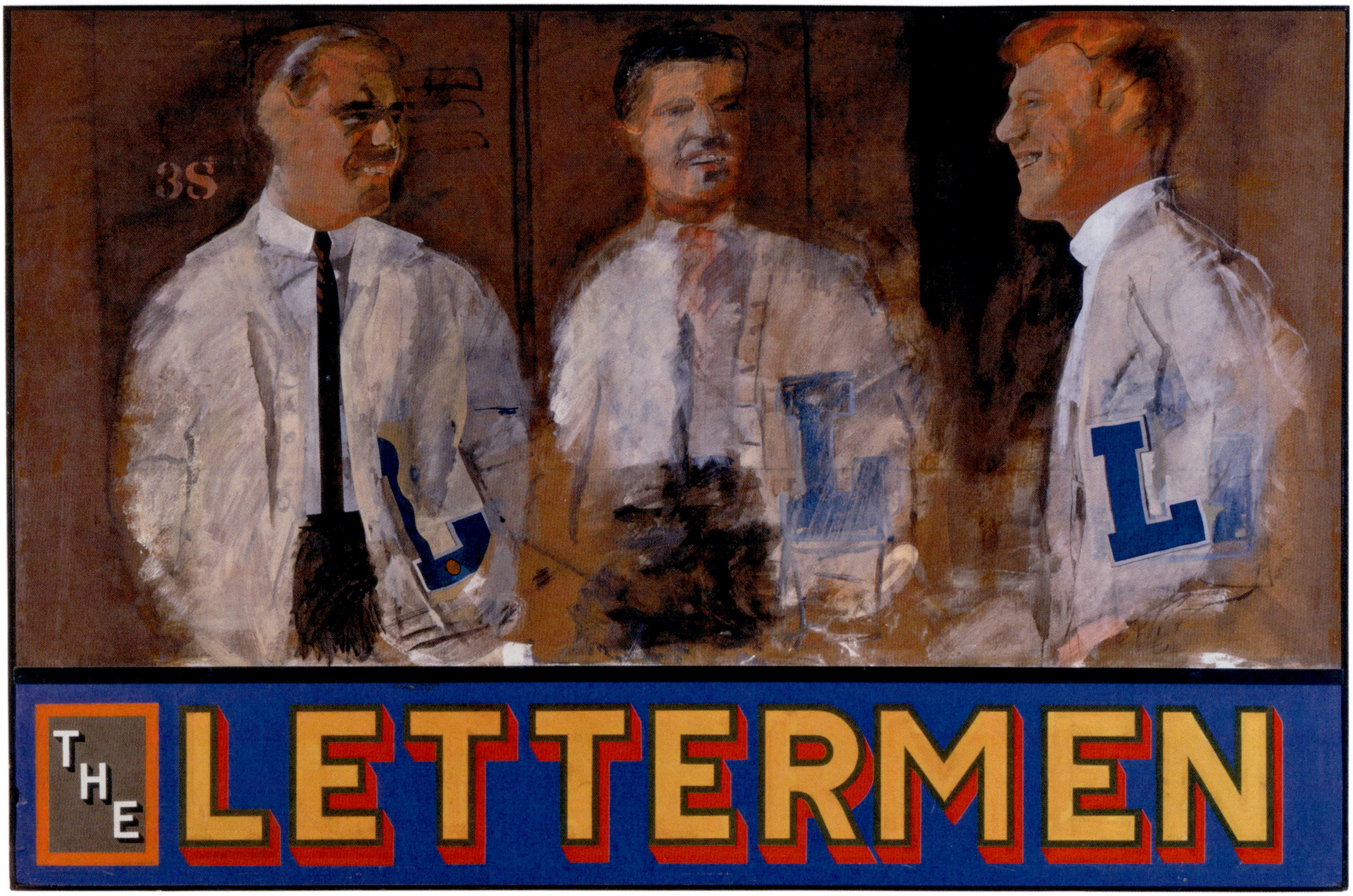

4 **The Lettermen**, 1963

of 1959, was to take his imagery ready-made from photographs, postcards, magazines and printed ephemera and to glue them onto hardboard supports painted in bright enamel colours and simple patterns to resemble fragments of doors or walls. Actual objects – including toys (for example, in *The Toy Shop* of 1962, Plate 61), a wax head and a real window (*Girl in a Window*, 1962, Plate 60), and store-bought lettering (as in *Tuesday*, 1961, Plate 47) – were soon added to the repertoire.

In the mid-1960s Blake began work on a series of large and ambitious paintings on canvas on which he was to continue to lavish his attention for more than three decades. These include *Portrait of David Hockney in a Hollywood Spanish Interior* (Plate 126) and *Tarzan and his Family at the Roxy Cinema, New York* (Plate 107), begun in 1964–5, and *A Mad Tea Party at Watts Tower* (Plate 169), begun about three years later. Their manifest skilfulness and finely rendered detail are in direct counterbalance to the overt simplicity and apparent effortlessness of the collage and found-object aesthetic of his most extreme Pop works. For these reasons alone, they deserve special attention, quite aside from their role in paving the way for Blake's 'Ruralist' style of the 1970s. Throughout his mature career, but particularly from the time of his retrospective at Bristol City Art Gallery in 1969, he had the habit of exhibiting works at different stages of completion and even of letting into the world works that he might still regard as unfinished (as he had with such apparently painterly pictures as *The Lettermen*, 1963, Plate 4). He has consistently taken a patient and unusually long-term view of his life's work.

These and related works in an essentially naturalistic style, including much later examples such as *'The Meeting' or 'Have a Nice Day, Mr Hockney'* (1981–3, Plate 180), and the considerable number of portraits painted on commission in the early 1990s represent the fulfilment of Blake's identity as a 'straight figurative painter'. With his appointment in September 1994 as the National Gallery's Associate Artist for a period of two years, he also sought to realise long-standing ambitions in relation to the Old Master paintings that had inspired him throughout his life. Although many of the paintings he made at this time were characteristically intimate and modest in scale, they reveal the depth of his feeling for traditions in western European painting established more than five centuries before his birth.

Of how many artists can it be said that inspiration has been drawn not only from such heroes of the Modernist avant-garde as Marcel Duchamp and Kurt Schwitters, but also from turn-of-the-century children's book illustrators and from Victorian fairy painters such as the obsessive Richard Dadd? As with his determination to explore different art forms, Blake considers diversity to be a virtue and one of the defining characteristics of his art. Though he may admire the single-mindedness of some of his fellow artists, he himself has always been convinced that he does not wish to be the type of painter who always does just one thing. Moreover, while other artists look constantly over their shoulders at what their contemporaries are doing, or act as self-censors of elements that might not be considered acceptable to the art establishment, Blake follows his intuitions and desires wherever they may lead him. His decisions are dictated by a single, unwritten rule: to make art that encompasses the whole of his experience, personality and view of the world. The virtues in which he sets store are almost embarrassingly old-fashioned ones – individuality, honesty, love, companionship, hope, kindness – relayed in a quiet but often humorous and self-deprecating tone.

Blake's art gains much of its strength from a vigorous interaction between public and intensely private spheres. His is a world in which we appear to be standing on firm ground, but in which strange and inexplicable events suddenly occur. By introducing us to characters in disguise, such as wrestlers notorious for playing on audience fantasies, he gently prods us to dig deep into our own imaginations and to restore something of the child still lingering within us. We may cringe at the idea of believing in fairies, but how can we remain unmoved by the magical atmosphere summoned forth in such Shakespearean paintings as *Puck, Peasebottom, Cobweb, Moth and Mustardseed* (1969–84, Plate 167) or the portrait of *Titania – Queen of the Fairies* (1977, Plate 162)? In more recent paintings, such as the *Madonna of Venice Beach* series (1990 and 1994–6, Plates 5, 195–8), he has turned his attention to other subjects deemed out of bounds in the twentieth century, again revitalising and reinventing a tradition in his own terms. The same principle by which he has revealed his works at varying stages of completion was now applied to the entire history of art as a single unit, existing in the present and in a constant state of flux: alive and kicking.

This book touches on every aspect of Blake's art over the whole of his career, but it departs continuously from a strict chronological structure. To attempt to present the work in the order in which it was made would bring up various dilemmas. Where, for example, should one situate a painting conceived in the mid-1960s but completed four decades later in a different spirit using techniques refined from a lifetime of experience? Or how can one discuss new works that reprise established themes without repeatedly going over the same ground? From a desire to be true to the spirit of Blake's creativity, and to reflect the diversity and the cyclical nature of his work, in which forms and subjects are constantly revisited, I have chosen instead to address myself to the most pressing and constant themes that have motivated Blake's creative process and that, in turn, provide the most enticing points of entry for an audience waiting to be entertained, amused, moved and dazzled by its endlessly shifting facets.

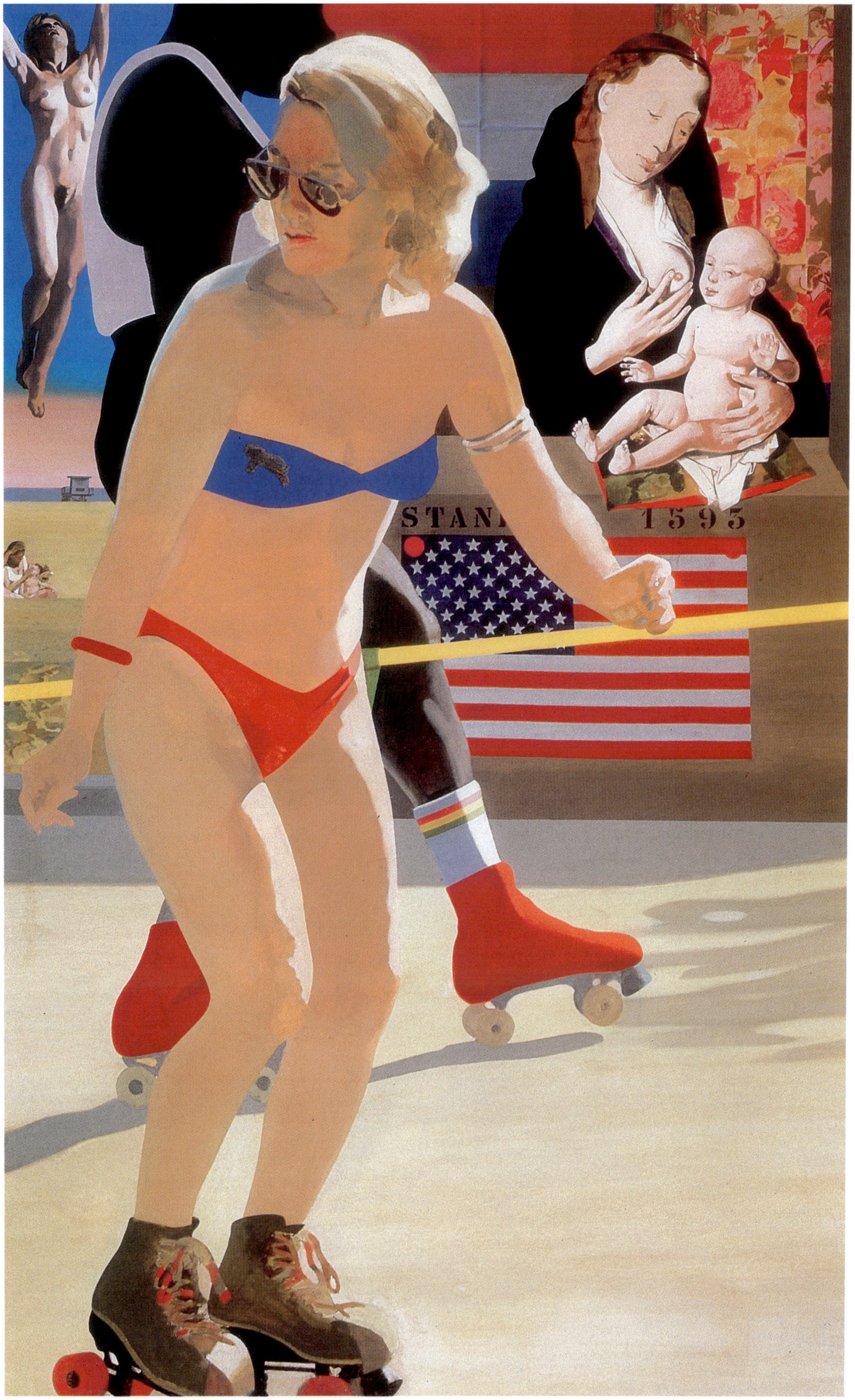

5 **Madonna of Venice Beach, No. 1**, 1994–6

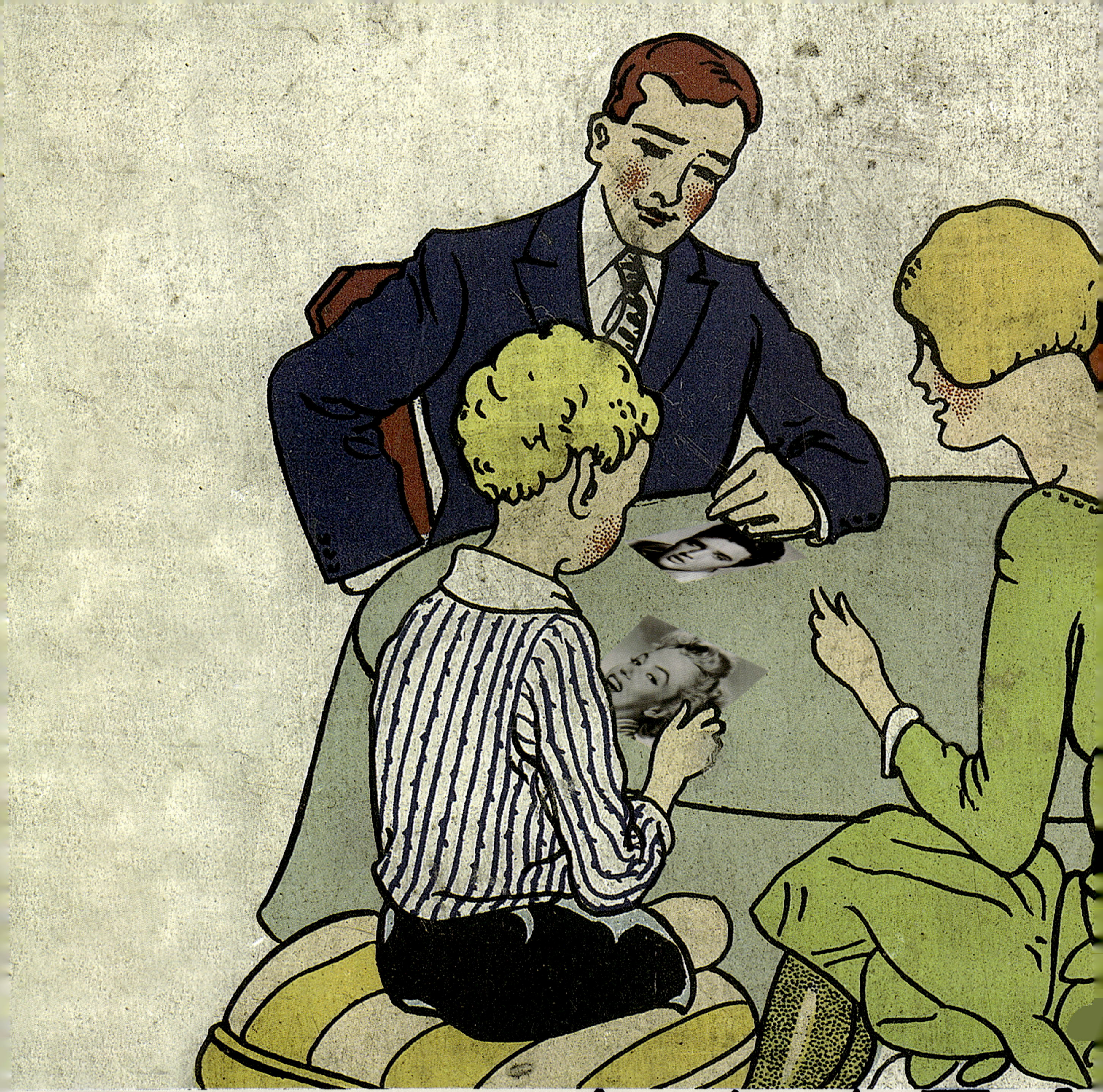

1 AMU

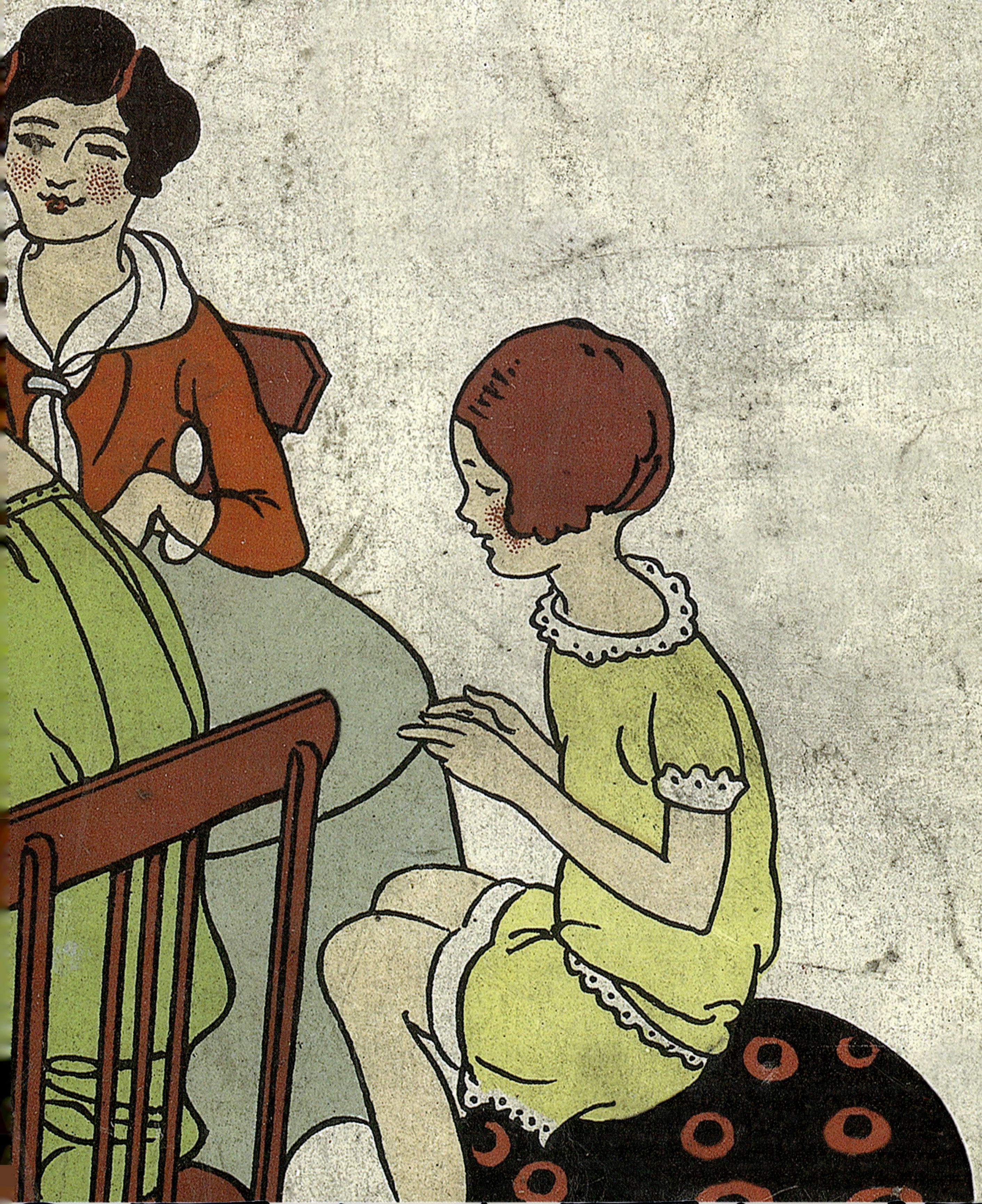

SEMENTS

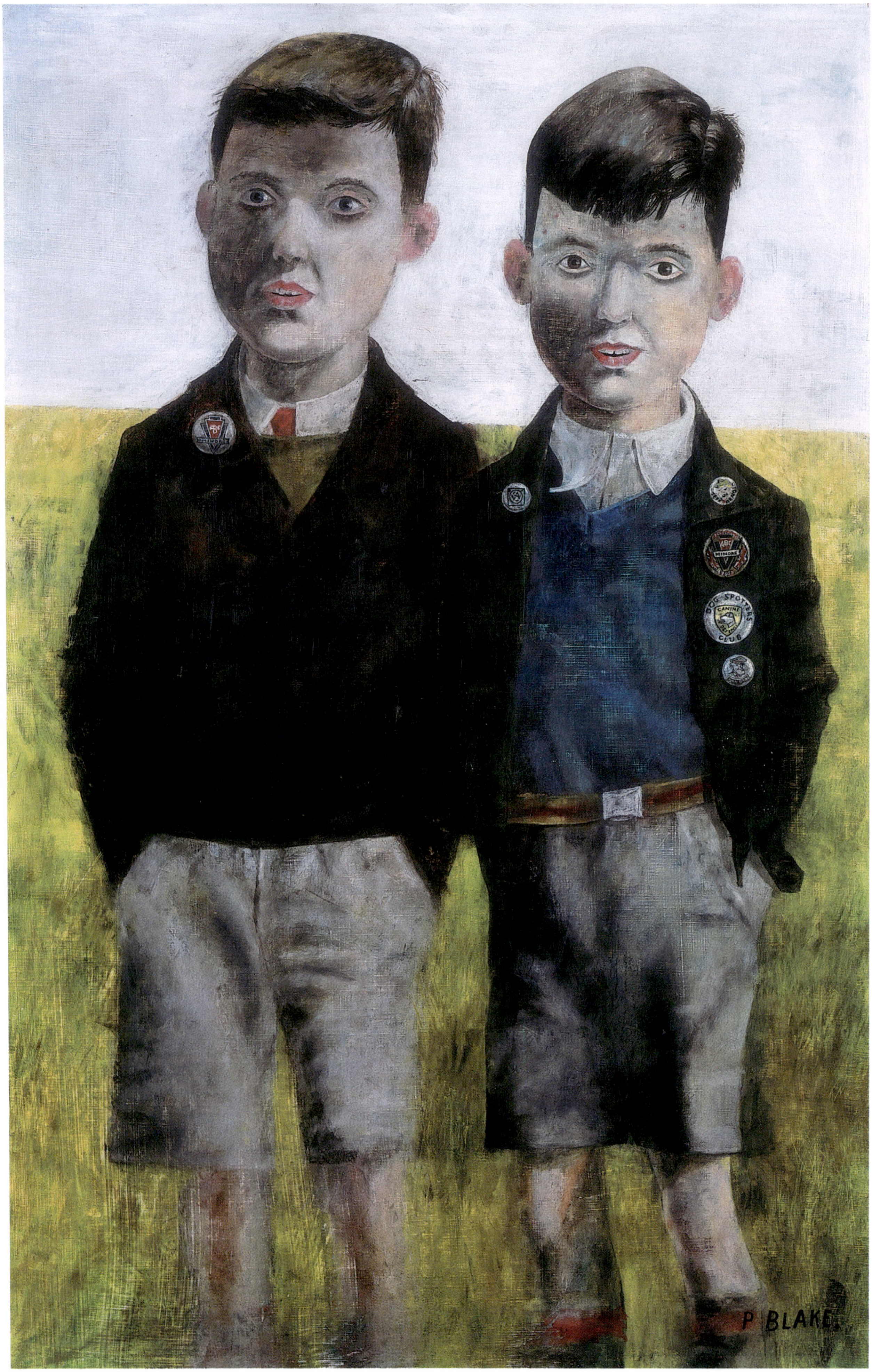

6 **ABC Minors**, 1955

1 Amusements

Childhood Memories and Youthful Experiences

Blake has vivid memories of his early life in Dartford, Kent. The house he remembers growing up in with his parents and sister Shirley (two-and-a-half years his junior) was at 9 Marcus Road. Just around the corner was the future rock star Mick Jagger, 11 years younger than Blake, who attended the same grammar school as Peter's younger brother, Terry (born on 13 September 1939, just days after Britain's entry into World War II). Blake's father, Kenneth, was an electrician, first at Vickers and from 1961 as head of his own firm. His mother, Elizabeth (known as Betty), who turned 21 a week after his birth, worked briefly as a nurse and later at Cable & Wireless as a teleprinter operator. The most significant event in his childhood was being twice evacuated with Shirley during the war, first at the age of seven, when they were placed with a rather strict family in Essex, and then when they were sent to their very eccentric grandmother's home near Worcester. Away from Dartford and from his parents and baby brother for most of the war, he consequently suffered a ruptured childhood. It is not difficult to see in these circumstances one reason for the atmosphere of deep nostalgia for childhood in Blake's mature art and even, dare one say, an element of arrested development in his innocent appreciation of toys and games, and what might be termed adolescent enthusiasms for pop music and a variety of popular entertainments.

A rather solitary boy, Peter was particularly close to his mother, under whose influence he first developed a passion for popular entertainments including the cinema, for which he has had a lifelong fascination. His oldest memories of films, which date from the age of three or four, came less than a decade after the advent of the talkies. He remembers seeing not only all the Shirley Temple films, but also *The Wizard of Oz* (still one of his favourites) and all the Walt Disney films, with Bowery Boys films always as the second feature. Many of his early heroes, as he later recalled, were these fantasy figures from the cinema: the Bowery Boys, Laurel and Hardy and, significantly, Tarzan, who was to become a recurring subject in his art from the mid-1960s onwards. When he was evacuated to Worcester in 1945, just before the end of the war, he began attending the 'ABC Minors' Saturday morning cinema club for children with his sister Shirley; his 1955 painting *ABC Minors* (Plate 6), which represents his brother Terry and a cousin, was a fond and nostalgic evocation of those often raucous occasions. From 1946, aged 14, when he was again living at home, he continued going to the cinema with his mother, though now sometimes in

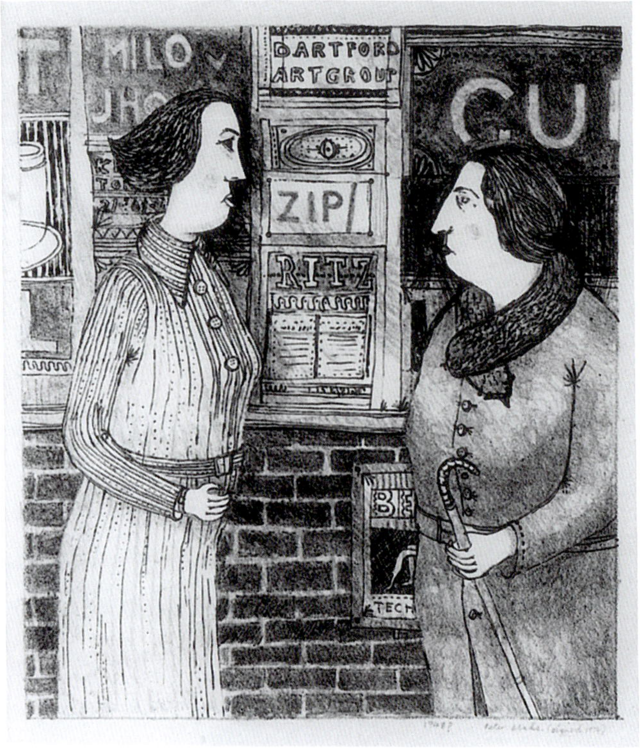

7 **Conversation**, *c.*1948

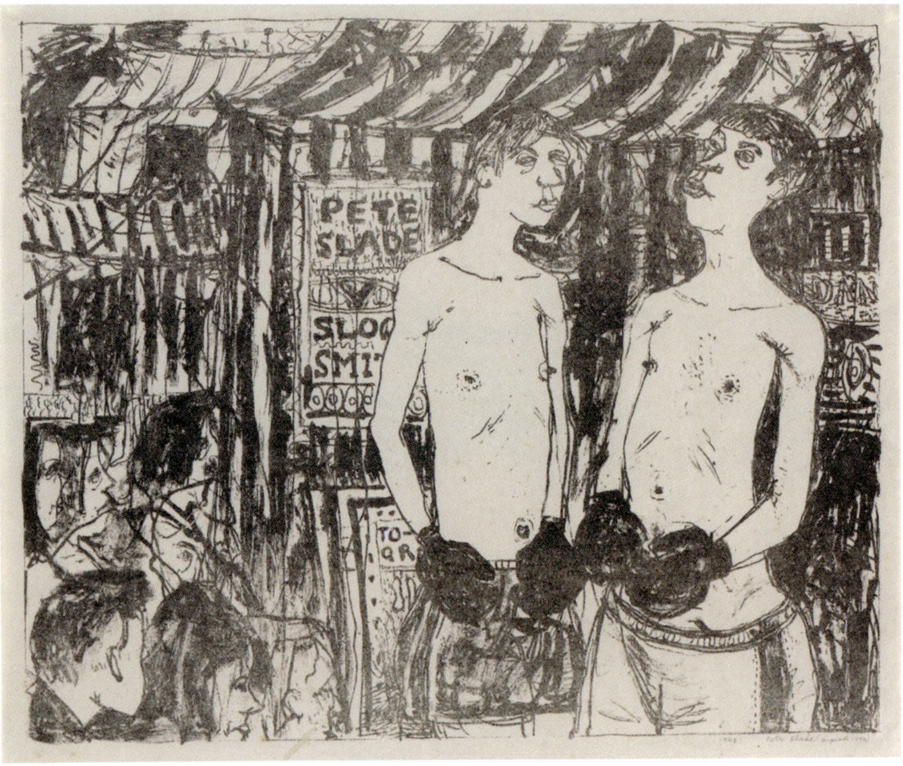

8 **Fairground Boxing Booth**, 1948

the evenings, as a regular part of his rather segmented life. By the time he was in his early teens, his life revolved around the art school, the youth club, the jazz club (usually on his own) and cycling as a sport. He also accompanied his mother (and other family members) to wrestling matches, which gave him such pleasure that they became, with the circus and the fairground, a major subject for his art.

Unlike his siblings, who both gained places at grammar schools, Blake attended a local Dartford comprehensive where a kindly headmaster encouraged him to take the technical examination. Given his parents' modest circumstances, he was awarded a grant to attend Gravesend Technical College. Once there, he discovered almost by chance that by taking a drawing examination, which he passed, he was also able to spend half his time in the Junior Art Department, and from 1949 to 1951 to study full-time at Gravesend School of Art. Thus, without having had any early ambitions to become an artist, he found himself through a curious combination of circumstances undergoing an artistic training of extraordinary thoroughness that would be pretty much impossible to replicate today. As Blake sees it – and he is not alone among his peers in having such a view – the explosion of working-class creativity in many different fields during the later 1950s and 1960s, and the creation in particular of the Pop Art of which Blake was to become one of the leading lights, owed much to these previously unknown opportunities for 'someone of his class'. It was to keep up the numbers after the loss of so many lives in World War II

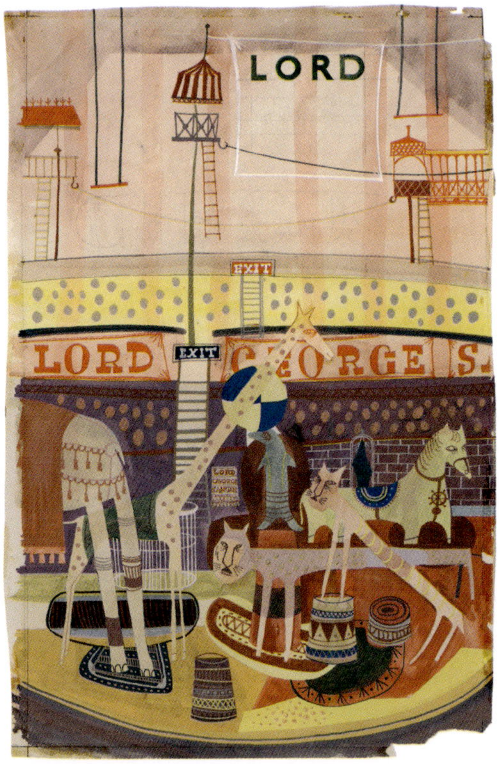

9 **Circus Poster**, 1949

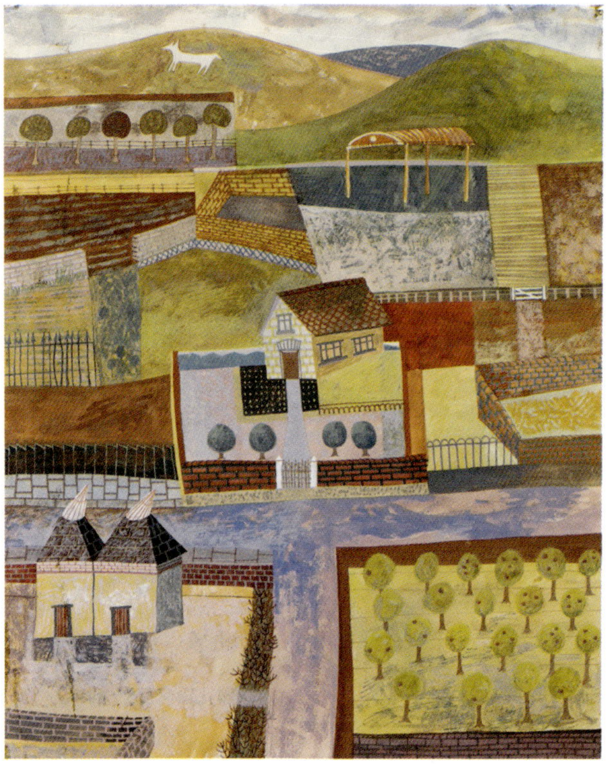

10 **Landscape**, 1950

that working-class men and women were suddenly allowed in more readily to the art schools. As Blake remarked in his Artists' Lives interview, he was one of the postwar generation that would not previously have been allowed to go to art school. It was not, in his view, simply a class issue; another kind of person now had the opportunity to train as an artist: 'In a way we were intruders. We were vulgar, we were common.' Thank goodness, is all one can say, that out of the terrible suffering created by the war, at least something of the previously crippling limitations of the British art world – polite, stuffy, genteel, proper and often upper middle class – was swept away.

Art school was an adventure and an introduction to an exotic side of life with which Blake would otherwise have had no contact. What impression could the flamboyantly homosexual Quentin Crisp, with his dyed hair and exaggeratedly effeminate manner, have had on the 14-year-old for whom he posed as a life model? Blake seemed to thrive on the challenge of set projects, as he was later to do when accepting commercial art commissions, always looking for a way of asserting his idiosyncratic personality and imagination into the most apparently dry of assignments. His first experiments with lithography, a medium in which he later demonstrated little interest, provided an early excuse for a tender examination of scenes from daily life, as in *Conversation* (*c.*1948, Plate 7) and *Fairground Boxing Booth* (1948, Plate 8). A *Circus Poster* (Plate 9) designed in 1949 for Lord George's Theatre, probably also in response to a set subject, is injected with the same warm, childlike humour

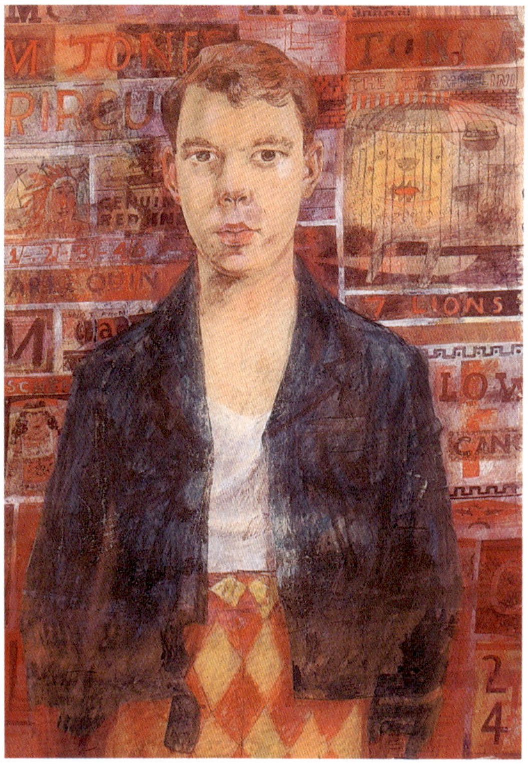

11 **Self–Portrait in RAF Jacket**, *c.*1952–3

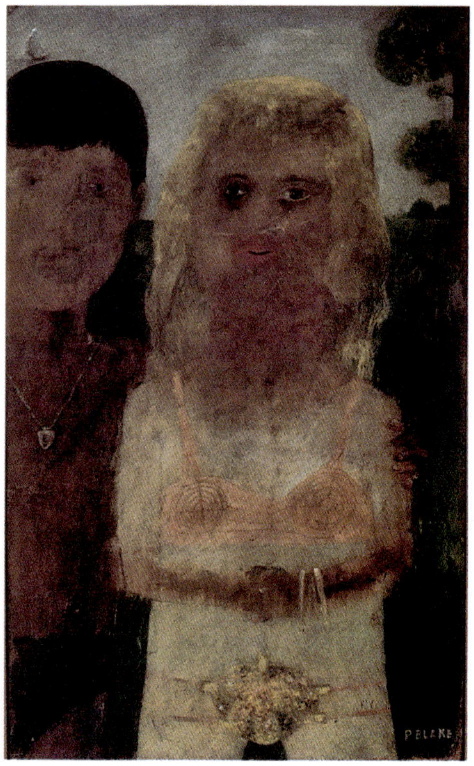

12 **Adam and Eve**, 1954–5

that came to be hallmarks of his mature work. Though the style is very much of its time, reminiscent for example of the work of Edward Bawden, one can almost hear the 17-year-old Peter chuckling to himself as he distends his skinny lions so that their bodies assume the same proportions as that of the neighbouring giraffe's long neck. The integration here of quirky hand-drawn typography (as intrinsic to the subject, rather than imposed onto it) also anticipates the striking marriage of word and image that was to become a notable feature of his art, long before he would have been well-informed about the precedents for such pictorial marriages in Cubism and other forms of modern art. Even in his guise as a naive artist, Blake was a natural sophisticate.

The real gift for Blake at Gravesend was the experience in 1950 of taking what was known as the Intermediate Course, which had been in operation for a good century, during the very last year in which it was taught. Only a small amount of his time was devoted to painting; his carefully delineated 1950 bust-length oil portrait of his sister Shirley, seen in three-quarter view against a dark background, was an attempt to paint in an Old Masterish style. He was given a thorough and very disciplined grounding in a very wide range of processes and crafts, including silversmithing, joinery, woodwork and wood carving, stone carving, modelling with clay, wood engraving, etching, life drawing, costume life drawing and anatomy. For his craft he chose Roman lettering, and he remembers doing a lot of hand lettering, typography and typesetting. All of these were to prove useful to him in his later professional life, giving him a solid base on which to build and enrich his vocabulary as an artist. Each of these areas was an important factor in his visual education in quite specific ways. The typographic exercises, for instance, trained him to notice that a row of ten storefronts might well exhibit ten different types of lettering, where other painters might choose to depict such a scene in a single typeface. Or, to take another example, the exercises in poster design were to be consciously echoed in his wrestling paintings of the 1960s. By contrast with such an elaborate tuition, an art student in Britain today is likely to be taught much more about public relations than about particular techniques, and to be left to his or her own devices in working out technical solutions.

In his late teens Blake began to educate himself about contemporary British art, in particular admiring the work of Bawden, Stanley Spencer and Eric Ravilious, and he soon knew that he wanted to be a painter. He was instead persuaded to take a commercial art course on the understanding that such a career would offer him a more secure livelihood than he could expect as a painter. In 1950 he applied to the Royal College of Art, a leading postgraduate school in London, a year before completing his studies at Gravesend. Taking his teachers' advice, he submitted an application for the commercial art course, but he also took with him one of his paintings, which he showed at the interview. On the strength of that one painting, which elicited the interest of the Principal, Robin Darwin, he was admitted instead to the Painting School and was led once again by improbable

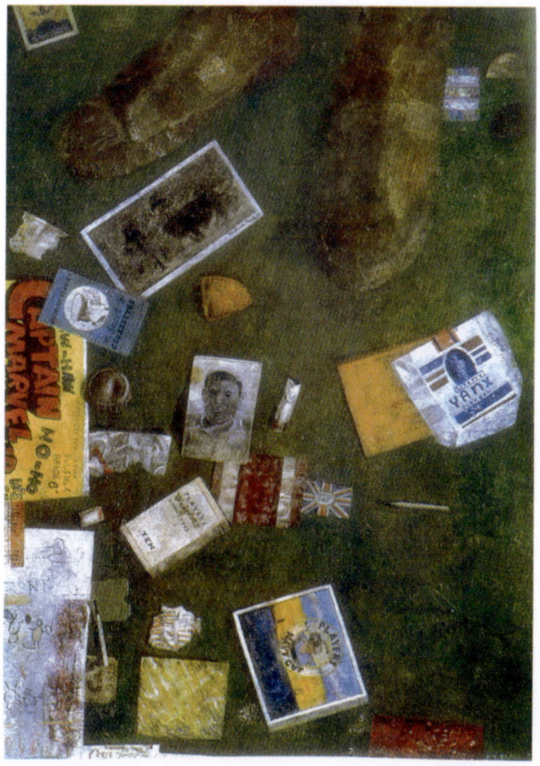

13 **Footsteps**, 1955

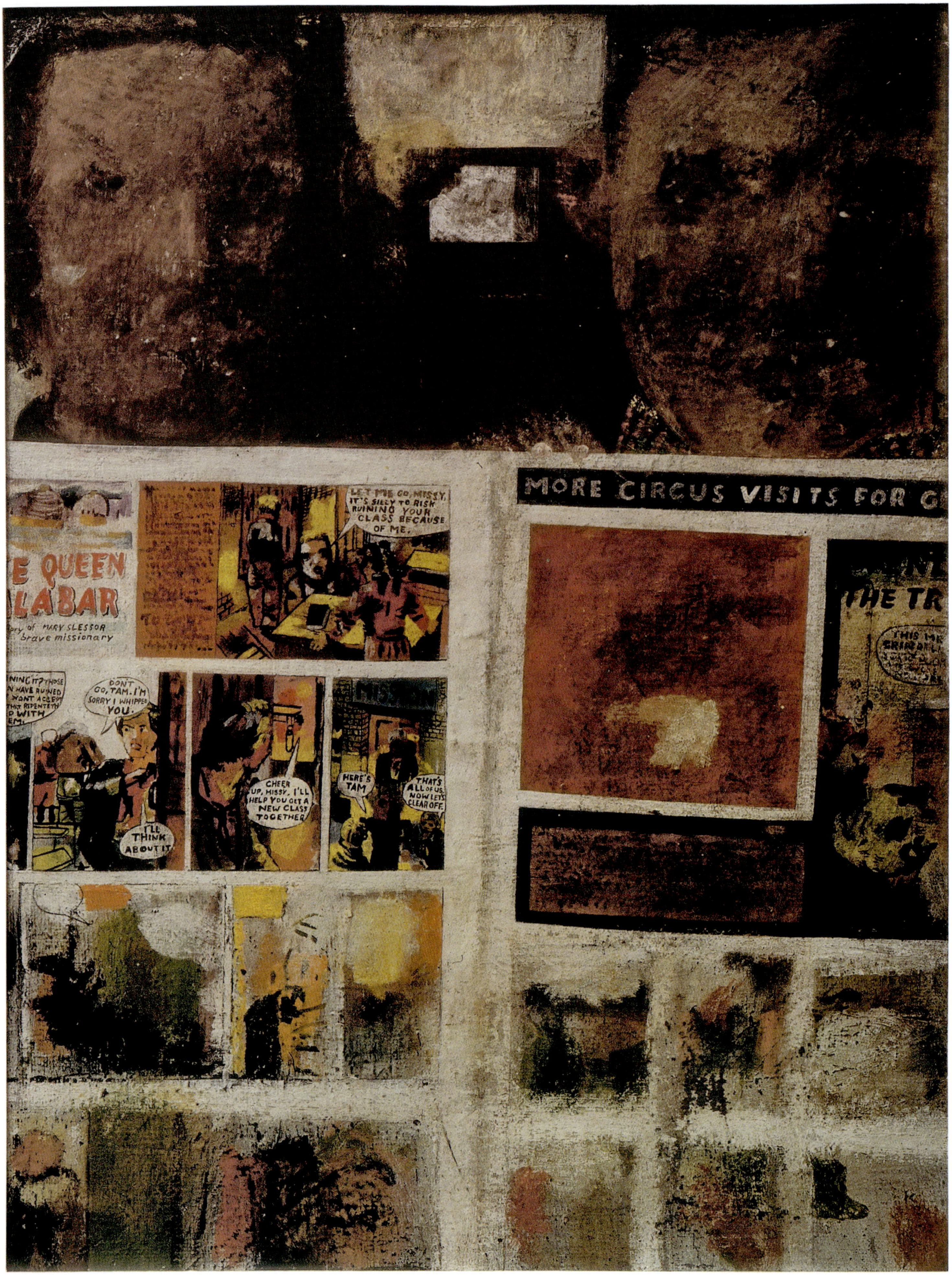

14 **Children Reading Comics**, 1956

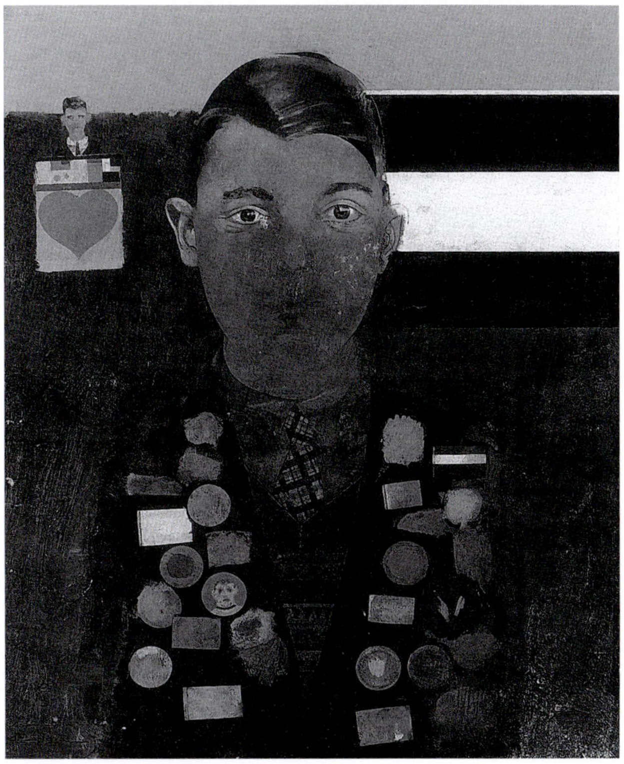

15 **Boy with Paintings**, 1957–9

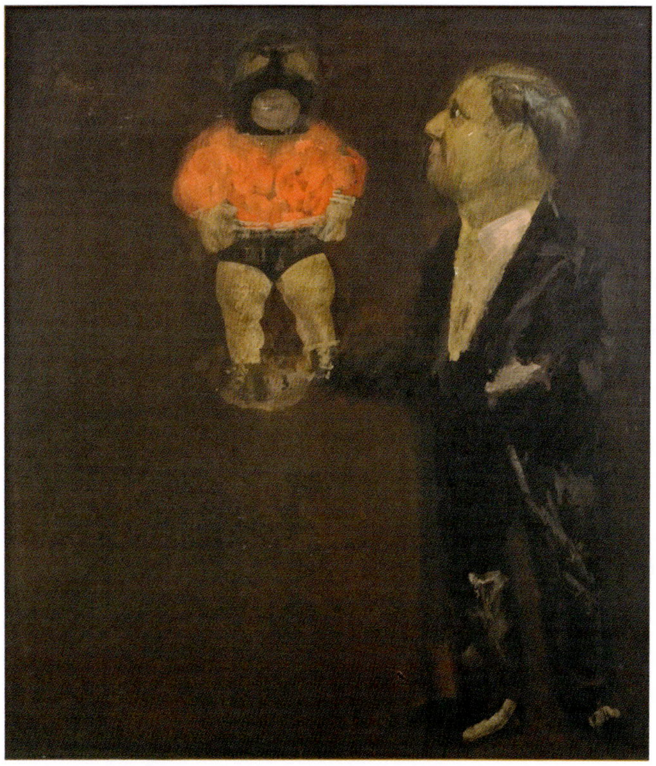

16 **Little Vigorous Daunt**, 1958 (unfinished)

circumstance into an unforeseen life as a professional artist. He was just 18 at the time. By then he felt equally comfortable with the idea of working both as a fine artist and as a graphic artist or illustrator, roles that he continued to view as interchangeable during his later life, the one informing the other.

A further three years were to pass before Blake took up his place at the Royal College, the second and third of those years being taken up by his obligatory National Service in the Royal Air Force. He was posted to various bases, including Padgate in Cheshire, Weeton in Lancashire, Compton Bassett in Wiltshire, Cirencester, Belfast and Lincolnshire. With their camaraderie, those years, too, were formative and character-building experiences, especially as they helped coax him out of his shell. In the summer of 1949, at the age of 17, he had suffered a serious cycling accident which left him facially scarred, intensifying his already shy and retiring nature. The friendships he formed in the RAF helped build his confidence, as did the sense of belonging. As he later recalled, in the RAF he lived in the same way as the others: his bed and his locker were his home, and it was in that small circumscribed area that he spent most of his spare time. It was only within those lockers that they were allowed to express their personality, for example by gluing pin-up images to the interior; the sense of comfort this gave him and the escape it offered into a fantasy life were directly alluded to in the sculpture with collage he was to make in 1959, titled simply *Locker* (Plates 1 and 55), made from a found object very like the one he had used in his late teens.

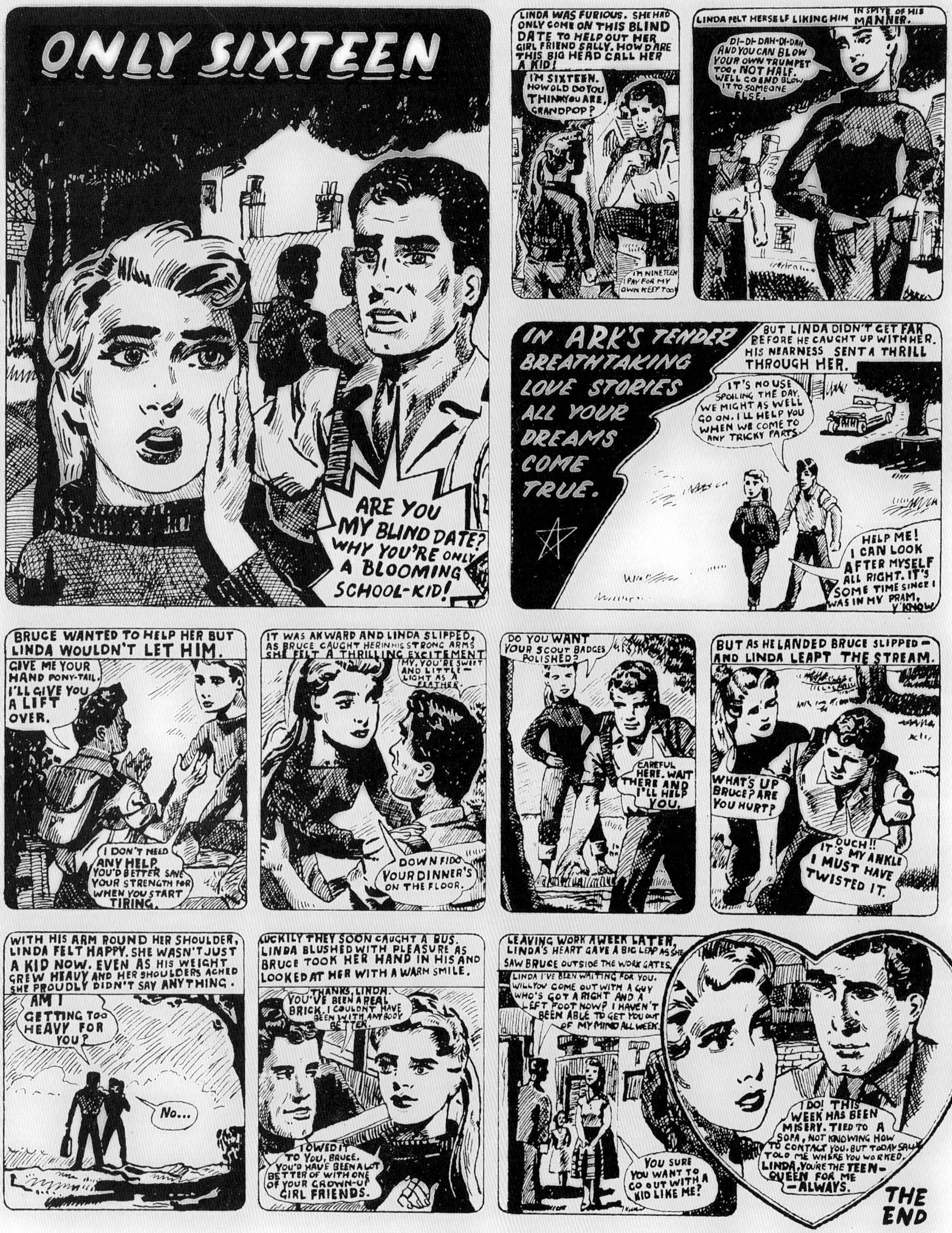

17 Only Sixteen, 1960

Even before studying art, Blake had been interested in fairgrounds and other forms of 'working-class' entertainment, discovering a particular love of sideshows and of painted roundabouts. Gravesend had been much bombed during World War II, and at nearby Tilbury he used to admire the Thames barges with their stencilled lettering. All these formative experiences were very visual as well as powerfully emotional for him, and they later entered into his art with an enviable naturalness. By the mid-1950s, when he was still a student at the Royal College of Art, Blake had made overt reference to popular culture – including comic strips, the cinema, the funfair and the circus – as an arena of escape and fantasy in such paintings as *Children Reading Comics* (1954, Plate 2 and 1956, Plate 14), *ABC Minors* (1955, Plate 6), *Dixie, Darling of the Midway* (1955–8, Plate 22) and *Cherie, Only Bearded Tattooed Lady* (1957, Plate 23).

The Circus, the Funfair and Popular Entertainments

Portraits of side-show performers, such as *Siriol, She-Devil of Naked Madness* (1957, Plate 20), were among the most original in conception of the works Blake made during and immediately after his period of training at the Royal College. Painted on planks of roughened wood so that they look indistinguishable from a found fragment of actual fairground art, they go beyond a straightforward representation of the subject in a frankly naive style and – with a rigour rivalling that of Jasper Johns's flag paintings of the same year – insist on a seamless identification of the painting with its subject. As Blake elaborated in 1989, when speaking to me of his early circus paintings: 'They were based on a known art form, on fairground decorations or canvases hung outside freak shows. They were not based on specific examples. Like with the wrestlers, I knew the language, but would invent them.'

The 'circus ladies' are among the most touching of Blake's early inventions, suggesting as they do a strong identification with misfits and social outcasts. Having sustained facial injuries from his bicycle accident, Blake had grown a beard at the earliest opportunity to hide his scars. His empathetic portrayals of people who are far from physically perfect yet bravely make their way in the world, and even present themselves as sexually alluring, clearly have their roots in his own vulnerability and self-consciousness about his appearance. *Loelia, World's Most Tattooed Lady* (1955, Plate 21) and *Siriol, She-Devil of Naked Madness* each face the spectator squarely and without apology, standing frontally to attention in a state of almost total undress. Both have rather flabby bodies and oversized heads, yet they seem conscious of their own glamour and offbeat erotic appeal: witness their extravagant hairstyles, the stylish sunglasses and jaunty sailor's hat, their little bikinis and the

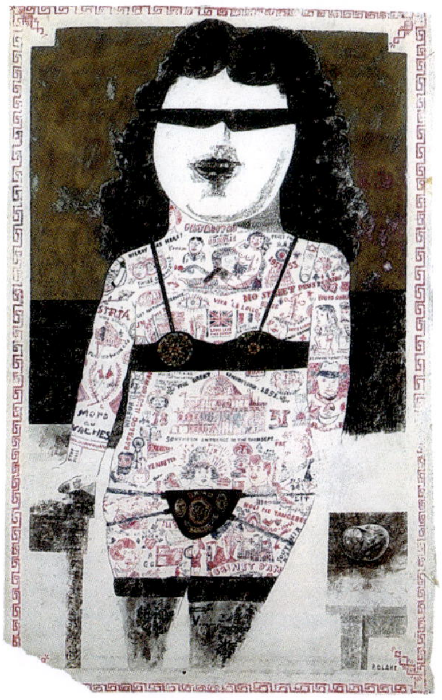

18 **Tattooed Lady I**, 1955

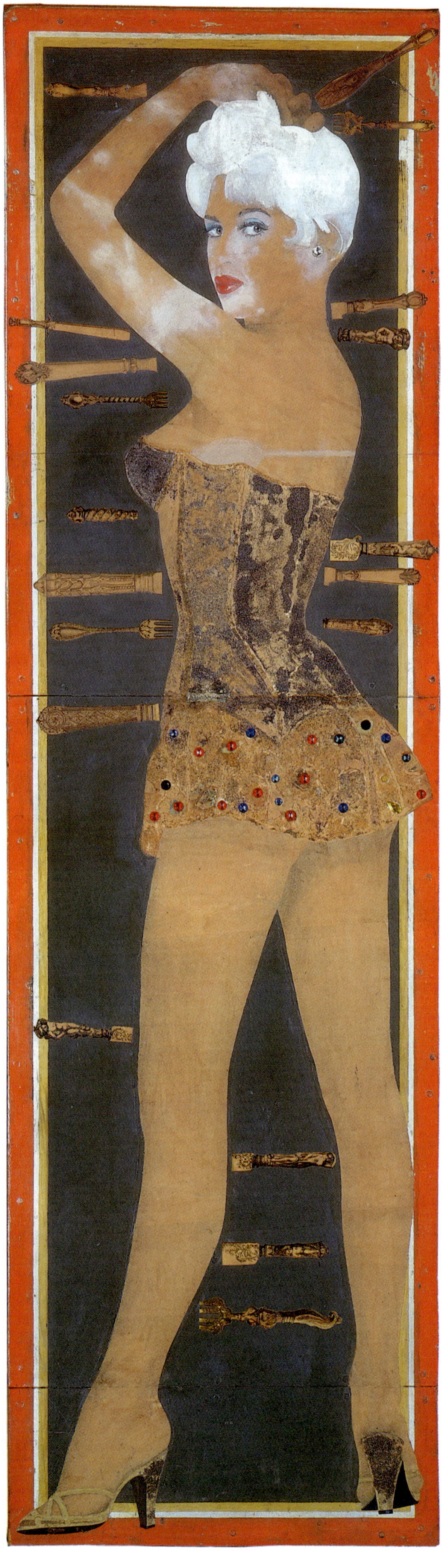

19
Knife Thrower's Board, 1957

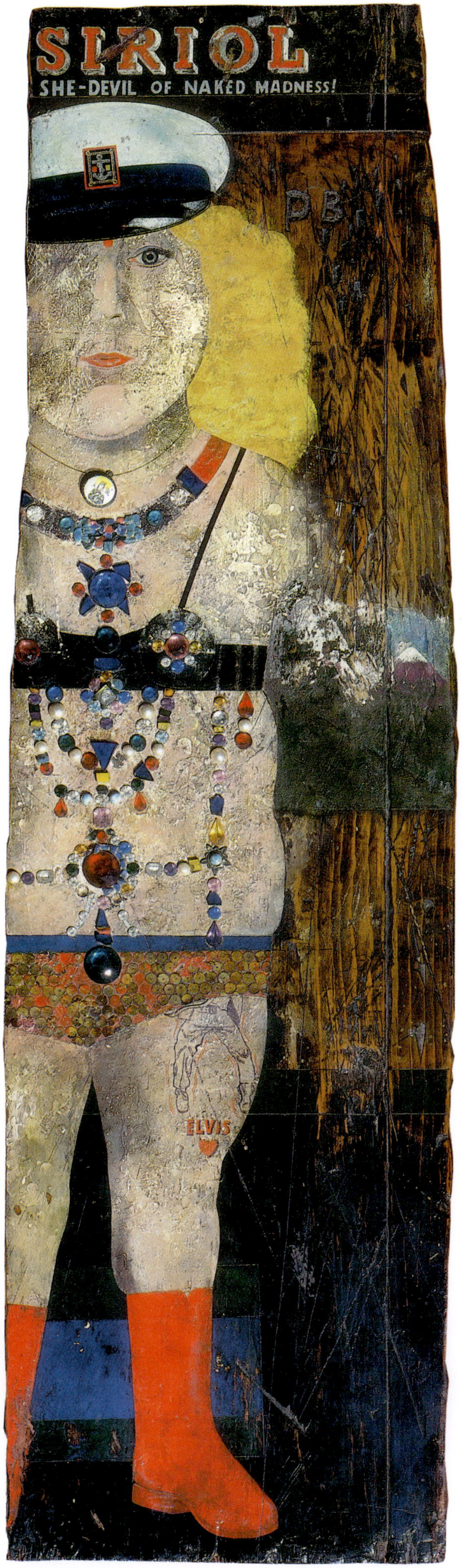

20
Siriol, She-Devil of Naked Madness, 1957

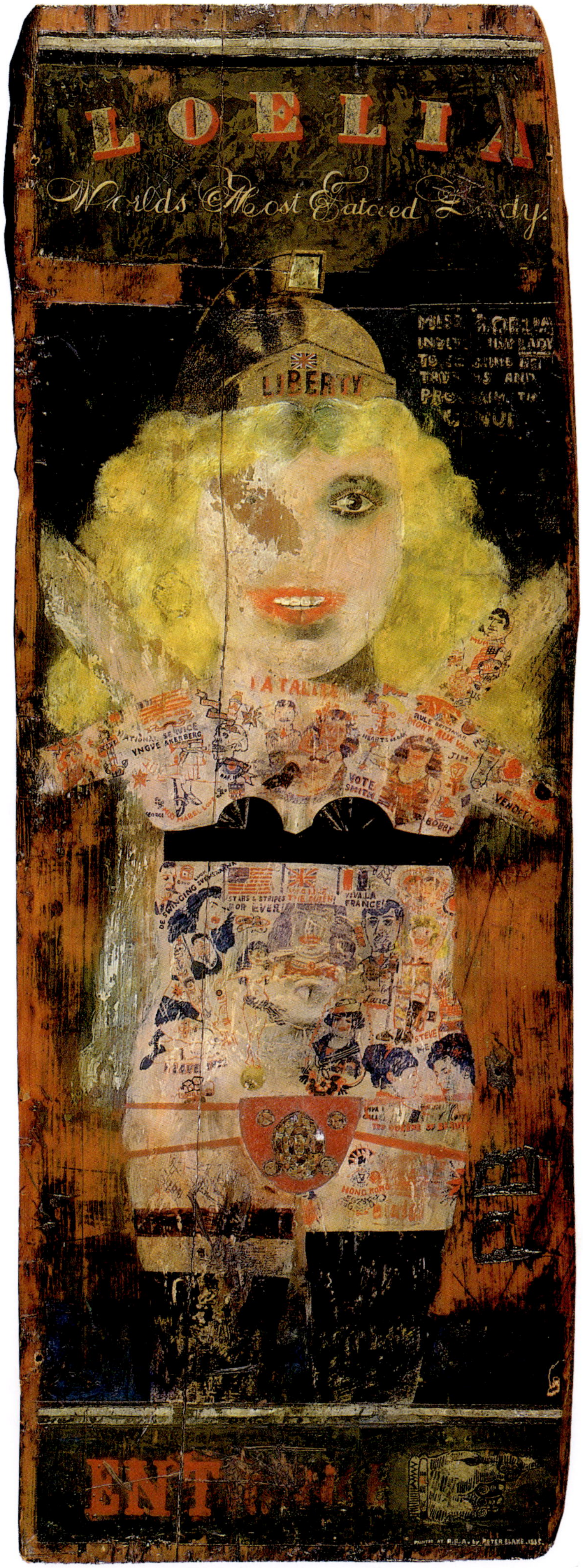

21
Loelia, World's Most Tattooed Lady, 1955

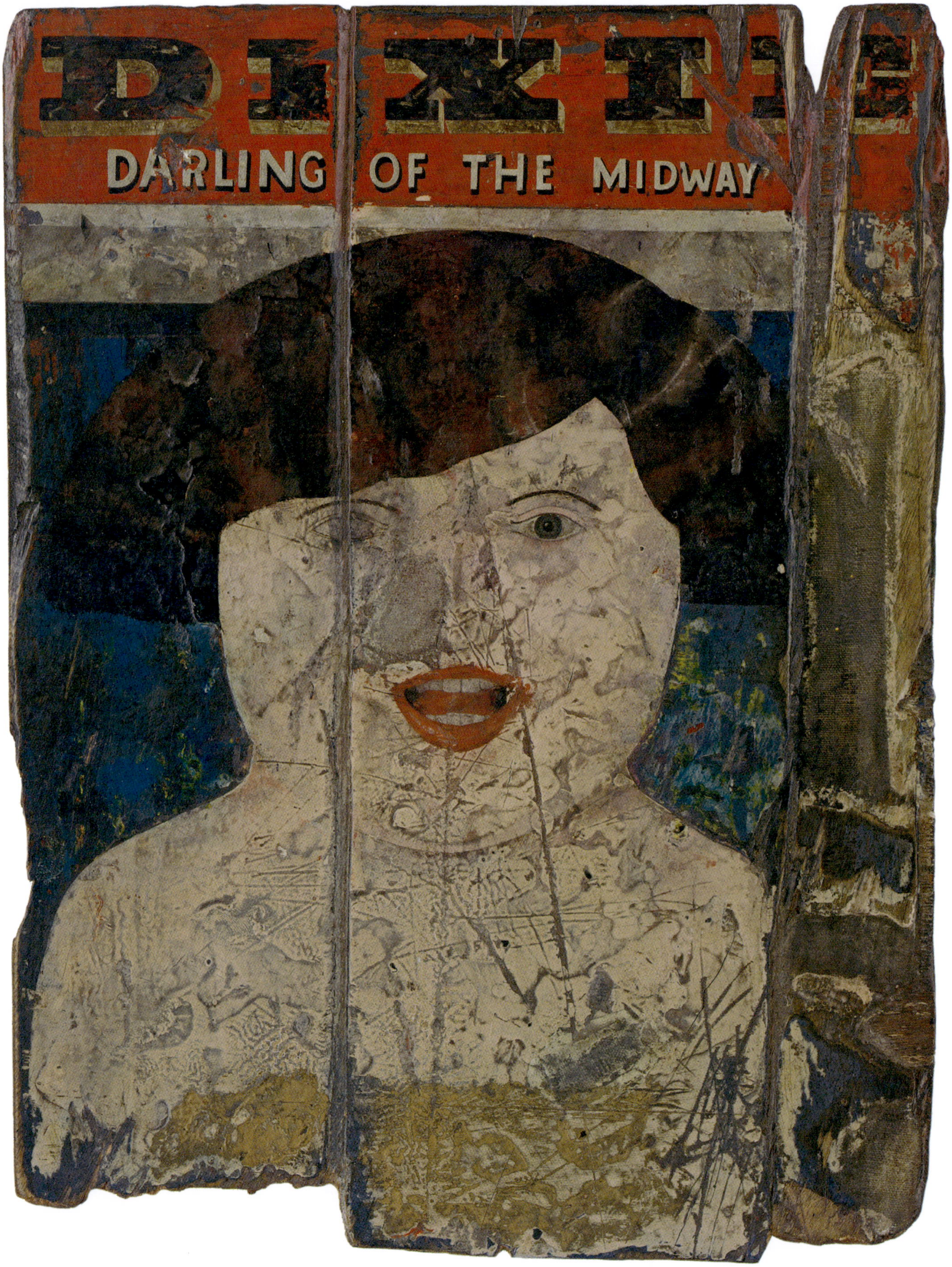

22 **Dixie, Darling of the Midway**, 1955–8

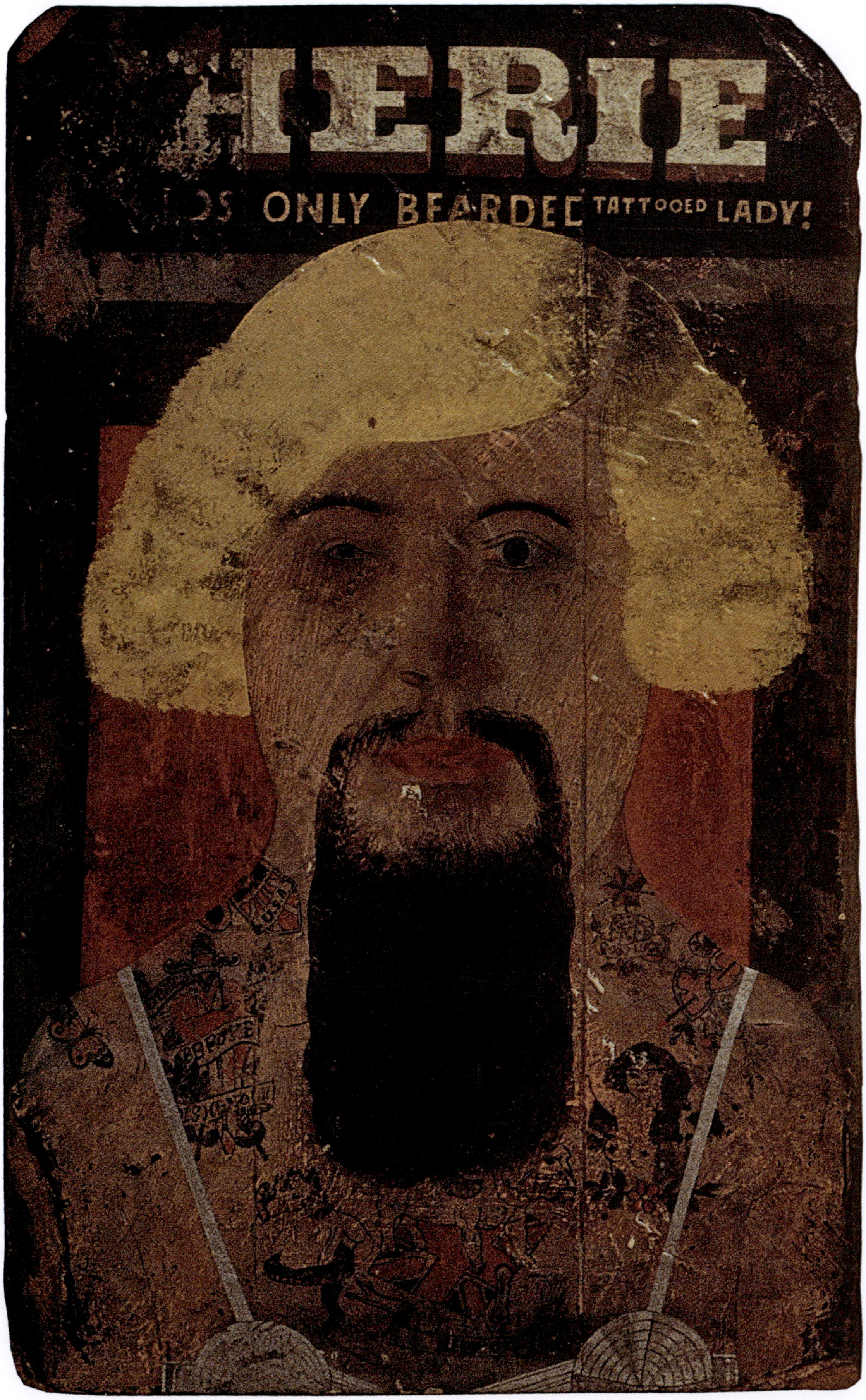

23 **Cherie, Only Bearded Tattooed Lady**, 1957

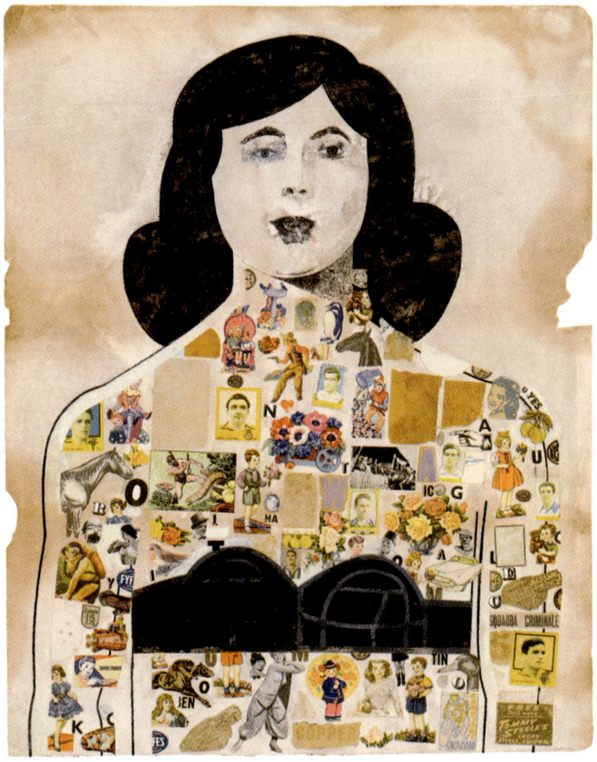

24 **Tattooed Lady with Collage**, 1958

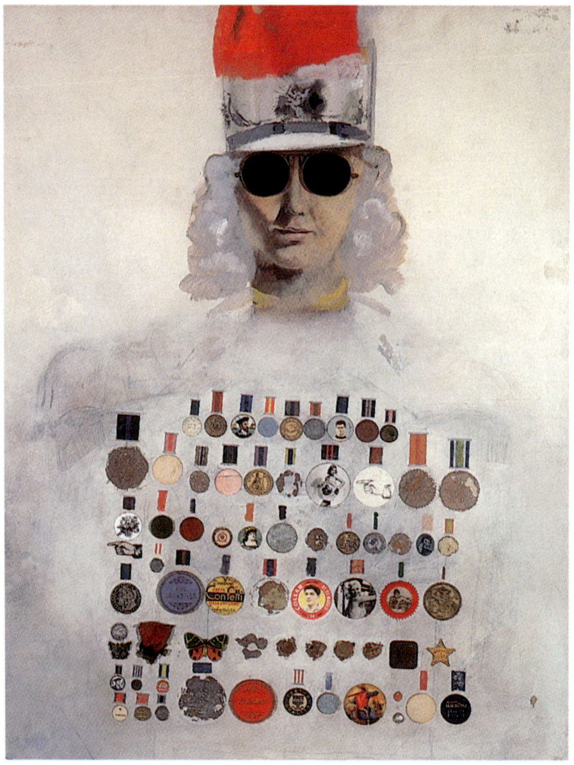

25 **Drum Majorette**, 1957

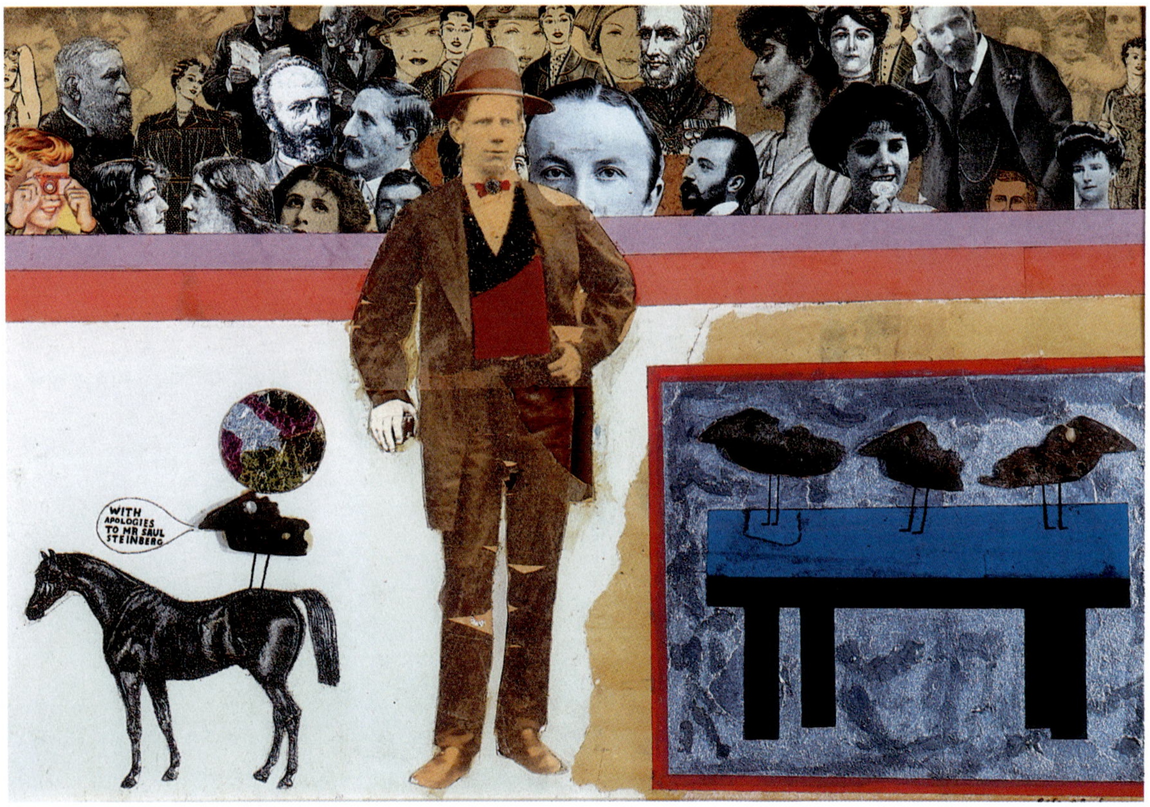

26 **Bird Act**, 1957

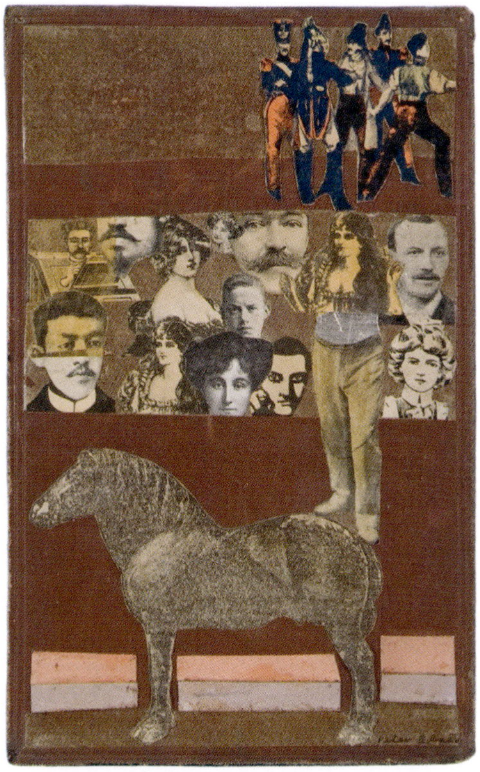

27 **Untitled Collage with Horse**, 1957

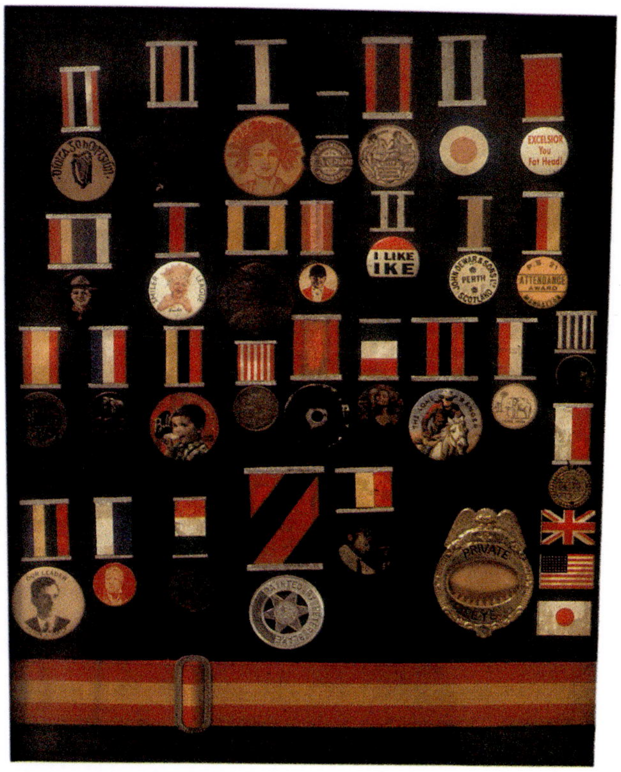

28 **Medals**, 1960

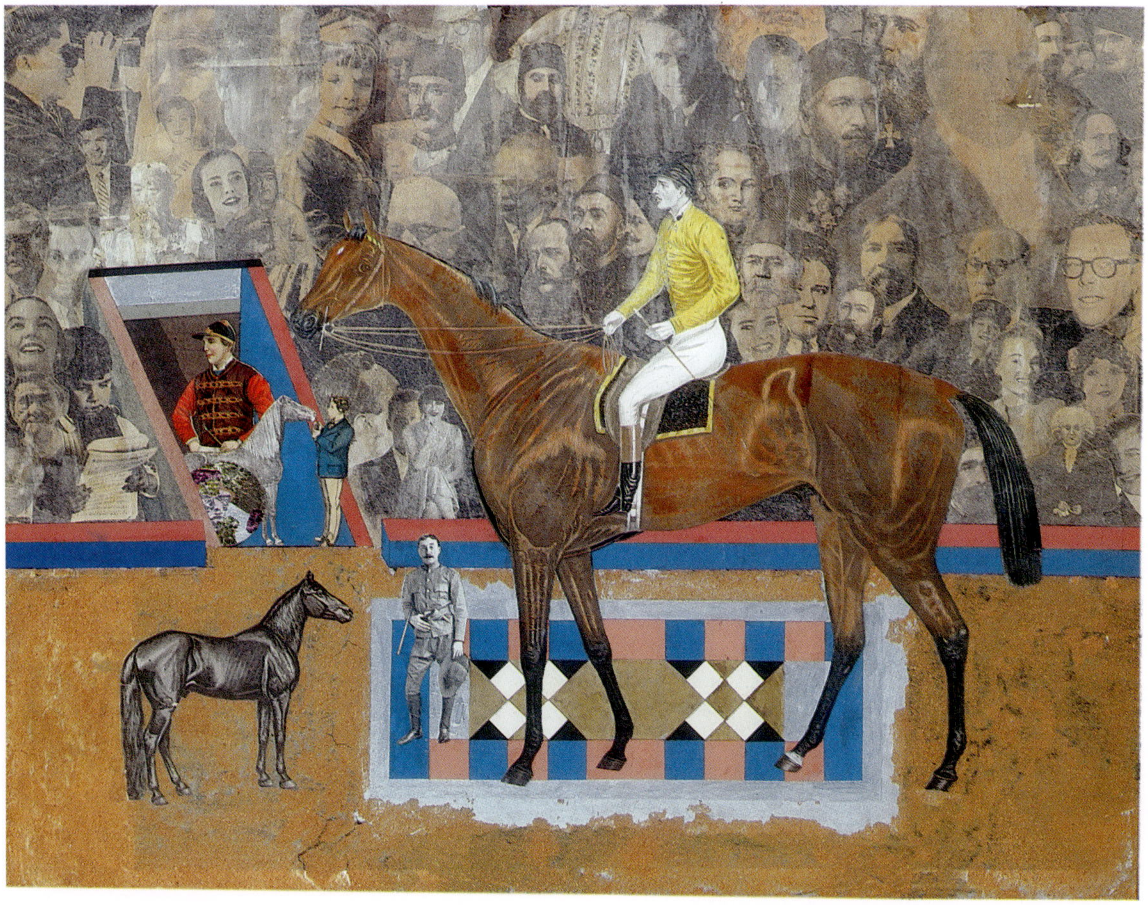

29 **Jockey Act**, 1957

jewel-encrusted adornment of their bodies. The tattooed lady's very skin has become a canvas for artistic expression. Like the pop stars and entertainers that Blake was to take as the subject for his Pop pictures of the early 1960s, these imaginary characters seem to revel in their own celebrity status, presenting themselves proudly for our adulation as queens in their own parallel universe.

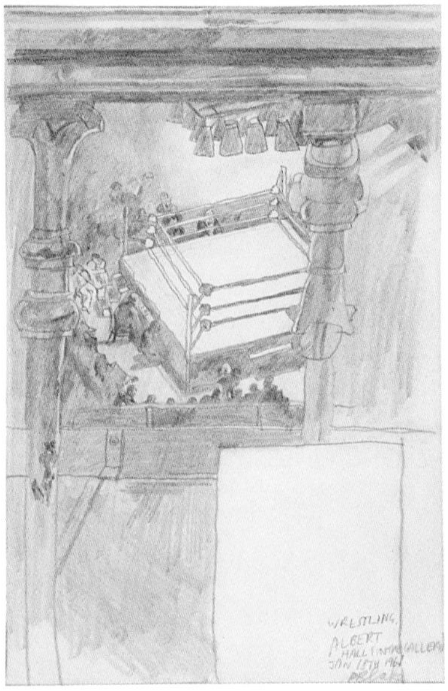

30 Wrestling at the Albert Hall, 1961

Blake's work of the 1950s, like much of what he has done since, is spirited, playful and full of humour. Much of it takes as its subject matter things and pastimes that ordinary people have experienced and enjoyed in their daily lives or as escapist entertainment, and they are presented not only as a part of life to be cherished but as worthy of elevation in a work of art. A great part of the affection that Blake's art instils in viewers arises from the tenderness with which he himself has treated his themes and the pleasure he takes in considering them. Blake is one of those rare artists whose work, notwithstanding the sophistication of his own concept of art, can be enjoyed and understood without much prior knowledge of other art because it touches so often, and with such depth of feeling, on shared human experiences.

Knife Thrower's Board (1957, Plate 19) is one of the largest and most imposing of Blake's works on circus themes, but it is distinguished from the others by incorporating a found object: a poster, printed in sections and given away with a special issue of the men's magazine *Reveille*, which depicts the great French film star of the period, Brigitte Bardot, life-size. Although presented in the guise of a painting, it is actually a giant collage, with forks and knives wittily inserted from engravings of cutlery snipped from the catalogue of the Great Exhibition of 1851; her costume is embellished with colourful, jewel-like decorations. Paint is sparingly applied to her face and hair. These fairly minimal but decisive alterations transform a simple pin-up poster into a subject picture in keeping with the artist's themes, while preserving the integrity of the main source. In this sense, this work comes closest to the pure found object among Blake's early paintings, paving the way for the more 'hard-core' Pop collage paintings and assemblages that marked a decisive shift in his art in 1959.

This area of Blake's imagery was particularly pronounced in his work through to about 1960, visible in paintings such as *Drum Majorette* (Plate 25) of 1957, in collages such as *Bird Act* (Plate 26) and *Jockey Act* (Plate 29) of the same year and in sketchbook drawings made in circuses or at wrestling matches. As with every aspect of his art, however, such subject matter continued to resurface in later years, invariably altered by his changing perspective as he grew older or by his investigation of new techniques or stylistic solutions. The most glorious resurgence of the freak-show imagery came more than a decade later in a set of five beautifully executed wood engravings – in my view, the masterpieces of his

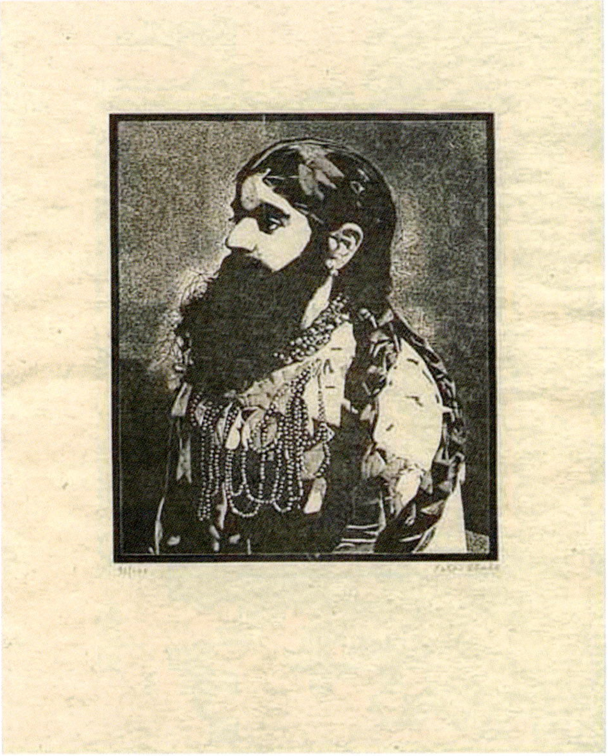

31 **Bearded Lady** from *Side Show Series*, 1974–8

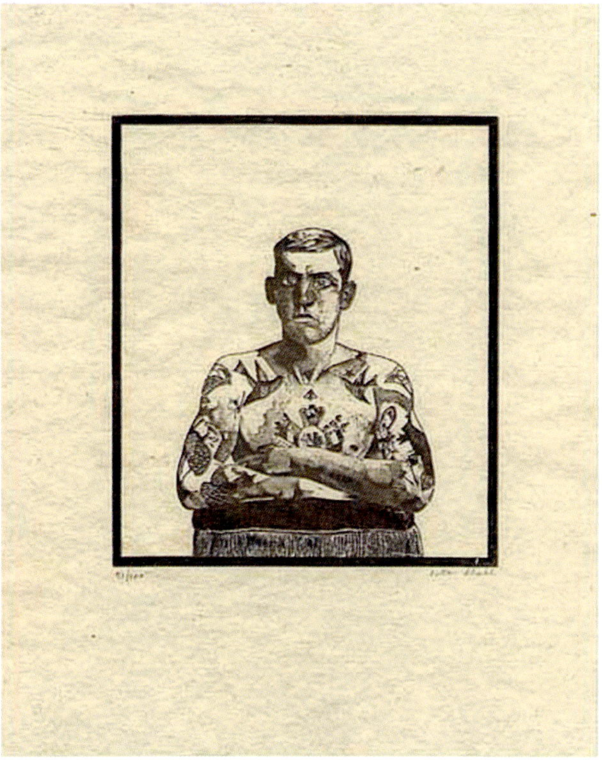

32 **Tattooed Man** from *Side Show Series*, 1974–8

printmaking – published by Waddington Graphics under the title *Side Show* (1974–8). The *Fat Boy, Midget, Bearded Lady* (Plate 31), *Tattooed Man* (Plate 32) and *Giant* all take us back to that politically incorrect era, so chillingly captured in Todd Browning's 1932 film *Freaks*, when it was considered acceptable to parade around unusual-looking people as objects of repugnant curiosity. In Blake's lovingly detailed portraits, as also in Browning's empathetic portrayals of these outcasts, it is not revulsion that comes across but affection and acceptance, even a sense of identification with the imperfections of his fellow man. As always with Blake, it is a deeply felt humanity that triumphs.

The Leverhulme Research Award: The Grand Tour, 1956–7

On graduating (with a First) from the Royal College in 1956, Blake was awarded a Leverhulme Research Award to study popular art in locations of his choosing around Europe. It was a sector of the visual arts that had long attracted his curiosity and for which there was at that time a considerable fashion, with such areas as barge painting, fairground art and shell grottoes attracting scholarly attention. He had even been taught for a short period at Gravesend by one of the experts in these fields, Enid Marx, co-author with Margaret Lambert of *English Popular and Traditional Art* (London: Collins, 1946). Within the graphic design community, there was no problem in making reference to such sources and within the

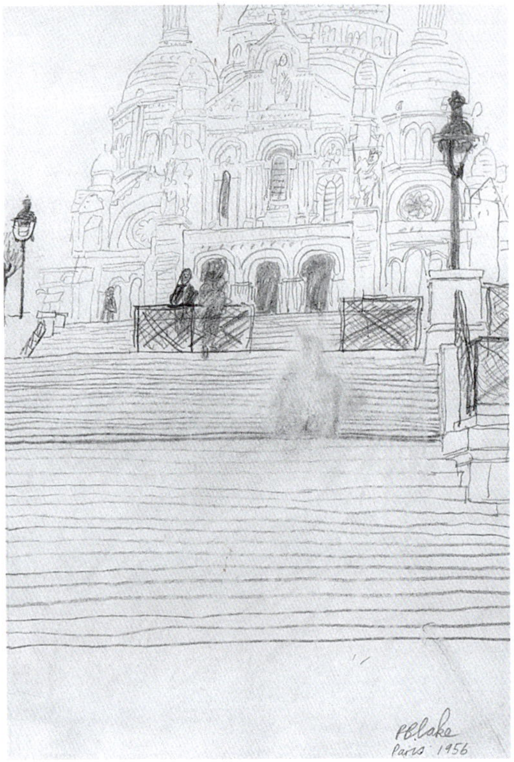

33 **Sacre Coeur, Paris**, 1956

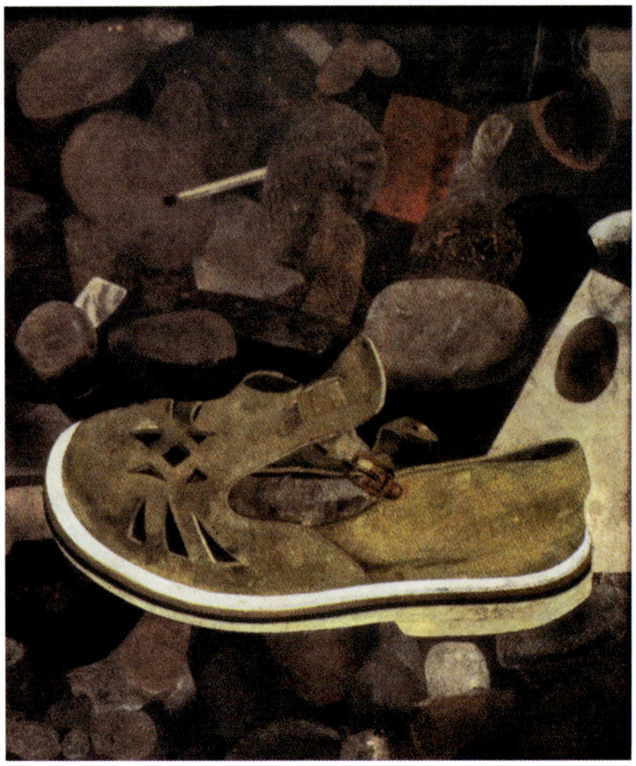

34 **Shoe on the Beach at Nice**, 1957

postwar fine-art context in Britain Blake found support for his enthusiasms in the work of such artists as Edward Bawden, Barbara Jones and the American-born Edward McKnight Kauffer. He remembers looking at, among other things, Bawden's posters for the Ealing Studios films, with their echoes of Victorian wood engravings. The vogue for Victoriana was indicated by the publication of an entire issue of the Royal College student magazine, *Ark*, on that subject just before Blake's arrival there as a student (*Ark*, 4, February 1952); that issue even included an article – 'The Spiritsail Sailing Barge' by Jim Lovegrove – on barge decoration.

Just before leaving for the Netherlands, Blake had the opportunity to see an exhibition called *This is Tomorrow*, which took place at the Whitechapel Art Gallery in London between 8 August and 12 September 1956. Now often cited as a key event in the prehistory of British Pop Art, this thematic group exhibition was organised by members of the tight-knit and essentially closed society known as the Independent Group, which included in its membership such artists as Richard Hamilton and Eduardo Paolozzi, two of the founding fathers of Pop Art, as well as architects, critics and historians. The Independent Group had been meeting at the Institute of Contemporary Arts (ICA) in London since 1952 and had displayed a great intellectual curiosity in areas of popular culture and design that were then normally considered outside the domain of fine art: automobile styling, science-fiction illustrations, the cinema and advertisements. Blake was vaguely aware of their existence but never attended any of their meetings, which were essentially open only to the group's own elite membership. *This is Tomorrow* prompted the making of a small but seminal Pop Art collage by Hamilton, *Just what is it that makes today's homes so different, so appealing?* (1956), for reproduction on one of the black-and-white posters; with its complex and wide-ranging iconography of popular culture – including comic books, the movies, television, space travel, convenience foods, consumer products and soft porn – this brilliantly condensed work announced many of the major themes that were to be mined by Hamilton himself and by other Pop artists during the 1960s. Without belittling the achievement of that collage, which measured less than a foot square, Blake was underwhelmed by the exhibition itself, joking with his friend Dick Smith (with whom he was soon to share a flat) that it should have been called *That was Yesterday*. Neither that show nor other work by the Independent Group's artists had any real impact on the Pop course of Blake's own work, which was deeply rooted in his own experience and enthusiasms. In conversation with me in 1989, he said that he 'did not feel very encouraged by it' and would allow only the possibility that he had been subliminally influenced by Hamilton's presentation of a life-sized photographic image of Marilyn Monroe in a billowing dress from Billy Wilder's 1955 film *The Seven Year Itch*.

Previously, only academics were in the running for a Leverhulme Research Award. Blake was one of the first to be given one as a practitioner. The grant of £500 gave him enough to subsist for an entire year, during which he travelled around Europe, usually staying in youth hostels and eating frugally. Aged 24, he had never before left the UK and he spoke and read no language other than English, though he soon learned at least how to order a beer in the language of every country through which he journeyed. Prior to his departure one of his tutors at the Royal College, Colin Hayes, gave him a list of museums, towns and cities to be visited to see in the flesh some of the great paintings from the history of art that he had previously known only in reproduction. This year-long voyage of self-education thus ended up being a grand tour not just of folk and popular art but of fine-art traditions as well, with Giotto's frescoes in Padua, the Piero della Francescas in Assisi and Velázquez's *Las Meninas* in the Prado making a particular impression. Referring now to that year of cultural self-education as a kind of finishing school, Blake consciously resisted taking on exotic foreign subject matter – finding himself resistant even to finishing a picture of a bullfight that his mother had wanted him to do for her – but admits that the Old Master paintings he saw during his many museum visits had an effect on the way he tried to paint. Having already experimented with a Realist style, he could not help but be affected, for example, by the fifteenth-century Flemish art he saw in Belgium. Something of the magic of artists such as Jan Van Eyck and Hans Memling somehow seeped into his own brushes, certainly setting a standard of careful technique to which he continued to aspire.

At first Blake travelled alone, starting in Rotterdam (with friends on holiday), Amsterdam and The Hague, and working his way down through Antwerp and Brussels to Paris, where he was particularly happy. He spent the weeks leading up to Christmas 1956 there followed by a further month after a short trip home. In Paris, he ran into a Scottish painter, Peter McGinn, whom he had met before and who was driving his own van to the British School at Rome. He offered Blake the chance to accompany him, so from Paris they proceeded to Nice and other locations in the south of France, including Antibes (where they failed in their hope of seeing Picasso at his favourite restaurant), through various parts of Italy including Tuscany and Rome, and back to the south of France. From there, Blake proceeded on his own to Spain, where he met up with his old friend Joe Tilson, who had recently married the artist Joslyn Morton and was living in primitive but idyllic circumstances on the Catalan coast.

Blake took a very wide view of what constituted research into popular art. His first stop in each city was often to the local folk art museum, where he would look at the artefacts, buy some postcards and perhaps do a bit of drawing. However, he would also look out for wrestling matches, boxing matches, bullfights and other entertainments, where he would buy the programmes or the posters. He also collected ephemera such as cigarette packets, sweet packets and other printed material that caught his eye, much of which – with his hoarding instincts – he has kept to this day and still uses. Some of the first Pop collage paintings made a few years later, such as *The Fine Art Bit* (1959, Plate 41) and *Couples* (1959, Plate 43), used postcards gathered on that trip. Since he had limited resources and even less space for accumulating things, he had to set aside his natural instinct to acquire more possessions and to content himself mainly with looking.

Although he did not have a camera with him, during the latter part of the journey Blake made perhaps eight small paintings, which he carried around with him from place to place. One of the first depicts a cheap plastic shoe washed on to the beach in glamorous Nice (1957, Plate 34). In Rome he painted the *Goldfish* (1957, Plate 36) in the pond of the British School, with a tiny leaf and floating matchstick adding a deliberately prosaic note. Later in the trip he made a portrait of Tilson while staying with him in Spain and another, also painted from life, of the local Guardia civil policeman (1957, Plate 35) in the village near Tarragona where Tilson was living. More to the point, he always carried sketchbooks and did a considerable amount of drawing. Some of that material was later lent to a publisher and never returned, and other sketchbooks were broken up during the 1960s and the 30 drawings sold to art dealer Robert Fraser for £3 each. The Royal College magazine, *Ark*,

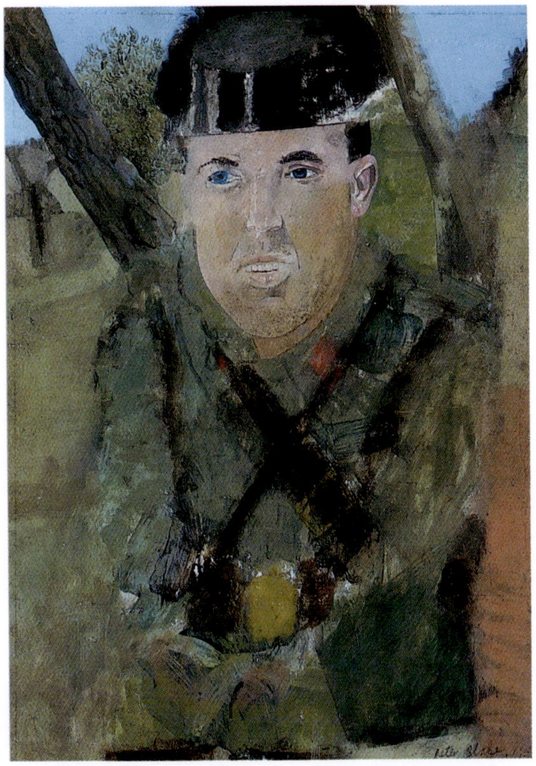

35 **Guardia Civil**, 1957

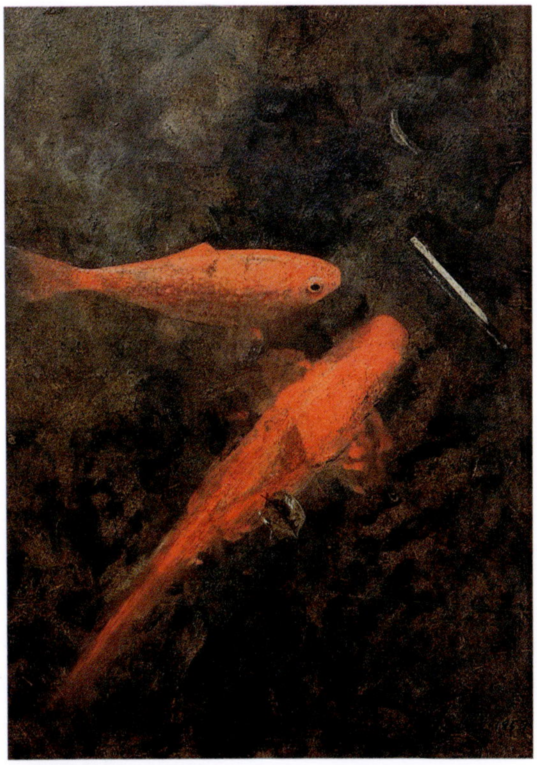

36 **Goldfish**, 1957

did however present a two-page spread in black and white in issue 20 (Autumn 1957, pp. 10–11) of 'drawings [made] especially for ARK on a recent visit to the continent'. Though uncaptioned, one of these drawings (dated 14 March 1957), of a camping site at Nice, anticipates by nearly a decade the look of David Hockney's topographical drawings in coloured crayons. Every line in it vibrates with life: one feels even the weight of gravity on the telephone wires suspended between poles. At once wonderfully spatial and graphically arresting as a flat design, filled with visual incident but brilliantly restrained, an observational drawing such as this one reveals Blake to be one of the outstanding natural draughtsmen of his time.

The year of travel around Europe did not produce much in the way of finished art, nor did it decisively change the direction of his work since he had made this research trip precisely because he was already interested in popular art. However, the journey did add to his information about these areas to which he was to continue to make reference, both in his subject matter and in his adoption of a variety of styles and modes of depiction. Perhaps more unexpectedly, it provided him with a real education in painting and the history of art, one which was to nourish him as a figurative painter in the years to come. In cultural terms, as he was the first to admit, this year out had an incalculable effect.

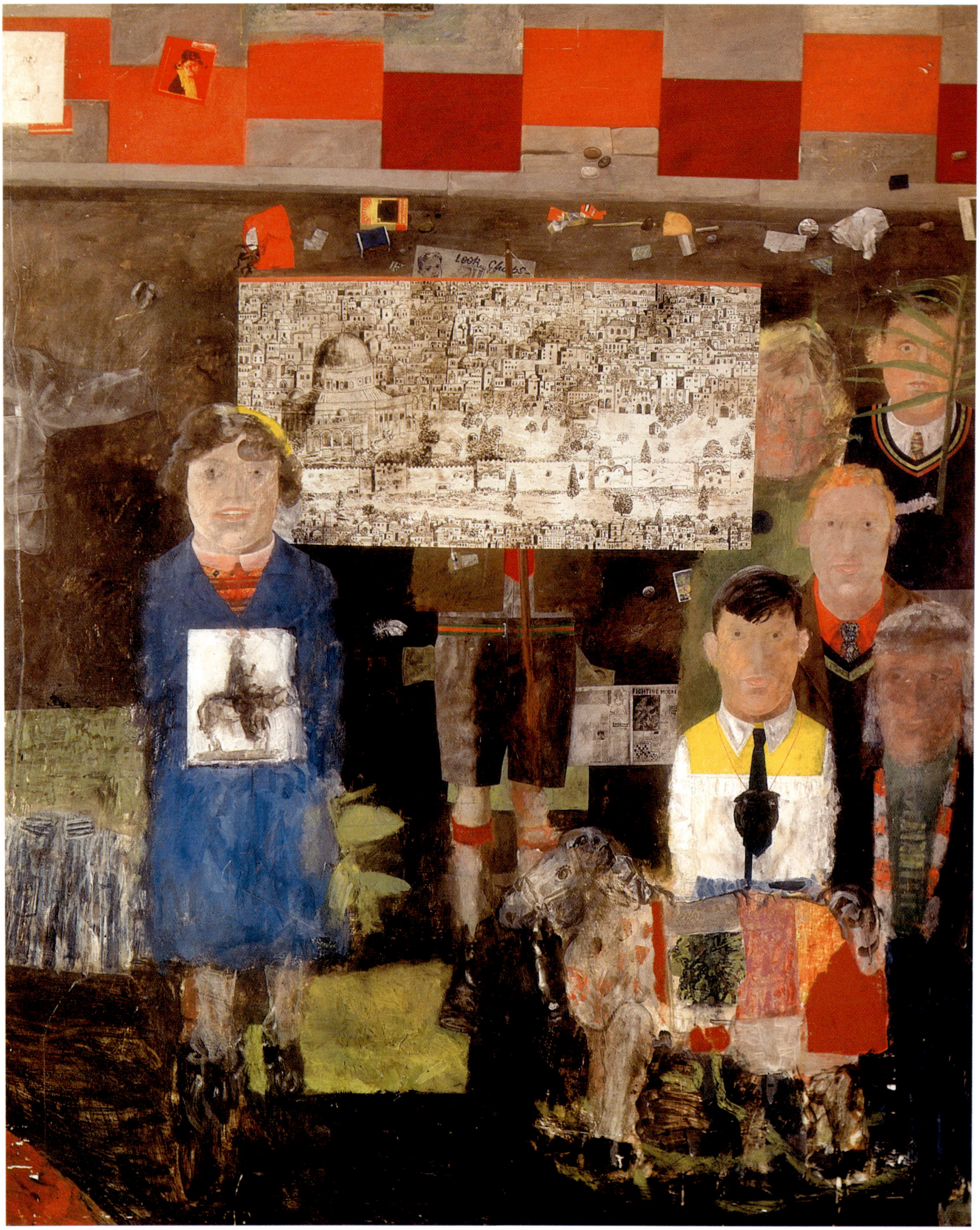

37 **The Preparation for the Entry into Jerusalem**, 1955–6

Subject Pictures

Blake was part of the first of many generations of art students who found it tempting to declare their modernity by responding almost exclusively to the work of their immediate predecessors or contemporaries, rather than to take a longer view of their chosen medium. For Blake, however, a working-class boy from the unglamorous fringes of London, the idea of being part of the community of painters represented by art history was always too exciting to be ignored. Not that he was capable of being unduly servile towards the Masters. It was simply that his love of pictures and representations of all kinds was so overwhelming that nothing could be excluded as potential inspiration. In student works such as *The Preparation for the Entry into Jerusalem* (1955–6, Plate 37) and *On the Balcony* (1955–7, Plate 39), both painted in response to set themes, allusions to Old Master precedents sit alongside references to contemporary art, magazine covers, postcards, comic strips and the cinema, all subject to a relentlessly frontal presentation of figures indebted to folk art traditions and to the bluntness of naive art by self-taught painters. In *On the Balcony*, for example, a handpainted reproduction of Edouard Manet's *The Balcony*, his famous painting of 1968–9, democratically shares the space with miniature paintings by fellow students such as Dick Smith, Leon Kossoff and Robyn Denny, but also with a bewildering variety of non-art visual material: handpainted reproductions of mass-circulation magazines, a Kellogg's Corn Flakes packet and other consumer products, badges and a tourist souvenir pennant. Black-and-white photographically derived images of the Royal Family, as stiffly formal before the camera as the awkward schoolchildren staring out from Blake's canvas, are understood to be part of the same media landscape as the screen goddess Marilyn Monroe, high-stepping it on a fan's garishly painted tie. Most poignant of all is the hand-painted facsimile of a black-and-white photograph of his old tutor, the painter John Minton, who had recently committed suicide.

Self-Portrait with Badges (1961, Plate 40), thinly painted in oils on untreated hardboard, was the last of a series of big subject pictures relating to the themes introduced during Blake's days at the Royal College. It was also one of the most overt in positioning itself in relation both to postwar Realist painting – including that of American artists such as Ben Shahn, Honoré Sharrer and Bernard Perlin, which he had seen in the exhibition *Modern Art in the United States: A Selection from the Collections of the Museum of Modern Art, New York* at the Tate Gallery from 5 January to 12 February 1956 – and to naturalistic styles of painting prevalent in the late nineteenth century. The range of reference subtly and undemonstrably embedded within this single work, and its concern with reinterpreting the idea of portraiture within a landscape setting, make it one of the most conceptually

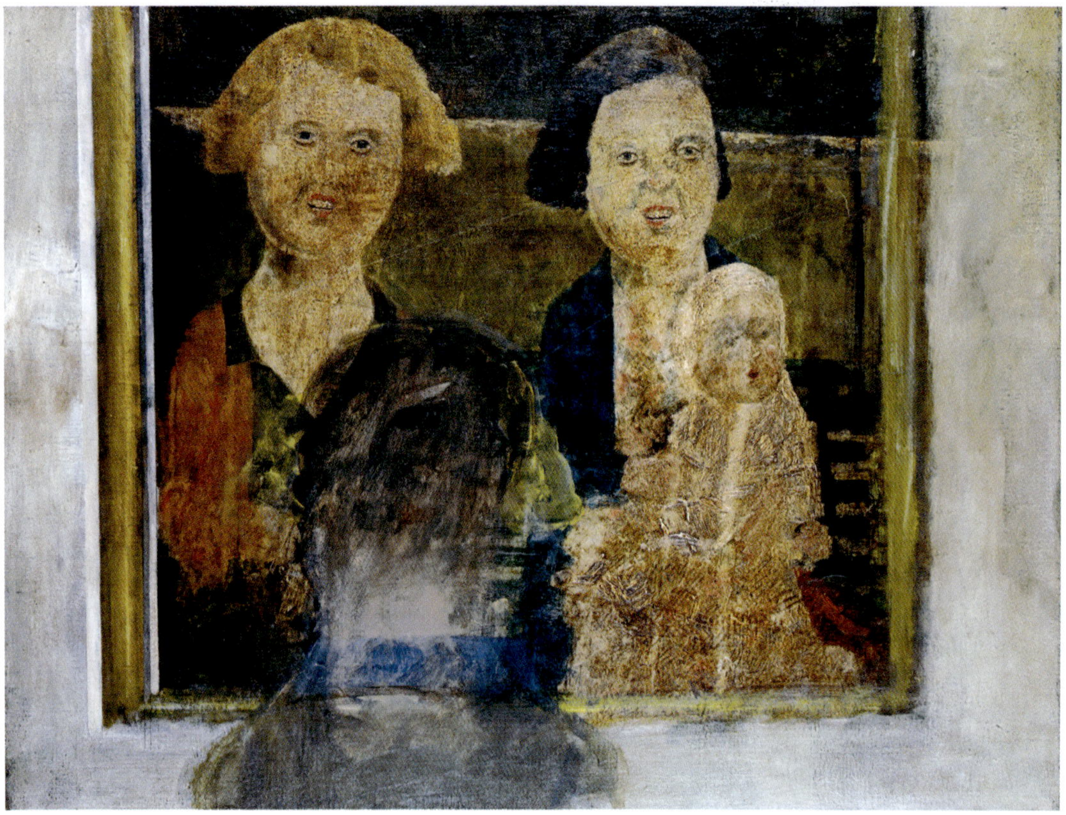

38 **Looking at Painting**, *c.*1955

layered of Blake's early paintings. The melancholic and solitary Pierrot figure of Jean-Antoine Watteau's *Gilles* (1721), which he had seen in the Louvre and to which he was to make reference over four decades later in *Marcel Duchamp's World Tour: The Artists' Fancy Dress Ball* (2004, Plate 209), was also in his mind: he took from it not only the frontal stance, the frank gaze at the viewer and the slightly dejected hunch of the shoulders, but even the splayed position of the feet. There is also an echo, so striking that it is hard to imagine it was simply unconscious or coincidental, of an 1882 painting, *Pas Mèche* (*Nothing Doing*), by the French Salon painter Jules Bastien-Lepage in the National Galleries of Scotland, which represents a street urchin standing in a similar position in front of an even more dilapidated fence. Fittingly, *Self-Portrait with Badges*, painted two years after he had produced the first of his 'hard-core' Pop collage paintings in bold designs and flat primary colours, is also the most frankly romantic and nostalgic in tone of the naturalistic paintings he had been making for nearly a decade. Looking back as it does to his childhood and adolescence in a working-class but aspirational suburban environment, it has a valedictory air, as if through it he was finally saying goodbye to his childhood in Kent while acknowledging the deep roots in that working-class upbringing that would continue to sustain him as an adult.

Where he had previously represented young children, including himself as recalled in memory, proudly sporting badges swearing their allegiances to Saturday morning film

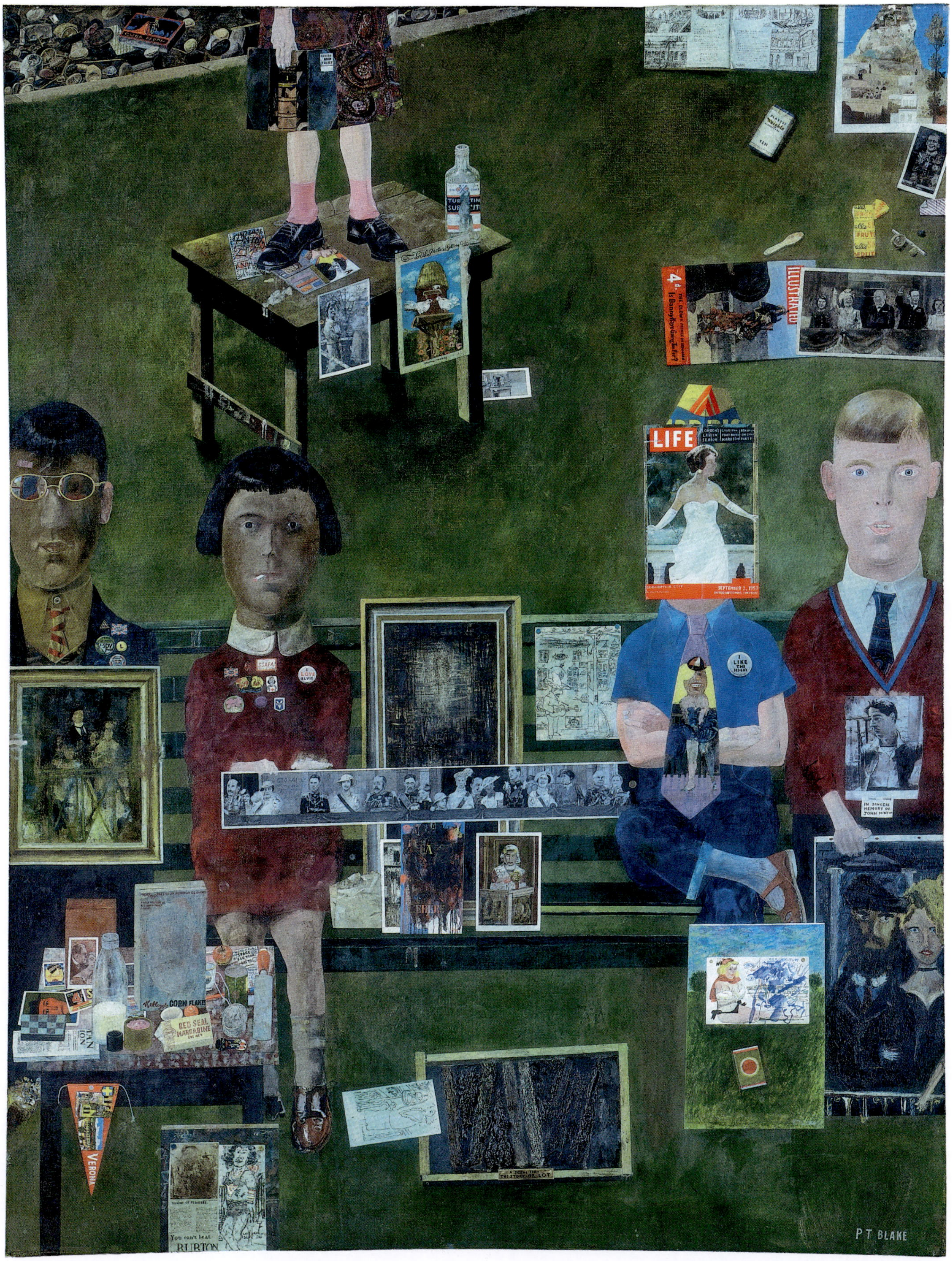

39 On the Balcony, 1955–7

clubs, dog-spotters' clubs, pop musicians, sportsmen, comic-strip heroes and the national flag, Blake now shows himself as a grown man still in thrall to such youthful enthusiasms. Standing stiffly to attention as he was to do in a lifetime of photographs for the press, he presents himself with the same forthright frontality as the denizens of his earlier pictures in a more naive style. He looks unblinkingly at us, as if attempting to give nothing away about his internal life. The rather lugubrious expression on his face, the product of scrutinising himself in the mirror for long periods rather than working from a photograph, reveals him in reflective mood rather than as revelling in terminal adolescence. When he painted this, at the age of 29, he was still experiencing the timorousness and lack of self-confidence that he had suffered since the bicycle accident that had left him facially scarred 12 years earlier: the resultant beard, as well as having five of his teeth knocked out (which has necessitated the wearing of dentures for the rest of his life), had the double trauma of making him look artificially old and of making him so cripplingly bashful with women that it was only in that very year that he finally had sex for the first time. The beard that he has worn ever since became for him a protective outer layer behind which he could conceal his more vulnerable self; it is little wonder that he has displayed in his art such a lifelong fascination with the power of masks both to conceal and to project a new identity or a fictional construct for the self.

In painting self-portraits, all artists are faced with the self-conscious decision about what clothes they should wear for posterity, while bearing in mind what image and signals they will project to the viewer. Blake here presents himself in denim jeans, denim jacket and basketball shoes, long before these became the uniform of the new youth culture, but he was far from being a teenager himself. A long-time habitué of jazz clubs, he clutches an Elvis fan club magazine not necessarily out of any overpowering emotional connection with the new rock'n'roll but because declaring such an affiliation might transform him from a lonely observer into an enthusiastic participant in the new, sexually liberated and joyful atmosphere such music conveyed. This painting of a boy-man, stranded in the suburbs while dreaming of the big city, is full of the very contradictions that were to continue to enrich Blake's art and to give it a bittersweet taste. It is at once touching and comical, humble and proud, unapologetically old-fashioned and coolly modern.

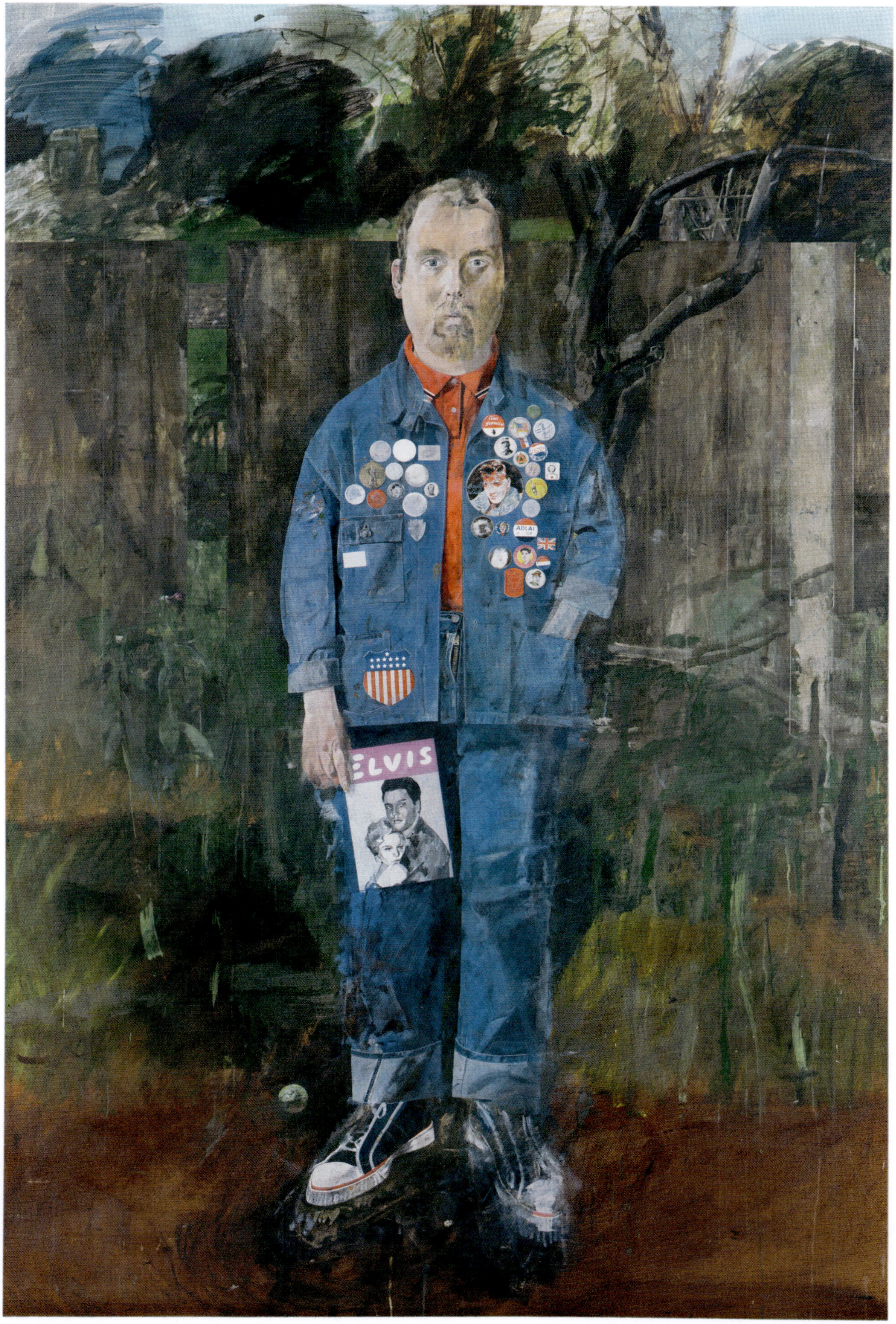

40 **Self-Portrait with Badges**, 1961

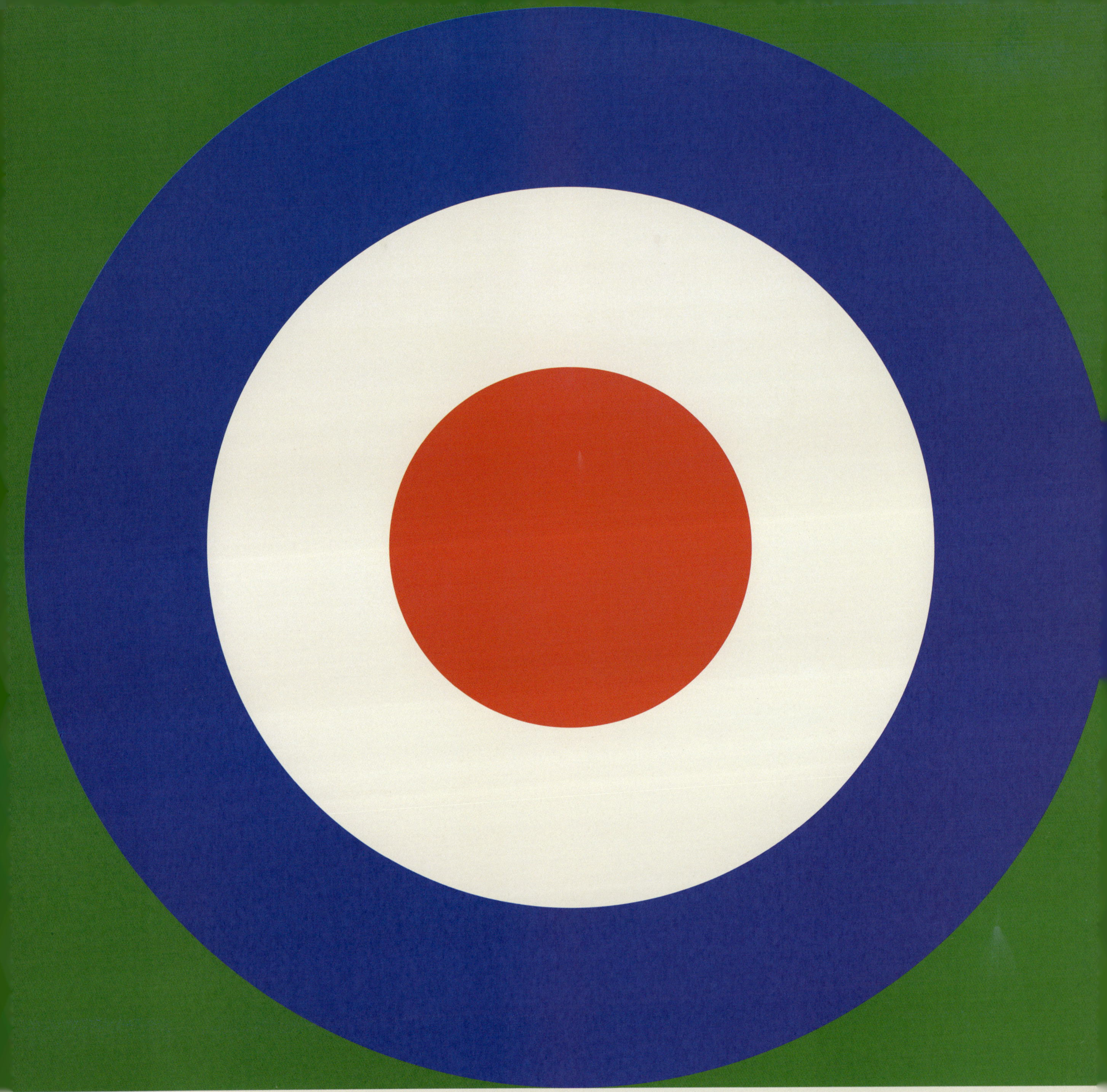

2

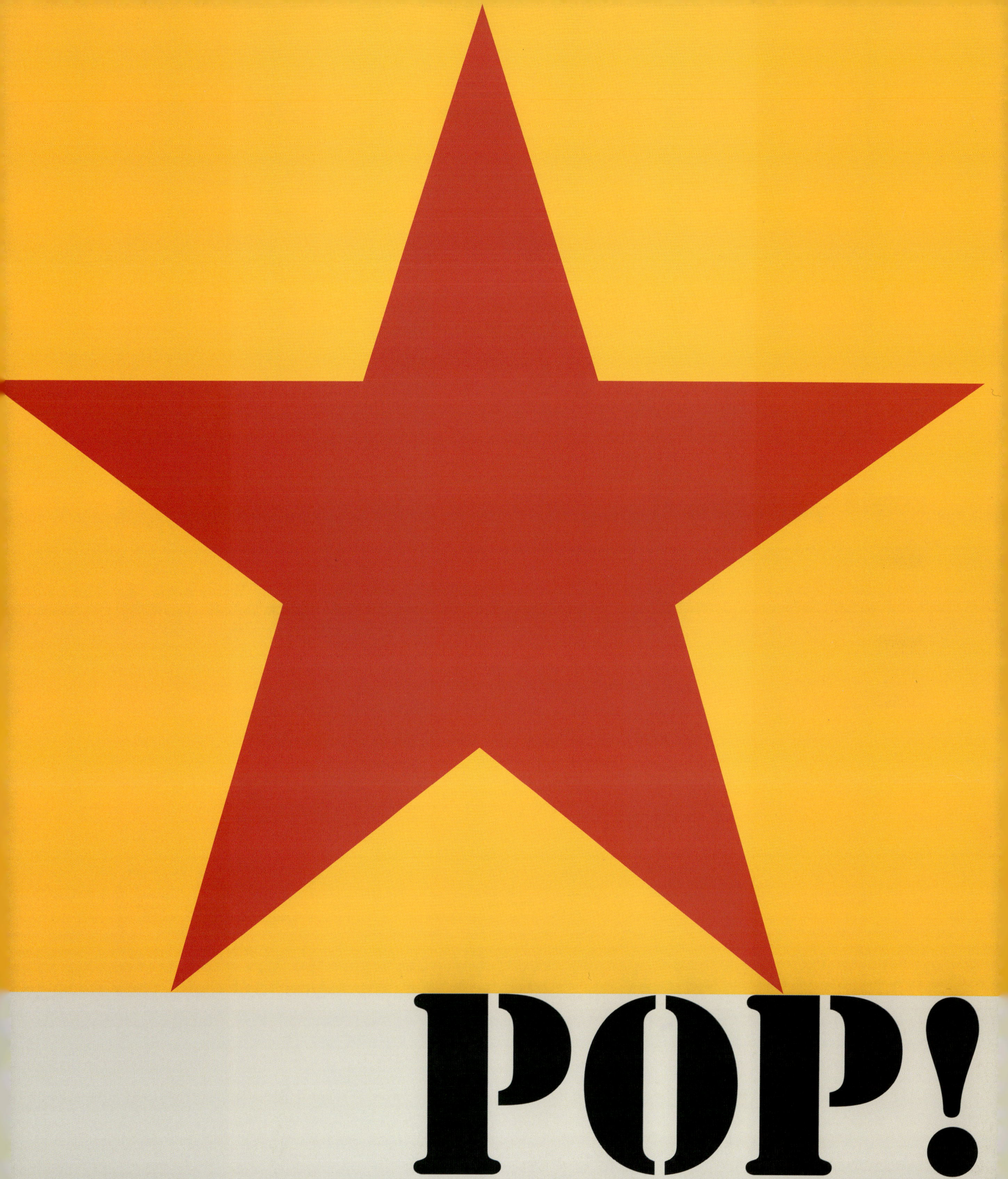

POP!

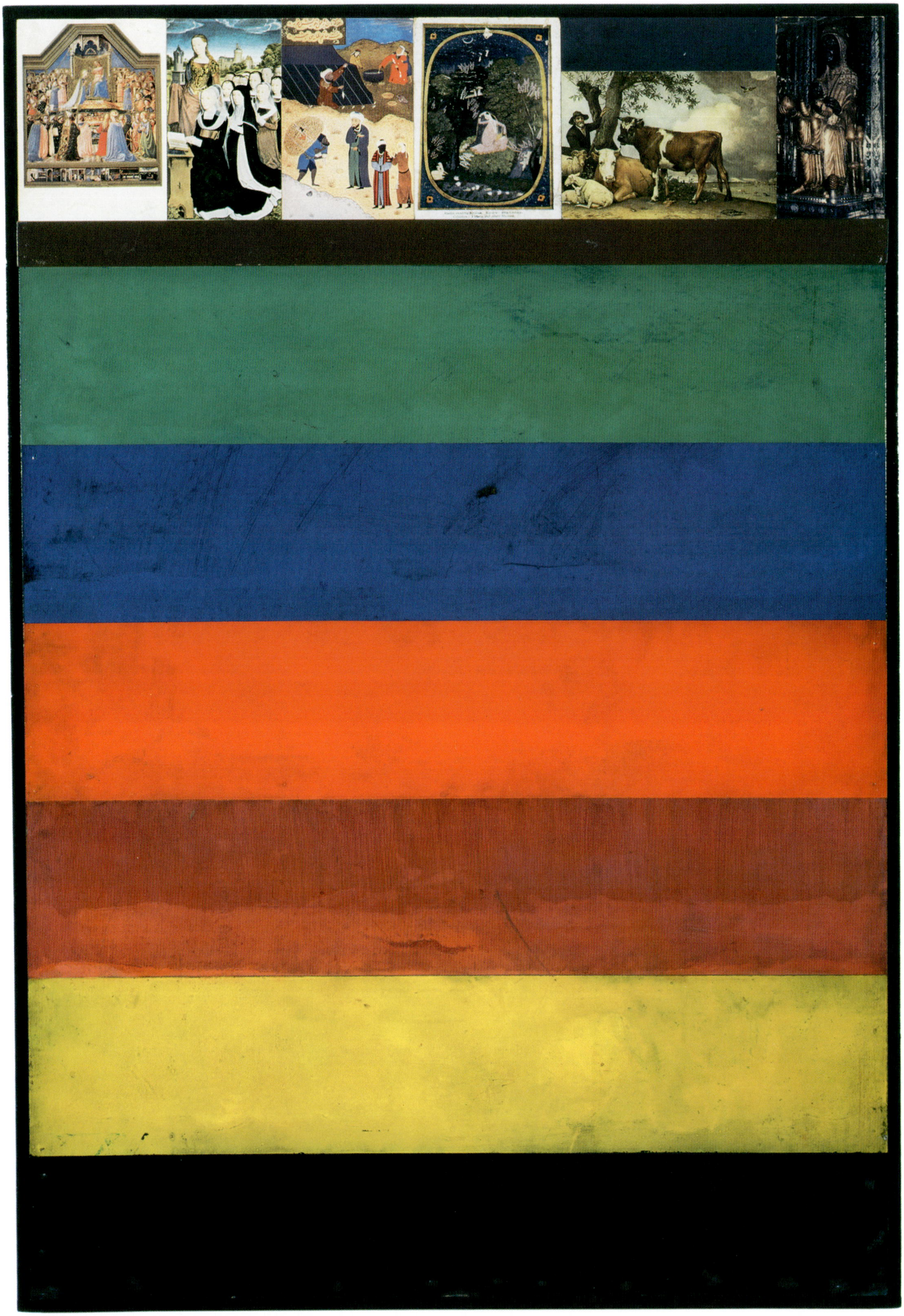

2 Pop!

Blake has wryly stated that in retrospect he sees 'staying ahead of the avant-garde' as one of his prime characteristics and ambitions as an artist. This is especially so in his pivotal role in the early history of Pop Art, an international movement that emerged only in 1961–2. The collage paintings that Blake began to produce in 1959 conform closely in their characteristics to the definition that I formulated for Pop painting in the introduction to my book, *Pop Art: A Continuing History* (London: Thames & Hudson, 1990). As I maintained there,

> this generally involves the use of existing imagery from mass culture already processed into two dimensions, preferably borrowed from advertising, photography, comic strips and other mass media sources; an emphasis on flatness and frontal presentation, characteristics which in modern representational painting had come to be associated largely with naïve art; an associated preference (especially in American Pop) for centralized composition and for flat areas of unmodulated and unmixed colour bound by hard edges, or for mechanical and other deliberately inexpressive techniques that imply the removal of the artist's hand and suggest the depersonalized processes of mass production; an unapologetic decorativeness; a delving into areas of popular taste and kitsch previously considered outside the limits of fine art; and a concentration on the contemporary subject-matter integral to the ready-made sources the artist has used.

Blake was already a kind of Pop artist, through the subject matter of his circus pictures and portraits of children reading comics, by the time of the first recorded use of the term in print in 1958 in an article by Lawrence Alloway. It was only after the term came into use, however, that Blake saw it as a challenge to reference popular culture more directly and to do so with the aid of materials and procedures closely associated with that culture, such as household enamel paint and colour photographs cut out of magazines and glued onto the surface of his pictures.

Blake anticipated Pop Art first through the popular subject matter of his mid-1950s paintings and collages, and then in 1959 in a new series of bold and brightly coloured paintings encasing appropriated photographic and printed imagery and found objects. His key and influential role in laying the groundwork for the movement is indisputable, as was evident in the television programme *Pop Goes the Easel*, filmed by Ken Russell in February 1962 and aired as part of the BBC's 'Monitor' series on 25 March 1962. In it Blake is seen as a friend and mentor to three other emerging Pop painters: Pauline Boty, Derek Boshier

41 **The Fine Art Bit**, 1959

and Peter Phillips. With a sprinkling of scripted realism and even a Surrealistic dream sequence, the film follows the young artists around the London of their inspiration, seeing them visiting Portobello Road and the Bertram Mills Circus, playing funfair games and letting their hair down at the film's climax, when David Hockney and others join them at a bohemian party for a bit of vigorous twisting. The first glimpse of Blake in the film is of him waking up from a dream about Brigitte Bardot, a conceit imposed upon him by the director but nevertheless one that was in keeping with the current subject matter of his art.

The other artists for whom a similar claim can be made as precursors of Pop Art were working at the same time (in the mid-1950s) but without initial knowledge of each other: Jasper Johns and Robert Rauschenberg were in adjacent studios in New York, while Richard Hamilton and Eduardo Paolozzi were members of the fairly enclosed society of the Independent Group in London. Whether one calls Blake a father of Pop, a grandfather of Pop or a godfather of Pop, the movement in its British incarnations would certainly not have developed quite as it did without his example. This is especially the case for the slightly younger artists who arrived as students at the Royal College a few years after his departure, all of whom looked up to him as a trailblazer: Pauline Boty in the 1958 intake (in the stained glass department, and belatedly as a painter), David Hockney, Peter Phillips, Derek Boshier and to a lesser extent Allen Jones among the 1959 arrivals, and Patrick Caulfield a year later.

The incorporation of different pictorial languages (including that of hard-edged abstraction) in Blake's 'hard-core' Pop pictures, and his readiness to question and even contradict his favoured naturalistic figurative style of painting with a stripped-down and brutally direct form of representation through found material, were part of a broader tendency on his part to investigate a multiplicity of ways of making art. In the space of a single year he would happily produce works in the guise of an academic, naive or naturalistic painter, as a sculptor, as a collagist and as a proto-conceptual artist, and to exhibit them separately, almost as if he were several different artists. In 1960, for instance, he showed in various contexts in five separate group shows in London, presenting objects at the Institute of Contemporary Arts, a series of gold-leaf paintings described as sections of Japanese screens in a two-person show at the New Vision Centre (a gallery for avant-garde art), and some of his more straightforwardly handpainted figurative pictures at the Portal Gallery (known for its promotion of naive painting). To operate in this way appealed to the mischievous side of Blake's nature, but it was in some way also a form of commercial and career suicide, since it risked confusing both the critics and the public and could be seen as suggesting a dilettantish lack of commitment to a particular idea of art.

What has taken time for some to understand and for some of his detractors to accept even today is that the astonishing variety of Blake's work comes from a single and very

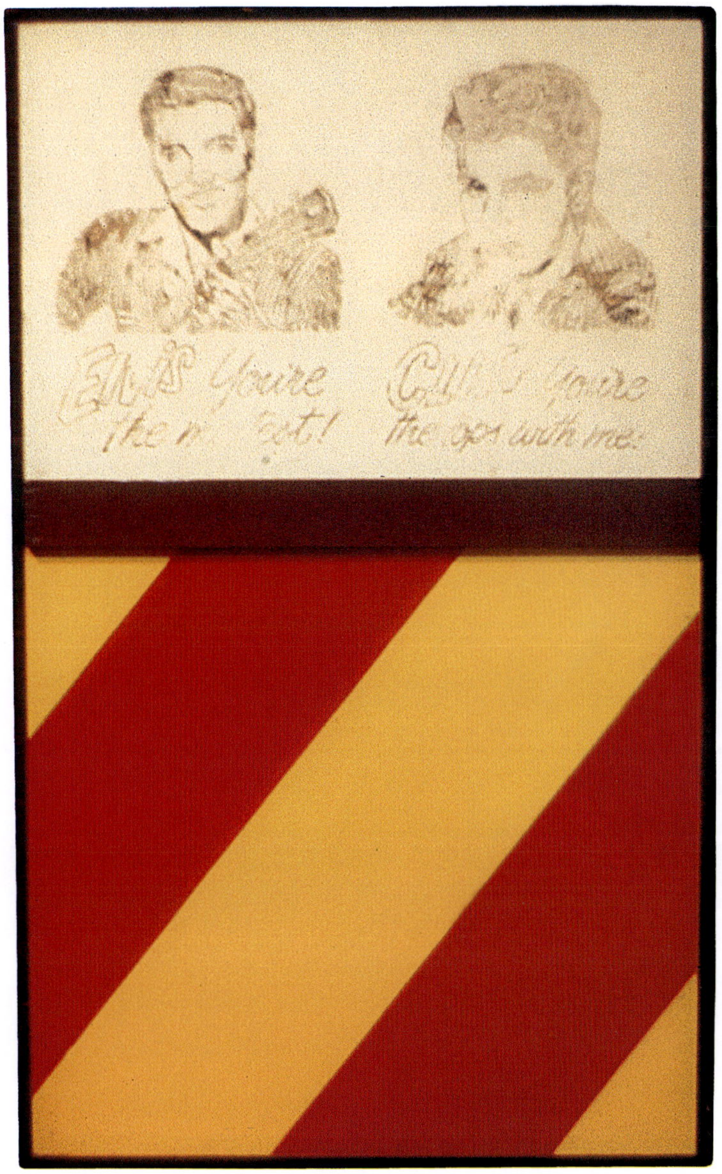

42 **Elvis and Cliff**, 1959

clear sense of purpose: that of investigating as many different ways as possible of making art and of finding a suitable form for his subject matter. Behind the abrupt changes of direction lies a solid conceptual project arising above all from the freedom he declared for himself as a young artist. He has repeatedly explained that he thinks of his art as a tree whose trunk is a certain kind of academic representational painting rooted in tradition, out of which grows a number of branches that take him in a variety of other directions. Thus it is that he is able to spend 30 years reworking a single picture and to paint with extreme delicacy and finesse in a manner that links to a realist tradition stretching back to

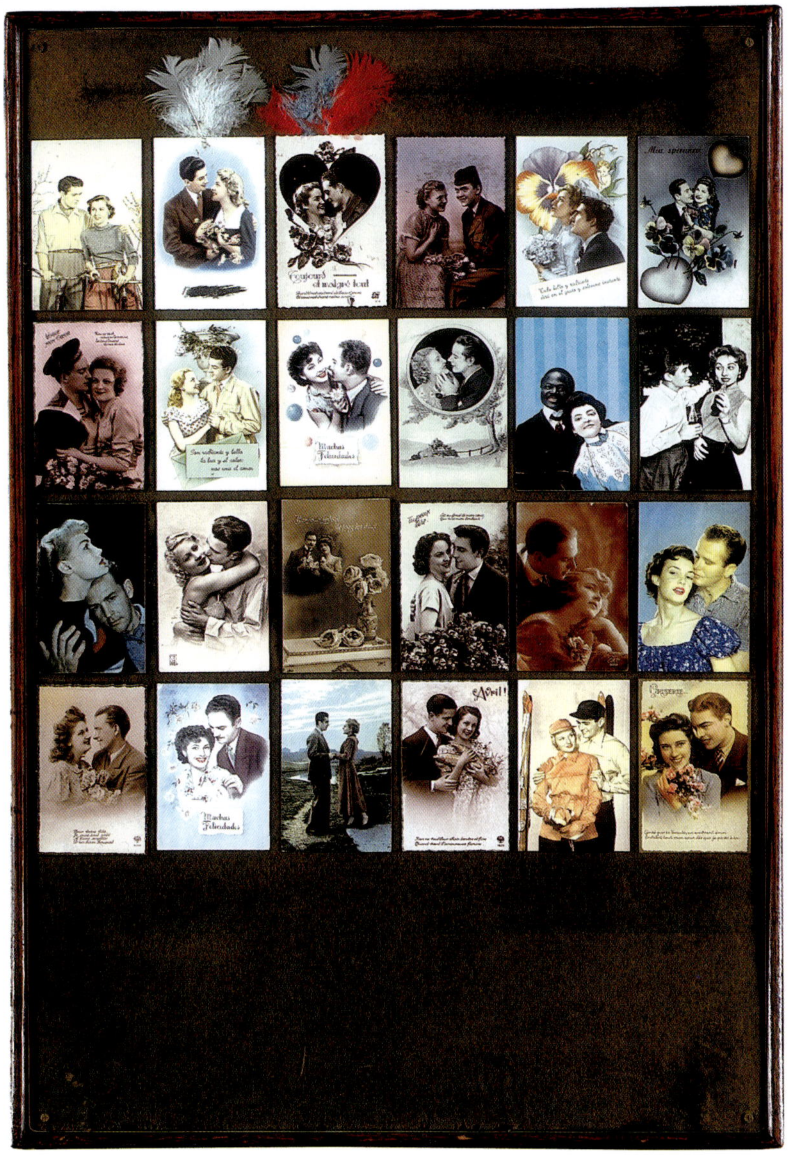

43 **Couples**, 1959

the great Flemish painters of the fifteenth century via Holbein, Vermeer and Ingres, while also producing pictures that seem almost to eliminate the hand, applying solid bands of uninflected gloss paint in the manner of a painter-decorator and then sticking photographs on top, completing the imagery in an instant with barely a hint of labour. Thus, too, he has been equally at ease declaring as art an arrangement of found manufactured objects, a meticulously rendered wood engraving, a screenprinted reinterpretation of one of his watercolours or a collage of printed ephemera.

Since the 1980s, when fragmentation, games with stylistic inconsistency and historical or stylistic quotations became accepted strategies arising from a 'post-modern' mindset, such a free-ranging approach has become very accepted, almost the norm. Now, indeed, it is almost expected that the same artist might paint, create video installations, take photographs, act in performances and have sculptural objects fabricated by specialist teams. During the 1960s, however, when an artist was meant to have a signature style, a favoured medium and a particular range of imagery and subject matter, it was problematic and troublesome to leap around in the way that Blake was doing. For him it was never a question of being fashionable. It was, rather, that with such a butterfly mind he was always thinking of different ways of making art and could not contain his enthusiasm for taking up a new project even if it meant having to set something else aside. Though working on commissions and towards exhibitions often helped to concentrate his attention, he was notorious for allowing delays to hamper the realisation of projects and for taking his time to bring various schemes, and even individual paintings, to fruition. Although he might take years to complete a work, and on many occasions (particularly during the 1950s and 1960s) ended up selling paintings in what he considered to be an unfinished state, he always maintained an enthusiastic embrace of spontaneity and a sense of play. Given the polished state of some of his best-known paintings, one cannot help but remark on the brushy look and sense of incompleteness that characterise some key works of the 1950s and 1960s, such as *Girls and their Hero (Girls with their Hero)* (1959–62, Plate 68), the *Captain Webb Matchbox* (Plate 58) of 1961–2 and the large 1963 painting *The Lettermen* (Plate 4). Such features cannot have been the result just of laziness, impatience or lack of time, but a conscious aesthetic decision – perhaps affected by the post-Abstract Expressionist casualness flaunted in the contemporaneous work of Larry Rivers and David Hockney – to present an image as if caught halfway through the process of being formed.

Collage Paintings

Among the most radically conceived of all British Pop works, and the flip side to the 'half-finished' figurative pictures, were the collage paintings initiated by Blake in 1959, a full two or three years before the term Pop was in common usage. They are characterised by a daunting simplicity and directness in their appropriation of existing photographs, glued onto surfaces that mimic ordinary walls and doors painted in flat bright colours with household gloss paint. To make paintings that looked like ordinary objects, and that were made with the same materials and processes as those things, was an extremely novel idea, notwithstanding the debt he himself acknowledges to Jasper Johns's paintings of such objects as flags and archery targets, which had been exhibited for the first time (and to immediate acclaim) in New York in 1958. Blake's *The First Real Target?* (1961, Plate 59)

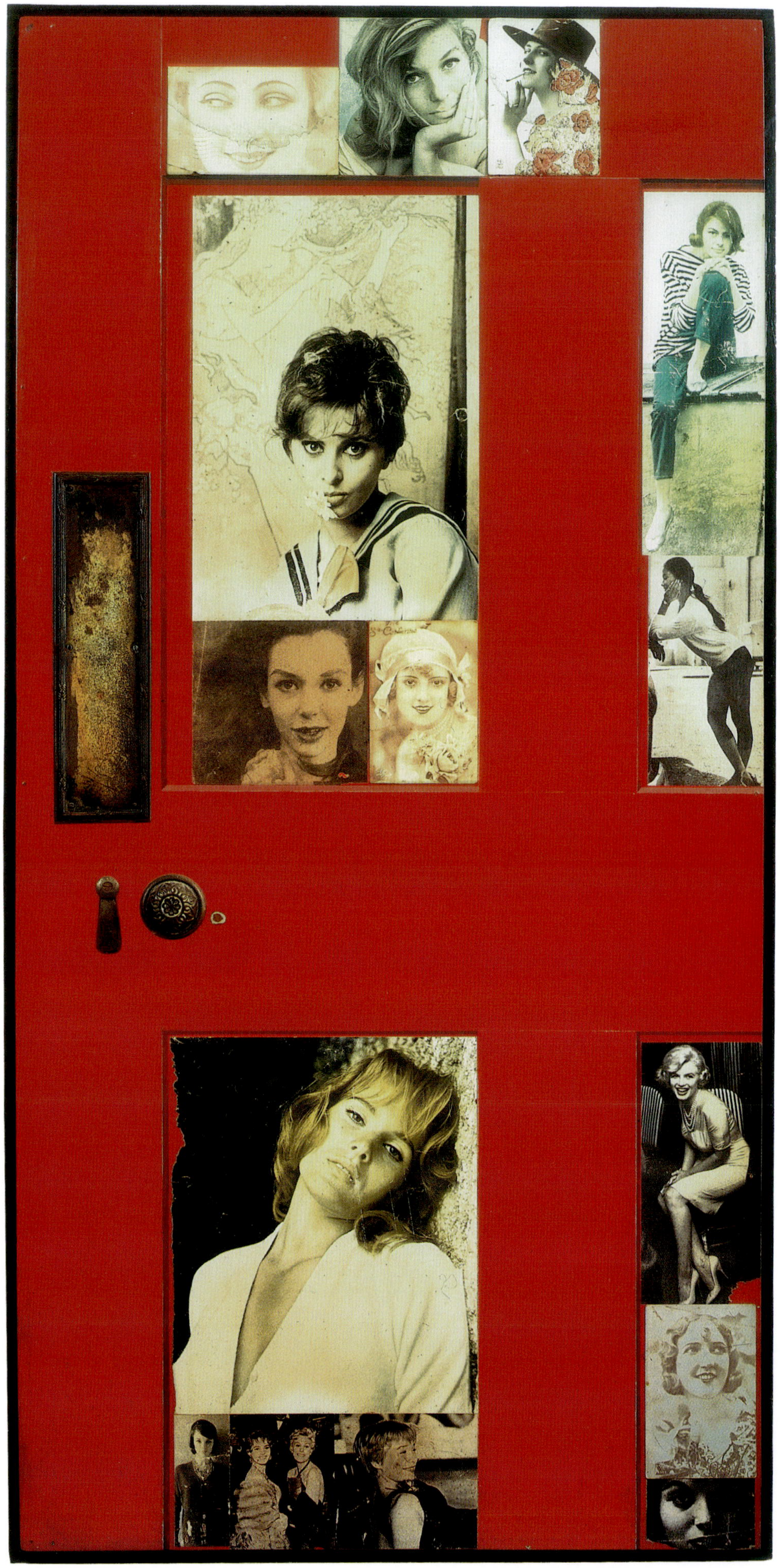

44 **Girlie Door**, 1959

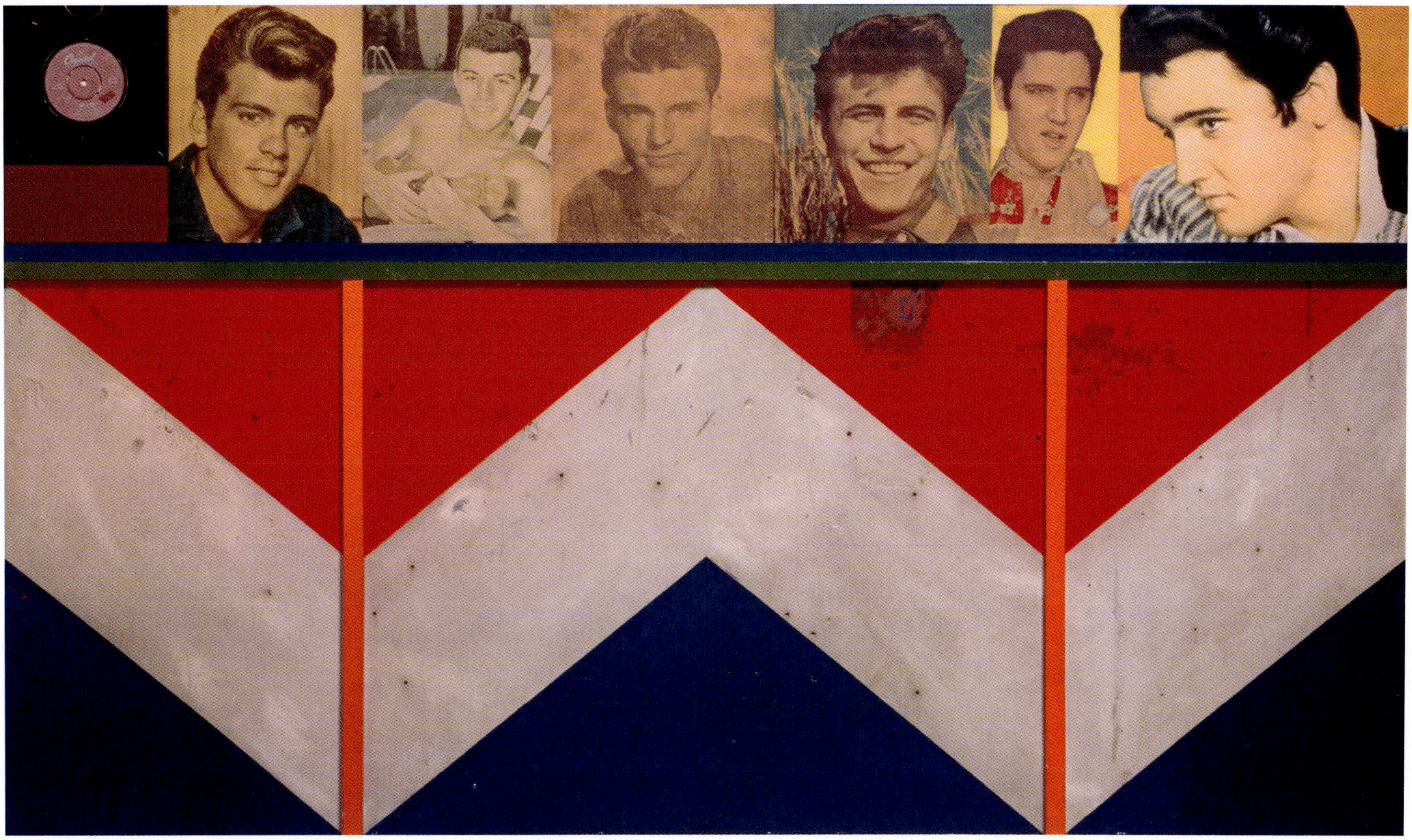

45 **Got a Girl**, 1960–61

was the most overt (and impudent) of his responses to the delightful shock he experienced on seeing reproductions of Johns's work. Instead of a handmade painting representing the simple concentric circles of a target design, Blake purchased an actual target and did nothing more to it than to frame it like a painting and to spell out its title – with a crucial final question mark – in the upper register, where Johns himself had placed plaster casts of the human face or body parts. In place of the trembling delicacy, vulnerability and poignant uncertainty of Johns's brushmarks, however, Blake in this case simply presented the actual object, bare, and in other works coated the support with a thick layer of flat, shiny paint that made it look more like a manufactured or functional object than a work of art. Such works by Blake, which are amongst his most distinctive and subversive contributions to the history of modern art, seemed to arrive out of nowhere, fully blown. How could it be otherwise, given the need for them to be painted boldly, unapologetically and without hesitation?

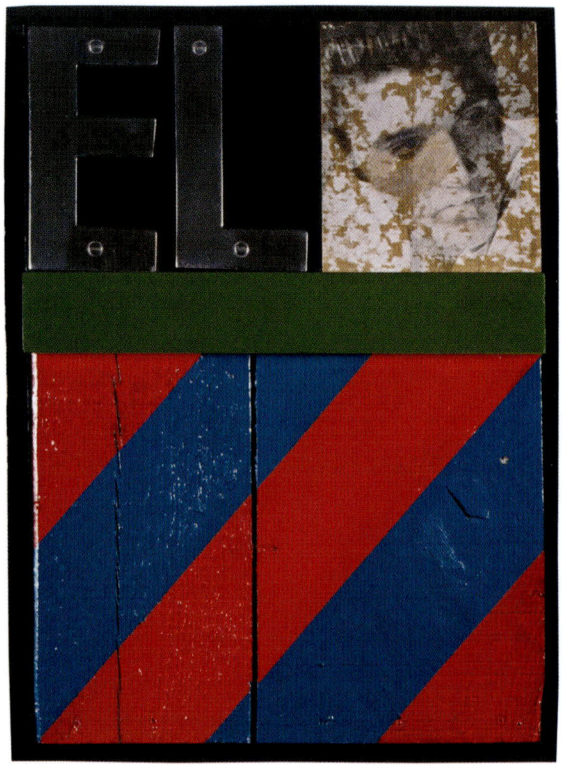

46 **EL**, 1961

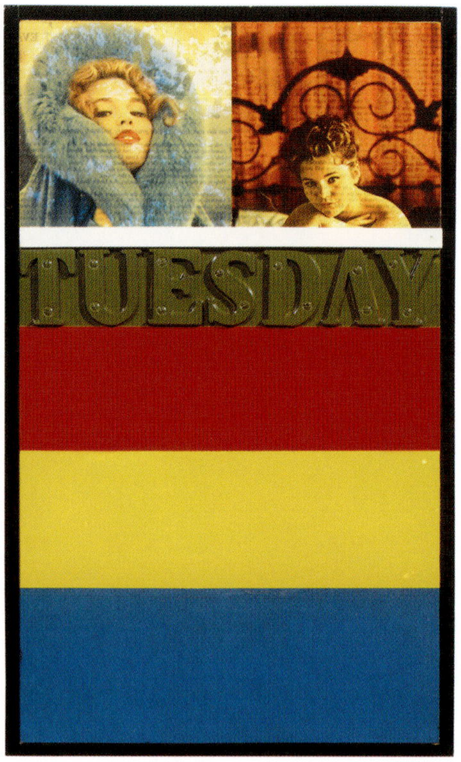

47 **Tuesday**, 1961

The reliance in these works on the ready-made and their elimination of obvious signs of skilful handiwork is all the more surprising given the ability already demonstrated by Blake for meticulous drawing and brushwork of a traditional, even academic, nature. Each picture is presented as a found object, although in fact it is essentially a brilliantly disguised illusion fabricated by the artist himself. Even small-scale paintings of this type have great presence thanks to the formal elegance and graphic verve of their compositions: witness *Kim Novak Wall* (1959) which pays homage to a beautiful Hollywood star as pictured in an official publicity still, or *Elvis Presley Wall* (1961), topped and tailed by a single sultry photographic image and by a quadrant representing the concentric wings of a target. Such is the case, too, with *Tuesday* (1961, Plate 47), which incorporates two magazine photographs of the then 18-year-old American film star Tuesday Weld, her name spelt out in store-bought plastic letters so that the whole also reads as a page in a pin-up calendar. The use of repetition and close-ups in works of this kind presage similar strategies in the silkscreen paintings of movie stars on which Andy Warhol embarked in New York in 1962; the concern with glamour and fame, too, anticipate classic Pop concerns not fully explored by other artists until some time later.

Girlie Door (1959, Plate 44), one of the largest and most impressive of these early works, uses scale not to overwhelm but as a way of ensuring an intimacy with the viewer appropriate to the subject matter. Here, various film stars seen at their seductive best,

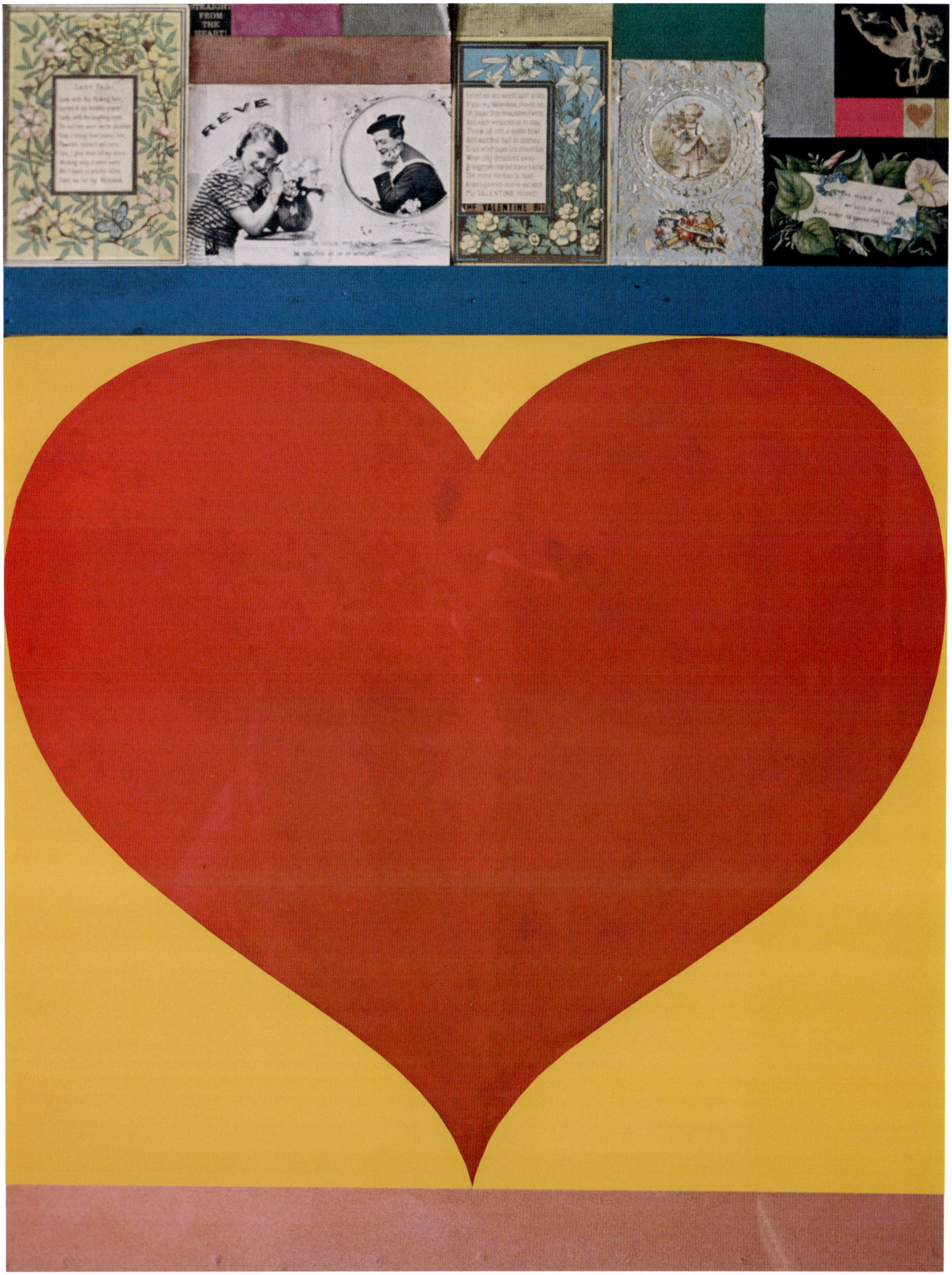

48 **Valentine**, *c.*1959–60

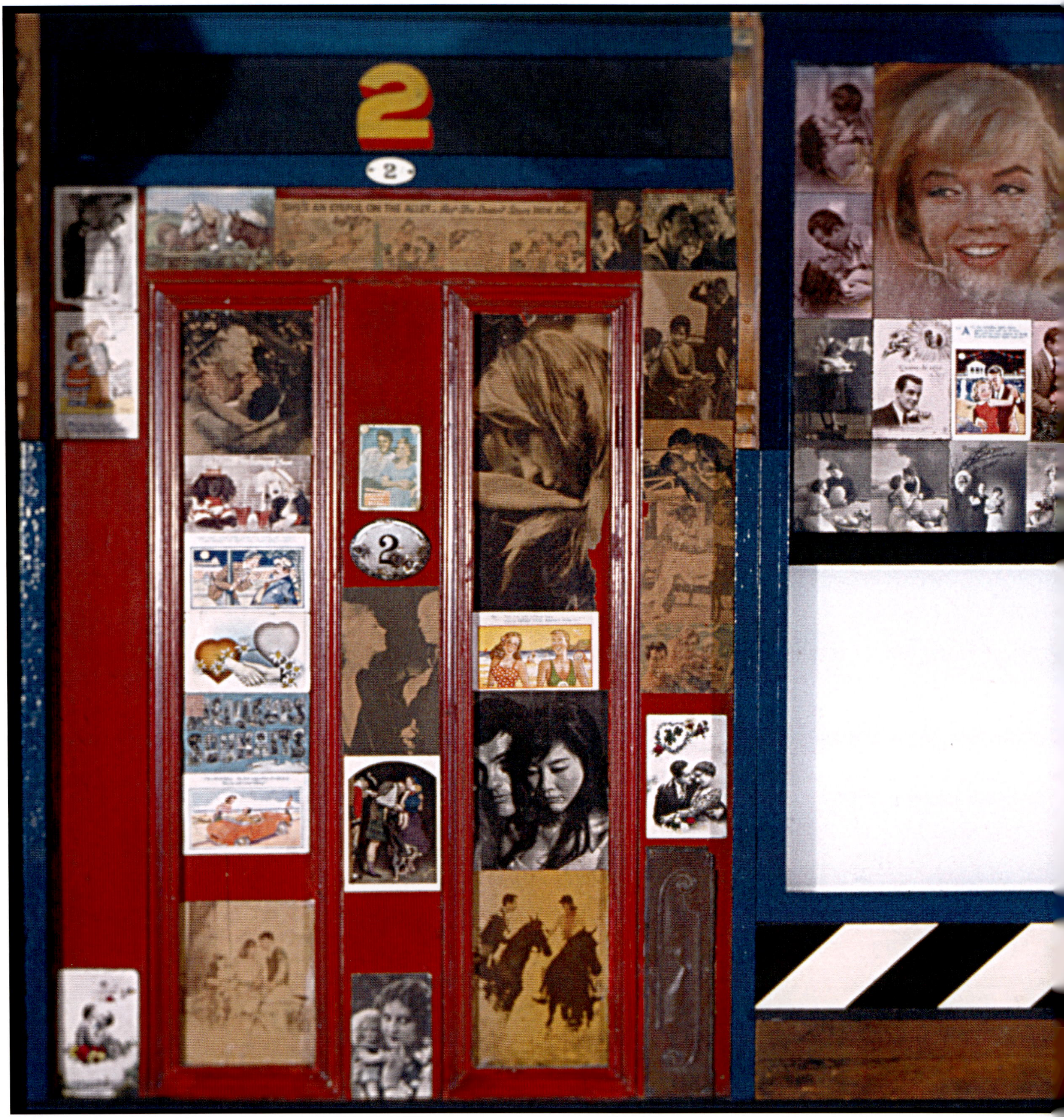

49 **Love Wall**, 1961

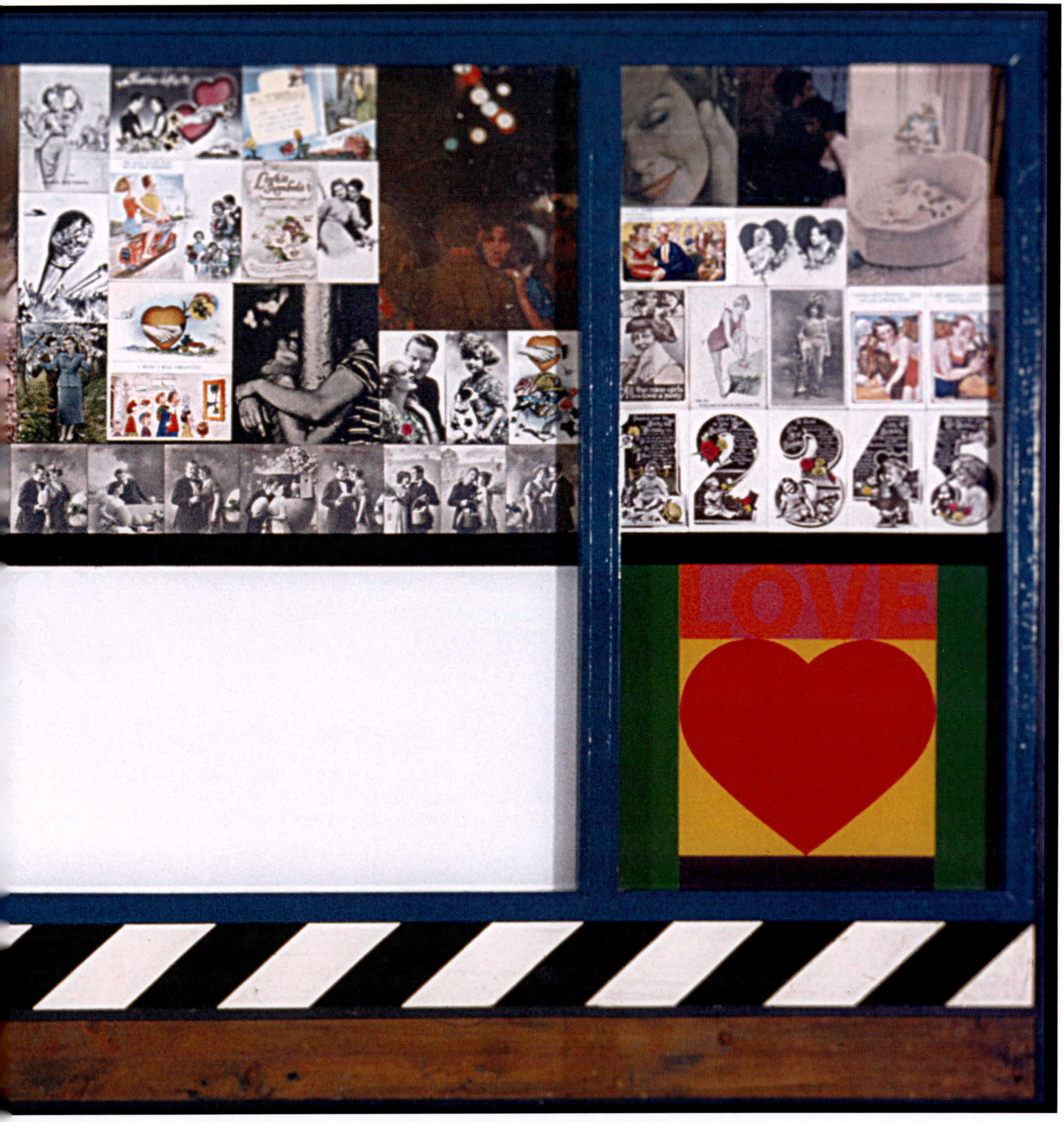
LOVE
12345

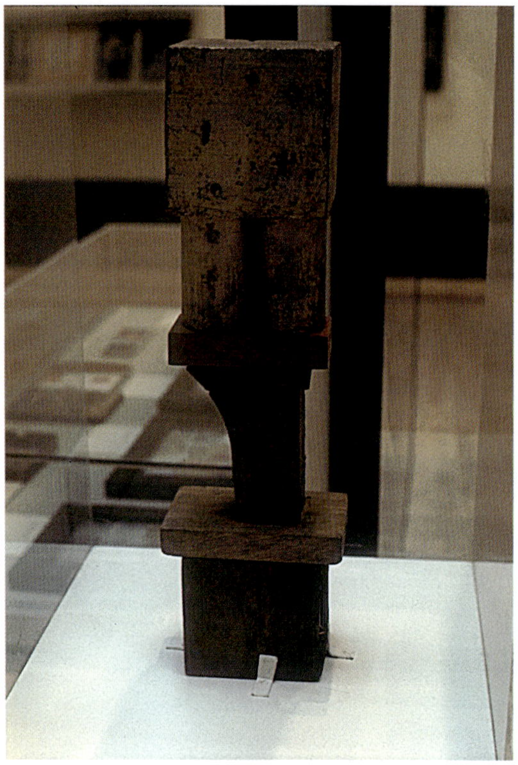

50 **Bodhisattva Sculpture**, 1959–60

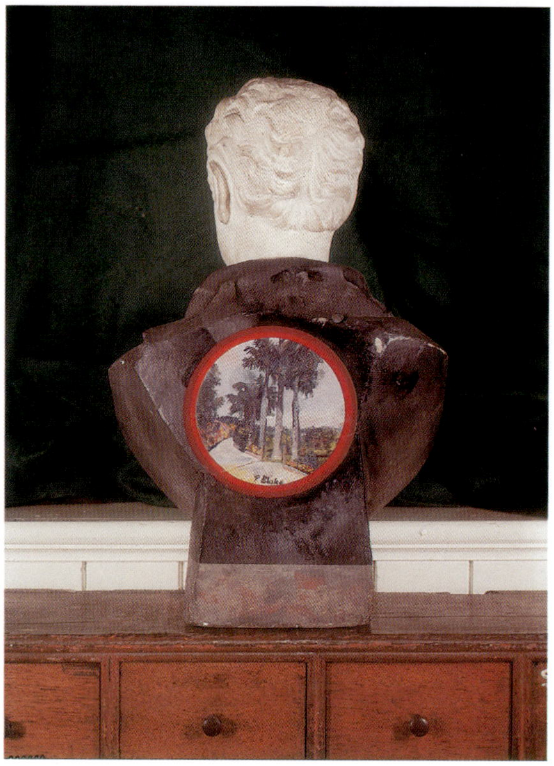

51 **Crazy said Snow White**, 1959 (detail)

including Novak again along with Gina Lollobrigida, Marilyn Monroe and Elsa Martinelli, are displayed in a more random arrangement as if pasted onto the bedroom door of a young male fan besotted with the movies. There is no irony in this, only an expression of genuine admiration. Such is the case, too, with the most densely inhabited and ambitious in scale of all Blake's early collage paintings, *Love Wall* (1961, Plate 49). This uses the distinct architectural sections of door, wall and windows as framing devices for a diverse collection of drawn and photographic postcards, magazine pages and a postcard reproduction of Sir John Everett Millais's painting *The Order of Release 1746* of 1852–3 (from the collection of the Tate Gallery); a painting by Blake in his customary bright colours, representing a Valentine's heart and emblazoned with the word 'LOVE', serves to tie everything together and brings this animated discussion of romantic love to a tranquil close.

Throughout his life, Blake has consistently chosen his imagery out of affection in a spirit of celebration, setting him apart from some of the more sceptical or caustic examinations of pop culture by his fellow artists. The survival of these instincts can be experienced with particular force in his periodic return to the principles of his collage paintings and constructions of the late 1950s and early 1960s, such as *Wall* (conceived in 1962 and finally completed exactly a quarter of a century later, Plate 53), with its bold presentation of a flag and photographs, and a group of entirely new works made for a solo exhibition called *Déjà vu* in Tokyo in 1988 (discussed in chapter 7). In 1972 he made a huge print, *Studio Tack-Board* (Plate 52), in a deliberately impersonal medium, that of offset lithography, as a summation and reflection of these methods and of their personal import in his art. As he wrote in a statement dated January 1972 for publication in the catalogue *Fourteen Big Prints* (London: Bernard Jacobson, 1972): 'This print is just [a] glimpse at one of my collections, postcards of circus "side shows" for instance, a few badges from the quite large collection I have, one or two photographs which I have taken myself, of my daughter, my wife and friends of mine. A glimpse at the usually private world of the artist[']s studio.'

Objects and Sculptures

Blake is always thought of first and foremost as a painter, but his fascination with objects – both as subject matter and as elements of his paintings, assemblages and box constructions – also brought him early to sculpture. Some of the first of these were shown as his contribution to a three-person show at the Institute of Contemporary Arts, London, in 1960: *Theo Crosby: Sculpture, Peter Blake: Objects, John Latham: Libraries*. Blake's choice there of the Duchampian-inflected 'objects' over 'sculpture' rightly stressed the nature of these works as things that he had bought or found rather than constructed, modelled or carved himself, and he presented them with relatively little tampering. The faux-beatnik title of the most elaborate of these works, *Crazy Said Snow White* (1959, Plate 51), came from a novelty record by the American musical comedian Stan Freberg; a bust is one of

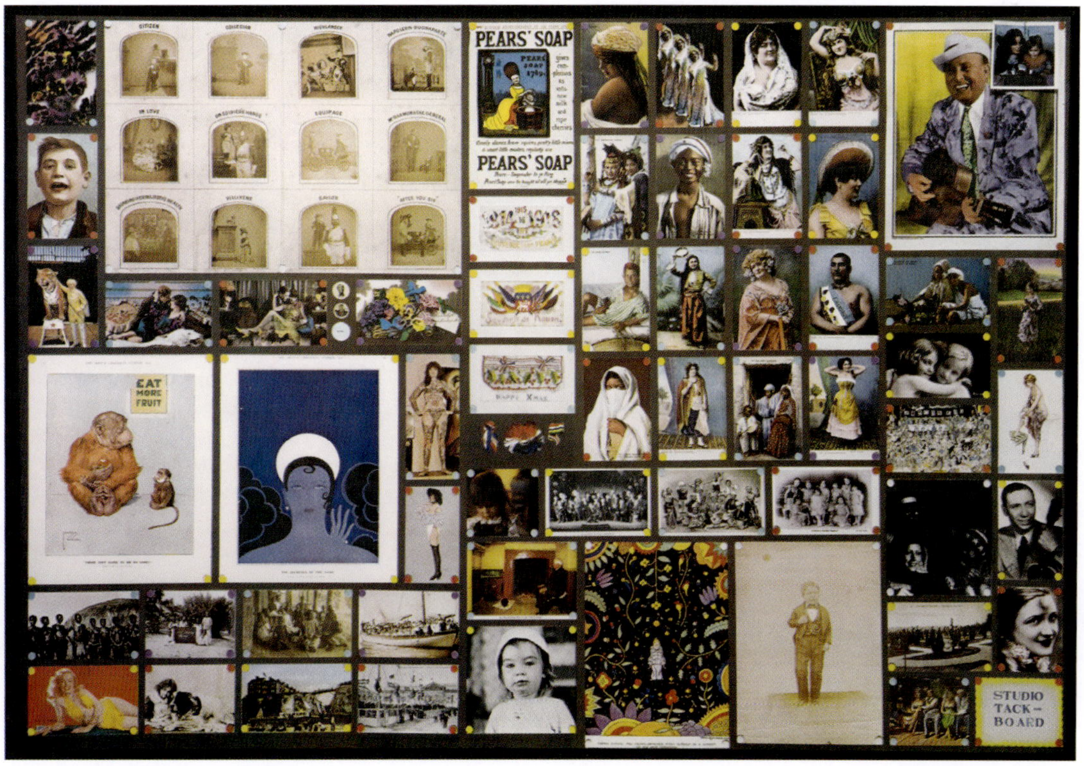

52 **Studio Tack-Board**, 1972

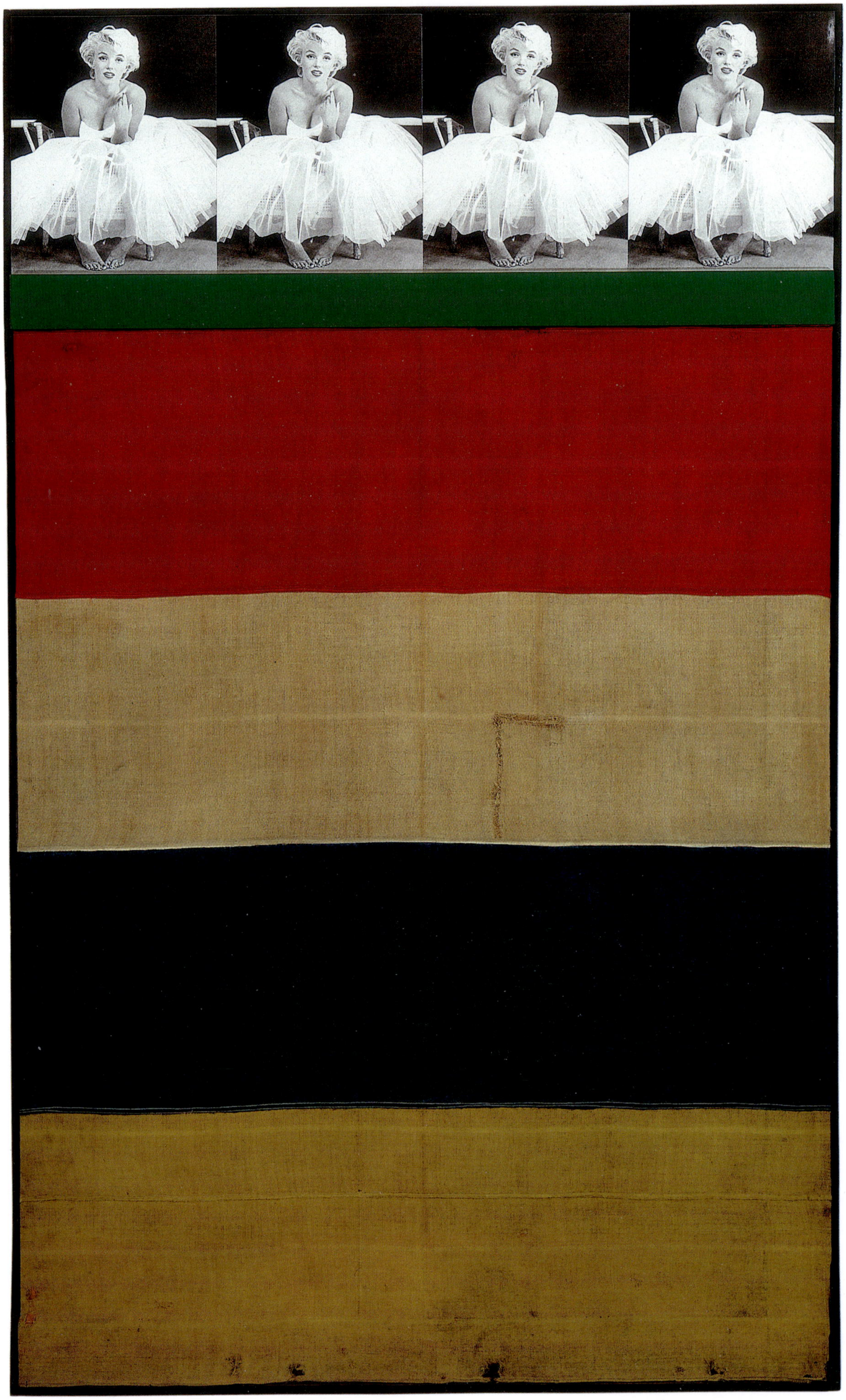

53 **Wall**, 1962–87

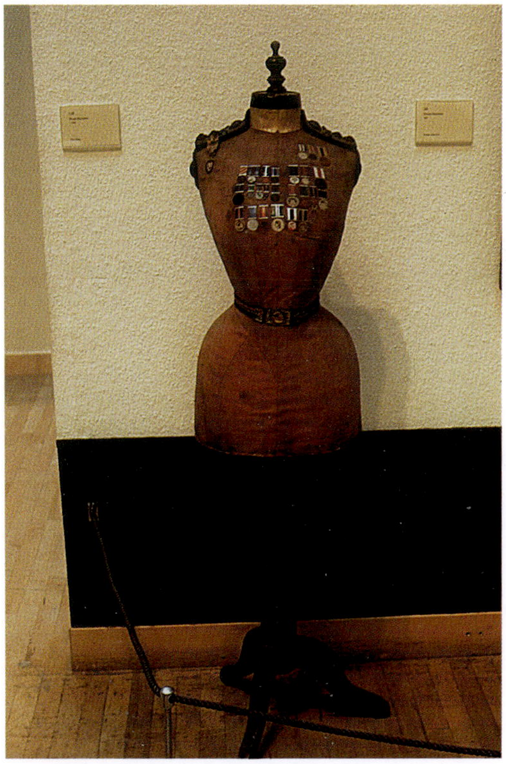

54 **Drum Majorette**, 1959

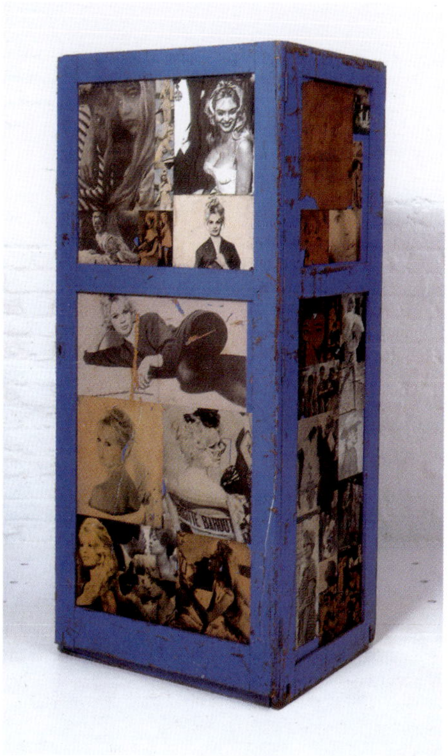

55 **Locker** (closed), 1959

the few fragments of it to have survived. The level of intervention in such works is kept to a minimum. *Bodhisattva Sculpture* (1959–60, Plate 50), for example, which takes on the fashion for Buddhism evident at that time in the writing of the Beats, including Jack Kerouac, is a devotional figure created simply by placing found blocks of wood on top of each other; its cheekiness is accentuated by the commentary it suggests on a sculptural cliché of the time, that of the totemic figure, as favoured particularly by members of the Independent Group including Paolozzi and William Turnbull. *Drum Majorette* (1959, Plate 54) must have appeared somewhat shocking at the time to anyone with a conservative view of sculpture, consisting as it does of nothing more than a dressmaker's dummy festooned with medals.

Blake effortlessly extended his notion of the collage-painting into three dimensions by gluing photographs onto objects, as in his jaunty redecoration of the Royal Air Force-type locker (*Locker*, Plates 1 and 55) in 1959, or by placing toys, printed ephemera and other found objects into box-like constructions sometimes presented in the guise of windows or storefronts. That he worried so little about conventional definitions of sculpture, or even about the degree to which he was simply reordering existing materials rather than inventing new forms, does much to explain their breezy cheerfulness and originality. It was a surprising, contradictory and – for some – outrageous notion of originality to have such temerity in claiming as one's own artistic property things that had been designed and

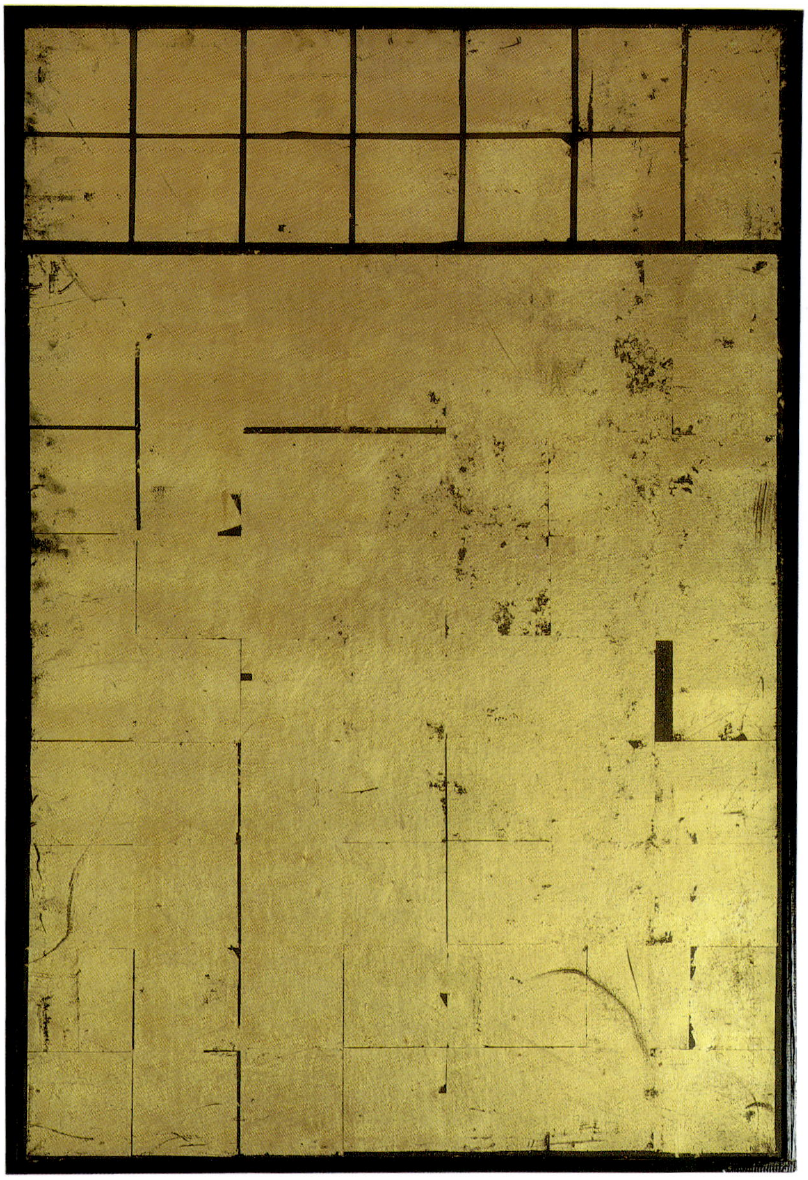

57 **Gold Painting (Piece of a Japanese Screen)**, 1959

56 **Untitled Gold Painting**, 1959

made by others and simply rearranged. Of course, Duchamp's notion of the ready-made was by then nearly half a century old, but Blake did not even feel the need to 'excuse' his simple strategy for sculpture by citing such serious art historical precedents. Instead, he presented himself as an avid consumer and collector, busily scouring the magazines and the junk shops for images and objects that caught his eye.

This was a truly democratic notion on Blake's part, a question of placing himself squarely within the visual culture of his time rather than looking down on the taste of the masses from his lofty position as a fine artist. By this I do not mean to give the impression that he even took a theoretical stance on the matter: he genuinely saw no dividing line between his popular tastes as a human being and his role as an artist. Mass entertainments such as the circus and wrestling matches, the new teenage rock'n'roll music, pin-up calendars and strippers, magazines, advertisements and the packaging of consumer products were all part of the visual spectacle that excited him in contemporary life, and which he sought to document and display in his own work. He never lost sight, moreover, of the personal import of the materials and images he used. The locker on which he pasted his objects of fantasy, though bought in a local junk shop, was an object freighted with associations. Blake has spoken frankly of his sexual inexperience at that age. The work itself, an empty container charged with unconsummated and sublimated desire, says it all.

The *Gold Paintings* (Plates 56–7) created by Peter Blake for a two-man show at the New Vision Centre in London between 18 January and 6 February 1960 were made in parallel with the sumptuously coloured enamel paintings representing doors and walls. The gold pictures, which play on the notion of the most advanced form of abstraction at that time, the proto-Minimalist monochrome, have a similarly prosaic second identity, this time because they pose as fragments of traditional Japanese screens. Amusingly, they came about partly because of Blake's habitual thriftiness: he had just been employed to help restore a mural with a gold background in a temple within the garden of an agricultural college, part of an eighteenth-century mansion designed by William Kent, and he wanted to find a use for the leftover gold leaf. The gold on some of these elegantly conceived object pictures has tarnished over the years, lending them (by happy accident) a patina of age in keeping with the artificially timeworn and pockmarked look of the wall paintings from the same period.

Following the example of the target and American flag paintings first exhibited by Johns only a year earlier, Blake equated the subject of the painting with its physical manifestation as an object. Conceptually, these painting-sculptures operate simultaneously on a metaphorical and literal level and are understood not just as representations, but as actual fragments, of walls or doors. *The First Real Target?* (1961, Plate 59), referred to earlier, is the most overt of Blake's references to Johns, conceived in a spirit at once of homage and of competition, since by implication he has taken the American's idea to a more radical level still.

Blake's pursuit in works such as these of a 'hands-off' look, which was to become a common feature of Pop Art only from around 1962, was all the more remarkable in his case for the ample evidence elsewhere in his work of his technical dexterity and devotion to an academic practice of drawing and painting from the motif. A more painterly side of his art is evident, indeed, in his *Captain Webb Matchbox* (1961–2) (Plate 58), a response to the painting-as-object equation formulated both in Johns's flag paintings and Larry

Rivers's paintings of commonplace objects. (The first of Rivers's own painted constructions, such as his *Dutch Masters* cigar-box reliefs, appeared only a year later.) In 1961, in shaped canvases such as Hockney's *Tea Painting in an Illusionistic Style*, younger British artists associated with Pop Art were also seeking ways to make an image more materially and tangibly present by generating the external outlines of the picture from the object it represented. Blake's *Matchbox*, however, which predated Warhol's *Brillo Boxes* and other sculptural facsimiles of supermarket cartons of 1964, would appear to be the first instance in which this strategy is taken to its logical conclusion in three dimensions.

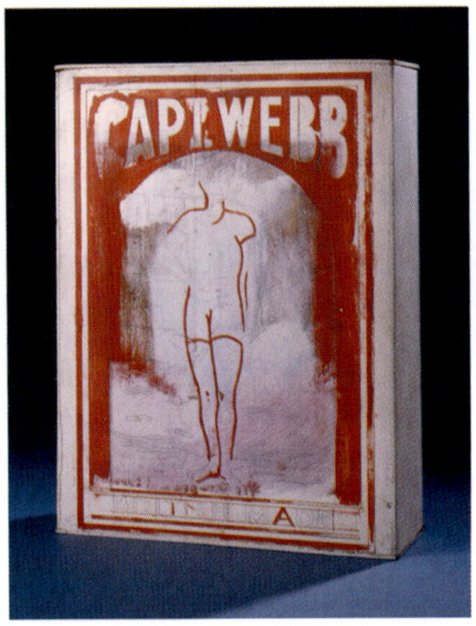

58 **Captain Webb Matchbox**, 1961–2

Together with the slightly sinister *Girl in a Window* (1962, Plate 60), with its almost Surrealist assortment of ready-made objects illuminated from behind the glass frontage, *The Toy Shop* (1962, Plate 61) of the same year represents the apotheosis of the paintings representing walls and doors that Blake had initiated in 1959, married to his collecting instincts and love of humble found objects and printed ephemera. Using an actual window and cupboard door purchased at a demolition site in Chiswick, West London, as the basic structural elements for the latter work, he created a child-sized storefront painted in bright colours with household gloss paint. The pristine and neatly packaged playthings are made to seem all the more alluring by the fact that these desirable objects, begging to be handled, are locked out of reach while remaining entirely visible behind the six panes of glass. The neat arrangement of the items – including artists' brushes, miniature dolls, puzzles and printed ephemera – not only mimics the appearance of a particularly fastidious shop window, but suggests museum methods of enshrining and categorising objects in locked display cases.

The conjunction between the ordinary, cheap and expendable consumer item on the one hand, and the precious artefact of a past civilisation on the other, lies at the heart of *The Toy Shop*'s fascination. This work touches on the ways in which all fabricated items eventually acquire value and historic importance, and also – on a more intimate and intensely personal level – how even the most commonplace and mundane objects become invested with the emotions and memories of the accumulated experiences we associate with them. It may be a cliché to speak of the child that remains within each of us as adults, but this work defies every spectator not to succumb to some degree to the sentimentality and emotion for our buried childhood memories at the sight of objects from our earliest years – like the dying tycoon muttering the name of his beloved sled Rosebud in Orson Welles's cinematic masterpiece, *Citizen Kane*.

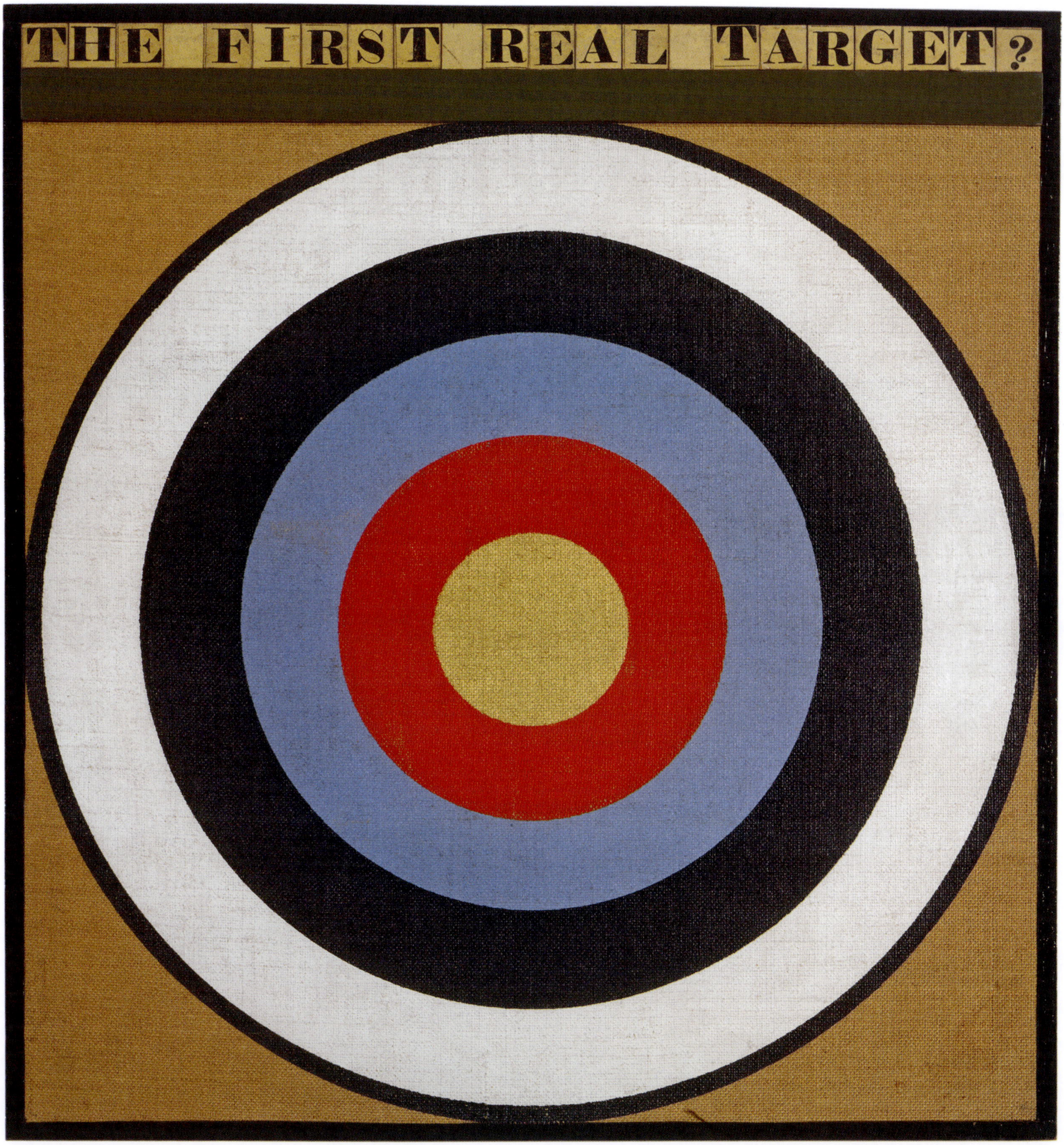

59 **The First Real Target?**, 1961

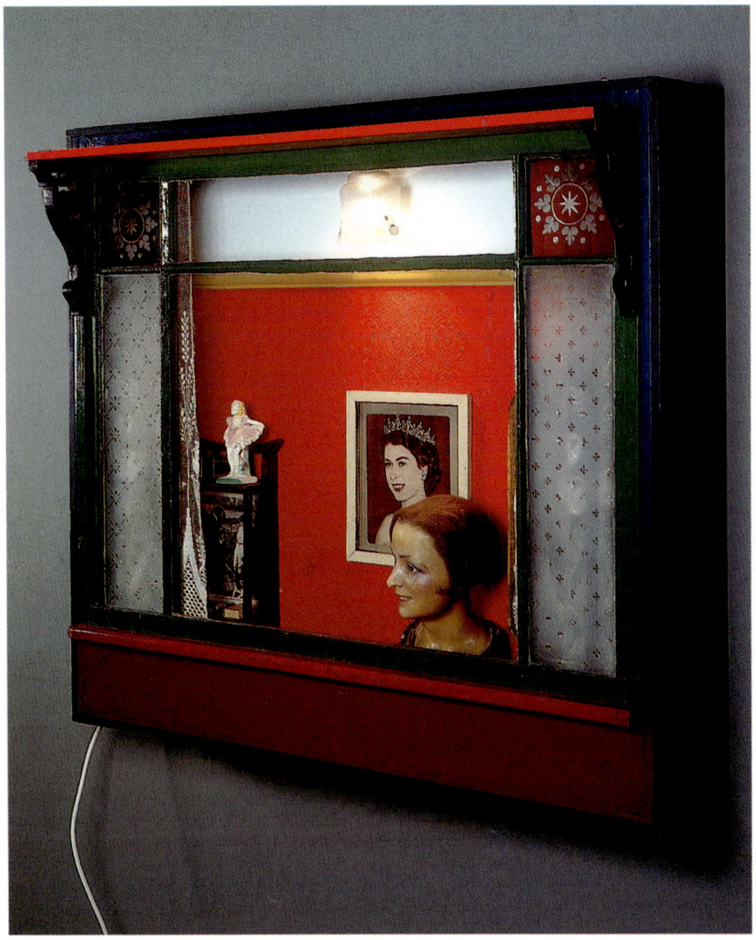

60 **Girl in a Window**, 1962

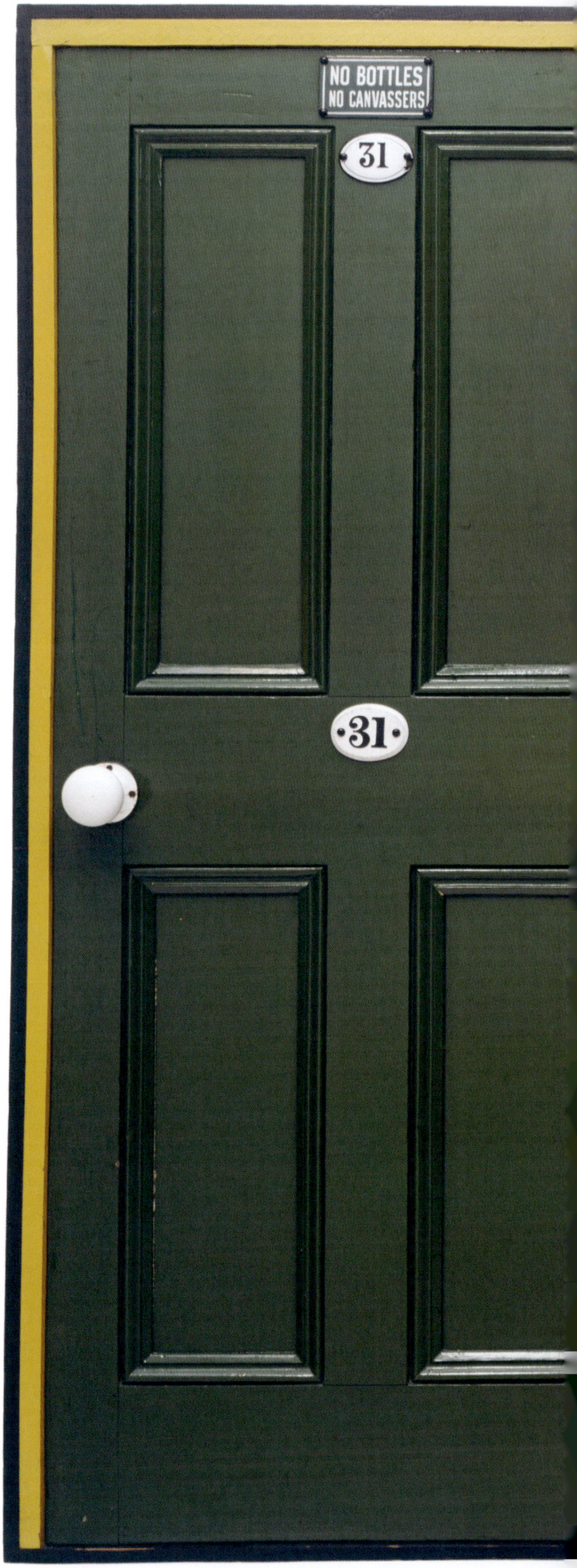

61 **The Toy Shop**, 1962

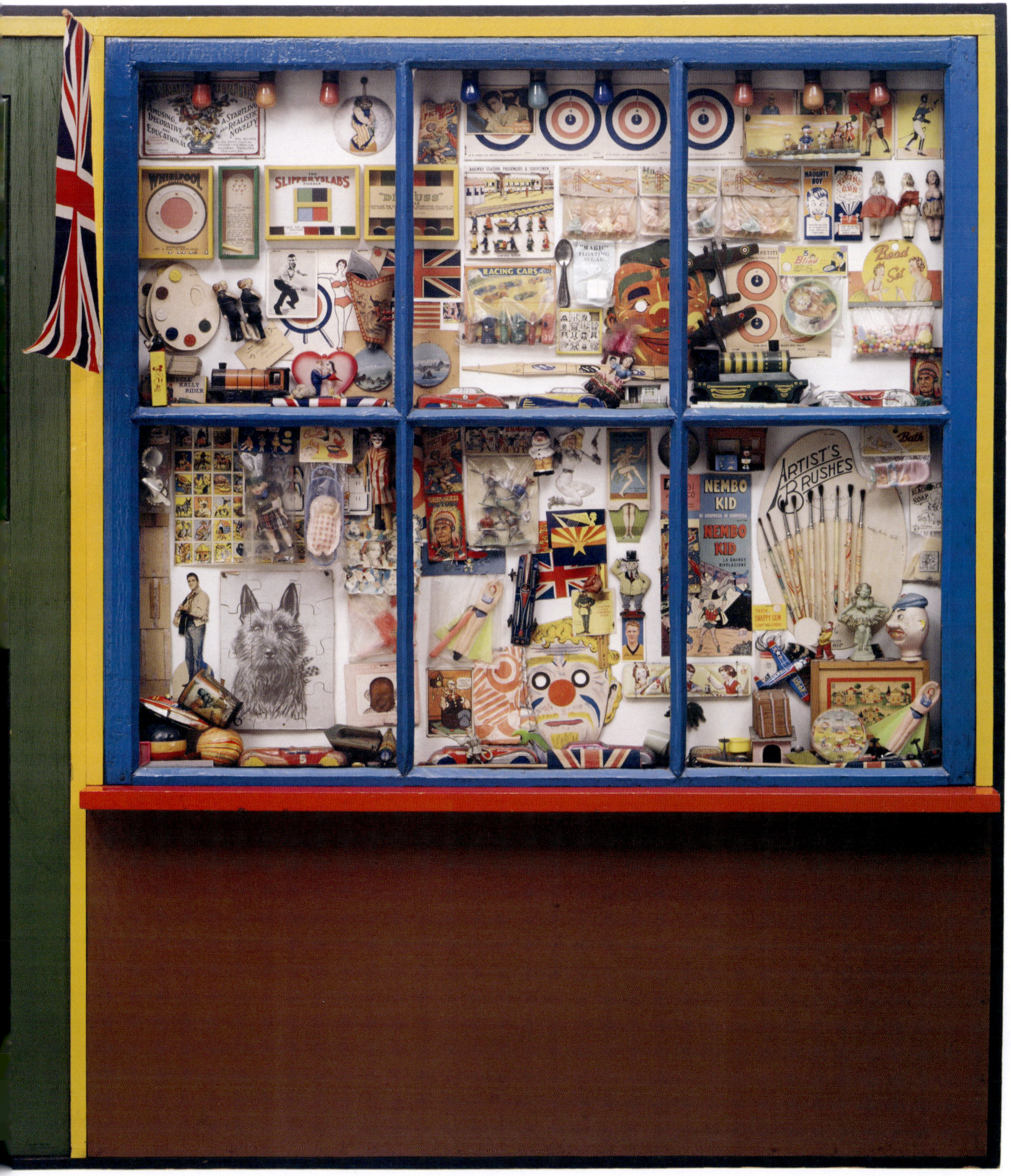
A STARTLING REALISTIC NOVELTY
AMUSING DECORATIVE EDUCATIONAL
WHIRLPOOL
SLIPPERYSLABS
RALLY RIDER
RACING CARS
"MAGIC" FLOATING SUGAR
NAUGHTY BOY
Bead Set
Blind
Bath
NEMBO KID
NEMBO KID
ARTIST'S BRUSHES

Postcards

Old postcards provided an occasional outlet for Blake's continuing fascination with printed ephemera, found imagery and Victoriana. He had collected postcards from an early age and had reproduced them illusionistically in handpainted form in his painting *On the Balcony* (1955–7, Plate 39), imitating the look of collage. As early as 1959, in paintings such as *The Fine Art Bit* (Plate 41), *Couples* (Plate 43) and *Valentine* (Plate 48), he had used them just as they were as collage elements laid out in neat rows, in the way that artists often pinned up favourite images for inspiration in their studios. (He later made this connection explicit in a large print, *Studio Tack-Board*, Plate 52, published in 1972.) *Couples* is perhaps the most extreme example in that even the surface to which the postcards are attached is an unaltered found object. However, the message on these English, French, Italian and German cards is unashamedly soft-hearted: the universality and timeless appeal of romantic love.

Postcards made available a potentially inexhaustible supply of imagery, from the erotic Belle Epoque poses replicated in his *Six French Postcards* (a set of offset lithographs created in 1969, Plate 64) to more obscure and mysterious glimpses into more exotic worlds. By 1961 Blake could not resist making grossly enlarged handpainted replicas of such items as independent paintings. A working-class Englishman of Blake's generation would never

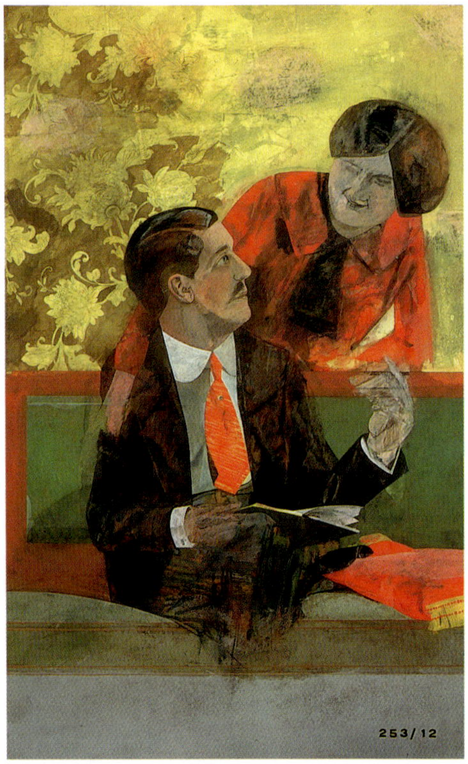

62 **Postcard**, 1962

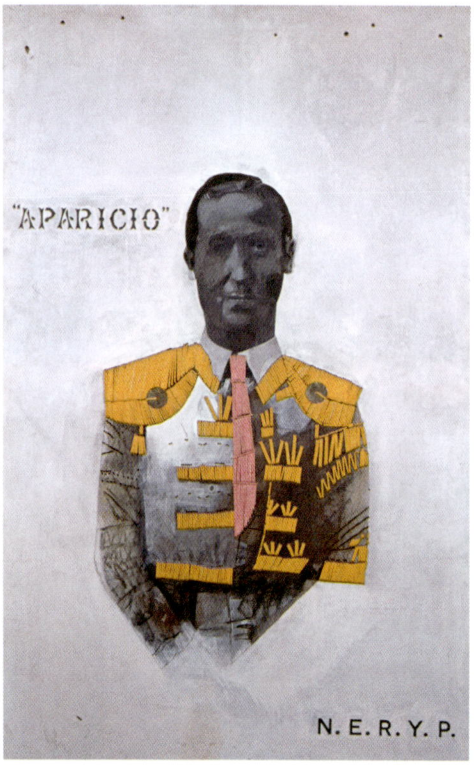

63 **Aparicio**, 1963

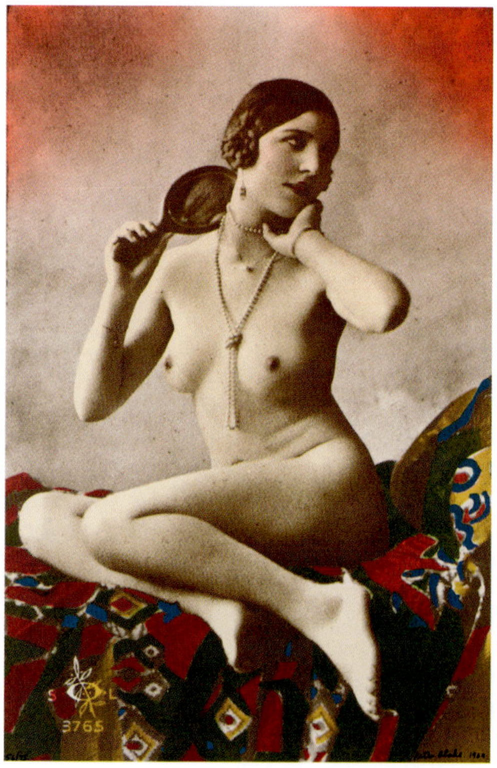

64 **3765**, from *Six French Postcards*, 1969

have dreamt of leaving the shores of his country in the way that has since become so commonplace thanks to cheap air travel and package holidays; his most accessible route to faraway places would have been in the form of postcards sent back to Britain by more prosperous or adventurous travellers, later picked up for pennies as curios in second-hand book shops and junk shops. *Le Petit Porteur* (1964–5, Plate 65), like another painting of the same size and date called *Bedouin* (Plate 66), was based on a set of picture postcards, 'Salut de Constantinople', printed in Italy but published in France in about 1900. Painted with Blake's habitual patience, it displays a subtle technical range from the superimposed layers of careful strokes that constitute the face to the wispy, virtually abstract marks that define the figure's left arm. The postcard allowed Blake to have his cake and eat it: to allude to the romance of another culture and to engage with a more traditional manner of painting, while at the same time ensuring a conceptual rigour entirely in keeping with Pop by presenting the final product as nothing more than a copy of a found object.

Pop Musicians, Entertainers and Film Stars

Rock'n'roll and the teenage-oriented pop music that came in its wake were central to Blake's enterprise as a Pop artist. His ambition was no less than to create the pictorial equivalent to these new musical forms, which in their simplicity and emotional directness appealed

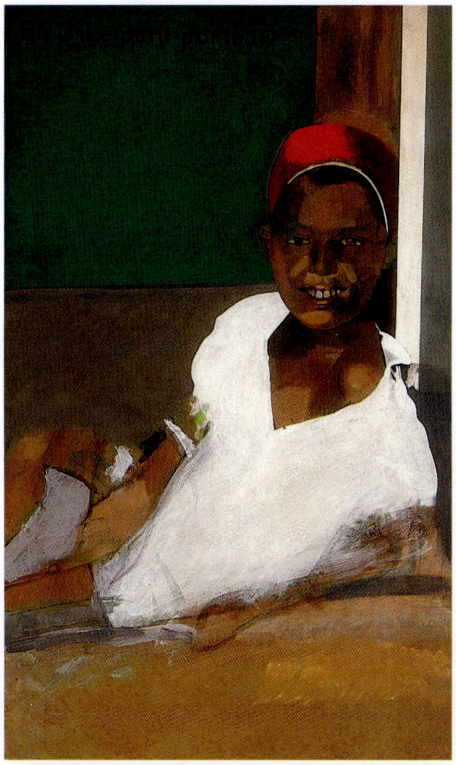

65 Le Petit Porteur, 1964–5

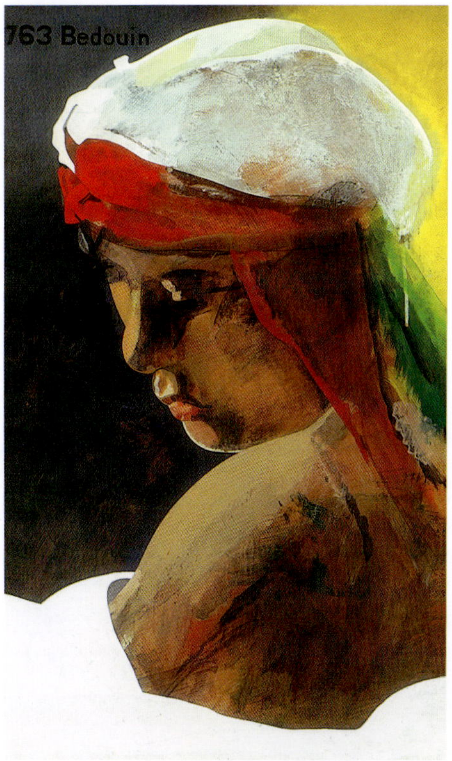

66 Bedouin, 1964–5

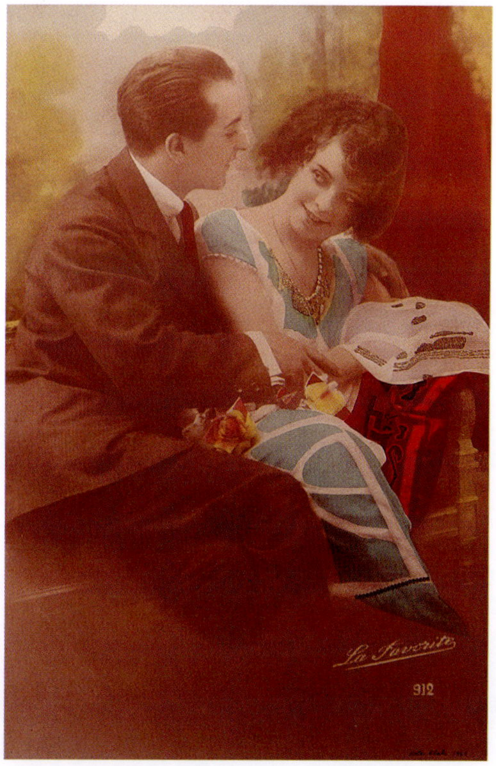

67 La Favorite, 1967

to a broad audience, and to reach that same audience by stripping away the pretensions and difficulty that made a non-specialised public shy away from 'fine art'. Blake was very clear on this in an interview conducted by Mervyn Levy, 'Peter Blake: Pop art for admass', published in the November 1963 issue of *Studio International*:

> I like to think my pictures can be enjoyed by young people who like pop music. At the moment I'm working on a large conversation piece of the Liverpool song group, The Beatles. Each of these chaps is closely associated with the city and I hope that local Beatle fans will find in this picture a visual significance that will somehow match the mood of Beatle music.

The goal may sound a little naively expressed to our ears nearly half a century on, and the artist himself considers his pop music pictures to have failed in securing the hoped-for converts to painting, but there is no doubting that the intention of matching the intensity, freshness and spirited vitality of the new music was instrumental in creating a vibrant art that successfully captured the optimistic atmosphere now associated with the early 1960s.

Elvis Presley had begun his singing career in 1954 with Sun Records and by 1956, after moving to RCA Records, he was an international star and the figurehead of the new rock'n'roll music. By the time Blake began painting *Girls and their Hero (Girls with their Hero)* (1959–62, Plate 68), the first of his pop music paintings, in 1959, Elvis had had hits in quick succession with 'Heartbreak Hotel', 'Blue Suede Shoes', 'Hound Dog', 'Love

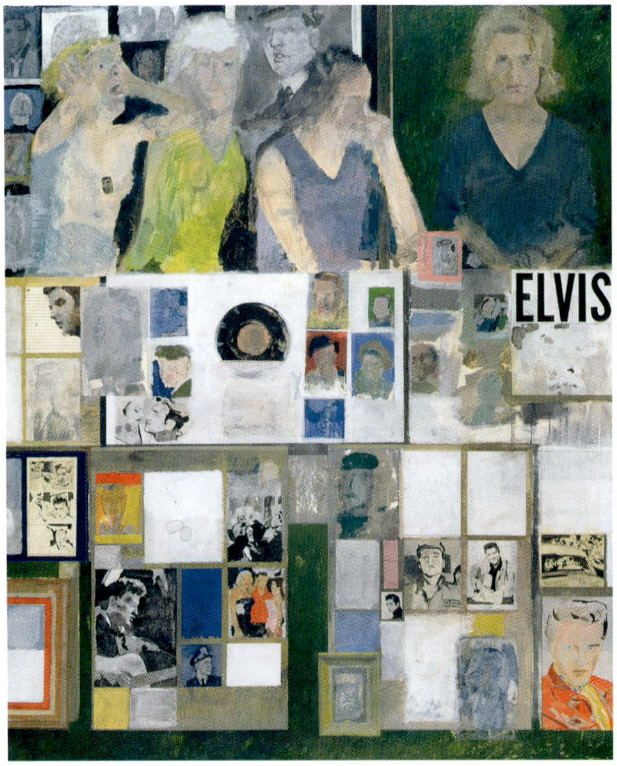

68 **Girls and their Hero (Girls with their Hero)**, 1959–62

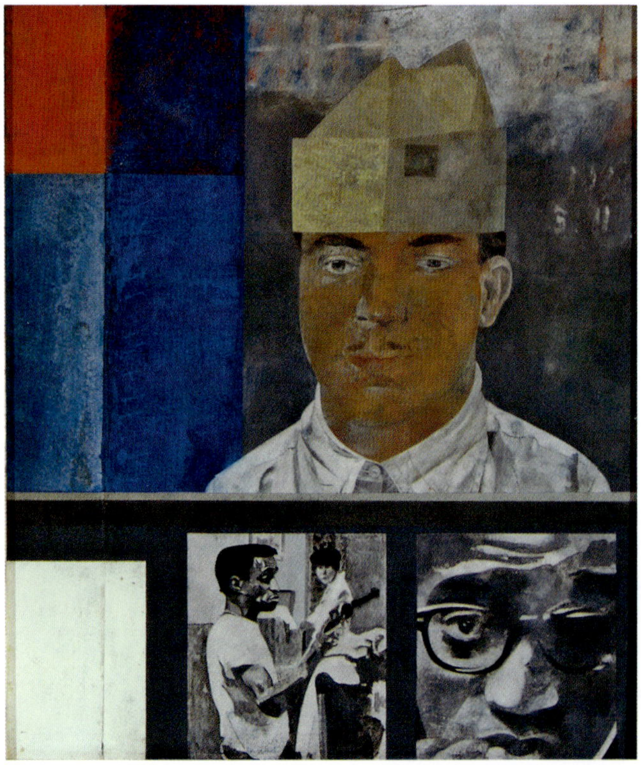

69 **Portrait of Sammy Davis Jr**, 1957–60

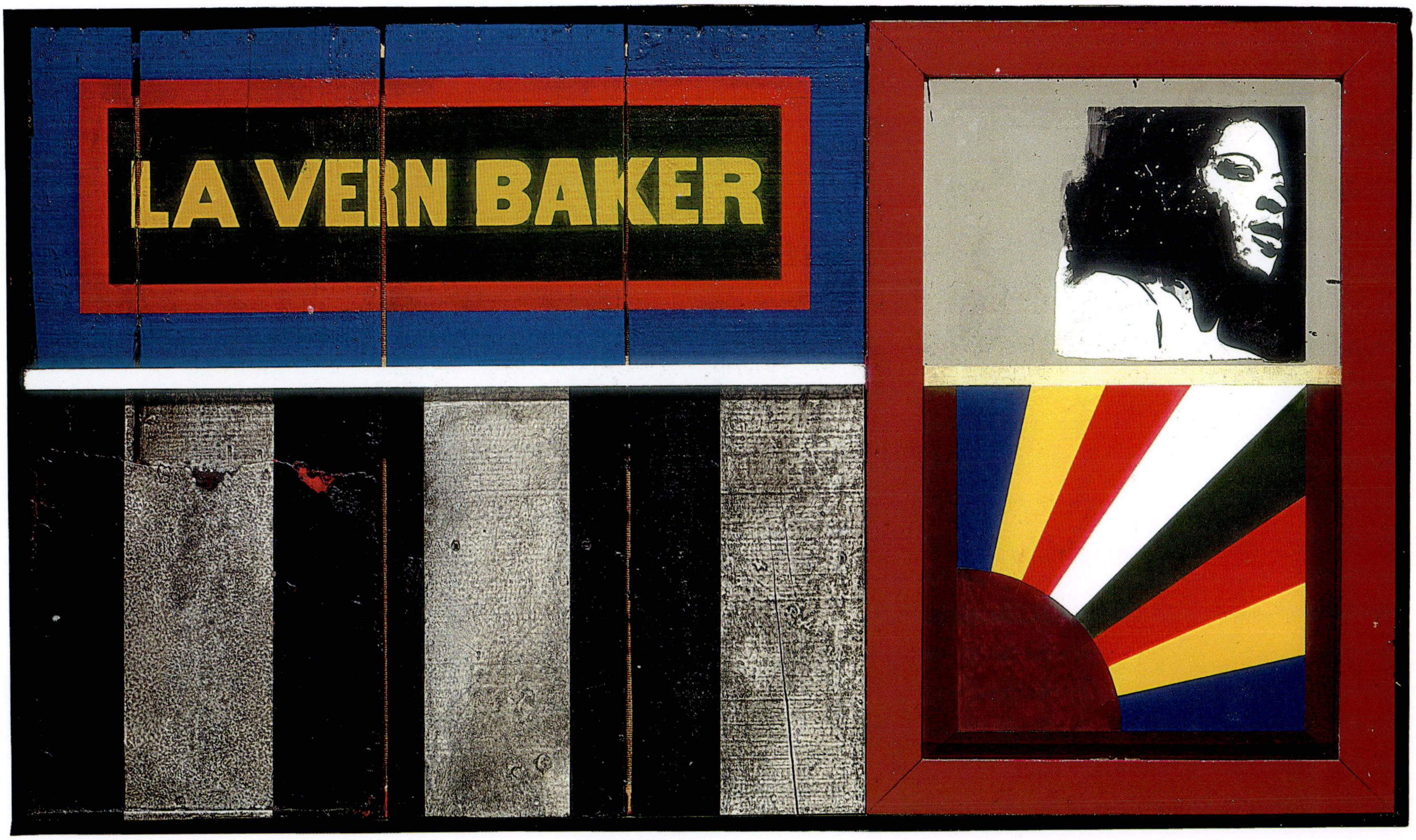

70 **La Vern Baker**, 1961–2

Me Tender' and 'Jailhouse Rock', to name just five. Returning to a conception of picture-making that he had employed in *On the Balcony* (1955–7, Plate 39), Blake arranged a selection of handpainted replicas of found photographs and printed images in rows across the surface, as if being held aloft by the fans depicted on a larger scale. The effect is like that of a shrine to an already iconic larger-than-life personality, simulating in paint the look of a teenager's room, festooned with record covers and photographic images cut out from magazines. The images are all presented frontally as if on a single surface, but also as if propped up against the legs of a table and on the tabletop itself. The dizzying accumulation of the musician's features testifies to his already unassailable position as one of the most photographed and idolised stars of the period.

Elvis was in the US Army (stationed in Europe) during the time that Blake worked on this picture and on *Self-Portrait with Badges* (1961, Plate 40), in which the artist presents himself shyly clutching an Elvis fan magazine. In both paintings there is an atmosphere

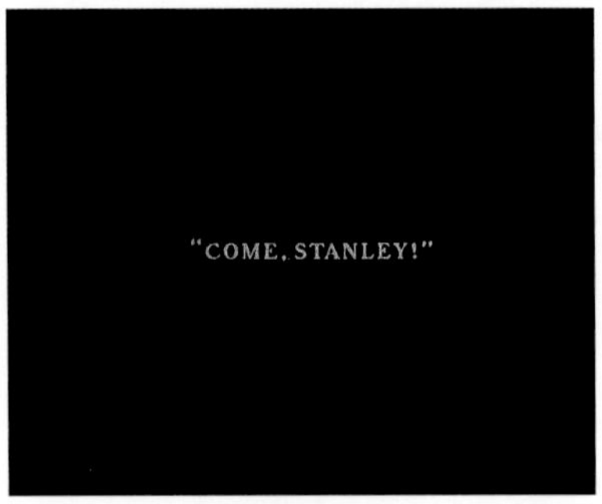

71 **Come, Stanley!**, 1962

of wistfulness, a sense of the remoteness of the man who was the object of such adulation: in spite of much speculation, Presley never visited or played in Britain. *Girls and their Hero* is painted more loosely than most of the pictures of pop musicians that were to follow, demonstrating a lingering allegiance to fine-art conventions and perhaps also a desire to convey, through the gestural handling, the excitement and emotional investment felt by the fans. Blake clearly had his finger on the pulse. As the painting testifies, he wasted no time in recognising Elvis as the first superstar of the new music, a man whose every public appearance was capable of sending his young female fans into an erotic frenzy.

Blake, as I have said, was quick to seize the implications of the works of Johns and Rauschenberg when he first saw them reproduced in the late 1950s, and under their influence took one stage further the object quality of his own earlier paintings. The decorative and dramatically simplified coloured backgrounds of his collage paintings of 1959–61 are as formally rigorous as any geometric abstraction, contributing forcefully to their eye-catching impact. The horizontal, vertical or diagonal bands of primary and secondary colours that give such heraldic impact to these pictures were intended, in part, as a comment on the hard-edged abstraction of the American painter Ellsworth Kelly and others whose work was just beginning to be shown in London and to be reproduced in international art magazines. Their immediate source, however, could be much more pedestrian. Such patterns could be seen, for instance, on railway rubbish bins, possibly as a visual code indicating a warning of danger. Perhaps this was Blake's gentle way of signalling the threat to traditional values in which he was engaged in these groundbreaking Pop pictures. The fact that these works were painted with household enamel paint on hardboard, as a deliberate gesture rather than as a money-saving solution, further insisted on the non-art associations that still endow these particular works with their heady mix of forthrightness, glamour and swagger. They get right to the point, with astonishing confidence and directness, and remain among the great icons of British Pop Art.

One such painting on a pop music theme, *Everly Wall* (1959, Plate 3), pays homage to the acclaimed singing duo the Everly Brothers as pictured in their official publicity stills. The geometric pattern of imperfect rectangles that covers most of the surface, recalling the use of sheets of gold leaf in paintings representing sections of Japanese screens that he was making during the same year, emphasises the object quality of the painting as a whole. These rectangles, cut by Blake from sheets of newsprint, surround a paper flag that he had found during his visit to Spain in 1957. It has recently been demonstrated that the black-and-white photographs of the pop stars were from the same photo session that produced the portrait for their 1959 single 'Cathy's Clown', their biggest hit. A vital feature of the picture as it now stands, and one which insists on that precious moment when a

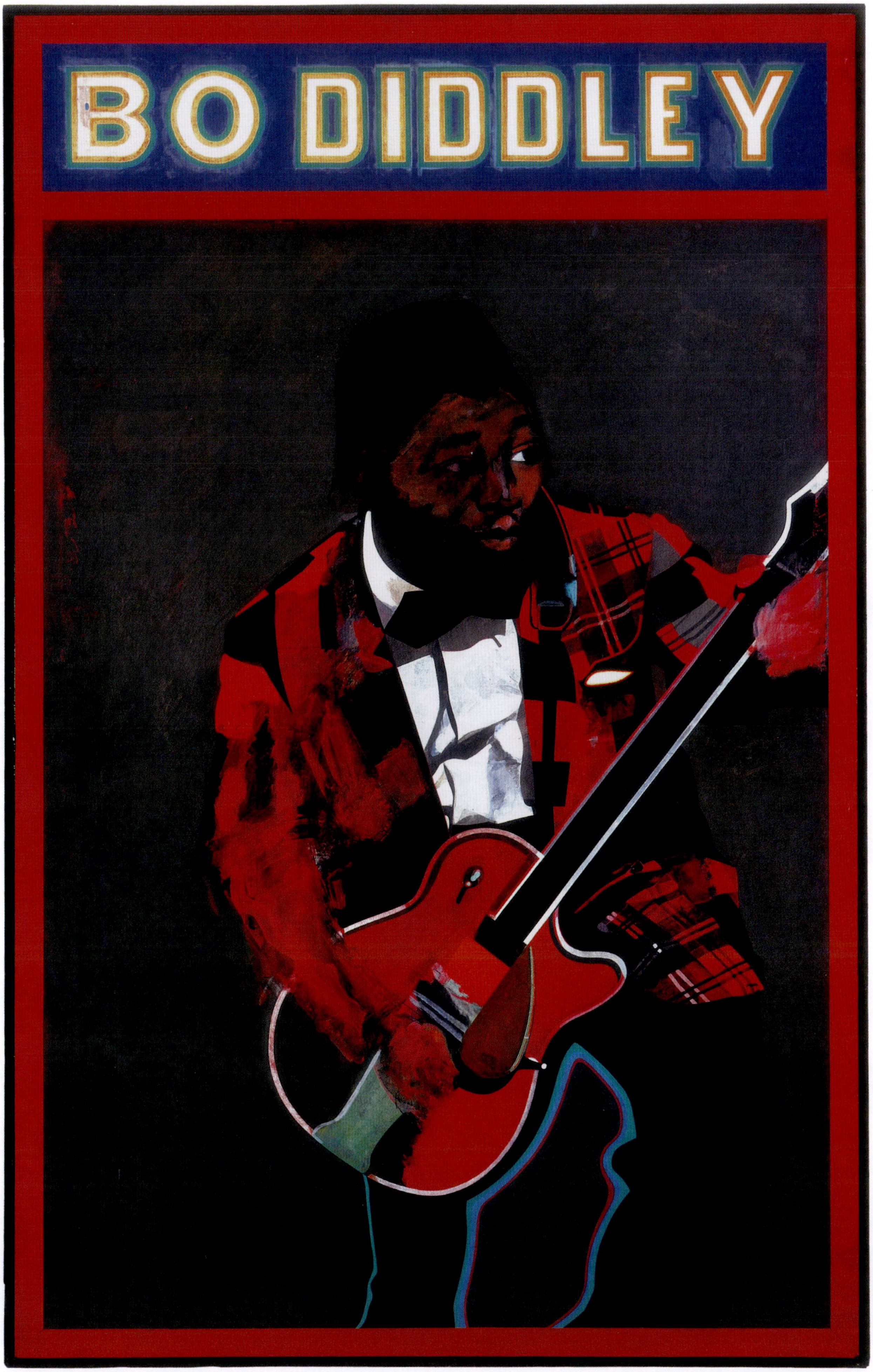

72 **Bo Diddley**, 1963

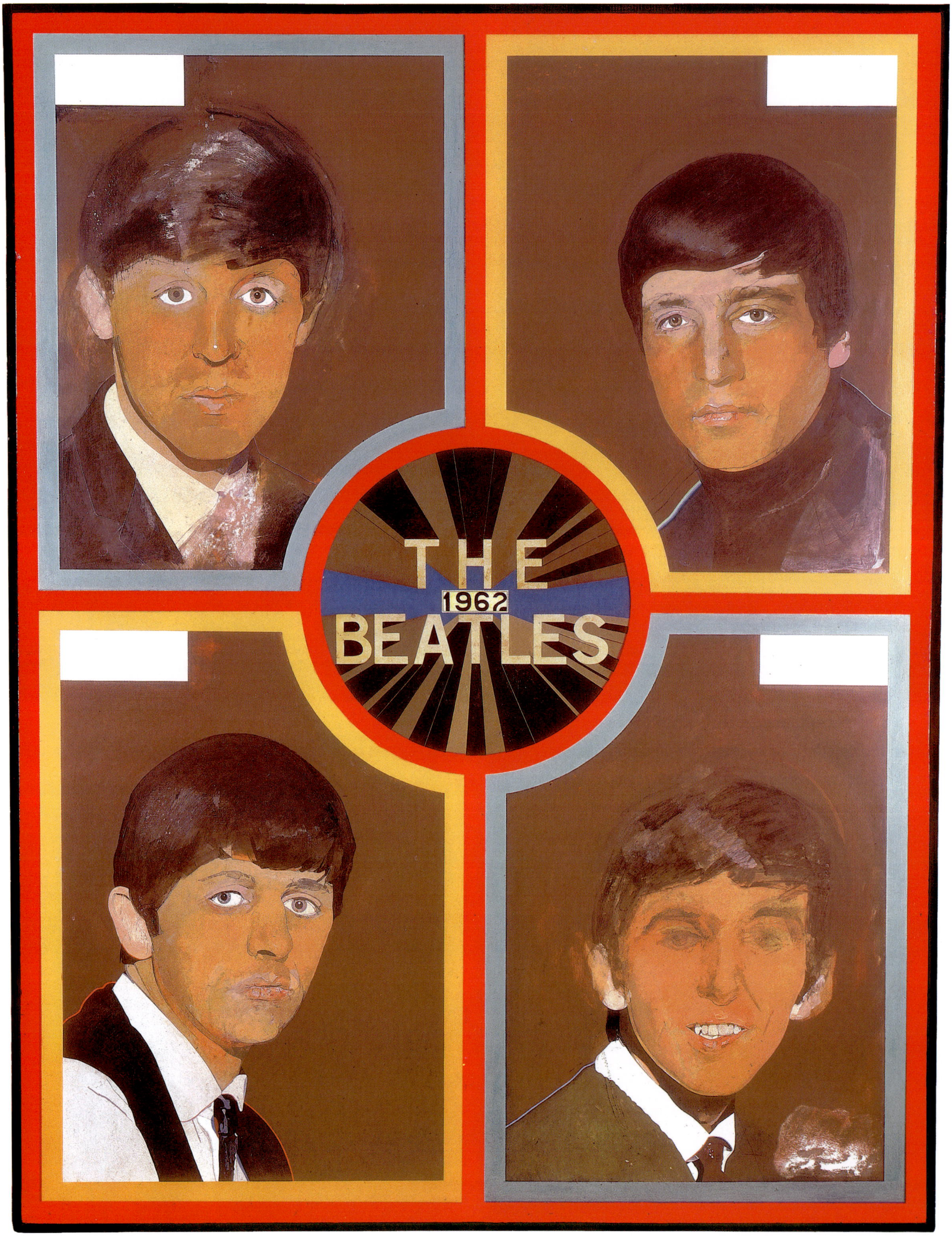

73 **The 1962 Beatles**, 1963–8

fan meets the object(s) of his or her adulation, is the autograph that proudly occupies central place; it was added 24 years later, when the artist's brother Terry, who had long owned the painting, met the singers and asked them to sign and dedicate the painting. As Peter by this time had been friends of theirs for many years, this was not quite as unexpected as it might appear, and seems a fitting final touch.

Bo Diddley (1963, Plate 72), *The 1962 Beatles* (1963–8, Plate 73) and *The Lettermen* (1963, Plate 4) are all painted in a much more restrained and realistic idiom than the homage to Elvis Presley, on which he had started work just four years earlier. The highly saturated colours and bold lettering, particularly on the Bo Diddley portrait, vibrate and resonate with the unrestrained energy of this new music. Although Blake is unlikely to have made the distinction at the time, these three major pictures represent the transference in popularity from the clean-cut, bland, middle-of-the-road American vocal harmony groups such as the Lettermen (formed in 1958) to the raunchy, blues-inflected rock'n'roll of Bo Diddley and the innovative and sexy post-rock'n'roll music of the Beatles, who were just breaking through to a mass audience in 1963. All three paintings had their origin in promotional photographs. The portrait of the American trio was based on the cover of their 1962 Capitol album, *A Song for Young Love* (as released in the UK), while Bo Diddley is shown vigorously strumming his guitar and sporting a red plaid jacket in a variant of the shot used on the cover of his second American album, the classic *Go Bo Diddley* (released on Checker Records in 1959).

The four Beatles are taken from the page of a magazine published in 1962 on their return to England after an extended residency in Hamburg. The 'Fab Four' are presented in identical quadrants that emphasise their equality within the band, notwithstanding the almost immediate acclaim accorded to John Lennon and Paul McCartney as the greatest songwriting team of the period. When painting in a painstaking, naturalistic mode, Blake always took his time: the '1962' added to the middle of the group's name in the title of the picture and right in the centre of its actual surface attests to the fact that, by the time he had stopped working on the painting in 1968, it faithfully represented them not as they looked in their later 'hippie' phase but in their original incarnation, with dapper suits and moptop haircuts. The small white rectangles above each musician's head were originally intended to bear their autographs. McCartney saw the painting in Blake's studio, and although he did not refuse to write his name on it, he left without doing so; the artist then abandoned his plan to get their signatures.

In her text for the 1980 Tate Gallery catalogue *Kelpra Studio: The Rose and Chris Prater Gift: Artists' Prints 1961–1980*, the scholar of printmaking Pat Gilmour noted that Blake's *The Beach Boys* (1964, Plate 74) – one of a portfolio, commissioned by the Institute of

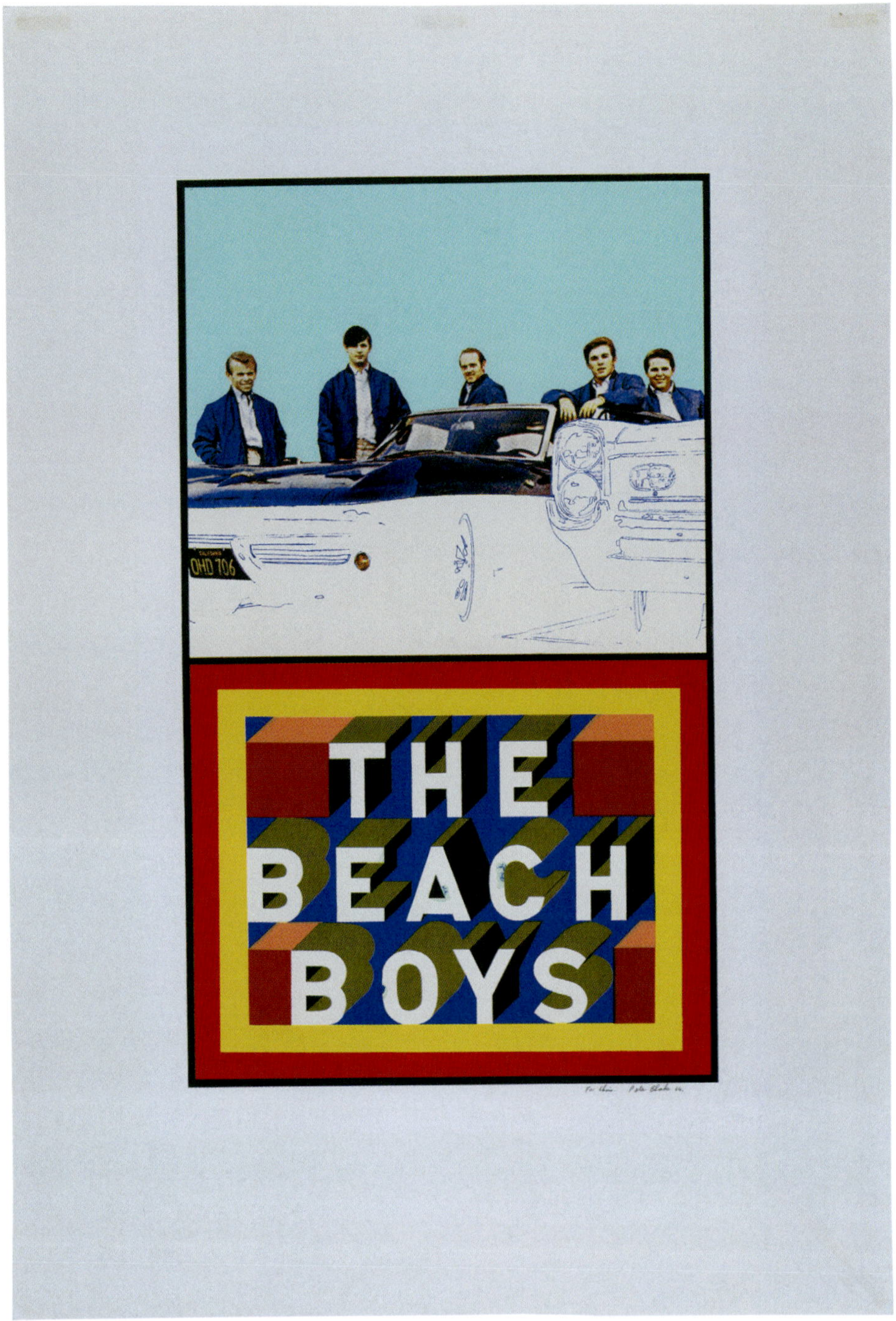

74 The Beach Boys, 1964

Contemporary Arts, to which 24 artists contributed one screenprint each – was the first trichromatic halftone to be printed by Chris Prater at his Kelpra Studio. This may sound like a rather arcane and specialised piece of information, but it is important to be reminded that it was only at that moment that the sophistication of such procedures was becoming available to fine artists. The almost square format of Blake's image of the group's members provides a clue to its source in an album cover: as any serious Beach Boys fan would immediately have spotted at the time, the picture is transcribed precisely from the front cover of their album *Shut Down, Volume 2* (released by Capitol Records in March 1964), which included two of their major hits, both of them touching on a love of cars: 'Fun, Fun, Fun' and 'Don't Worry Baby'. The only liberty taken with the design, apart from the removal of the typography, was the slight cropping of a strip of sky along the top. Part of Blake's print consists of a straight photographic reproduction of the five musicians and part of one of the cars; the traced outlines of the remainder of the image, while drawn by hand, remain equally faithful to the source. Only the multicoloured lettering of their name, in the manner of an illusionistically painted sign, was wholly the artist's invention. Married together, the adapted image and the heraldic typography celebrate the fresh, youthful, joyful and exuberant music of the quintessential Californian band of the 1960s.

It was not just pop musicians whom Blake celebrated in his Pop Art portraits. From 1957 he had also paid tribute to stars of the Hollywood film industry as well as to the great female European film stars of the period, first in *Knife Thrower's Board* (1957, Plate 19) and two years later in collage paintings such as *Locker* (Plates 1 and 55), *Kim Novak Wall* and *Girlie Door* (Plate 44). He had also made handpainted portraits of other celebrities, such as the entertainer Sammy Davis Jr in 1957 (Plate 69). Consequently, in 1964, he accepted with alacrity the opportunity to paint an earlier goddess of the silver screen, Jean Harlow, for the cover of the *Sunday Times* colour magazine (Plate 75). Having studied both commercial art and fine art, Blake continued to feel perfectly at home in both worlds, distinguishing himself among Pop artists with the collages and illustrations that he continued to produce throughout his career in response to commissions. Jean Harlow, the 'blonde bombshell', was one of the legendary actresses he would have first seen performing during his weekly visits to the movies as a child: she died in 1937 at the age of just 26. To dwell on her image again in his early thirties was therefore in part an exercise steeped in nostalgia. Blake worked from a black-and-white official publicity still, inventing the colour much as a commercial artist might have hand-tinted a photograph for reproduction on a postcard; the actress's signature, faithfully copied from a separate photograph, not only identifies her but adds to an already glamorous image a gentle reminder of her celebrity and of our own much more humble status as autograph-seeking fans. Fashionably and elegantly dressed in such a way as to accentuate her beauty and sex appeal, Jean Harlow flashes her radiant smile to an unseen public with the confidence of a star who knows that her image will continue to dazzle audiences on cinema screens well after her life on earth has come to an end.

Celebrity culture has now taken over to such a degree that it is difficult to remember, let alone for anyone born after 1970 to fully understand, a time when celebrities were people who were admired for their achievements as actors, musicians or sportsmen rather than just being famous for being on television or having their photographs printed in gossip magazines. Blake, like Andy Warhol in the US, anticipated this apotheosis of the celebrity in the late 1950s and early 1960s out of a very personal response to the glamour of stardom most associated with the Hollywood film industry. Independently of each other, both artists kept magazines and scrapbook cuttings of the film stars with whom they were besotted. They were not the first or the only artists to do so: as unlikely a candidate as Edward Burra, for example, had collected such material as long ago as the 1920s. What was new, however, was both Warhol's and Blake's blunt and undisguised incorporation of this imagery into new forms of portraiture. In the American's case, this involved the replication of photographic imagery through the process of silkscreen printing laid over a base of acrylic paint in luridly coloured stencilled shapes corresponding to the eyes, mouth, hair and facial contours of Marilyn Monroe, Elizabeth Taylor and other immediately recognisable stars. In Blake's hands, where the photographic derivation is equally important for the instant identification of the object of fan worship, the photograph was either presented as found, as a collage element (often in the form of commercially produced postcards) or conscientiously replicated by hand through the intermediary of tracings that assured a good likeness.

Blake's identity as a Pop artist was most pronounced in the works he made during a short period in the late 1950s and early 1960s, but the concerns that animated the paintings and sculptures of that time have continued to resurface in his art in every subsequent decade. Without Pop, it would be difficult to imagine the existence of the fantasy portraits of pin-ups, strippers, boxers and wrestlers that became such a rich arena for his imagination. Through the Pop-saturated designs made on commission for record covers and other commercial work, including posters and magazine illustrations, he broke through to a mass consciousness in a way that most fine artists could only dream about. He has continued to draw sustenance from his Pop past, at times explicitly referencing the boldly conceived and dazzling works that he had made by the age of 30 (as with the *Déjà vu* works of the late 1980s, as discussed in chapter 7). Though there have been many divergent aspects to his art, some of them made in apparent contradiction to Pop precepts (like the Ruralist pictures of fairies), Pop Art has continued to provide the vibrant and ever youthful framework for much of Blake's later work.

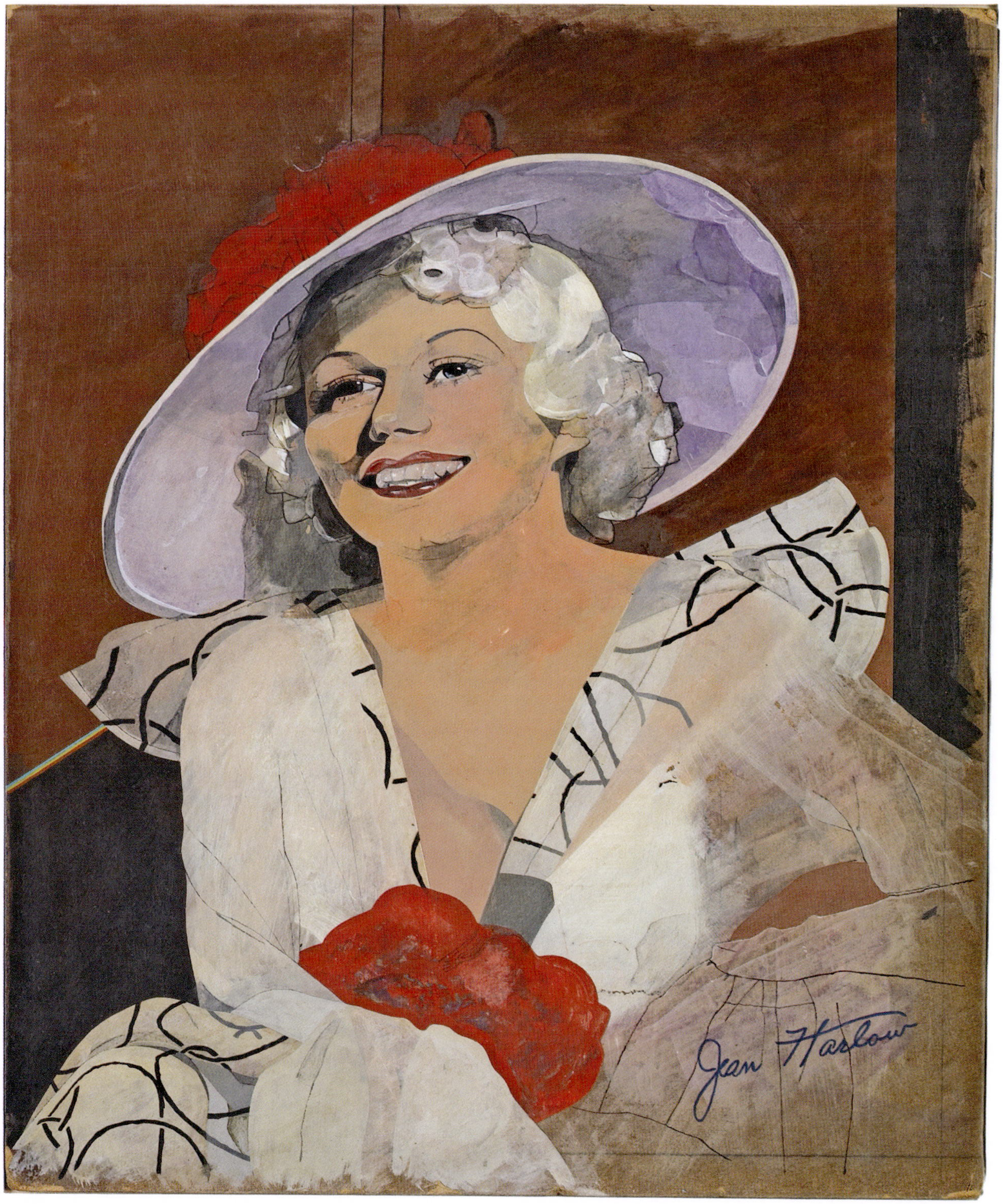

75 **Jean Harlow**, 1964

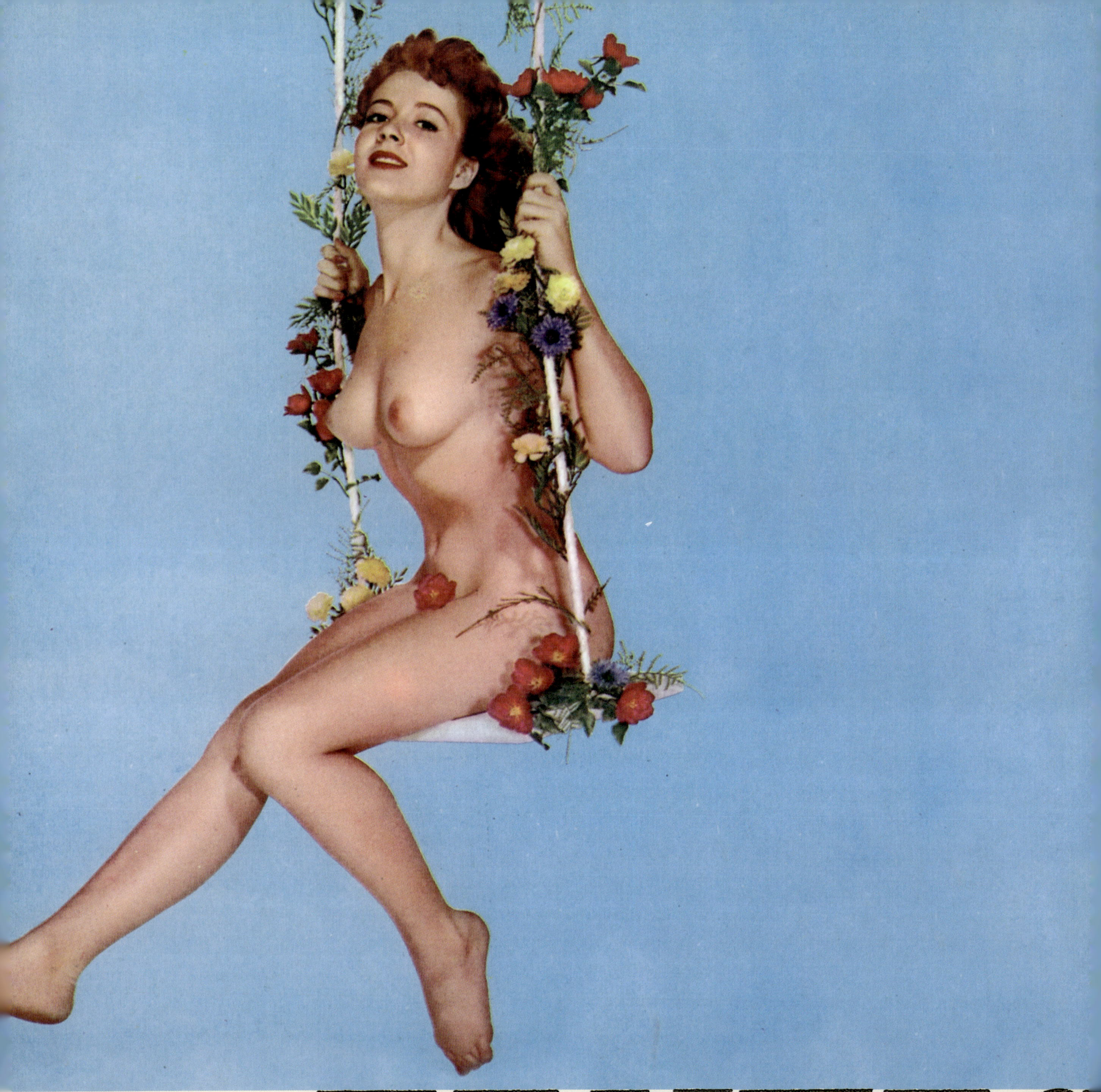

3 FANTAS

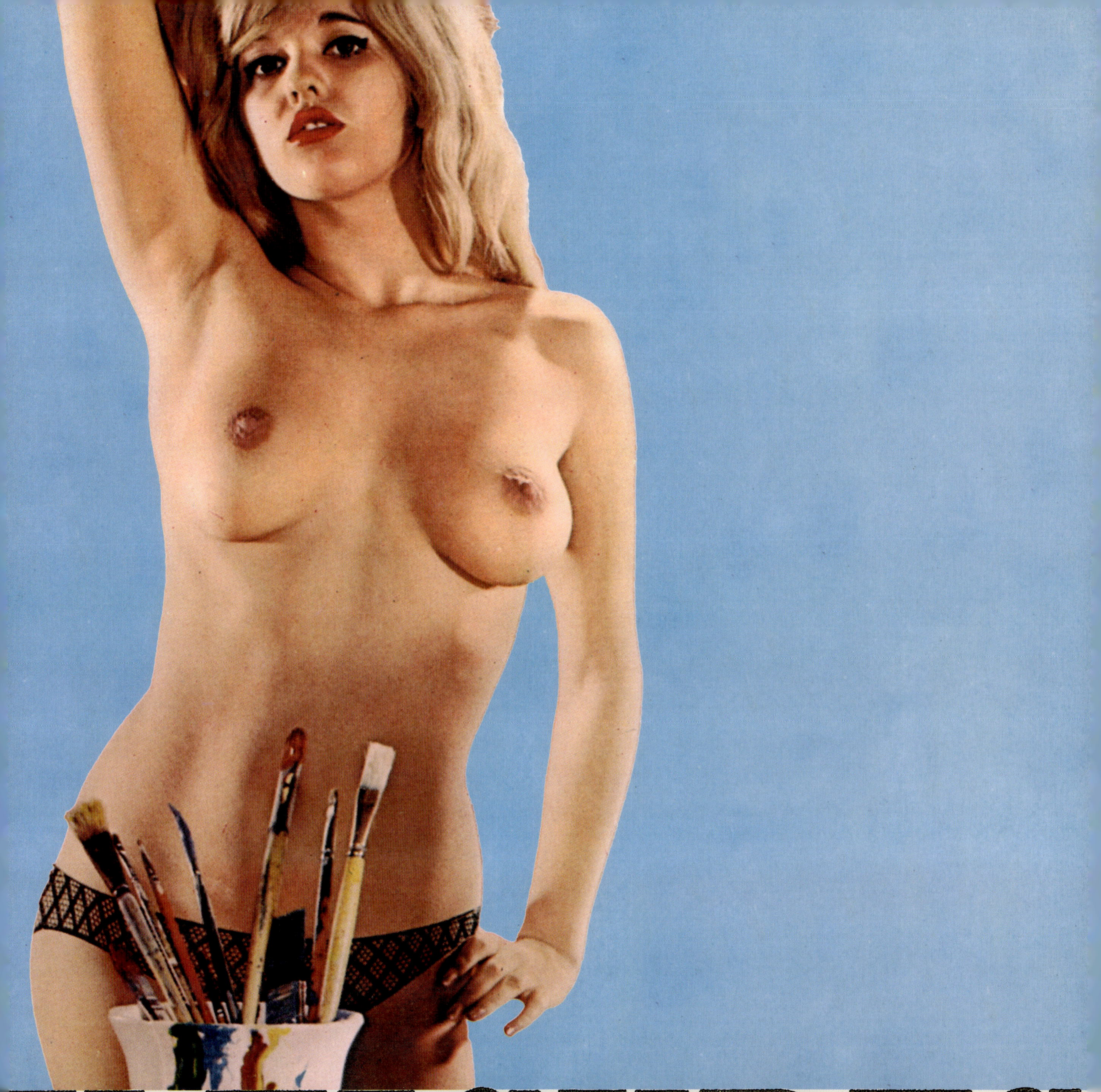

Y FIGURES

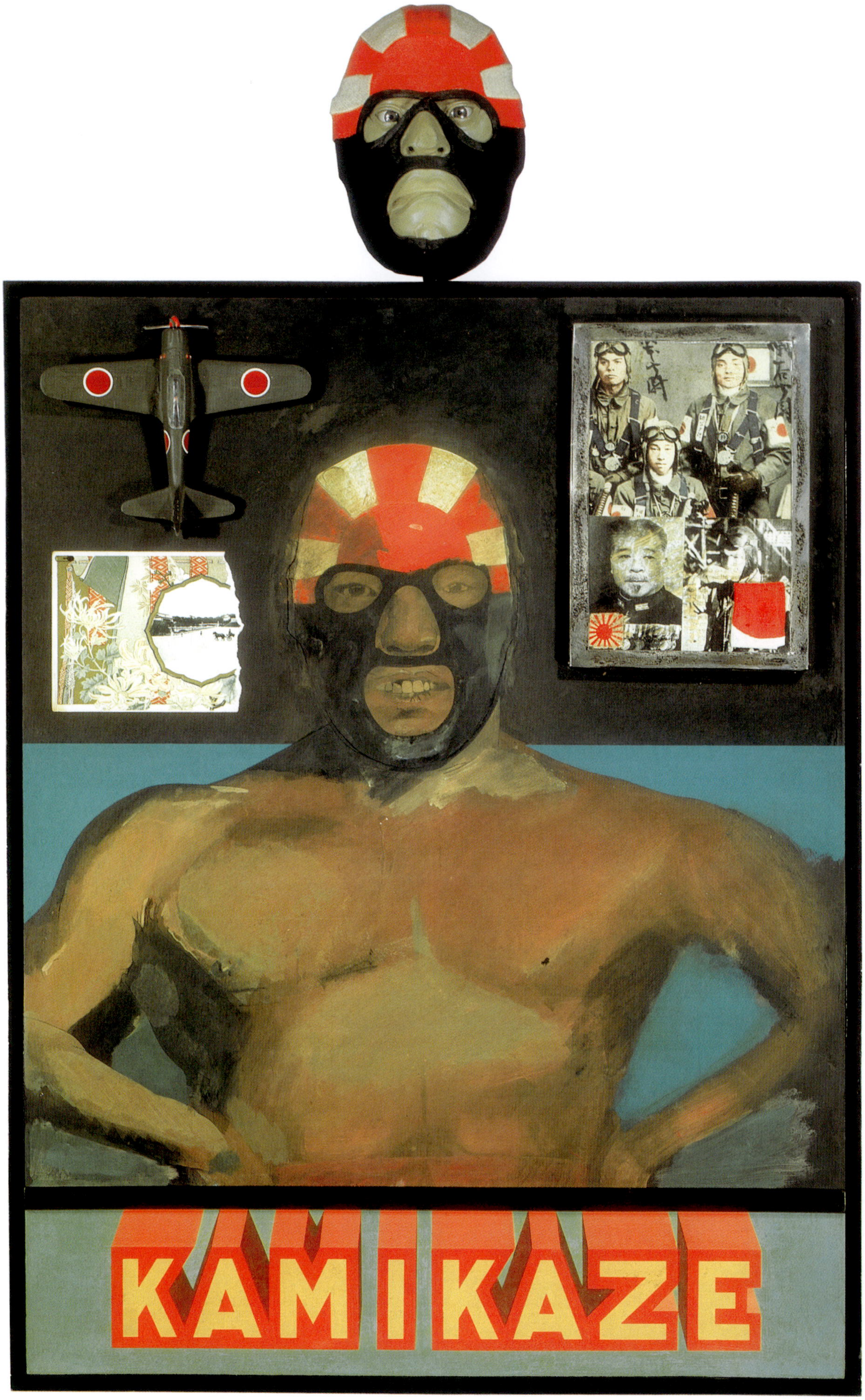

76 **Kamikaze**, 1965

3 Fantasy Figures

The interest in popular entertainments displayed by Blake in the 1950s was treated with renewed vigour during the 1960s, notably in his series devoted to wrestlers and to strippers, and later still with an acute and exquisite sensitivity in his *Side Show* wood engravings of 1974–8. These and other images produced after Blake's concentrated Pop phase of 1959–63, such as the elaborately worked pencil drawings of female nudes executed in the mid-1970s after photographs published in 1928 (Plate 158), provide evidence of the continuous threads linking his art during the first three decades of his career.

Though rightly acclaimed as one of the originators of Pop Art in Britain, Blake remains one of the most stubbornly unclassifiable of contemporary artists. However vividly the term Pop encompasses a specific group of works produced by him in the late 1950s and early 1960s, it is not wholly adequate as a label with which to describe his art as a whole, either in terms of his subject matter or his passionate devotion to the traditional virtues of drawing and small-scale easel painting. By the same token, though, Blake's own estimation that the main thrust of his work lies in a straight, naturalistic figuration also fails to take into account the strong visionary impulse and elements of heightened fantasy and nostalgia that have consistently coloured the ways in which he conveys his experience of the world. A close, clear-eyed observation has alternated – and often mingled with – childlike invention and an unbridled imagination. He has turned his attention repeatedly to the exotic in the everyday, as in his portraits of imaginary and larger-than-life wrestlers with such preposterous names as *Pretty Boy Michael Angelo* (1972, Plate 90) or *Mambo Rambo* (1987) or of Arab girls and nubile nudes brought into existence from photographs.

Pin-ups and Strippers

Images of unavailable, sexually alluring women had featured in Blake's work long in advance of the series of *Pin-up Girl* paintings (Plates 77, 78) on which he embarked in 1962. Even before his incorporation of collaged photographic portraits of screen goddesses in works produced in 1959 such as *Locker* (Plates 1 and 55), *Kim Novak Wall* and *Girlie Door* (Plate 44), there was the stunning standing figure of Brigitte Bardot brought ready-made into *Knife Thrower's Board* (1957, Plate 19). Earlier still, in affectionate parodies of such vixens and sex kittens, were such paintings in a faux-naive style as *Loelia, World's Most Tattooed Lady* (1955, Plate 21), *Dixie, Darling of the Midway* (1955–8, Plate 22) and *Siriol, She-Devil of Naked Madness* (1957, Plate 20). All of these, it has to be said, were created

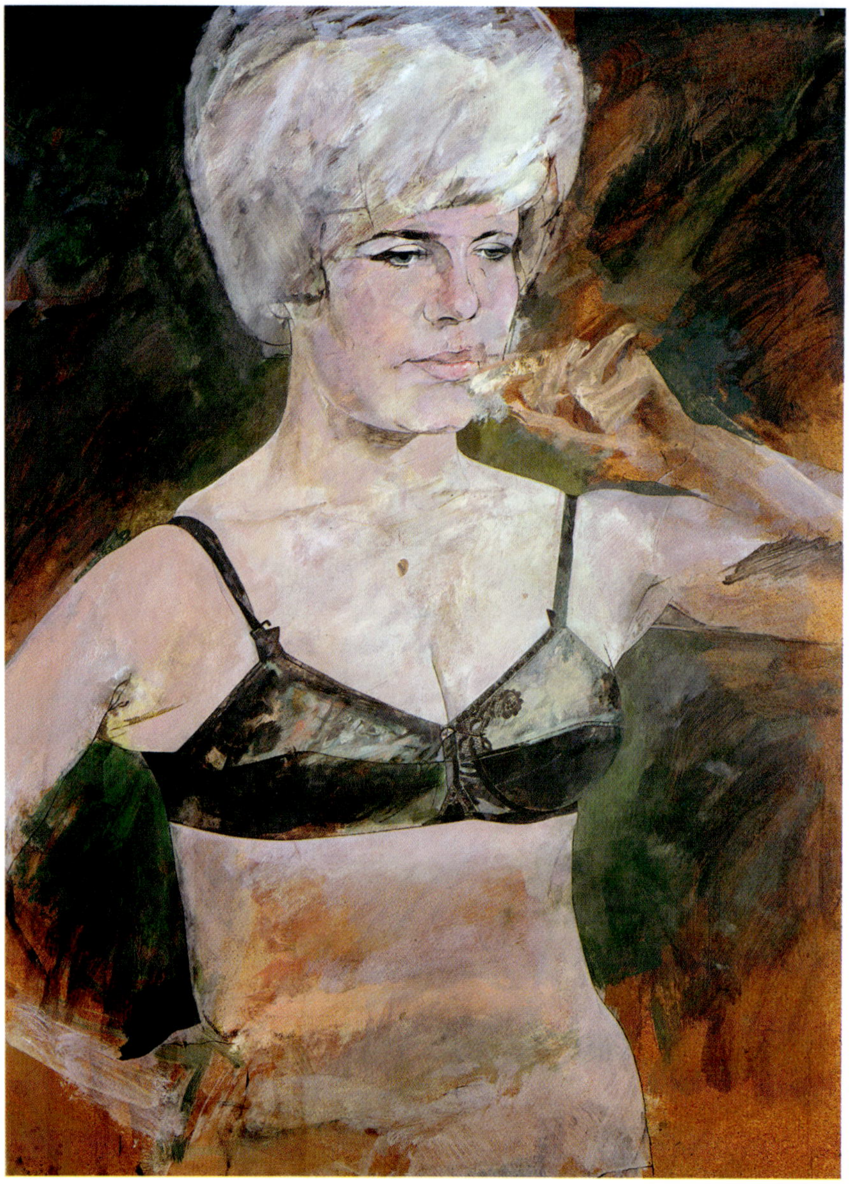

77 **Pin-up Girl**, 1962

when the artist was still sexually inexperienced and (in his own words) 'pathologically shy', and it is therefore more than simple conjecture to view them as filled with a young man's longing, curiosity and pent-up desire. As he recalled in his interviews for the Artists' Lives archive, before meeting and then marrying the American sculptor Jann Haworth in 1963 he had been in love several times – notably with the painter Pauline Boty, who began her studies at the Royal College in 1958 – but those were all unrequited. Until he was seduced by a model at the Slade in 1961, sex for him existed solely on the level of fantasy. His loss – his frustration and sense of exclusion from this most elemental of human pleasures – became

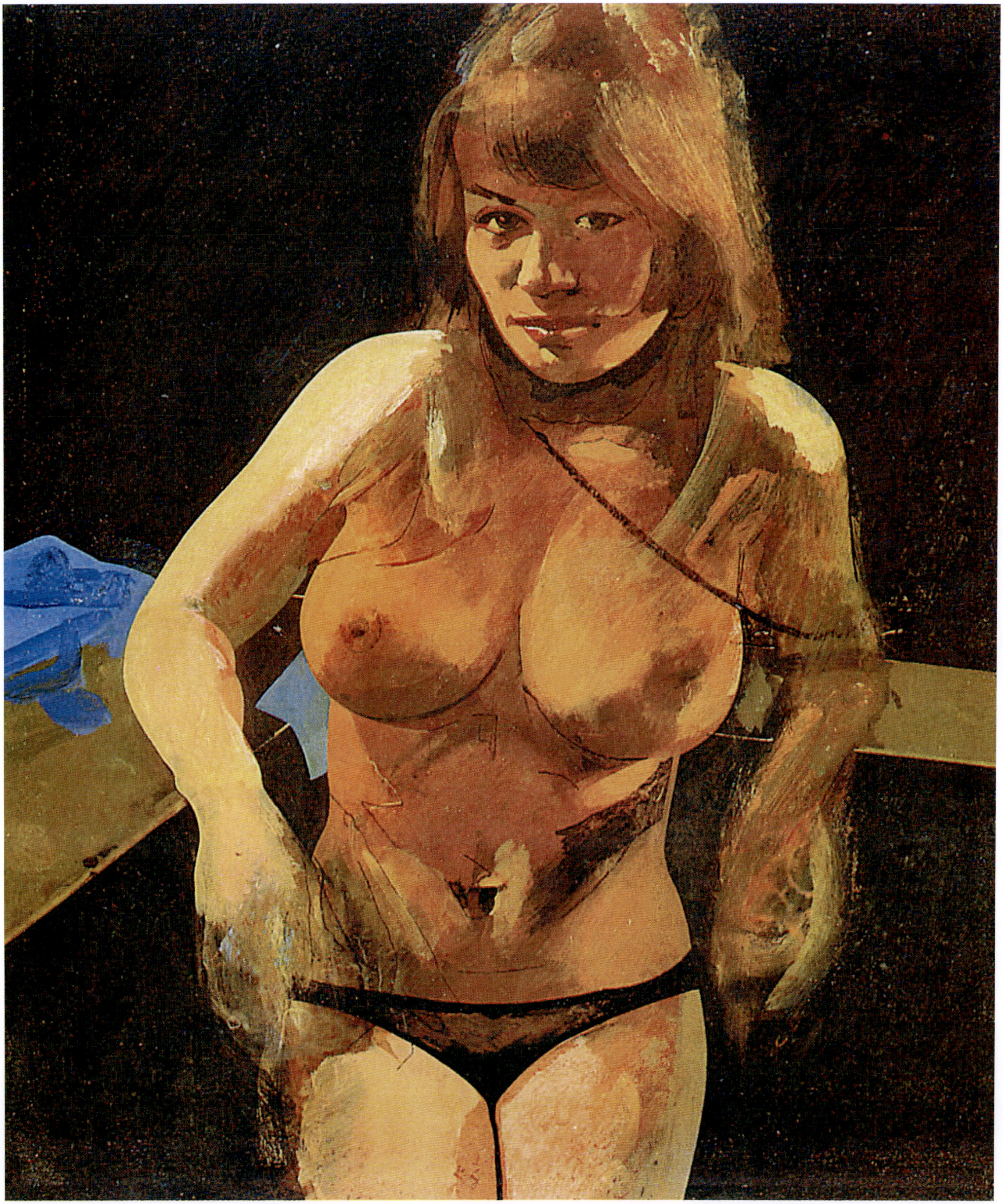

78 **Pin-up Girl**, 1965

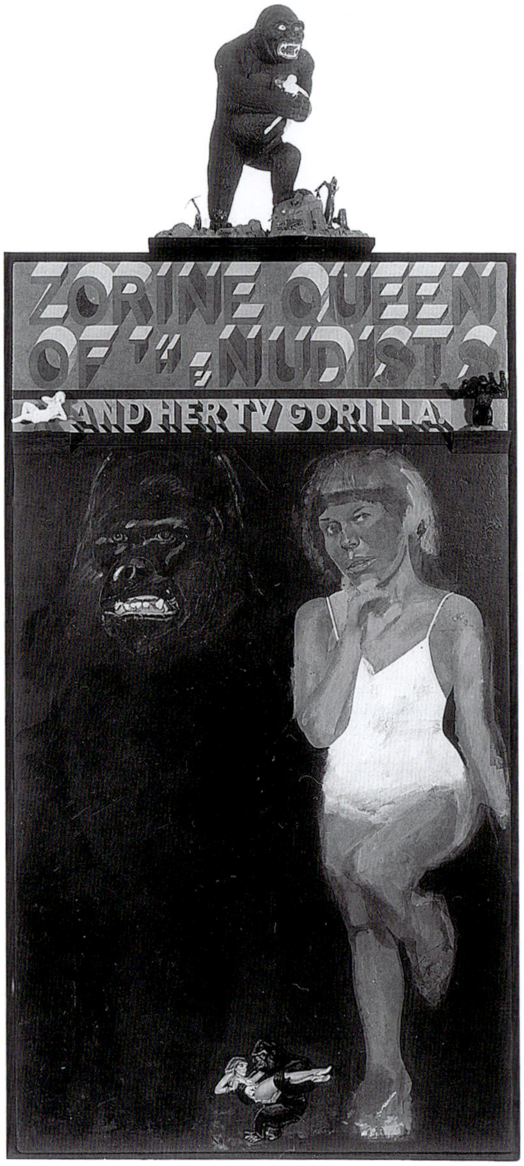

79 **Zorine, Queen of the Nudists and her TV Gorilla**, 1961–5

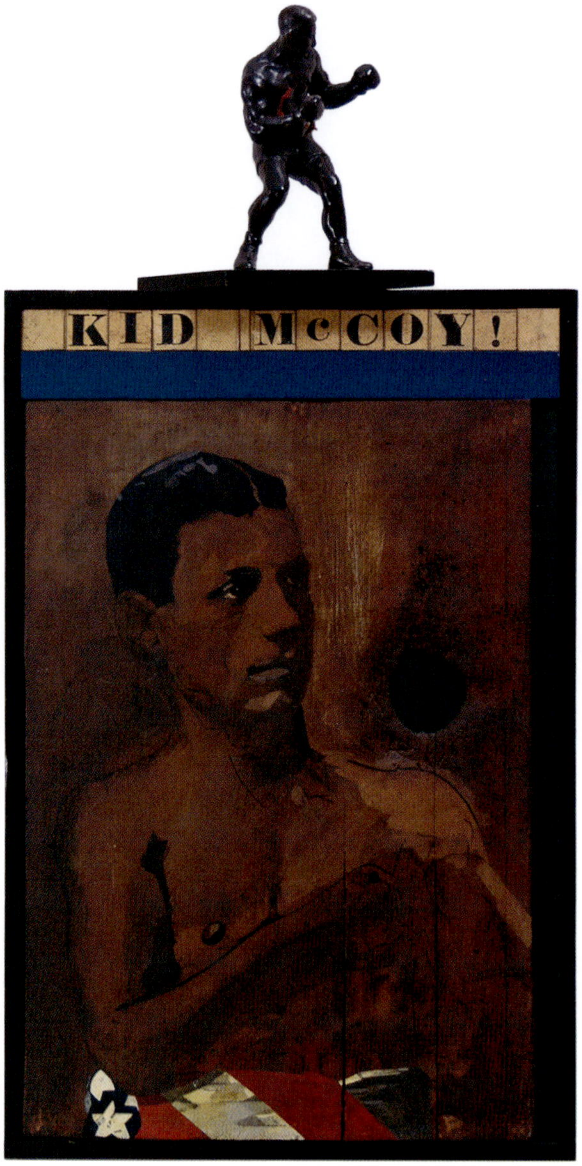

80 **Kid McCoy**, 1961–5

our gain, given the way in which those impulses were channelled into his art, injecting the pictures with an intensity and sense of urgency.

While he was at the Royal College, Blake had chosen to write his thesis, entitled 'Don't Point, it's Nude', on a topic of particular relevance to an emerging area of his subject matter: the decline of the nude in the music halls. With the arrival of television, the music halls themselves were on the way out, since the comics and other performers were finding it difficult to continue touring with the same act once they had been seen doing it on TV. Whereas fellow students found themselves researching in libraries or museums, Blake cleverly found a way of mixing work with pleasure, as he was to continue do throughout his life, by frequenting places for popular entertainment and using these visits as first-hand evidence. Among the acts he witnessed were Peaches Page, the fan dancer Phyllis Dixie (the English equivalent to Gypsy Rose Lee) and the suggestively named Jane and her little Fritzie. Though his thesis was stolen from his degree show and all the material he had thus collected was sadly lost, the stage shows he visited two or three times a week during that period left an indelible impression.

There is a poignancy and tenderness to Blake's portrayals of even those who present themselves as hard-bitten, tough and worldly: whether this be the female strippers and pin-ups or the male and female wrestlers who populate two of the extended series of paintings on which he was engaged during much of the 1960s. The women he had displayed as objects of unrequited desire in the collage paintings – unapproachable film stars and sex goddesses – are separated from mere mortals not just by their fame and wealth, but also by their habitation of a make-believe world that we can never expect to penetrate. The strippers and pin-up girls to which he turned his attention in the early 1960s are painted as flesh and blood, but we understand them, too, to be materialisations of fantasy brought to life from photographs printed in the pages of men's magazines. The first three such paintings to be completed by Blake, dating from 1962 and 1965, were each called simply *Pin-up Girl* (Plates 77, 78), conferring on them the same anonymity as those women shown projecting themselves, semi-naked, to satisfy men's desire in the soft-porn 'girlie magazines' of the period. One of these paintings, however, which depicts a blonde in a black bra, was actually from life. The others, despite their photographic derivation, look just as convincing as flesh and blood. Though undoubtedly vampish and sexual, even (one has to admit) a little slutty, they are not just sex objects. Their facial expressions and body language make them appear self-possessed and in control, but also vulnerable. That is to say, they come across as complex human beings, with conflicting needs and personae, rather than just as ciphers of desire.

Even before painting these *Pin-up Girls*, Blake had started work in 1961 on a painting with the extraordinary title *Zorine, Queen of the Nudists and her TV Gorilla* (Plate 79), which he completed four years later. The comical title was, in fact, derived from a real act he had heard about, though he has elaborated it to his own ends and paired the painted couple – a reworking of the Beauty and the Beast legend – with a collaged image of Fay Wray in the arms of King Kong (from the celebrated movie released just a year after Blake's birth). This single work, considerably larger in scale than many of those that were to follow, features all the elements of the key works in this series: a figure painted from a photograph but remodelled in his imagination, circus-type lettering and an extension of the imagery outside the painted picture frame in the form of plastic toys glued onto the surface.

Many equally fancifully named beauties with improbably voluptuous bodies and large breasts were to follow. There is the top-heavy, virtually naked *Kandy!*, for instance, in a painting of 1963–5. With her swaggering posture and the promise of excitement indicated by the exclamation point after her name, she is aptly christened after the heroine of a Terry Southern novel, *Candy*, which was considered so scandalous and licentious that it was not published in New York until 1964, six years after its first publication by the Olympia Press in Paris. Many imaginary portraits of this type were to follow in later decades. During the 1960s alone we have *Nudina*, an imaginary stripper in a painting of 1961–4; *Babe Rainbow* (Plate 89), star of a silkscreened multiple published in 1967 (which enters the territory of female wrestling); and *Selina Silver*, who is spied primping herself in a small oil with lettering, from 1968–77. These are all women that we know we can never meet even though some of them may have counterparts in the real world. They are forbidden fruit as much to married men as to pubescent boys, but as objects of desire – like the 'Pictures of Lily' in the Who's hit single of 1967 – can still have 'made my life so wonderful'. Are they soiled by this objectification? For some feminists, that may be so. However, there is too much tenderness in these pictures for them to be seen as merely lewd, too much strength in these women for them to be dismissed as passive victims and too much personality for them to be dismissed as empty vessels. What comes across, to me at least, is the fullness of their humanity.

Wrestlers, Boxers and Other Fantasy Portraits

The wrestlers that Blake began painting in 1961, as a continuation of the vein of escapist entertainment celebrated in his circus pictures of the previous decade, provide an aggressively male counterpart to the cast of characters in the stripper and pin-up paintings. With only a few exceptions, these larger-than-life figures are all inventions of the artist. Two wrestlers, *Masked Zebra Kid* (1965, Plate 85), whose authentic autograph appears as a trophy item in the centre of collaged photographs, and later *Kendo Nagasaki* (1992, Plate 103], were men he had seen perform. He also made portraits of two boxers from decades past: *Kid McCoy* (1961–5, Plate 80) (from the Edwardian era) and *Joe Louis, Brown Bomber* (1975–99, Plate 102) (world heavyweight champion from 1937 to 1948). In flaunting their toughness and masculinity to the point of self-parody, Blake's wrestlers and boxers play on boyhood fantasies of super-heroes and super-villains. Their often brutish appearance, like their hilariously over-the-top stage names redolent of power, evil and outlaw status – *Baron Adolf Kaiser* (1961–3, Plate 81), *Doktor K. Tortur* (1965, Plate 84), or *Franck and Jesse, The James Brothers* (1966–83, Plate 88) – masks the suspicion that they are really just big

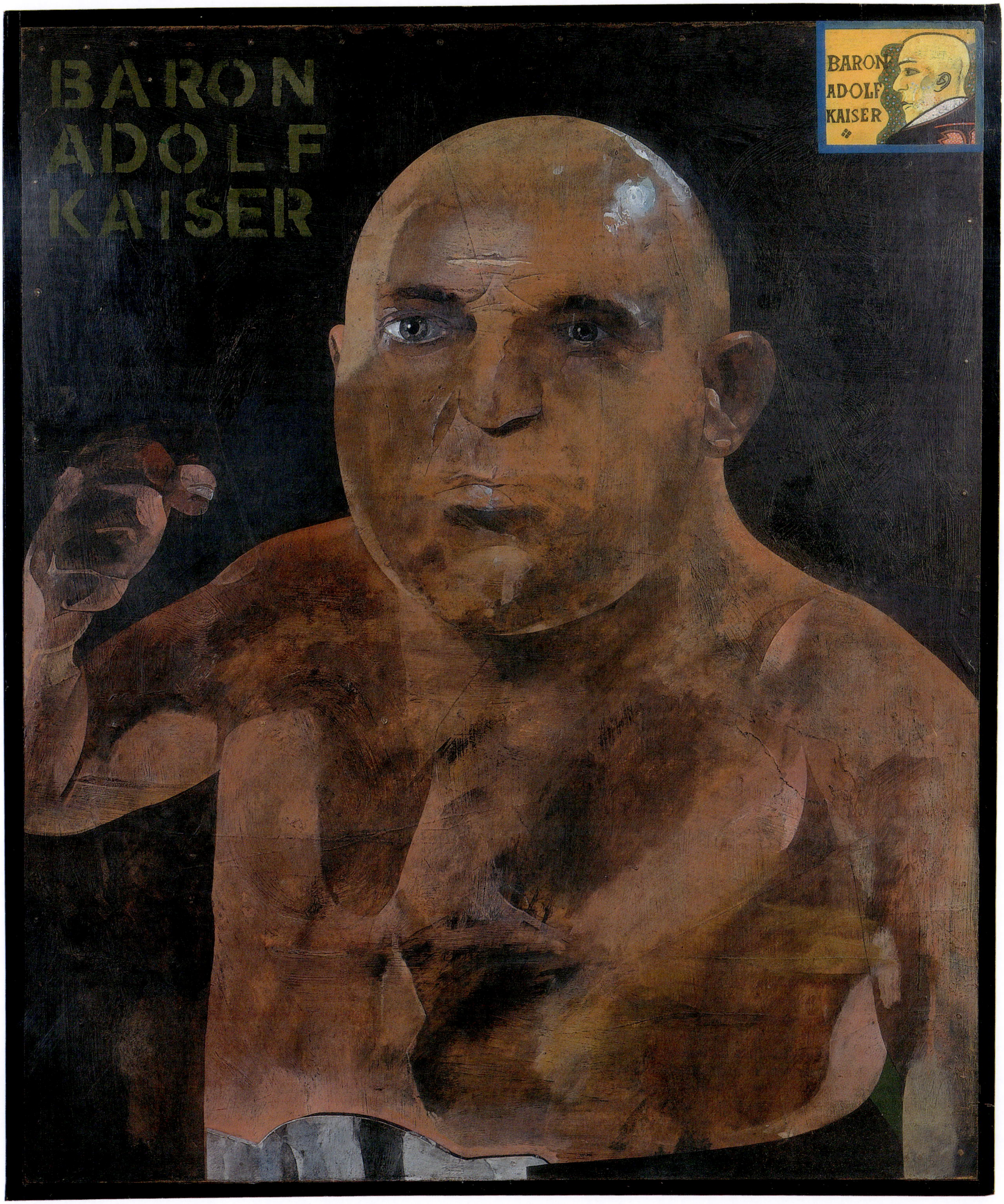

81 **Baron Adolf Kaiser**, 1961–3

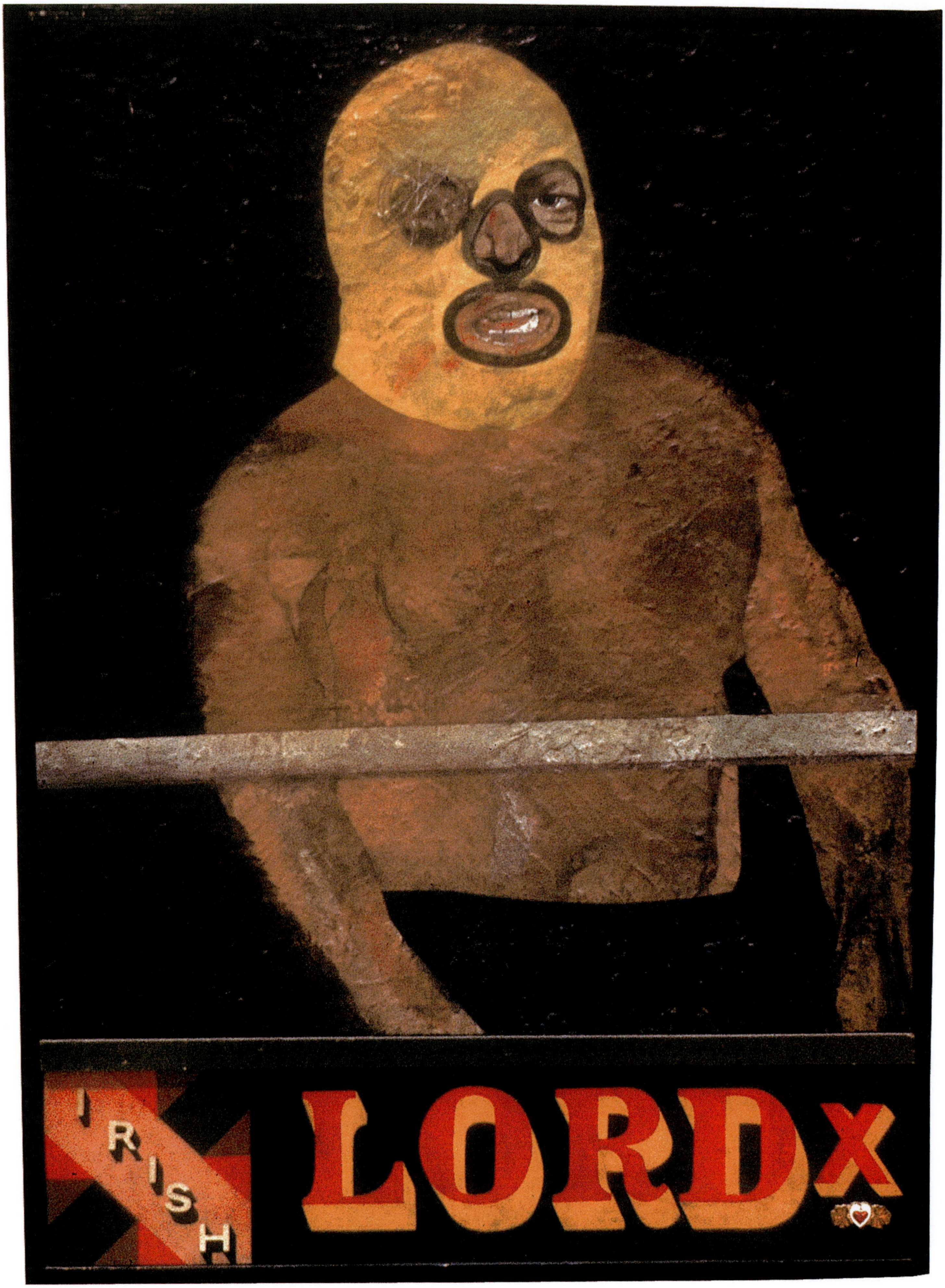

82 **Irish Lord X**, 1963

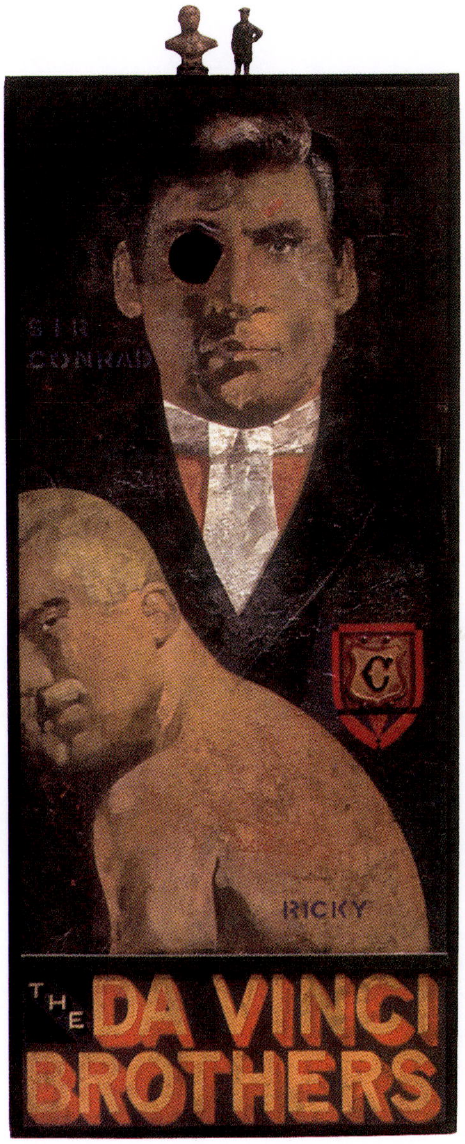

83 **Da Vinci Brothers**, 1963

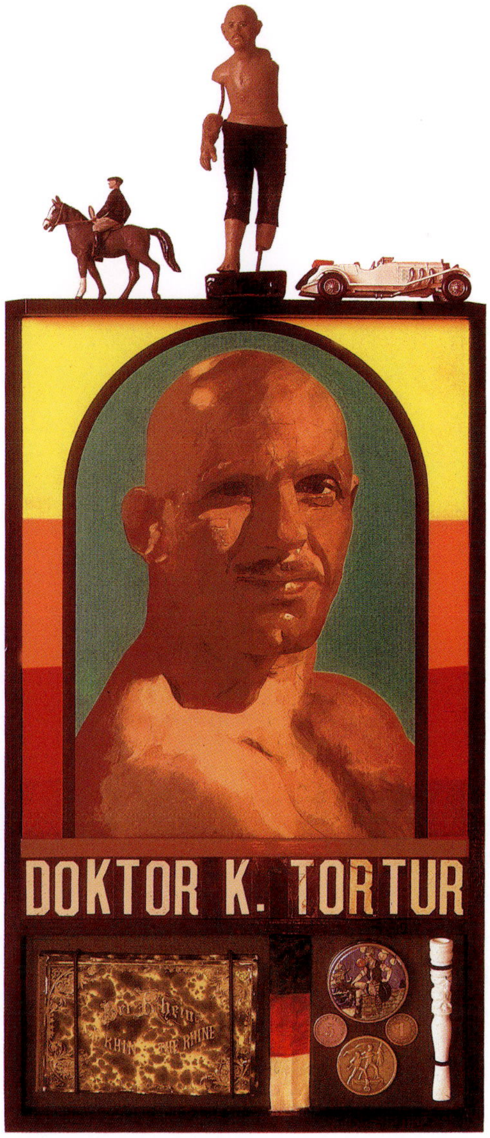

84 **Doktor K. Tortur**, 1965

softies underneath, acting out an assumed identity just as they choreograph their acts of combat in the ring for the entertainment of mere mortals.

Blake had begun going to wrestling matches from about the age of 15 in the company of his mother and other relatives, so he fully understood that the deception was carried out in full view of the audience and with their tacit collusion. He also appreciated the essentially comic thrust of the whole spectacle, the sending up of masculine stereotypes, which brought these burly men back to earth with a mighty thump. Blake clearly enjoyed

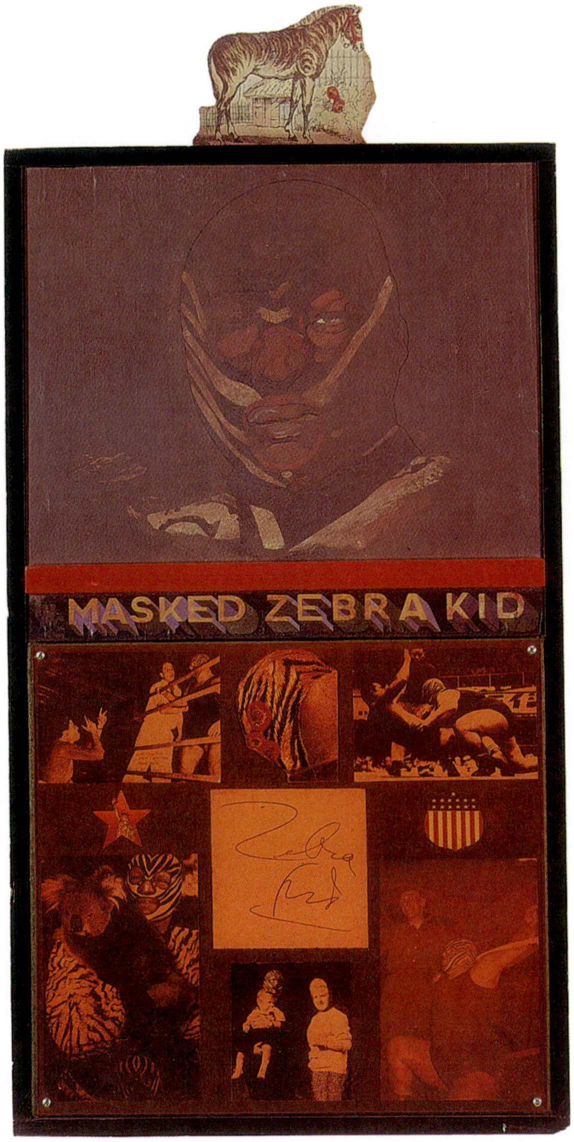

85 **Masked Zebra Kid**, 1965

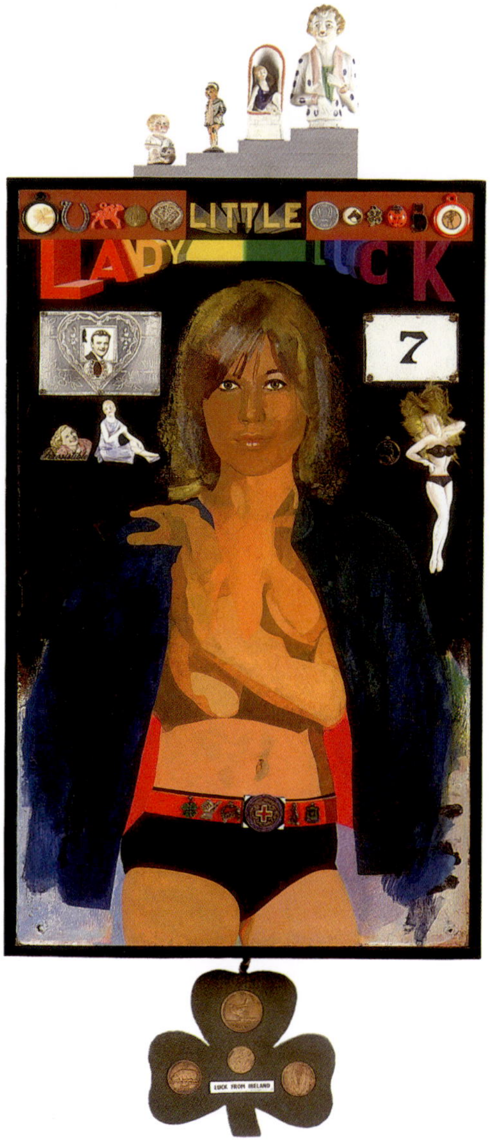

86 **Little Lady Luck**, 1965

inventing preposterous stage names and identities, such as the *Da Vinci Brothers* (1963, Plate 83), who are presumed Italian mafiosi named preposterously in honour of the painter of the *Mona Lisa*. In spite of their masks, their muscles and their threatening demeanour, there is nothing very frightening about any of these men. It is more tempting to smile at their posturing than to find them intimidating. Moreover, they are all painted with the greatest delicacy of touch that the artist could muster and on a small, intimate scale that emphasises that behind their costumes they are just human beings. One could go so far as to say that these *Übermenschen*, through being painted in this way, have been tamed and to some extent even feminised.

That many of the wrestlers also hide behind masks hints that beneath the bluster they may suffer from the same shyness as Blake himself who, as we know, grew a beard in his late teens in order to cover the scars of his cycling accident, in effect creating a life-long mask for his own face. The wrestlers emerged as a subject in the same year that he painted *Self-Portrait with Badges* (1961, Plate 40). Was this just coincidence? It suggests at least the possibility of a direct link between his representation of himself – and his adoption of multiple guises in a constantly shifting artistic identity – and his creation of an endless cast of compelling characters that function on at least a subliminal level as the exciting alter-egos for a man who knew himself to be quiet, retiring and self-effacing. Just as the wrestlers are understood to derive some of their power from the creation of a fictional identity that supersedes that of their hidden selves, so Blake gained strength as an artist through a constant return to what might be mistaken for an eccentric or wayward strand of his subject matter. As one of his obsessive themes, the wrestling pictures must be understood as being as central to his artistic identity as his Pop Art or his evolution of naturalistic figuration.

Like the circus paintings of the mid-1950s, Blake's wrestling pictures combine the naive look of old posters and sign-painted advertisements with a trained illustrator's sophisticated touch and eye for detail. As with much of Blake's art, there is a nostalgic, wistful atmosphere,

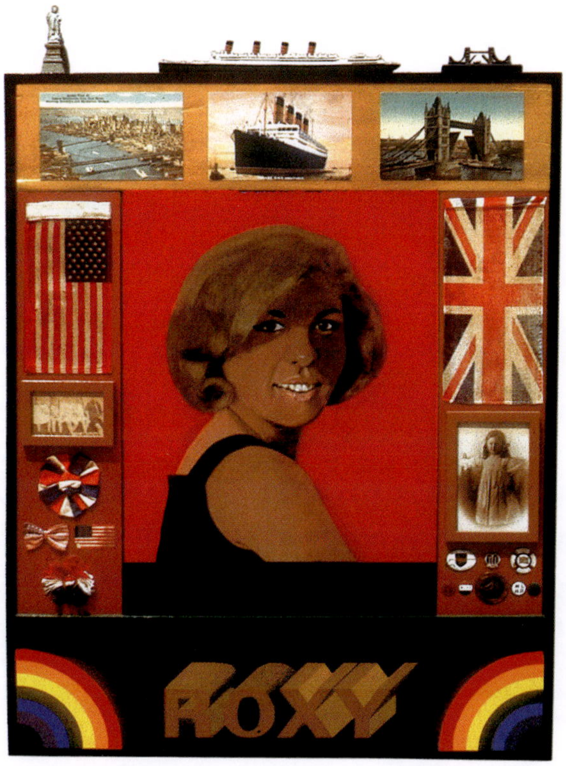

87 **Roxy Roxy**, 1965–83

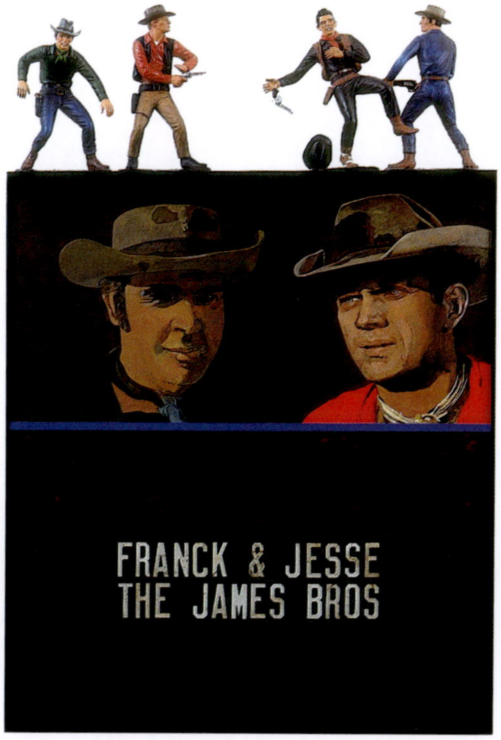

88 **Franck and Jesse, The James Brothers**, 1966–83

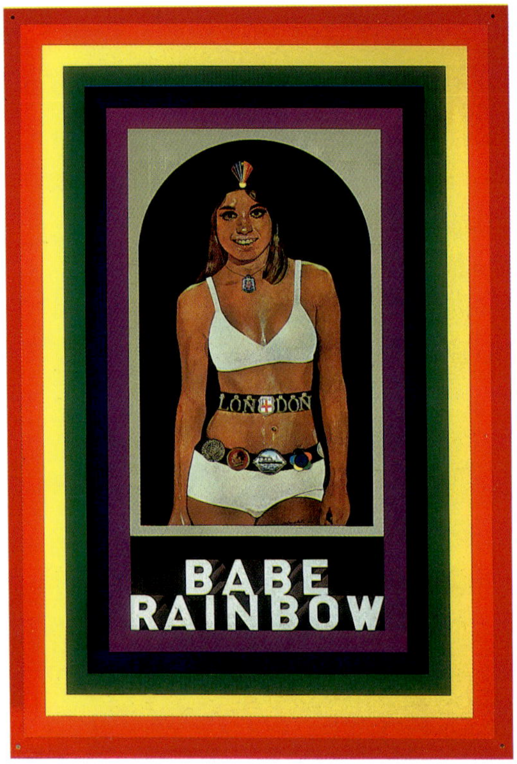

89 **Babe Rainbow**, 1967

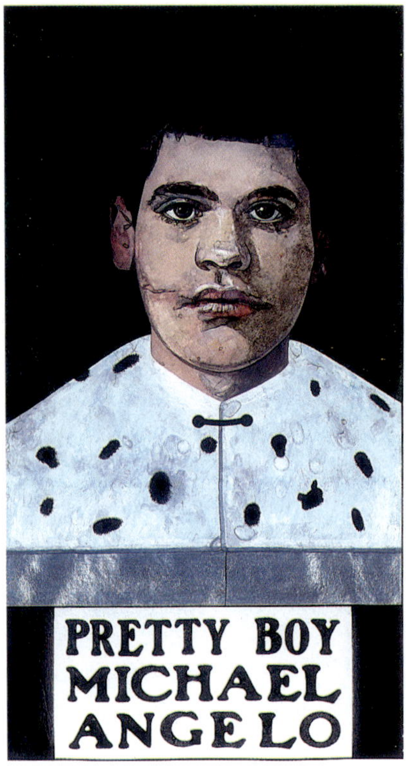

90 **Pretty Boy Michael Angelo**, 1972

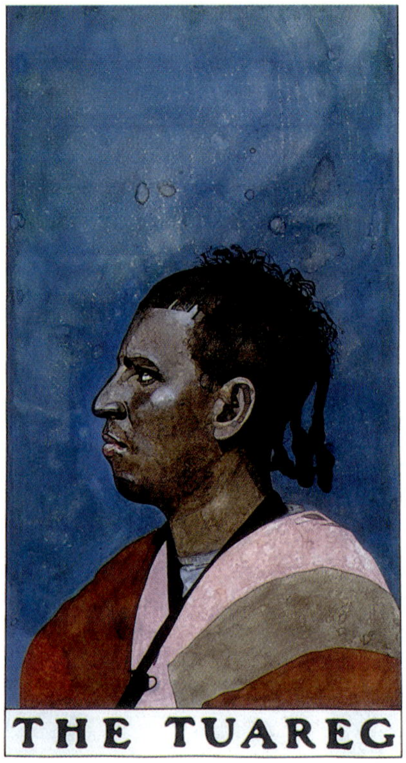

91 **The Tuareg**, 1972

both through the association with childhood and as a result of a regret that certain popular pastimes were already beginning to be made redundant by the glossier, more high-tech entertainments offered by the mass media. The small scale suggests a humility in the face of larger-than-life characters, at once honouring them for their exploits and humanising them. Typically, he used this subject matter to give free rein to his own humour and fantasy, inventing picturesque identities that were exaggerated but no more preposterous than those adopted by many stars of the ring.

Baron Adolf Kaiser (Plate 81), which Blake began in 1961, was the first of his wrestling pictures and it is simpler and more direct in format than those that followed. It presents an imaginary and rather comically villainous bald-headed fighter in a theatrically aggressive stance. This portrait, adapted from an image that the artist had found in an American wrestling magazine, is paired only with a second perfunctory representation of his features in profile, in the guise of a card similar to those that were collected by young boys. The stencilled lettering that identifies the man, reminiscent of the use of words on Jasper Johns's canvases, situates the painting in the traditions of medieval and early Renaissance portraits and of Victorian and modern posters bearing the likenesses of popular entertainers. As Blake himself has noted, these wrestling paintings, in their adoption of the presentation methods used in commercial poster design, are among the works most indebted to his early training in graphic design.

It is not just in their brazen illustrational qualities that the paintings of wrestlers comprehensively resist all the purist, Modernist conventions deemed proper for advanced art at the time, when abstract painting was in the ascendancy and even to be a figurative artist was to break the rules. Like his friends R.B. Kitaj and David Hockney, and like a few other renegades of the period such as Paula Rego, Blake took a delight in suggesting narrative possibilities. The idea of using a painting to tell a story was considered by many of his fellow artists – not least by Francis Bacon, author of the most imposing figure paintings made in Britain in the late 20th century – to have become totally unacceptable, even taboo, suggestive as this was of the literary inclinations of the Victorians. Blake had a natural affinity with much Victorian art and went on his merry way, well aware of such charges but heedless of them. In fact, he rebelled against these strictures by inventing

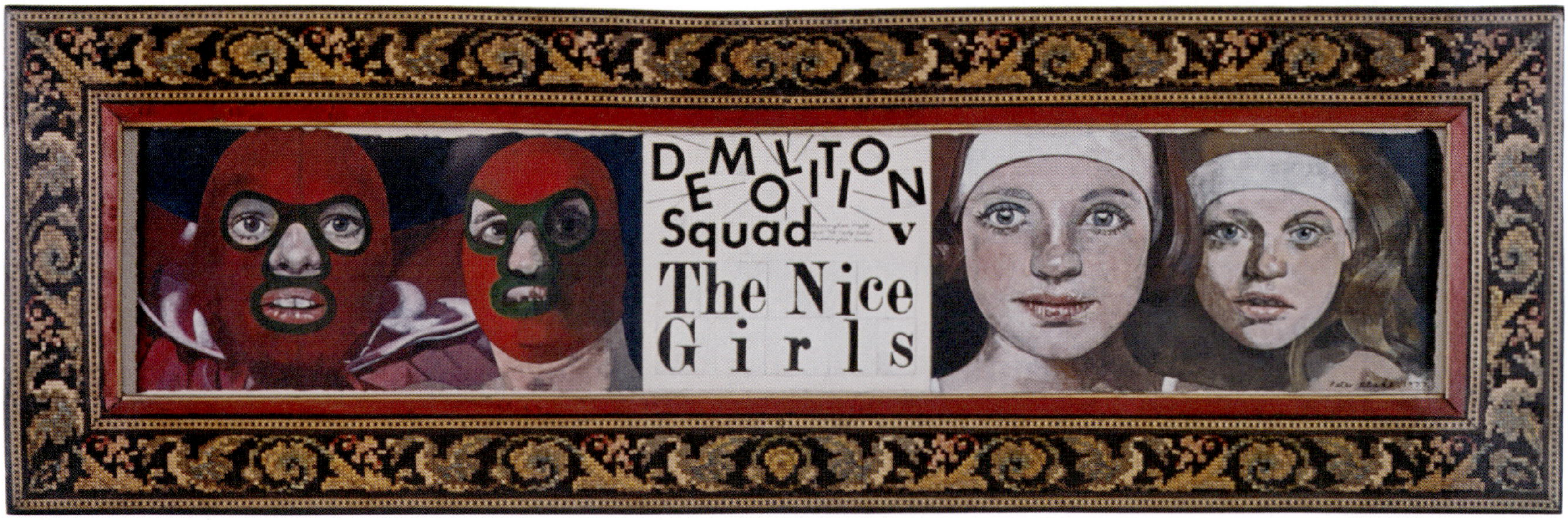

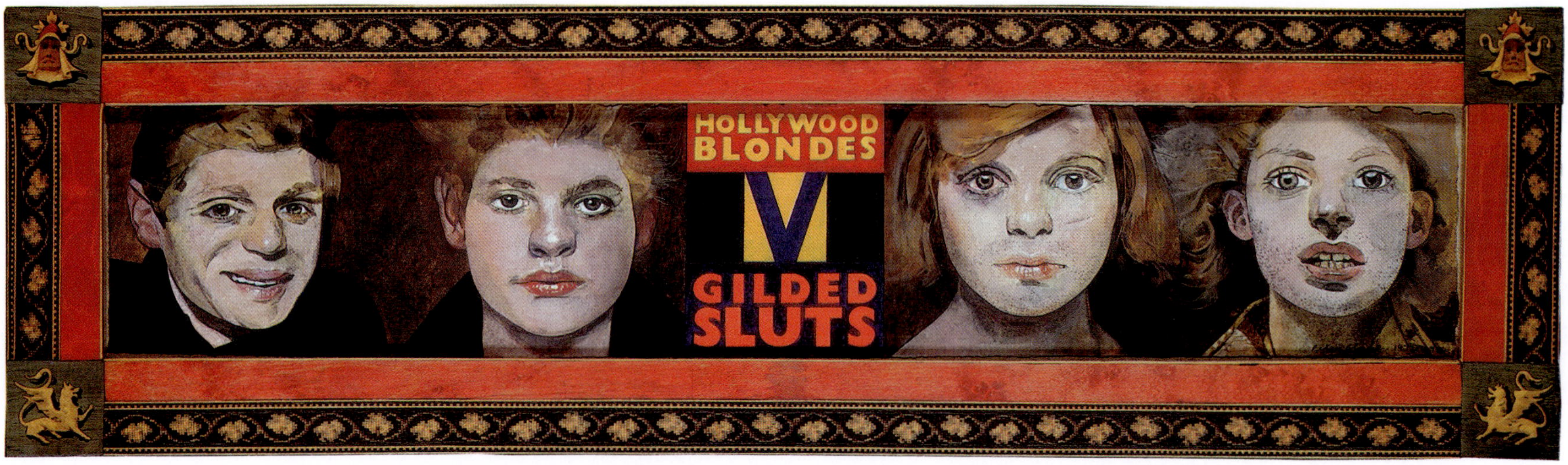

top **92** **Demolition Squad, Birmingham Drizzle and the Lady Doctor Versus the Nice Girls**, 1977
bottom **93** **Hollywood Blondes Versus the Gilded Sluts**, 1977–84

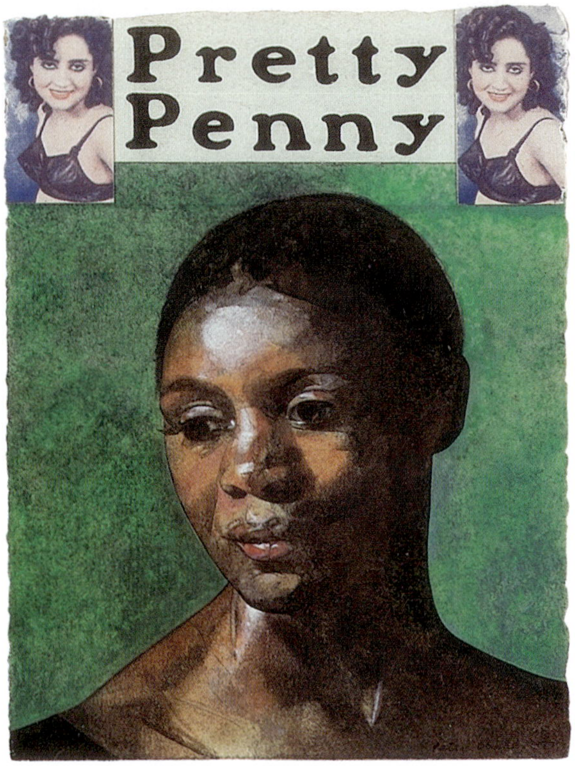

94 **Pretty Penny**, 1977

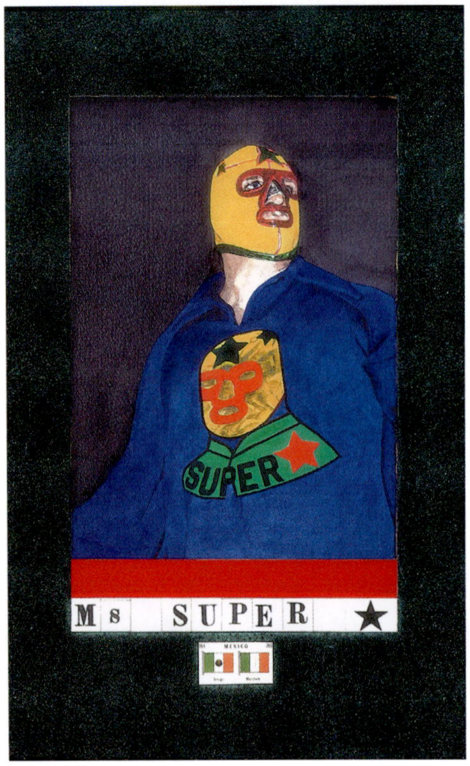

95 **Ms Super**, 1987

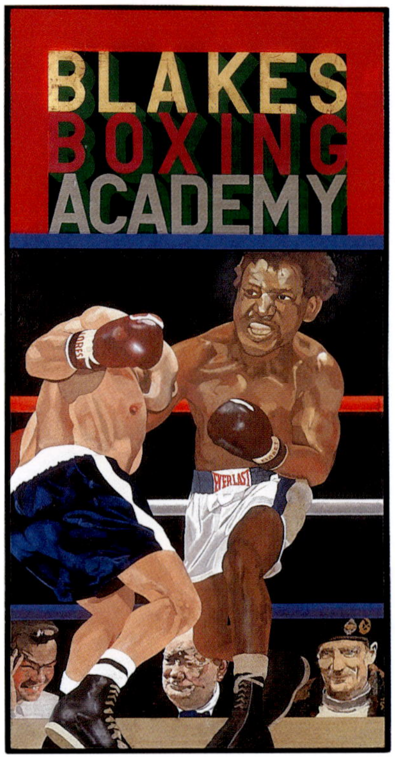

96 **Blakes Boxing Academy**, 1988

characters to whom he could ascribe an imaginary life history, as in the case of *Irish Lord X* (1963, Plate 82), an aristocrat forced to wear a mask in the ring so that he would not be disowned by his family, or *Kamikaze* (1965, Plate 76), a masked Japanese-American wrestler named after the suicide pilots of the Second World War. It can hardly have been accidental that Blake chose to counter the aesthetic prescriptions of the time by using some of his most aggressive imagery. The self-effacing humour with which all these pictures are tinged, however, takes some of the sting out of them, suggesting a constitutional inability on the part of this gentle humanist to express real anger or violence. Any pugilist aggression on his part – just like in the kind of wrestling as entertainment that he watched in the ring or on television – is merely play-acting. The atmosphere of combat is not meant to be taken too seriously or at face value in either the sport or the art. This is not, however, to devalue the deadly seriousness with which both wrestler and artist have carried out their allotted roles.

The figures portrayed in the *Da Vinci Brothers* (1963, Plate 83) may suggest closer affinities to organised crime than to their Renaissance namesake but, however threatening their demeanour, the air of menace is undermined by the illusionistic three-dimensional lettering that spells out their name below, which presents them unequivocally as entertainers. Another nasty character, with a shaved head and the Germanic name of Doktor K. Tortur in a painting of 1965 (Plate 84), is more overtly villainous, all the more so for the hints of an ill-begotten access to the high life (as represented by a 1930s Mercedes and a

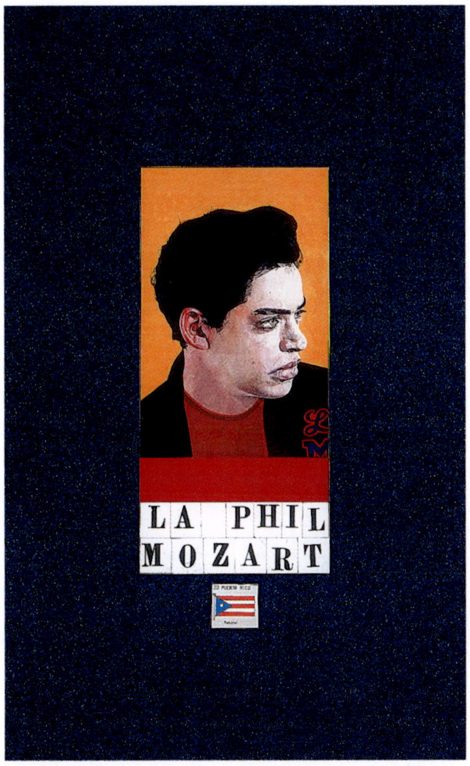

97 **L.A. Phil Mozart**, 1987

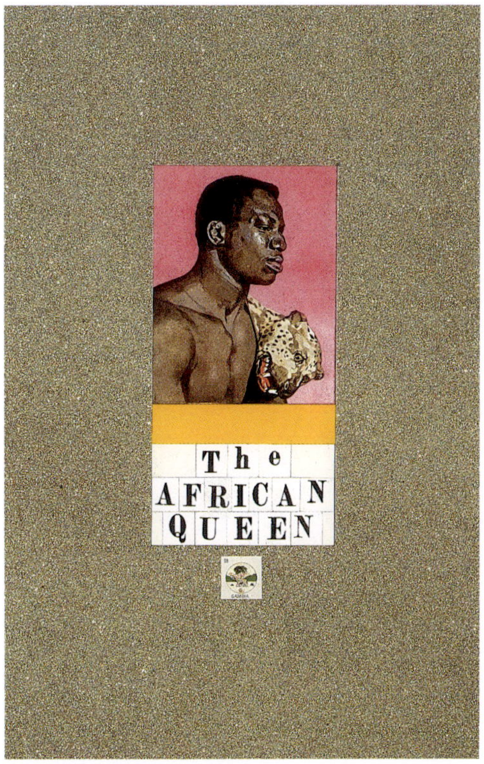

98 **The African Queen**, 1987

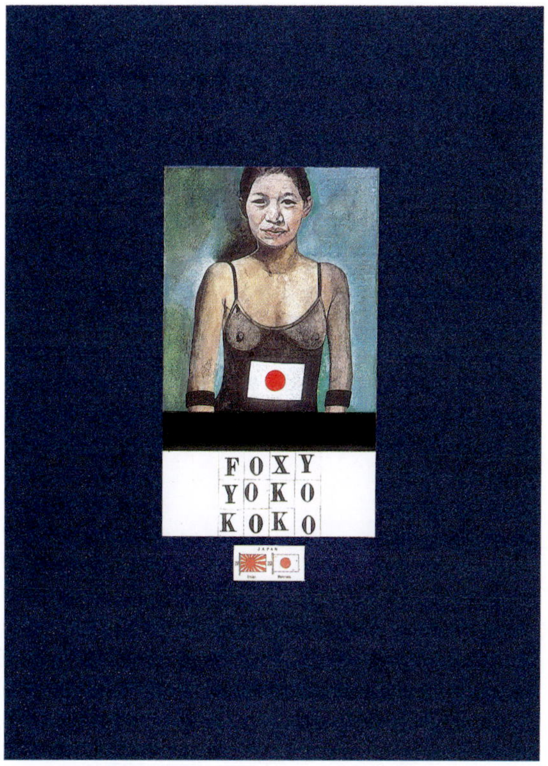

99 **Foxy Yoko Koko**, 1987

racehorse ridden by Doktor K. Tortur). In the end, he is no more frightening than the 'baddies' portrayed in comic books or the evil geniuses featured in the James Bond movies that had first appeared in cinemas in 1962. The small found objects placed along the top edge of many of these pictures serve a similar role to the attributes of saints in Renaissance paintings, identifying the persons portrayed but also amplifying one's understanding of their tastes and complexity as fully rounded individuals.

An equal-opportunity employer and a subverter of gender stereotyping even before the advent of late-1960s' feminism questioned assumptions about which jobs and careers were appropriate to men and women, Blake also created a number of portraits of female wrestlers. The earliest of these are two pictures begun in 1965 and later altered, *Little Lady Luck* (Plate 86) and *Roxy Roxy* (Plate 87). If the nubile young woman in the former resembles the earlier *Pin-up Girls* (Plates 77, 78) this is hardly surprising given that she is a reinvention from a photograph found in the same kind of magazines that were used as a source for those pictures. Accompanied by the lucky number 7, an Irish three-leaf clover and a variety of other amulets and charms, she strikes the viewer as a woman supremely confident in herself and in the prospects of a continuous winning streak. With her black, sleeveless dress and careful coiffure, *Roxy Roxy* – so good they named her twice? – looks more like an English débutante than a tough cookie ready for a good grapple. The collaged postcards, flags and badges, together with the trio of objects glued to the top edge, suggest

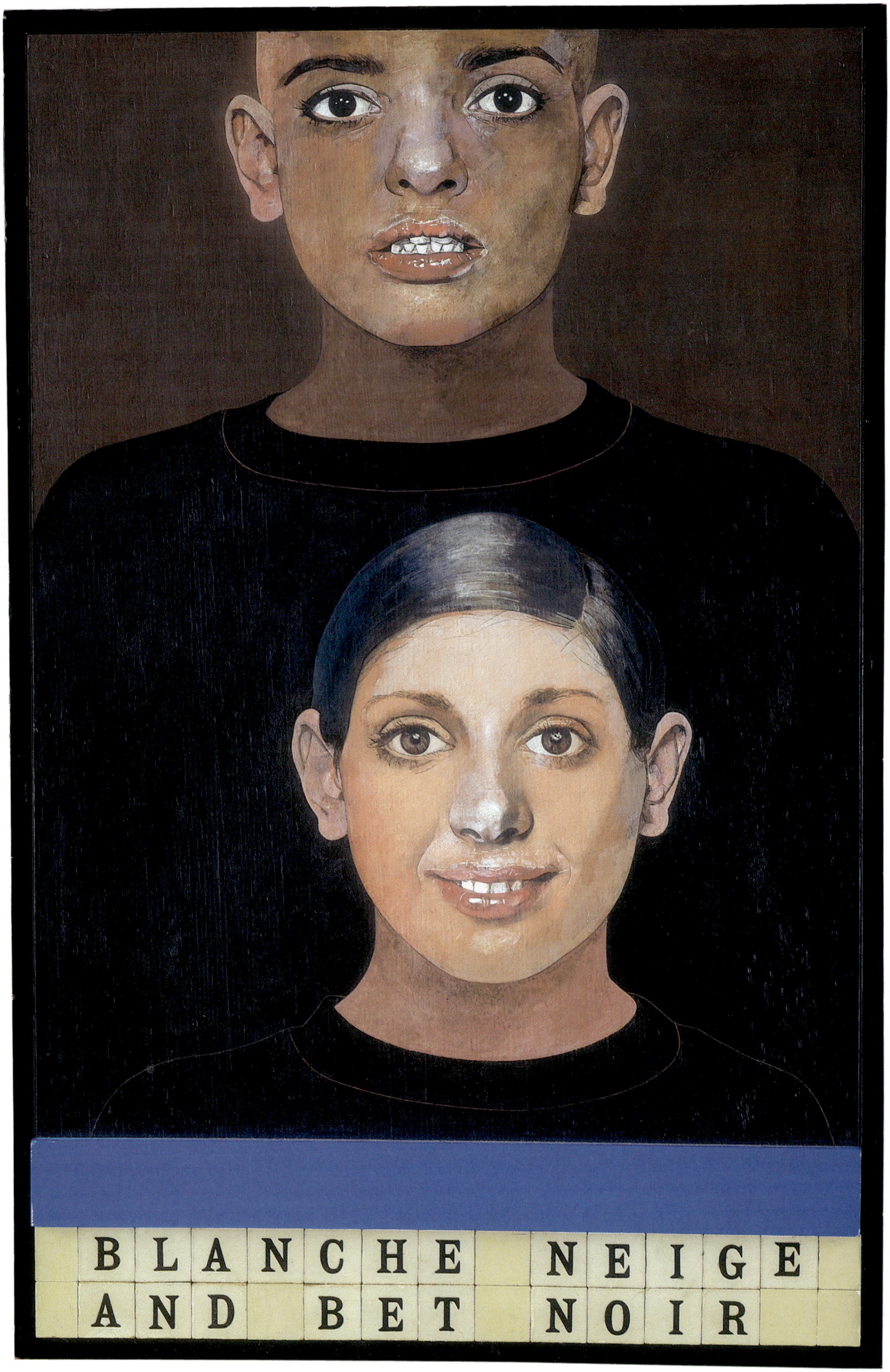

100 **Blanche Neige and Bet Noir**, 1976–81

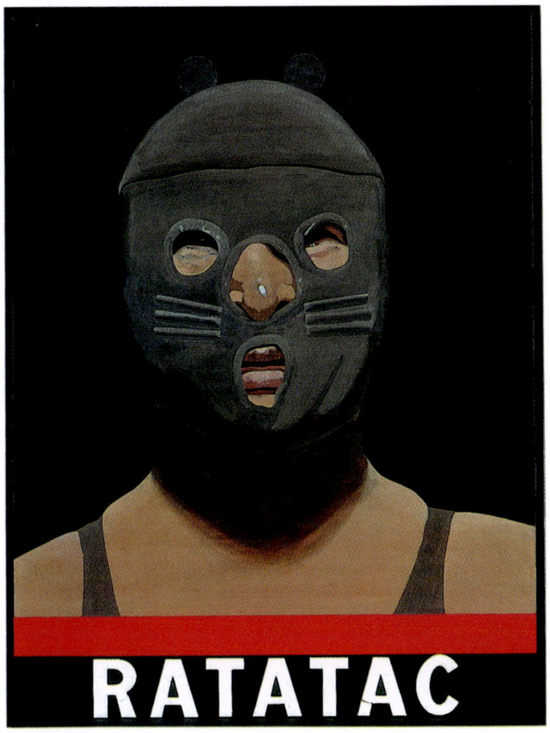

101 **Ratatac**, 1997–2003

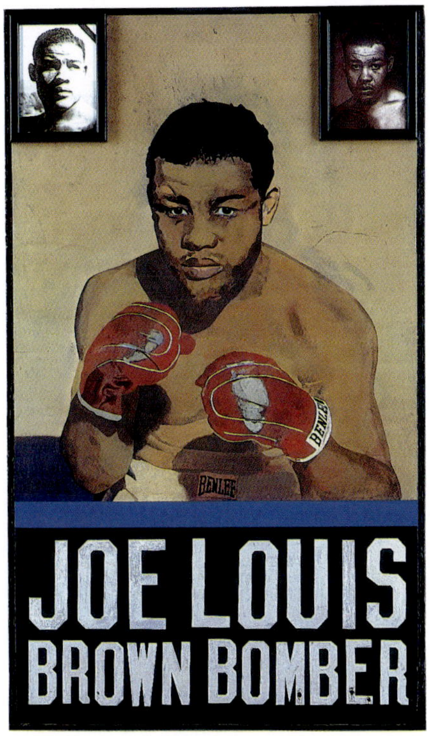

102 **Joe Louis, Brown Bomber**, 1975–99

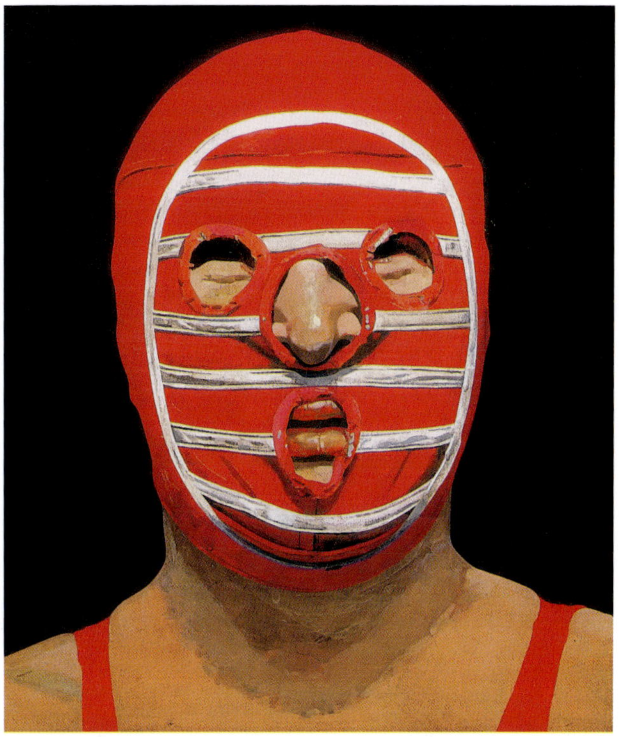

103 **Kendo Nagasaki**, 1992

that she is on her way from London to New York in order to make her name in the United States and to crown herself with more glory.

Another memorable addition to Blake's growing cast of characters in the wrestling series was *La Petite Reine Africaine* (1968–83), based on a photographic portrait of a male American civil-rights campaigner but reimagined as an African princess. Probably the best known of all his portraits of female wrestlers, however, because of its ubiquity as a multiple screenprinted on tin in an edition of 10,000, is *Babe Rainbow* (1967, Plate 89). The image was adapted by the artist from a cover of the women's magazine *Marie Claire*. In its daring use of an industrial process adapted from old-fashioned packaging, it appears to be a curious marriage of nostalgia and avant-garde effrontery: the biscuit tin turned into high art for the masses. In the accompanying explanatory text published with the print by Dodo Designs, Blake helpfully explained the place of this archetypal 1960s' 'chick' within his art and sketched out a brief biographical note to flesh out her identity:

> Babe Rainbow, a fictitious lady wrestler, is the most recent in a line of wrestlers I have painted. These include Irish Lord X, Doktur K. Tortur, Kamikaze and Les Orchidées Noires. She is twenty-three years old and has broken her nose in the ring. She was born in New Cross, London and wrestles mainly in Europe and the U.S.A. as there have been only a few contests between lady wrestlers in London. She is the daughter of the notorious Doktur K. Tortur.

Many of Blake's later fantasy portraits have continued to be devised for this arena of the imagination, the wrestling ring. In 1972 he created a set of six of his richest watercolours as a series of imaginary wrestlers corresponding to national types: *Pretty Boy Michael Angelo* (Plate 90), *Ebony Tarzan*, *Red Power*, *Penny Black* and *The Tuareg* (Plate 91). They were also disseminated as limited-edition silkscreen prints published by Waddington Galleries in the same year. One can almost hear the artist chuckling as he devises such new characters as Blanche Neige and her punningly named adversary Bet Noir, for a painting of 1976–81 (Plate 100), or the male and female gay tag teams represented in a pair of watercolours begun in 1977, *Demolition Squad, Birmingham Drizzle and the Lady Doctor Versus the Nice Girls* (Plate 92) and the more snappily titled *Hollywood Blondes Versus the Gilded Sluts* (Plate 93). We also have *Bernie Berni – Jewish/Italian Mat Star* (1977) and *Pretty Penny* (1977, Plate 94), two tiny but elaborately framed and beautifully rendered paintings on paper.

Periodically, Blake has produced new series of imaginary wrestlers, such as those made between 1985 and 1987 as watercolours collaged onto a variety of sparkling and decorative backgrounds and accompanied by their names and the national flags of their presumed origin: *Ms Super* (1987, Plate 95), *Dex and Lex Lisowski Junkyard Dogs* (1986), *Lucky Boy Fit Kelly* (1987), *Mambo Rambo* (1987), *L.A. Phil Mozart* (1987, Plate 97), *The African Queen* (1987, Plate 98) and *Foxy Yoko Koko* (1987, Plate 99) were added to this ever-growing throng. Much of the fun for the artist (and consequently for the consumer of the pictures) seems to have been in referencing popular culture, including classics of the cinema and more recent blockbusters by the likes of Sylvester Stallone, or in allowing an idea for a new character to be sparked by some flight of the imagination when encountering an object or image in the public domain. Such was the case with the painting *Baby Ruth* (1972–89, Plate 105), named after an American chocolate-covered candy bar which itself possibly derived its name from a baseball hero (Babe Ruth) of the 1920s, and *L.A. Phil Mozart*, a conjunction of words spotted on a poster advertising a Mozart concert by the Los Angeles Philharmonic Orchestra.

It is not always a question of jolly japes and hijinks in this area of Blake's art. For example, despite the cartoonish whiskers displayed on the male wrestler's mask in the painting *Ratatac* (1997–2003, Plate 101), the concealment here of the face and starkness of the presentation introduces a sinister atmosphere rarely seen in his work. There are also at least two fairly straightforward homages to great sportsmen in his later work. The first of these was the painting of *Joe Louis, Brown Bomber* (Plate 102), which he started in 1975 and finally completed 24 years later. The second, *Kendo Nagasaki* (Plate 103), was made under the glare of the spotlight for a BBC2 documentary programme screened in January 1992 under the title *Masters of the Canvas*, during which Blake fulfilled his

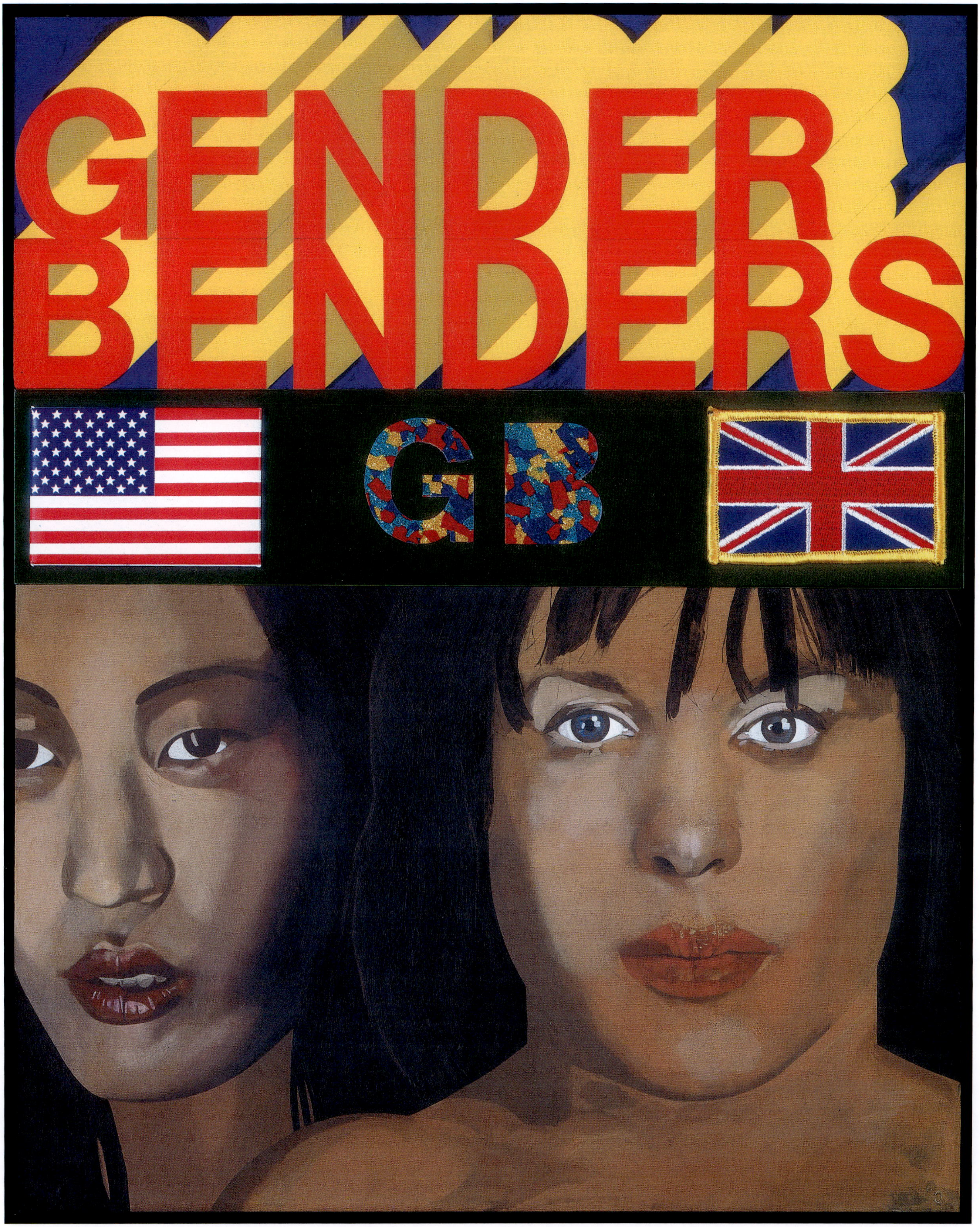

104 **Gender Benders**, 2002–3

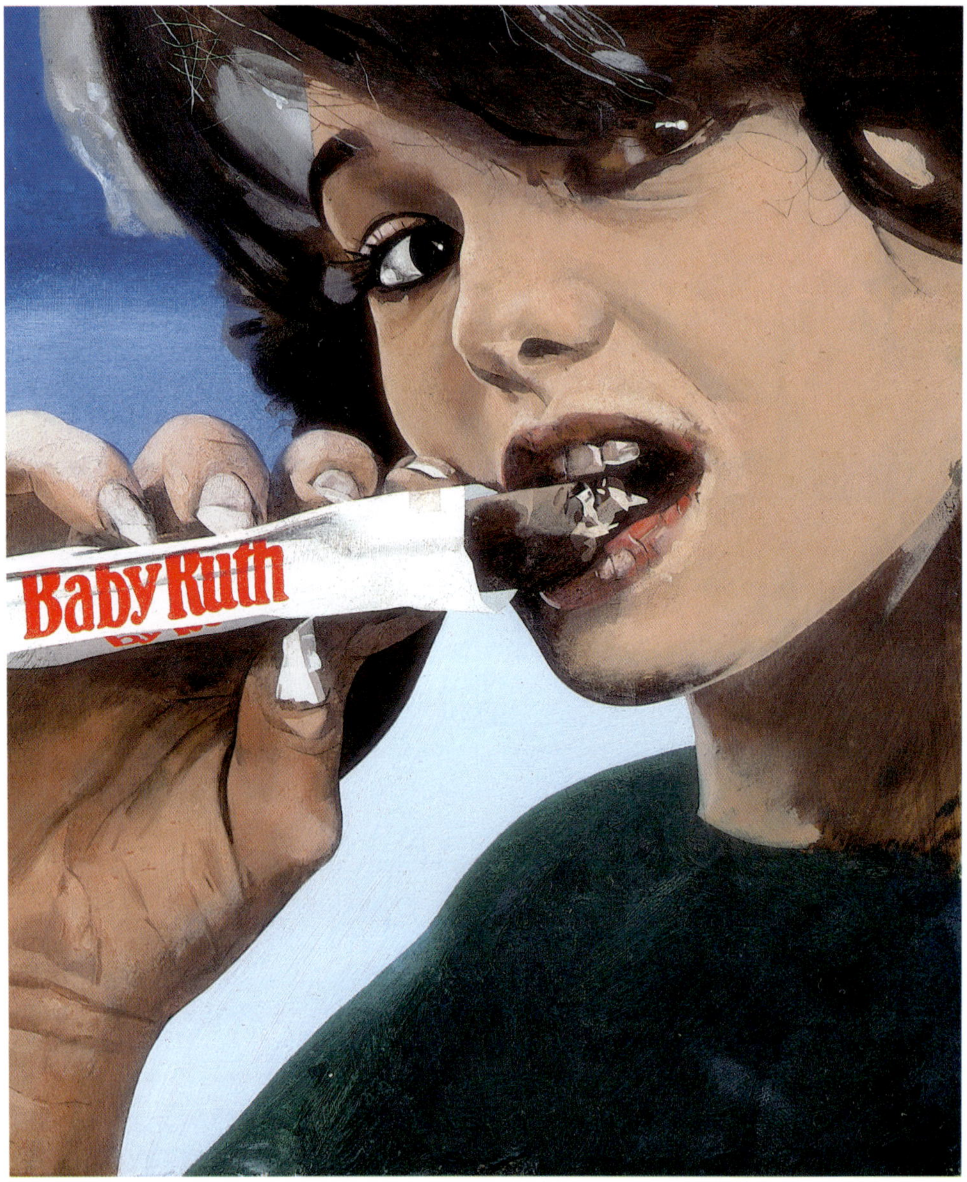

105 **Baby Ruth**, 1972–89

ambition to meet and paint the British masked wrestler Peter Thornley, better known by his Japanese stage-name. Among the most recent additions to this highly entertaining lineage is a colourful lithograph on tin that Blake created in 2001 to raise funds for Pallant House Gallery, Chichester. Printed in a signed and numbered edition of 2,000, it explicitly recreates the look and spirit of *Babe Rainbow*: as well it might, since this young woman, identified as *Bobbie Rainbow*, is Babe's daughter, proudly carrying on the family tradition. In 2008 Blake began work on a further print, this time of Bobbie's long-lost, gay twin brother, Billy Rainbow, adopted at birth.

Tarzan and his Family

Literature has been a natural ally for Blake, as has the twentieth-century reinvention of the narrative impulse in the movies. This now seems a foregone conclusion, given the importance he has attached in his art to the imagination and to the creation or elaboration of fictional characters who take on a life of their own, reappearing in many different guises and contexts. In his mind, both real people (including Hollywood actors and pop musicians) and purely invented characters become part of his repertory company once they have entered his work. Given their status as players in his pictures, they can be invited back whenever necessary, their lives constantly extended in new directions. From the 1950s much of his subject matter has hinged on an escape into make-believe, into the worlds of the circus, the funfair and wrestling and also into the movies. Lewis Carroll's *Alice in Wonderland* and *Through the Looking-Glass* (which he came to illustrate in a series of eight watercolours in 1969–71, Plates 168–75) held a particular appeal for him, as did the 1939 movie based on Frank L. Baum's 1900 novel *The Wizard of Oz* and the day-long journeys of James Joyce's *Ulysses* and Dylan Thomas's *Under Milk Wood* (Plate 143), proposing as they did an invitation to a parallel universe: a place of wonder, discovery and enchantment where one can escape the humdrum reality of ordinary existence.

In a sense, everything Blake makes in his studio is part of the world of the imagination that he is able to create for himself there, locked away from the grubby realities of the 'real' world, in a state of heightened and prolonged fantasy. There are no-nonsense and

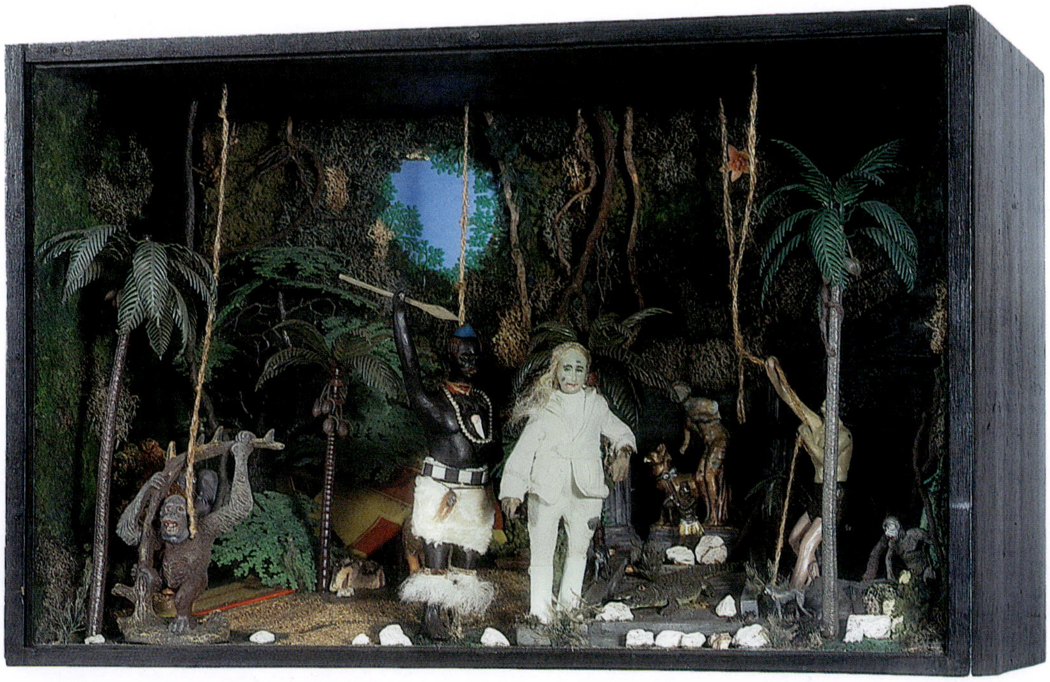

106 **Tarzan Box – 'Big Iron Bird She Come'**, 1965

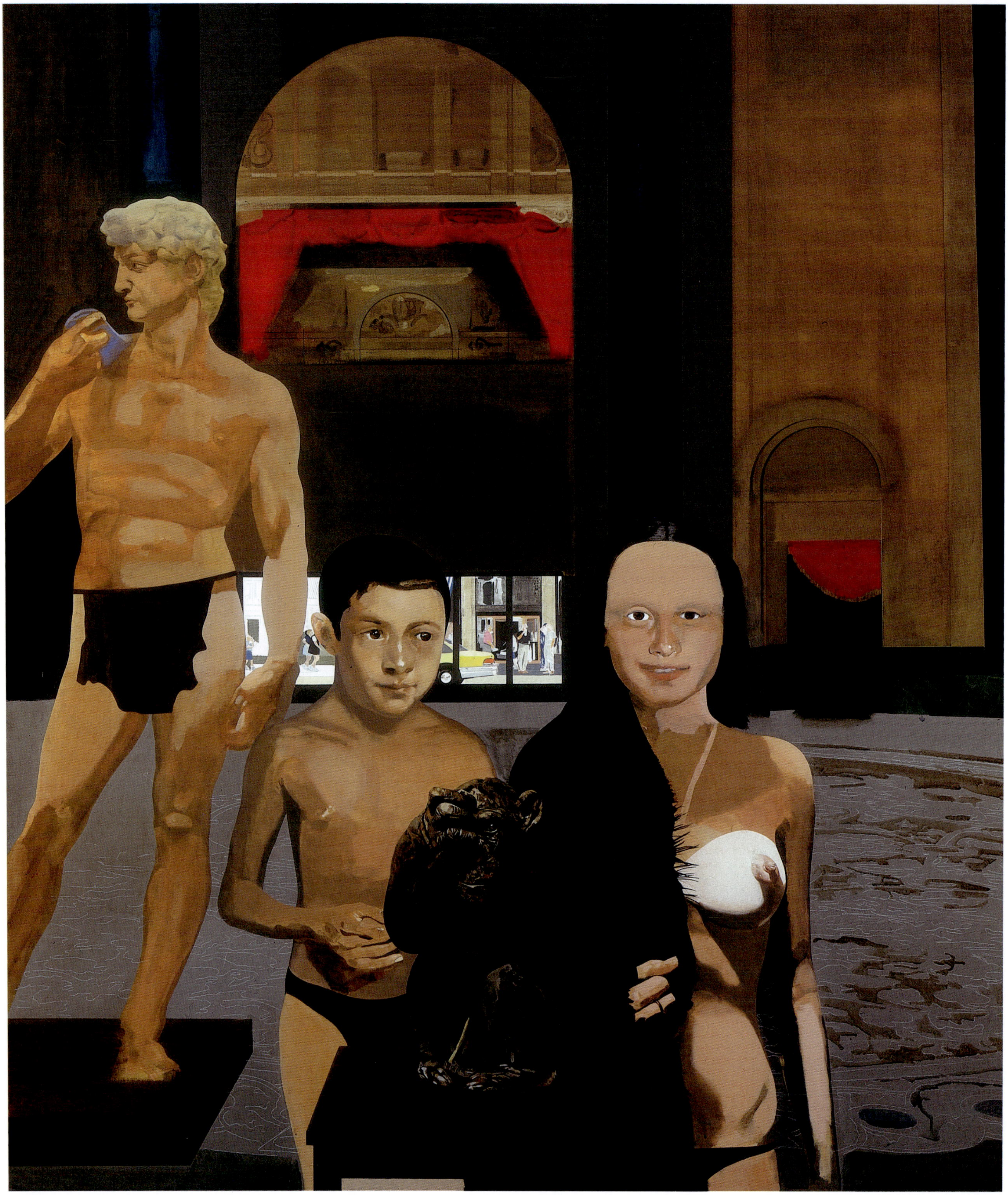

107 **Tarzan and his Family at the Roxy Cinema, New York**, 1964–2002

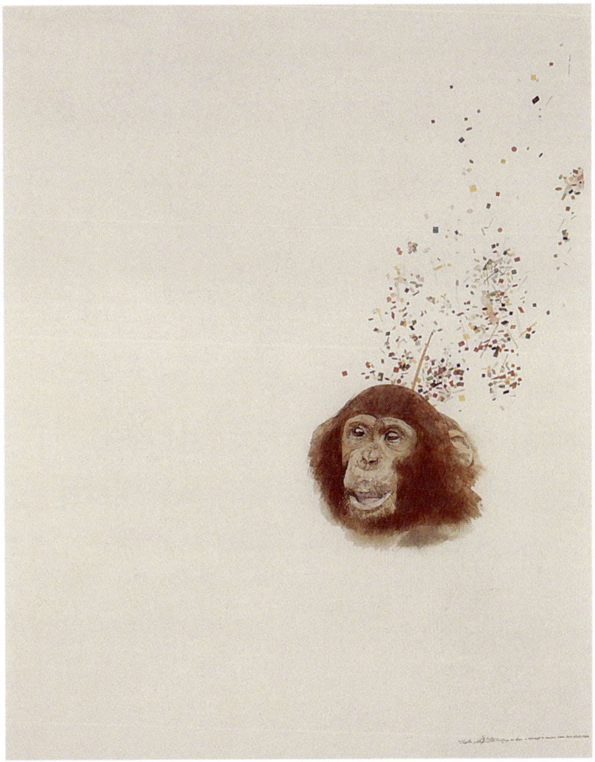

108 Cheeta with Confetti Falling on Him – A Tribute to Lawson Wood, 1969

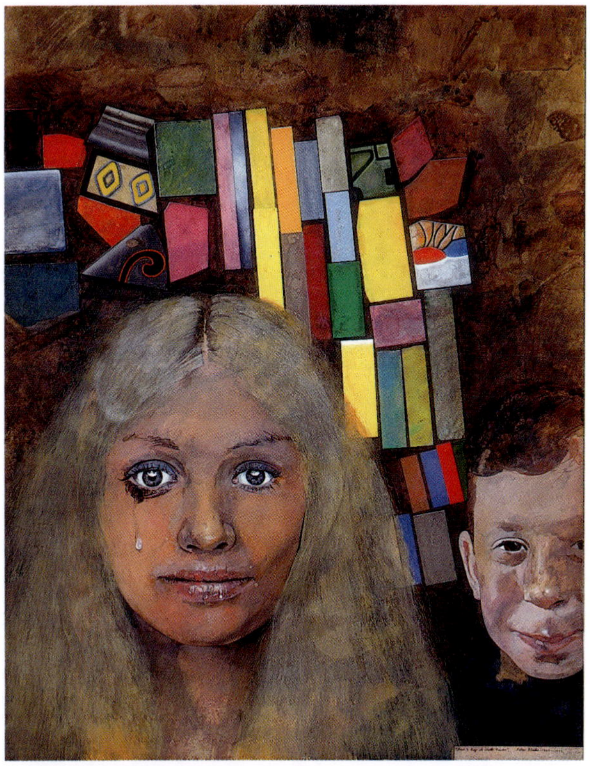

109 Jane and Boy at Watts Tower, 1969–76

pragmatic people, of course, who find all this hard to take and who become irritated and impatient with the fancifulness and whimsy of Blake's art in its most dreamlike dimensions; we need such down-to-earth people in this world, but Blake's art does not necessarily need them (nor they his art). I am the first to understand the toe-curling embarrassment that some experience when hearing talk of 'finding one's inner child'. However, those of us who find our lives enriched by the imagination, and who can still tap into that 'willing suspension of disbelief' that made the stories of our early years seem so magical, will not need to have all this explained. When you bring yourself to accept even the most outlandish premises in Blake's work, such as the existence of fairies, you can experience a sense of well-being, a deep-rooted happiness and comfort, that might seem out of proportion to the circumstances. Even or perhaps especially at its most illustrational, his art transports the viewer, at least momentarily, to another (perhaps better) world. The only catch is this: just as a hypnotist depends on his subject's desire to submit to another person's will, so Blake's art will fully cast its spell only on those who are prepared to give in to it without making too many conditions.

Tarzan and his family have been favourite subjects for Blake since just after his first trip to Los Angeles in 1963. *Tarzan of the Apes*, published in 1912, was the first of some two dozen Tarzan novels by the American writer Edgar Rice Burroughs (1875–1950), but it was the first six Tarzan films released by MGM between 1932 and 1941, starring Johnny Weissmüller as Tarzan and Maureen O'Sullivan as Jane, which provided Blake with much of his inspiration. Years later he was tickled to discover that the chimpanzee that played Cheeta in most of these movies was born in the same year as him, and – even more aptly – had taken up painting.

The first work on this subject actually to be completed was a small sculptural object, *Tarzan Box – 'Big Iron Bird She Come'* (1965, Plate 106), containing an arrangement of found objects in a glass case. As a sculptural form this owes something to the work of two American artists whom Blake admired: H.C. Westermann (two of whose witty and humorous sculptures he was later to own) and the Surrealist sculptor and collagist Joseph Cornell, whose box constructions had a secretive and magical quality that he particularly appreciated. The narrative solution proposed by Blake, however, is very much his own, conceived somewhat in the manner of the dioramas in natural history museums or the penny entertainments associated with the amusement arcades on Victorian piers. Using plastic toys and other materials, he has created a miniature tableau in which the key events from Tarzan movies are amusingly condensed into a single action-packed scene: a recently crashed plane, a rapacious lion, an overactive gorilla, a fearsome warrior with spear poised over a frightened Jane and Tarzan himself about to swing from a rope in time-honoured fashion. With a characteristically generous and humble spirit, Blake continued to find ways of proposing serious artistic questions. Under the guise of humour and a shared memory of a childhood entertainment which is likely to have spurred our own fantasy and imagination, *Tarzan Box* constitutes a provocative artistic gesture in disclaiming the sculptor's traditional manipulation of materials, while subtly proposing a new definition for sculptural composition through the precise arrangement of found objects in a delimited space.

Blake had begun his first Tarzan painting, *Tarzan and his Family at the Roxy Cinema, New York* (Plate 107), in 1964, but left it in a very unfinished state and substantially reworked it during his residency at the National Gallery in London between 1994 and 1996; it was finally brought to a conclusion as late as 2002. His willingness to reinterpret existing images so as to breathe new life into them extends here to his own art. In deference to his new proximity to the great masters, he reworked Jane's face so that it resembled that of the *Mona Lisa*, though viewed head-on and with her lips parted into a toothy smile, and that of the boy after a painting by Titian. Tarzan himself, still but a shadowy figure when this painting had last been exhibited, at the *Pop Art* survey presented at the Montreal Museum of Fine Arts in late 1992, now emerged in the guise of Michelangelo's *David*, completing the sense of each character as a star making 'a special guest appearance' from exciting foreign locations such as Paris and Florence. Giving these new inflections to a

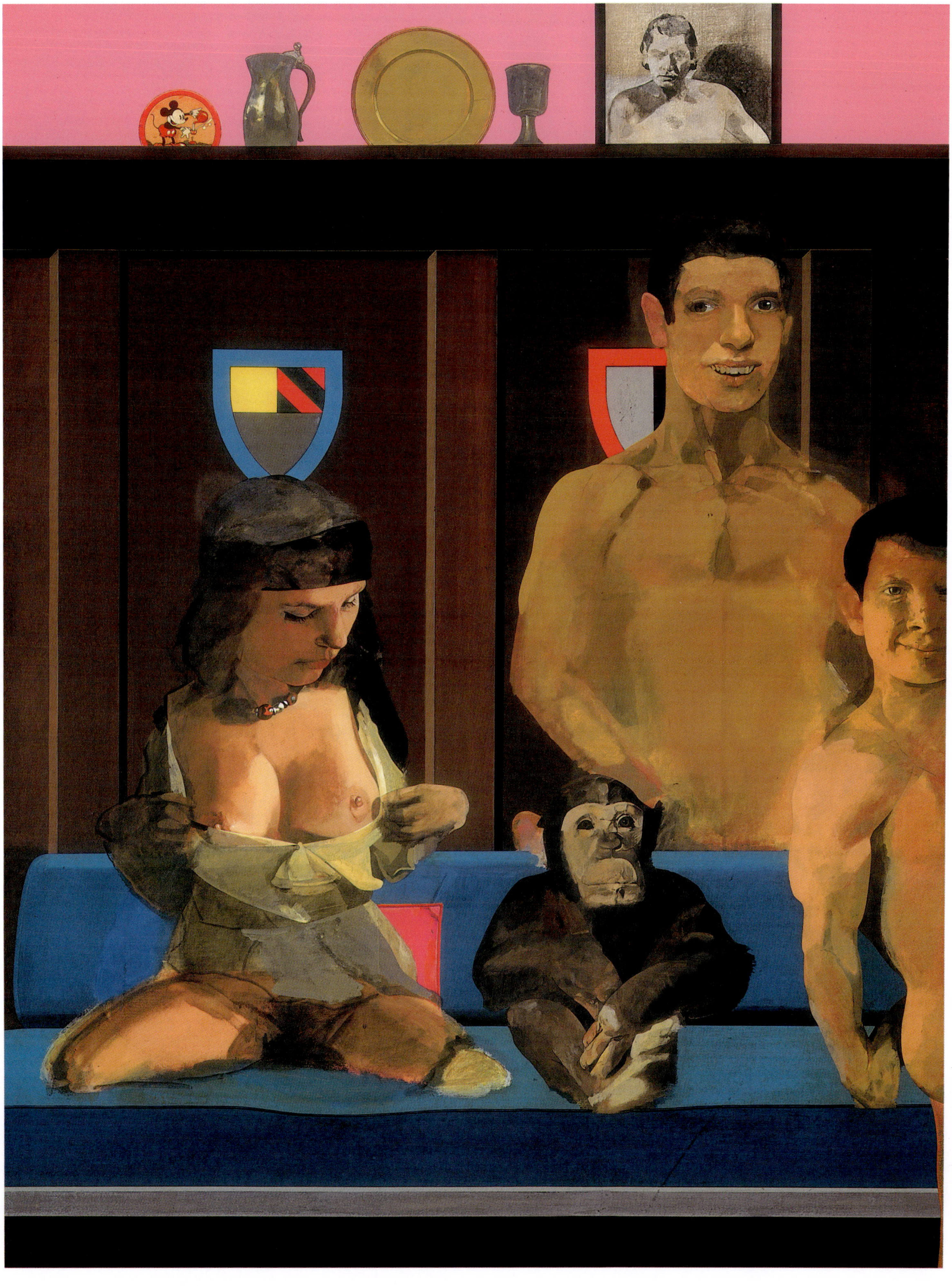

110 **Tarzan, Jane, Boy and Cheeta**, 1966–75

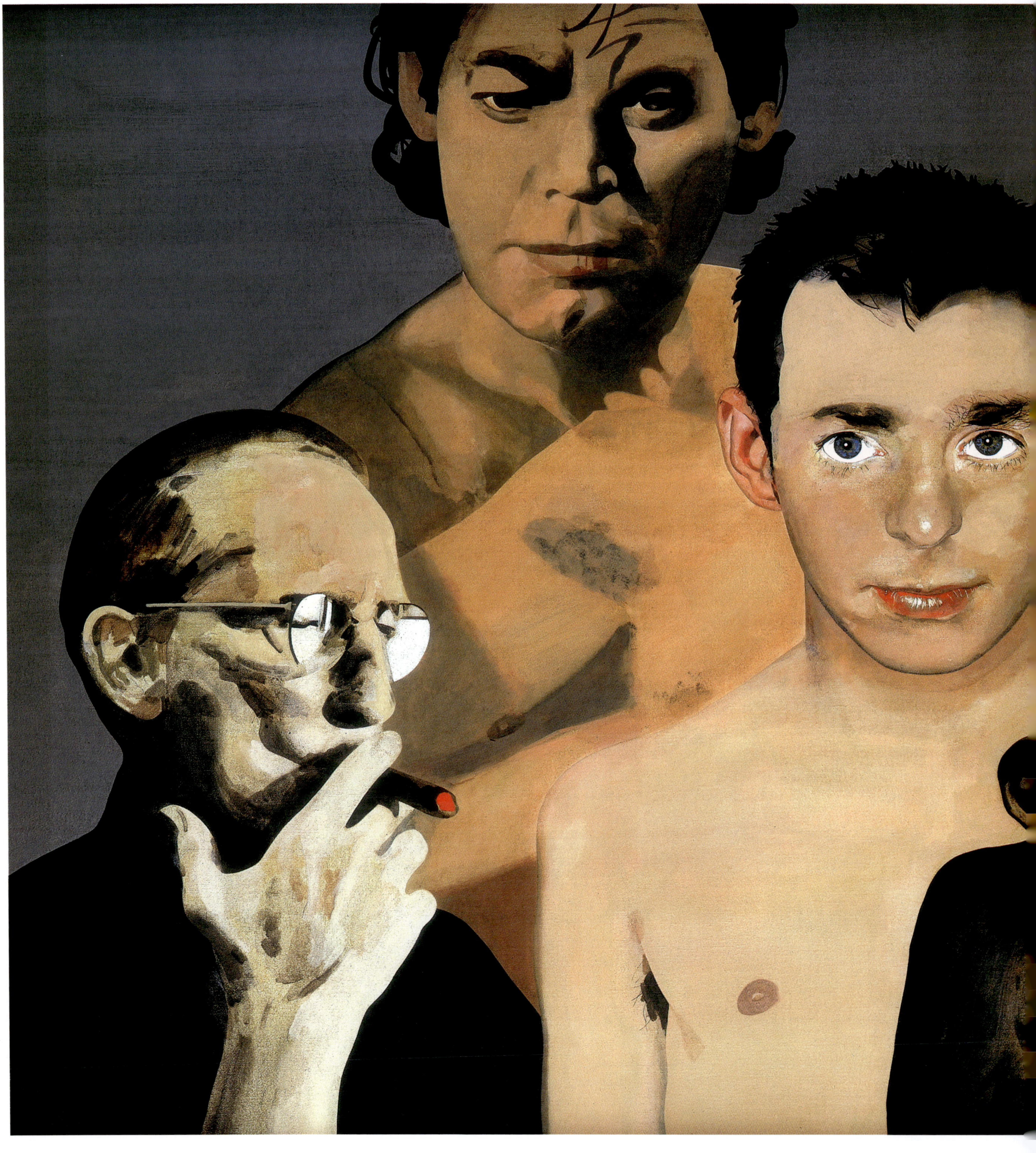

111 **Marcel Duchamp's World Tour: The Tarzan Family**, 1995–2005

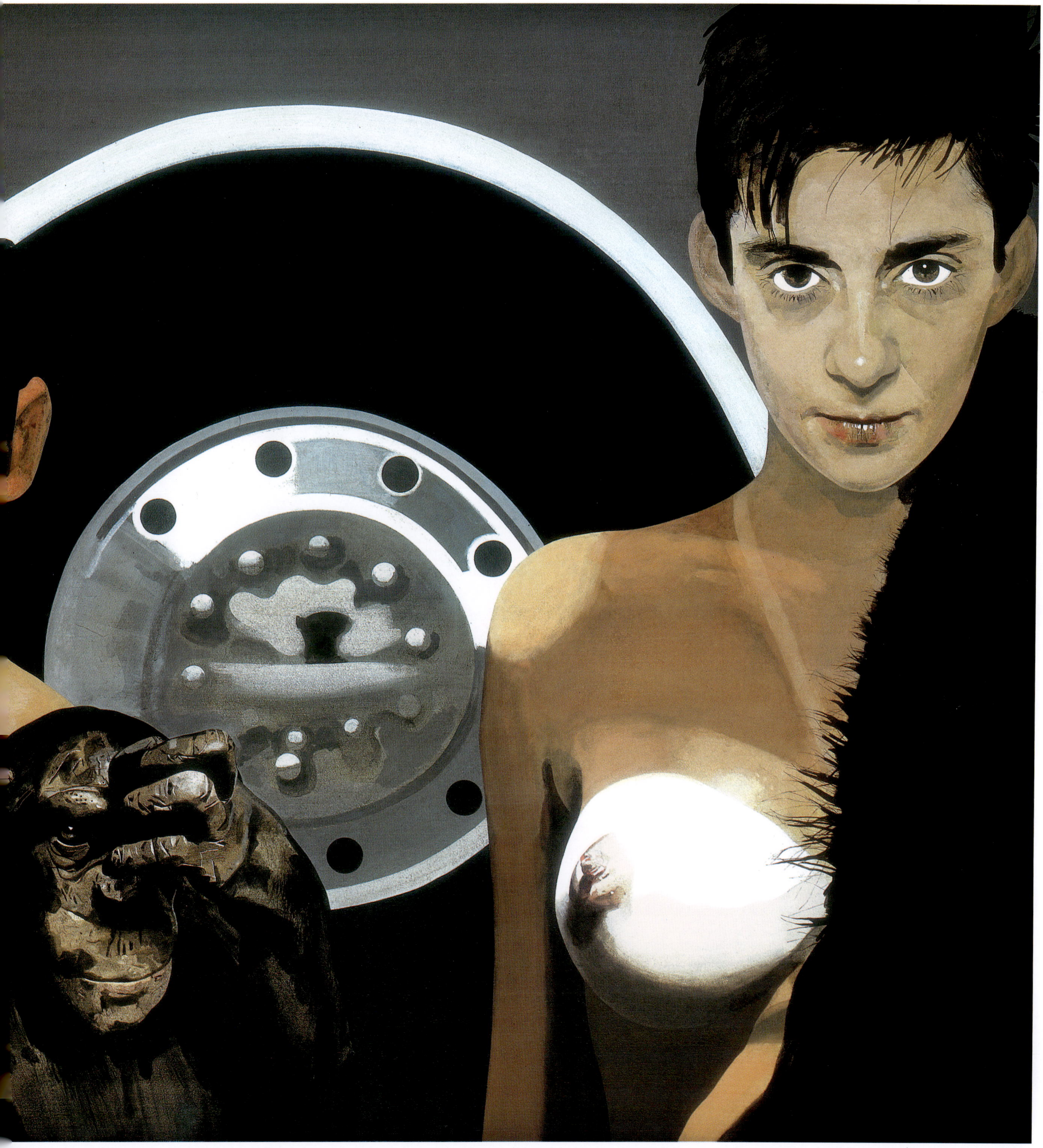

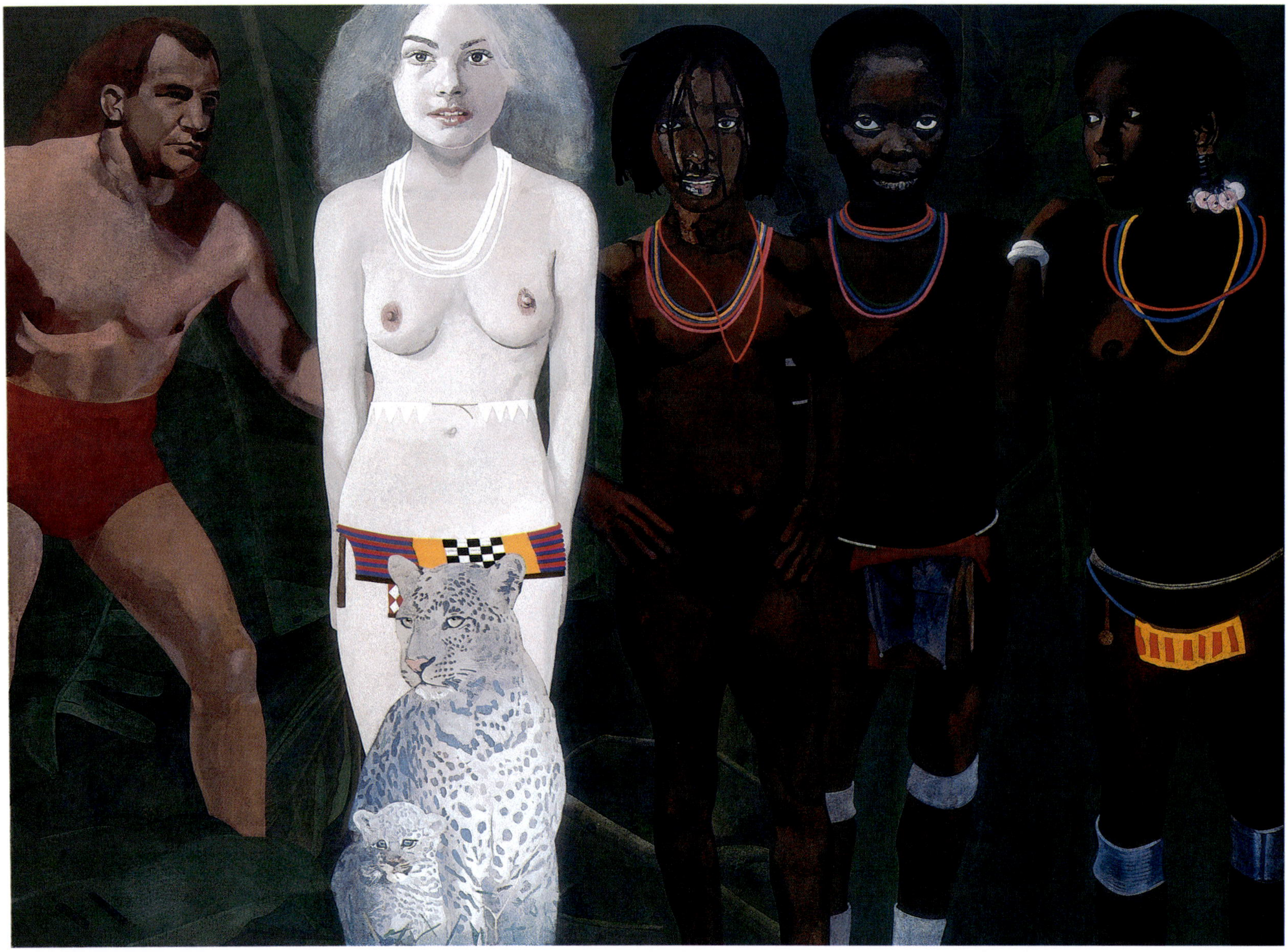

112 **Tarzan Meets the Jungle Goddess**, 1970s–94

painting that had been in the making for over three decades, Blake keyed the changes of style and motif to reinventions of each of the figures.

Tarzan, Jane, Boy and Cheeta (1966–75, Plate 110), the second of the two large Tarzan paintings begun in the mid-1960s and worked on intermittently for years, typifies the way in which Blake re-imagined the fictional hero and his family by reference to different sources. In this work, the figures are consistently depicted with the same veracity he has lavished on portraits of real people. A handpainted rendering of a black-and-white photograph of Johnny Weissmüller appears amusingly as a family snapshot propped up on a shelf behind the naked family; its presence not only acknowledges Blake's use of photographic sources but also integrates a further layer of play-acting into a 'conversation piece' already teeming with assumed identities and steeped in make-believe. Over the years Blake continued to revisit these characters, as if popping in on old friends, seeing them in a variety of contexts in watercolours such as *Cheeta with Confetti Falling on Him – A Tribute to Lawson Wood* (1969, Plate 108) and *Jane and Boy at Watts Tower* (1969–76, Plate 109), and in oil paintings such as *Tarzan Meets the Jungle Goddess* (Plate 112), begun in the 1970s and completed in 1994. As imaginary characters they are, of course, blessed with a kind of eternal life – much as any painted figure, in fact, becomes frozen in time and immortal. That they do not need to age is part of their attraction.

In their most recent sighting, in *Marcel Duchamp's World Tour: The Tarzan Family* (1995–2005, Plate 111), the members of an entirely naked family group present themselves to our gaze as if posing for a family portrait. Blake takes us time-travelling to an indeterminate moment when the great artist/*provocateur* has momentarily descended from his tour bus to smoke a cigar in their company. The real star and focus of attention here is not Tarzan, seen in his beefy prime, nor the intelligent Cheeta, lost in thought, nor the tomboyish Jane with a fleshy exposed breast picked out in the sunlight. It is the often marginalised boy, here depicted with a hallucinatory intensity, who now holds our gaze. With this head, with its ruddy ears, moist lips and acutely rendered eyes, Blake brings his brand of realism to a new level of accomplishment just when it is most needed: to persuade us that a figure devised for a work of literary fiction, and re-imagined by an actor in films now decades old, can be convincingly brought to life. Here, as so often before in his art, fantasy and reality become so intertwined that it becomes irrelevant to ask where one ends and the other begins. Instead, we are left suspended, with our eyes wide open, in a delirious dream state from which one might be tempted never to re-emerge.

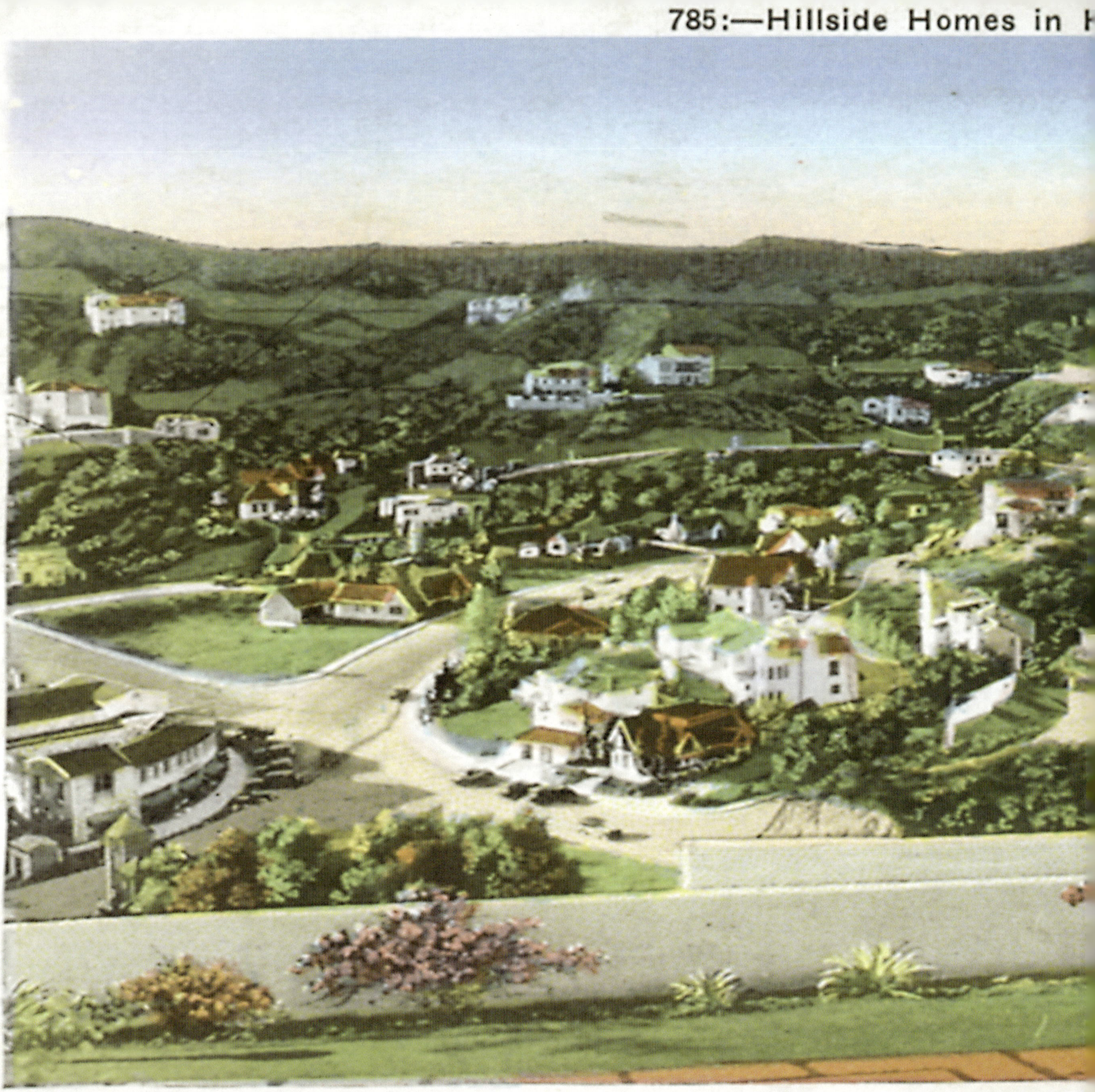

4 OBSERV

llywoodland, Hollywood, Calif.

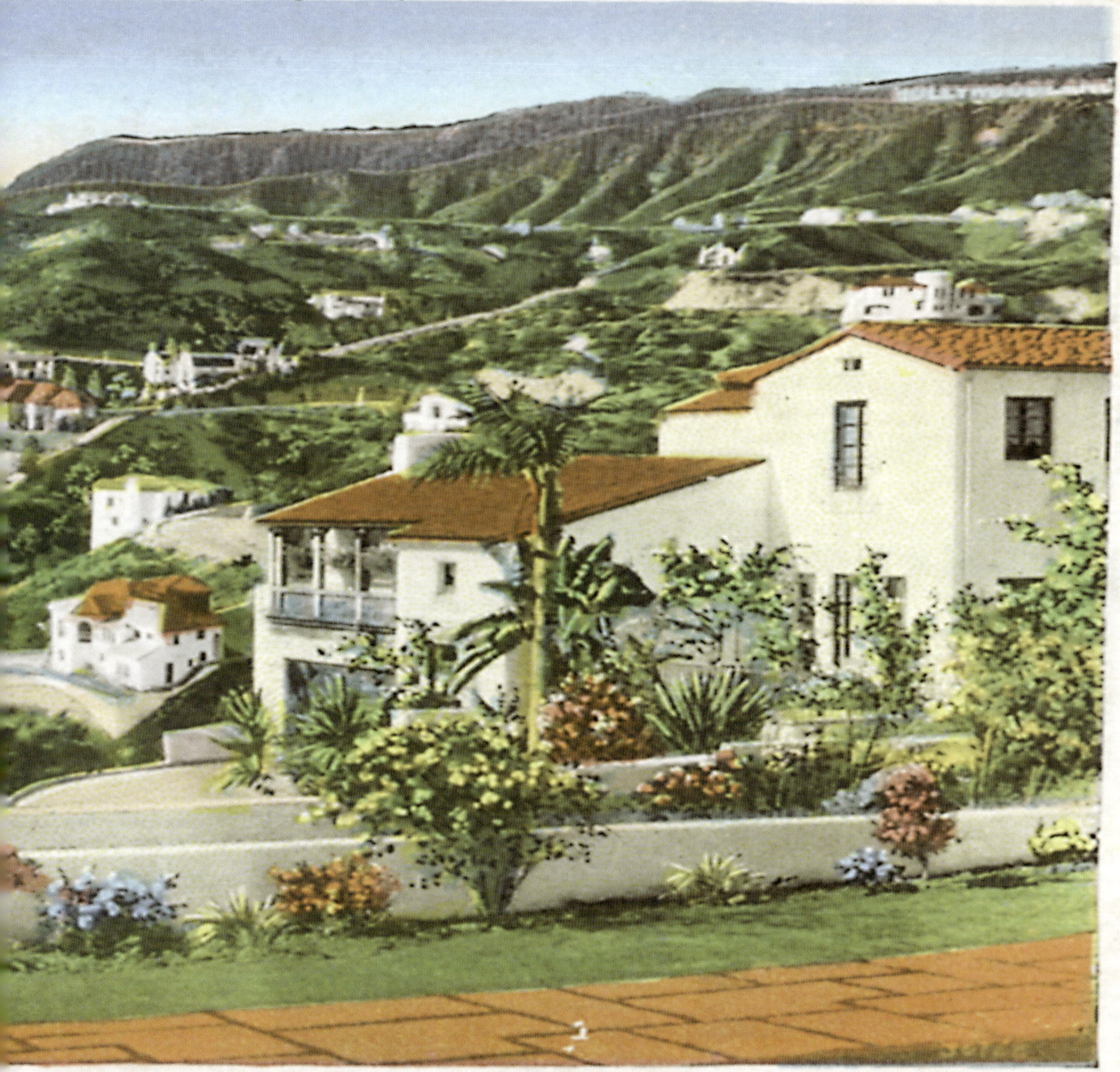

VATIONS

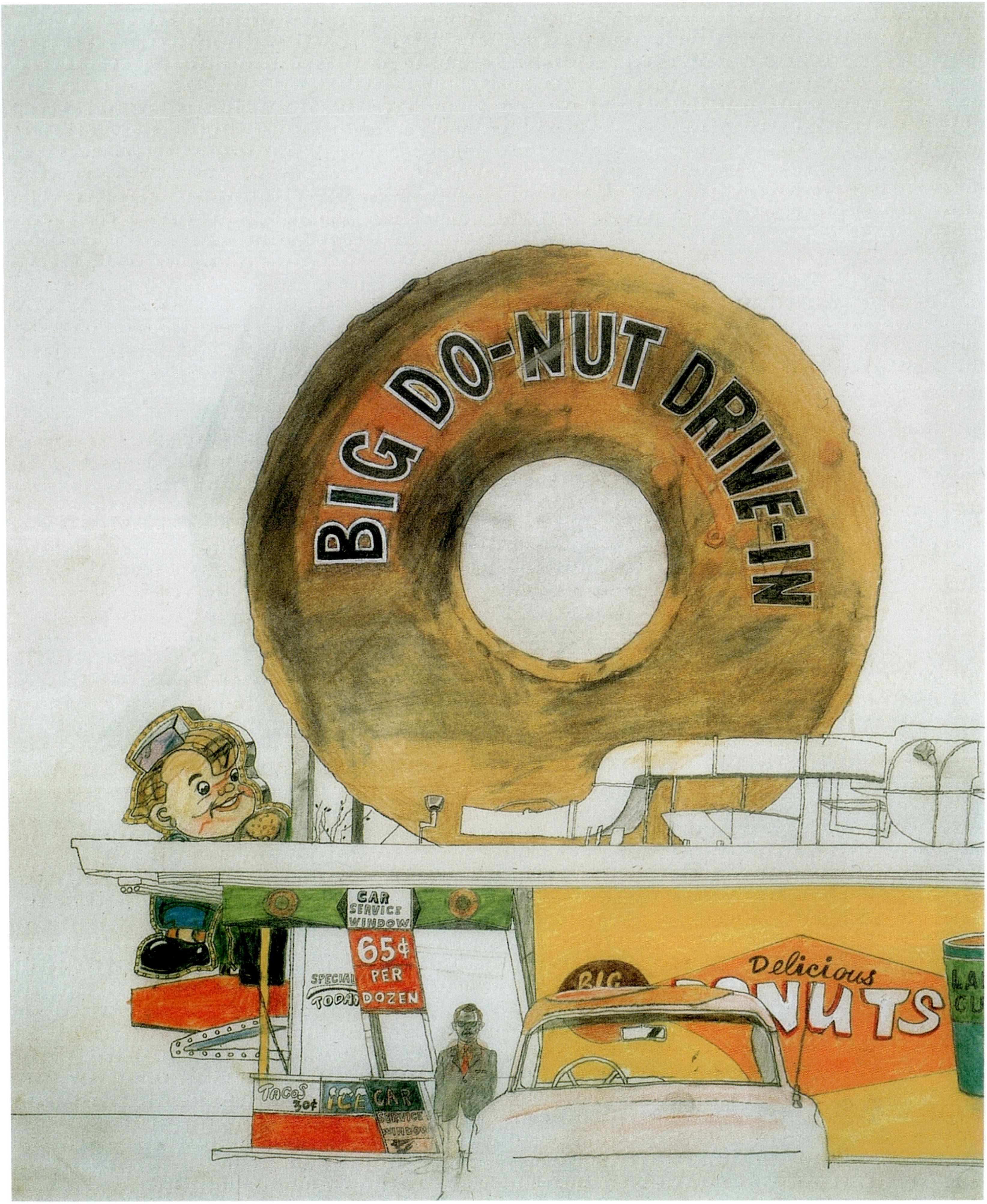

113 **Big Do-Nut Drive-in, Los Angeles**, 1963

4 Observations

Drawing was central to Blake's education as an artist and has remained an integral part of his practice ever since, not just in the importance attached to drawings as ends in themselves but also in the linear structure underpinning almost all of his paintings. Though he frequently draws from photographs, he has always also sketched from direct observation. Almost the whole of his first year at the Royal College was devoted to working in the life room, as was then required, both for drawing and painting. He remembers sitting at a distance from his fellow students Frank Auerbach (a year ahead of him) and Leon Kossoff, both of whom drew so expressively and with such vigour that they produced a storm of charcoal dust around them while Blake sought to observe the figure with the reticence, meticulous accuracy and delicacy he admired in artists such as Ingres and Degas. Almost all of this first year's production by Blake disappeared when he left it in his locker at the end of the final term, not realising that the lockers were meant to be left empty over the summer; sadly, it seems that all that work, evidence one longs to see today, was simply discarded. Perhaps it was subconsciously a desire to replenish this lost resource, but also to reconnect with this essential aspect of his formation as a painter of the human figure, that led Blake half a century later to meet with several friends every week to draw the human body again from life. This time he imposed a conceptual structure on the activity, setting himself the task of producing 1,000 life drawings, each of which he assiduously labelled with the date, the number of the drawing and the length of the pose.

At least from the time that he was a student at the Royal College, Blake had also been in the habit of making topographical drawings in sketchbooks that he carried with him to any locations where he was likely to find subject matter that interested him: circuses, funfairs and wrestling matches, among others. Although this was a particularly frequent activity for him during the 1950s and early 1960s, and was especially useful when travelling (as he did with his Leverhulme Research Award) without the usual paraphernalia of the studio, the making of such drawings has remained part of his language to this day. Together with the even more private notebooks in which he jots down thoughts and ideas, and with the tracings that he produces from photographs or printed matter as a preparatory stage in the making of paintings, watercolours and certain drawings, these sketches from observation are an important resource as part of his constantly expanding vocabulary of subjects and images. At their best, and in their more ambitious incarnation as larger and more finished observational drawings, they are beautiful things in themselves and a frequent reminder of the strength Blake draws from traditional artistic practices stretching back many centuries.

Los Angeles 1963 and Later Observational Drawings

In 1963, Blake received an invitation to go travelling and to produce a visual account in the form of drawings to be published in the *Sunday Times* magazine. The invitation came from the art critic David Sylvester and Mark Boxer, the editor of the recently established colour supplement which was the first of its kind to appear alongside a national newspaper. He was given a fee to cover both his travel expenses and his permission to reproduce the resulting work. David Hockney, who had been asked at the same time if he would return to his native Bradford, Yorkshire, eventually went instead to the much more exotic location of Egypt. Blake, newly married to Californian native Jann Haworth, had never been to the United States, so he chose to travel to Los Angeles, where she had family and where he could see at first hand the setting of the Hollywood film industry which had long exerted such a hold over his imagination. Hockney himself was to make his first extended visit to L.A. at the end of that very year, remaining in the country until the following December. He returned to Los Angeles for the latter half of 1965 and again from summer 1966 to summer 1967. For Blake, by contrast, memories of that single eventful visit proved enough to sustain his imagination and he was not to return for 16 years.

The Hollywood-born Jann had studied at UCLA in Los Angeles from the fall term of 1959 and had arrived in London on 29 December 1961. She was accepted for a place at the Slade School of Fine Art, which had long had what Blake terms a 'cross-town rivalry' with the Royal College and where she studied for the 1962–3 academic year. As a present

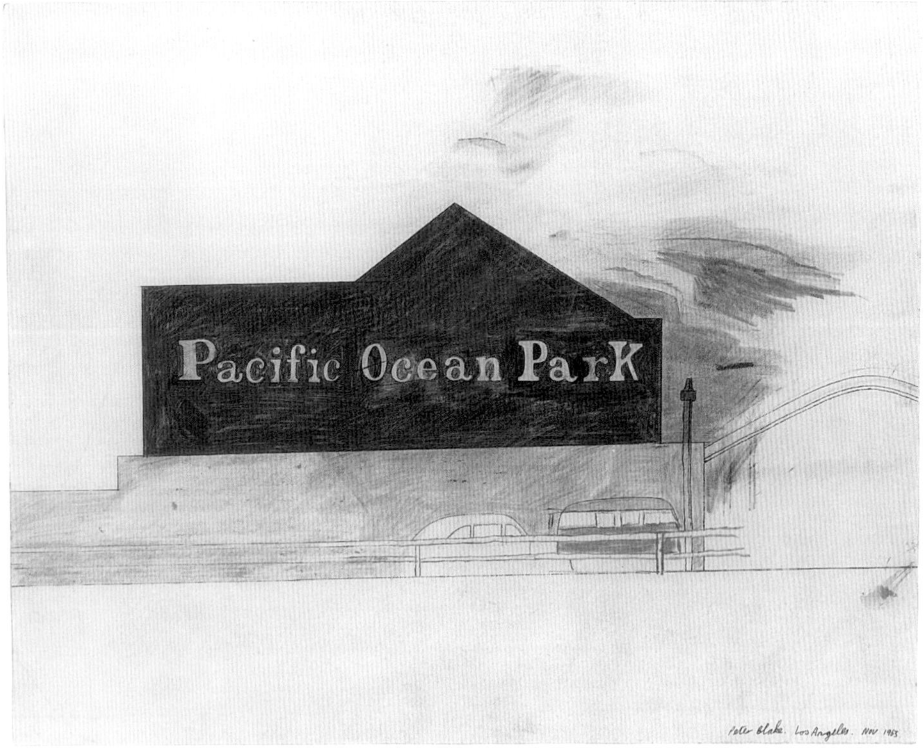

114 **Pacific Ocean Park**, 1963

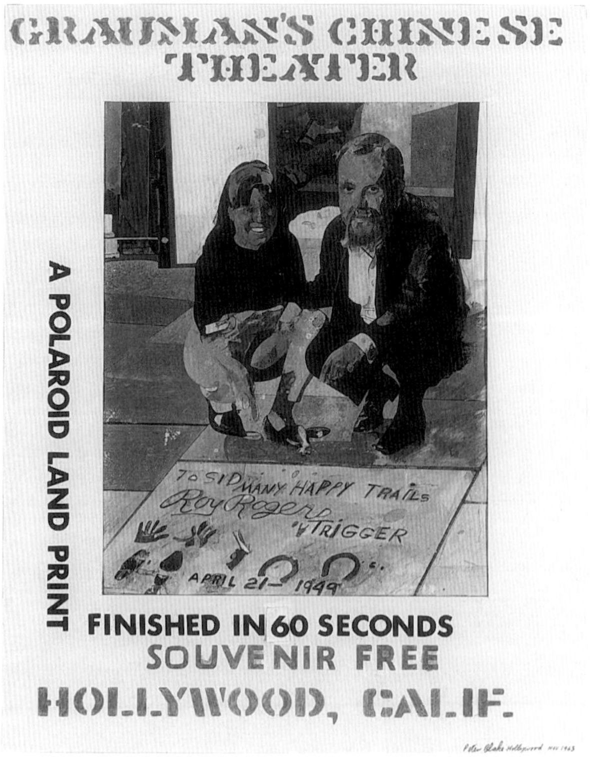

115 **Outside Grauman's Chinese Theater, Hollywood**, 1963

in advance of her birthday on 15 March, her mother had given her a copy of the winter 1962–63 issue of the magazine *Motif* (issue 10), which featured a cover article on Blake that reproduced his *Self-Portrait with Badges* (1961, Plate 40) and other works and also included a set of original Blake prints bound into the magazine. Jann made a sculptural portrait of Blake in the form of a doll, in keeping with the work she was then making, and asked Joe Tilson to pass it on to him. It was soon after this that she met Blake, probably around February or March 1963, after asking him and other artists – including Tilson, Hockney, Derek Boshier, Pauline Boty, Allen Jones and Dick Smith – whether they would consider participating in a group exhibition with her and fellow students such as Gerald Laing from St Martin's and Colin Self from the Slade. Once all the artists had given their assent, the proposal was sent to Whitechapel Art Gallery director Bryan Robertson, with whom she had previously discussed it, but he decided against proceeding with it. Instead, he curated his influential exhibition *The New Generation* (March–May 1964), which included a strong Pop contingent of Boshier, Hockney, Jones, Patrick Caulfield, Antony Donaldson and Peter Phillips as part of a selection of 12 painters.

Jann and Peter starting seeing each other and it was she who invited him to judge a 'sketch club' at the Slade; it was there that he first saw the work of a younger artist, Colin Self, who was about to be failed but whose great originality Blake was quick to recognise with a prize. After a brief courtship, Jann and Peter married on 12 July 1963. She was so fresh out of California that she was keen to go back to tie up some unfinished business now that she found herself settling in the UK, and Peter was equally eager to visit it for the first

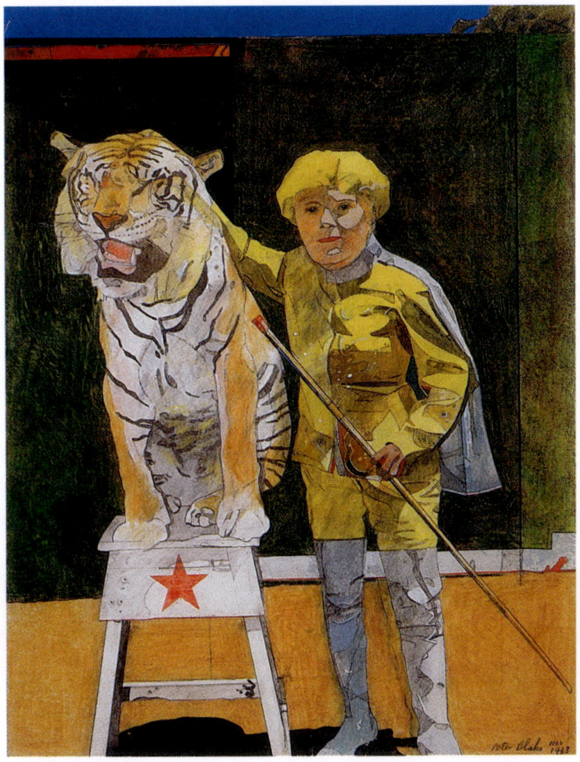

116 **Mabel Stark, an 80 Year Old Lion Tamer at Los Angeles**, 1963

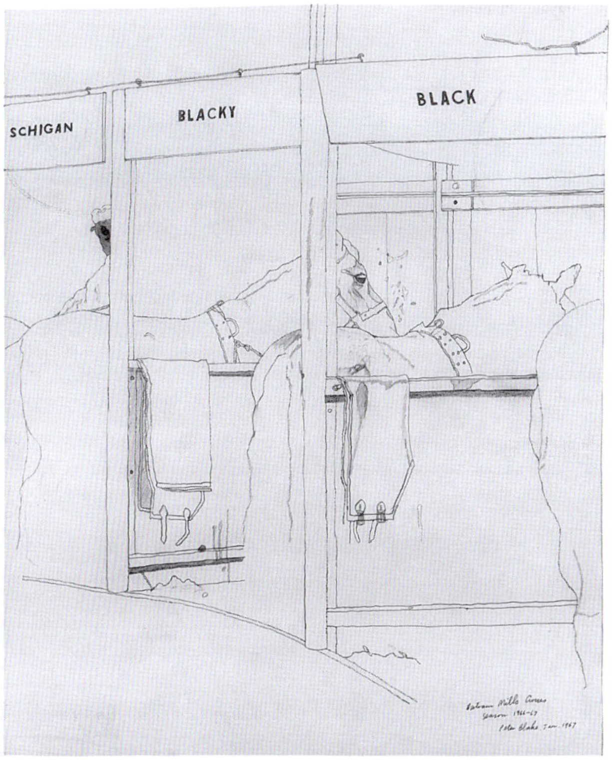

117 **Bertram Mills Circus, Season 1966–67, no.1**, 1966–7

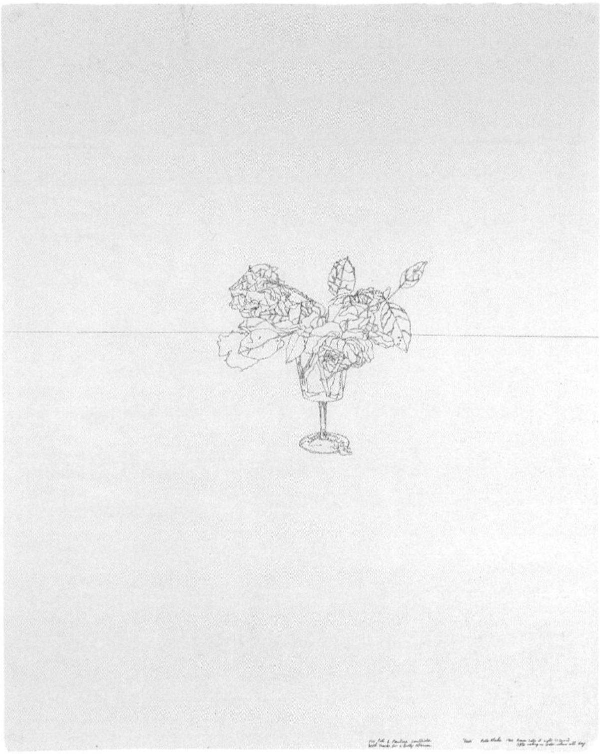

118 **Roses**, 1969

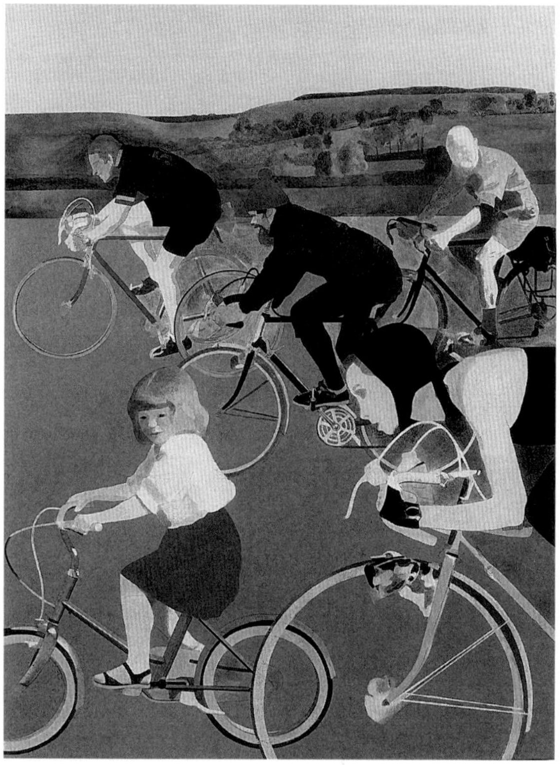

119 **Bristol Bicycle Race**, early 1980s

time. Jann's mother, Miriam, who settled in England with her second husband soon after Peter and Jann married, was an artist working especially as a printmaker and ceramicist; her father, Ted, worked in Hollywood as an Oscar-winning Hollywood production designer, providing another point of contact for Blake's fascination with movies, the star system and the Hollywood film industry. (Among the films Ted worked on was the Billy Wilder comedy gem *Some Like it Hot*, in which Marilyn Monroe gave one of her greatest performances.) Blake professes a love/hate relationship with Los Angeles, which he was not to visit again until very soon after splitting up with Jann in 1979. Among his most vivid memories of that first trip he recalls driving along Venice Beach in his father-in-law's streamlined Corvette Stingray, with the ecstatic pop songs of the Beach Boys playing on the radio: the whole fun-loving ethos of the city wrapped in one glorious package.

Since the new Mrs Blake hating flying, they crossed the Atlantic instead on the SS *France*. The journey had a tragic start, with Jann miscarrying on their first night at sea, so their arrival in sunny southern California (after a further three days and two nights on a transcontinental train journey) was tinged with great sadness at their loss. It was during their stay also that John F. Kennedy was assassinated on 22 November 1963, a deeply traumatic event for many. Nevertheless, Blake had a job to do, so he continued drawing. Jann proved to be the perfect tour guide, taking him to key tourist destinations such as Grauman's Chinese Theater (the Hollywood cinema outside which the great stars imprinted

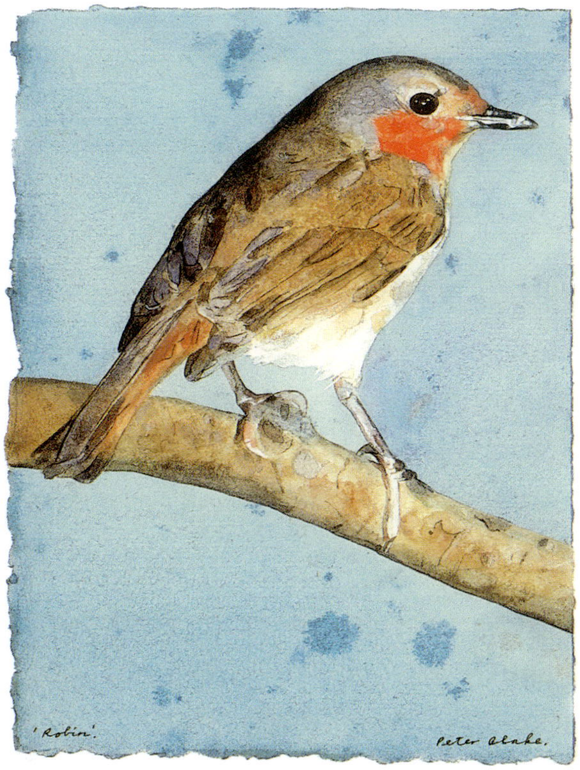

120 **Robin**, 1984

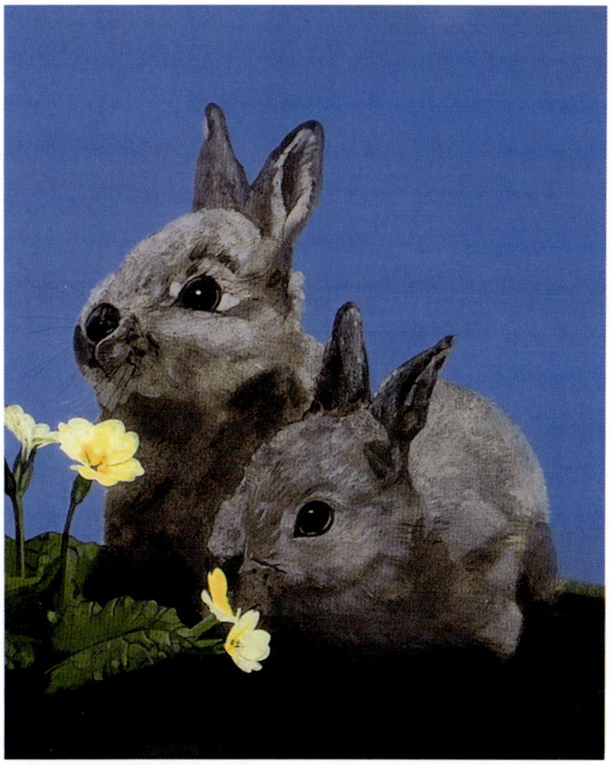

121 **Baby Rabbits**, 1984

their hands and signed their names in cement, Plate 115) and to other places that she knew would inspire him to draw. These included the giant amusement park called Pacific Ocean Park (Plate 114), the initials of which, as Richard Hamilton wryly noticed during a visit there in the same year, spelt out POP, and iconic examples of the city's playful, pop-sculptural architecture such as the Big Do-Nut Drive-in (Plate 113). All of these became subjects for wonderfully scrutinised, economical but precisely delineated drawings buzzing with the excitement of discovery at such vibrant visual treasures.

Six of the resulting L.A. drawings were eventually published in the 15 November 1964 issue of the *Sunday Times* magazine under the title 'Peter Blake in Hollywood'. The images were made with a variety of media including watercolour, pencil and coloured inks. Particularly successful are those in coloured pencils, such as the glorious *Big Do-Nut Drive-in*, which anticipates the drawings that Hockney began making of Los Angeles streets and architecture early in the following year, also from life and in coloured pencils. Taken as a group, these works on paper play brilliantly on Blake's strengths as a draughtsman, combining as they do a graphic artist's flair for composition and decorative appeal with a refinement of line, colour and surface. However, it is not just on a technical level or in terms of design that they work. It is because they conjure up the atmosphere and look of this most open-air of cities with affection and immense good humour that they remain a touchstone for all his later sketchbook and larger scale observational drawings.

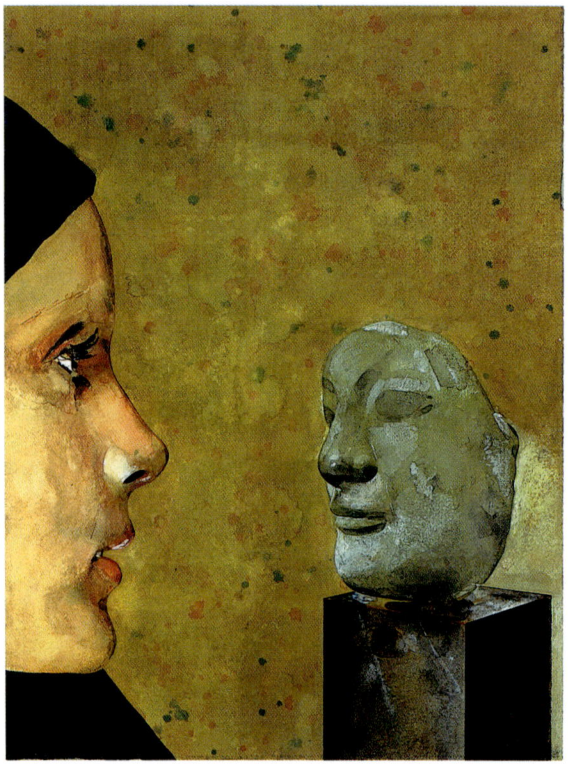

122 **Girl Looking at Sculpture**, completed 1984

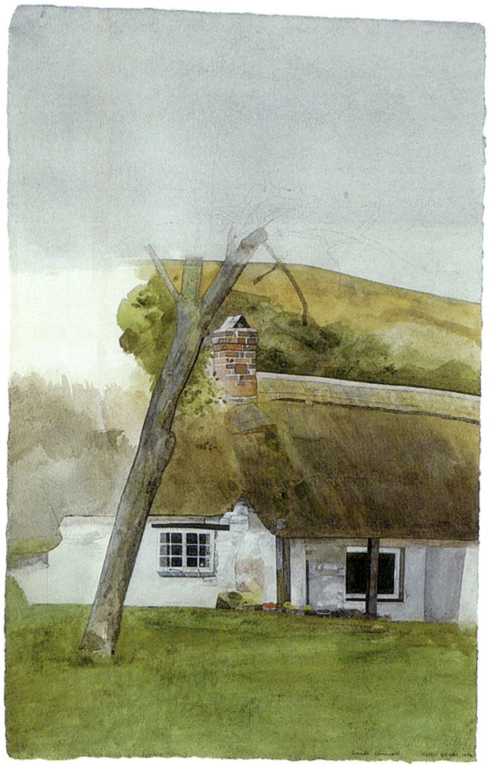

123 **Ford Cottage, Coombe**, 1976

Blake continued to draw in sketchbooks on his return from the Los Angeles trip, much as he had done during the previous decade, for example on outings to the circus. The sketch in pencil and coloured pencils of *Bertram Mills Circus, Season 1966–67, no.1* (1966–7, Plate 117) is not precisely dated but is typical of these larger, more accomplished drawings made in such circumstances. Other works on paper suggest a spontaneous decision to record something that struck him as beautiful. An intricate pen-and-ink study of *Roses* (Plate 118) made in 1969, for example, scrupulously records the arrangement of the blossoms, leaves and stems in a wine glass against a bare tabletop, with the motif accentuated compositionally by the exposure of so much of the sheet of paper on which it sits; the inscription indicates that it was made in a gesture of appreciation following dinner with his friends Patrick and Pauline Caulfield.

Often there is an ambiguity, as in so much of Blake's work, between what was drawn or painted from life and what was actually based on photographic evidence. This is especially true of the watercolours, whether of simple and soft-hearted subjects suggestive of tranquil rural life or of more intricately visualised interiors and landscapes, such as *Commissionaire, British Museum* (1970) or *Bristol Bicycle Race* (Plate 119) of the early 1980s. The cute and friendly animals depicted in *Robin* (Plate 120), *Ducklings* and *Baby Rabbits* (Plate 121), all from 1984, were conceived as studies for a painting, to be called *Once upon a Time,* which he had no intention of making: the project simply gave him an excuse to produce these overtly sentimental pictures. The date given to *Girl Looking at Sculpture* (completed in 1984, Plate 122) provides a clear clue that this, like many of Blake's water-colours and paintings alike, was made over a long period in his studio rather than in a single burst of activity. In that sense it is not, strictly speaking, made from life – though, critically, pictures such as this might easily be misconstrued in that way. Certainly at their best, as in the case of a wonderfully achieved watercolour such as *Ford Cottage, Coombe* (Plate 123), painted in 1976 during a holiday in Cornwall, the fact that he might have supplemented direct observation with information from his own photographs becomes something of an irrelevance. What one feels while looking at this, or at paintings such as *Girl in a White Chair* (1986, Plate 124), is the visual and emotional truth of what he has pictured. They persuade the viewer that, without a doubt, he was witness to what he is showing us, even if on occasion it has been recalled (with the assistance of *aides-mémoire*) at another time and in another place.

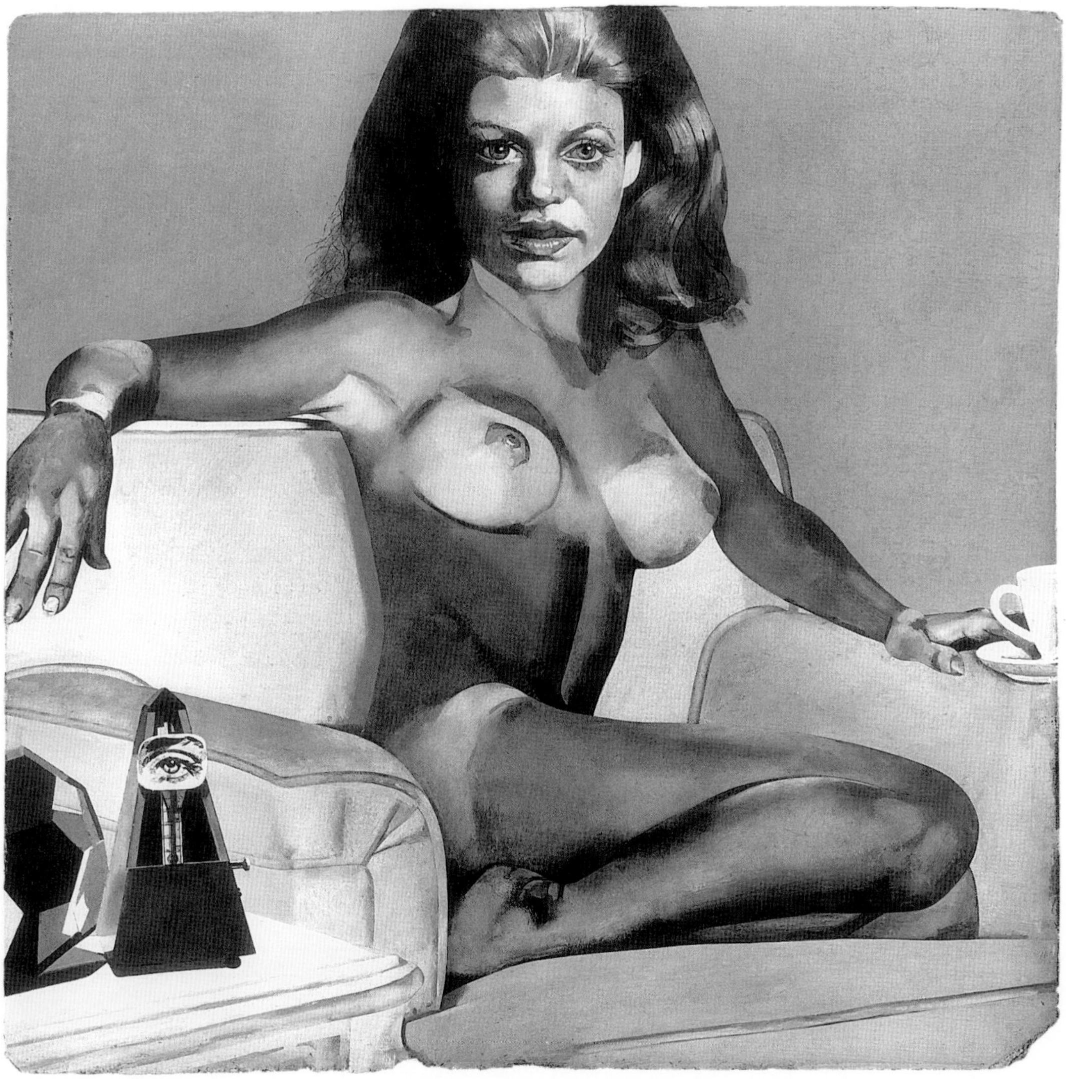

124 **Girl in a White Chair**, 1986

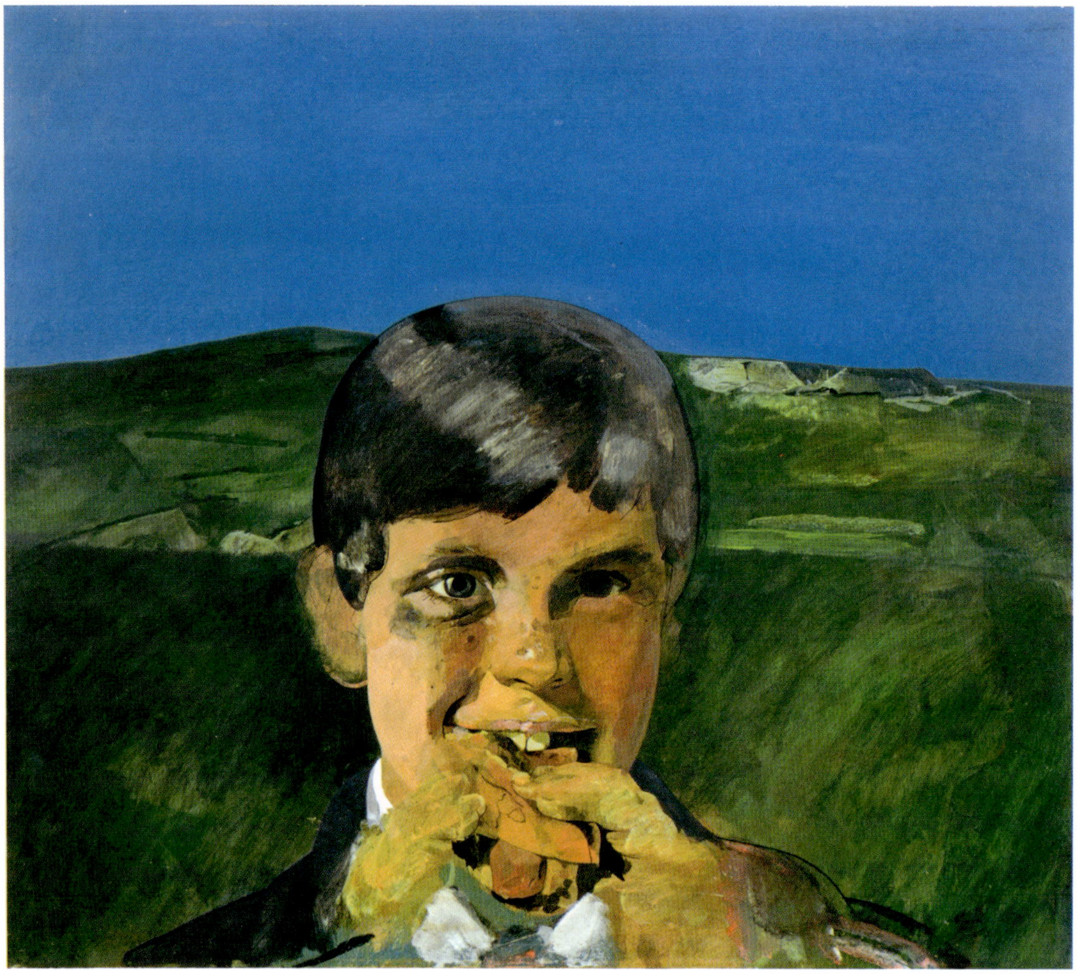

125 **Boy with Hot Dog**, 1960–65

Portraits

Portraiture has been a sturdy thread right through Blake's art from the late 1940s and early 1950s, when he first represented himself and family members, including his sister Shirley. Already in those youthful works he favoured showing the person straight on, with the sitter's gaze meeting that of the viewer. These are conventions one often finds in folk art or naive art, connoting a straightforwardness and lack of guile. This approach to the figure is one that characterises not only the early circus pictures and tattooed ladies and the more complex contemporaneous subject pictures, such as *On the Balcony* (1955–7, Plate 39) and *The Preparation for the Entry into Jerusalem* (1955–6, Plate 37), but also the portraits of real people recalled from old photographs, as in *Children Reading Comics* (1954,

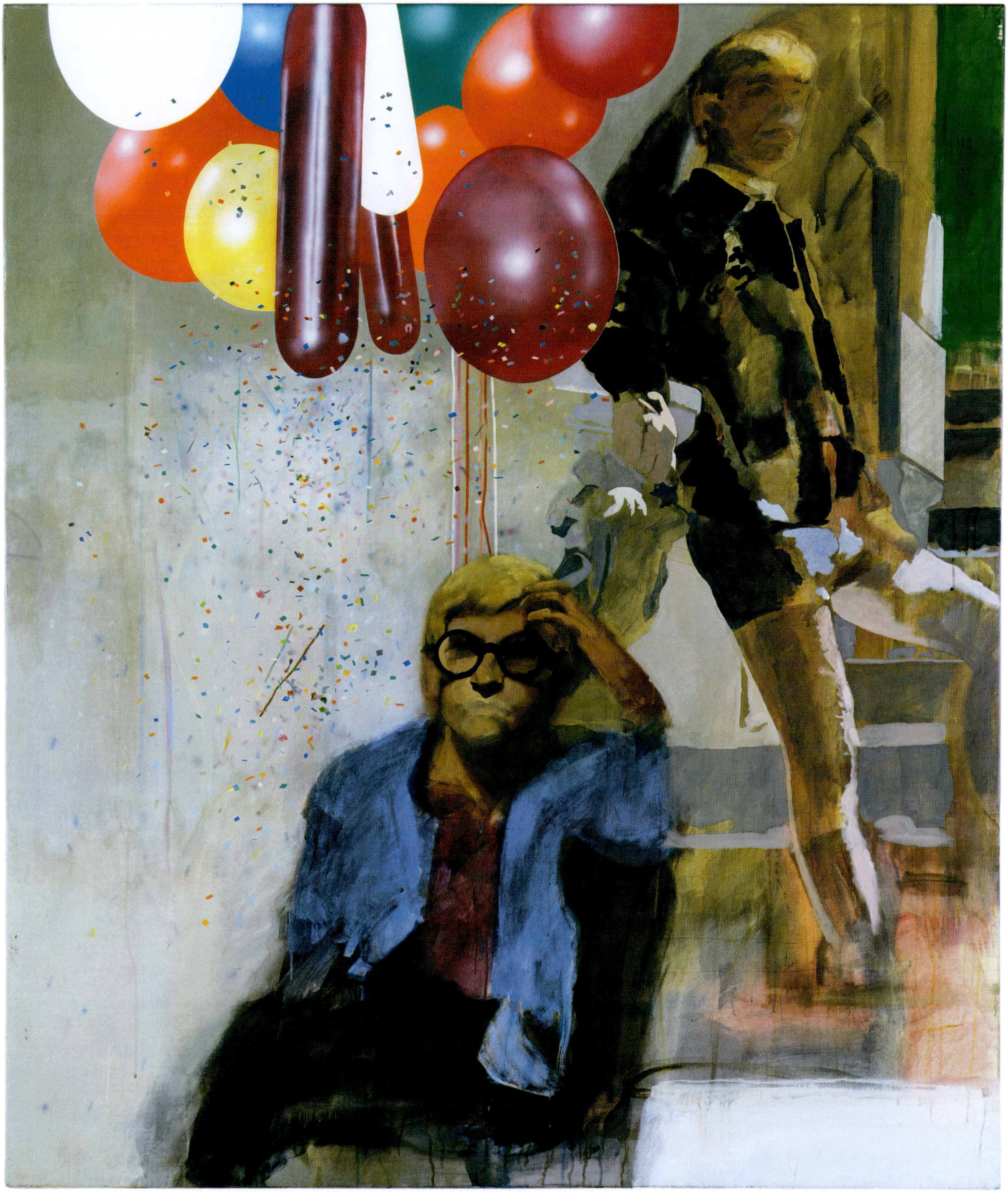

126 **Portrait of David Hockney in a Hollywood Spanish Interior**, begun 1965

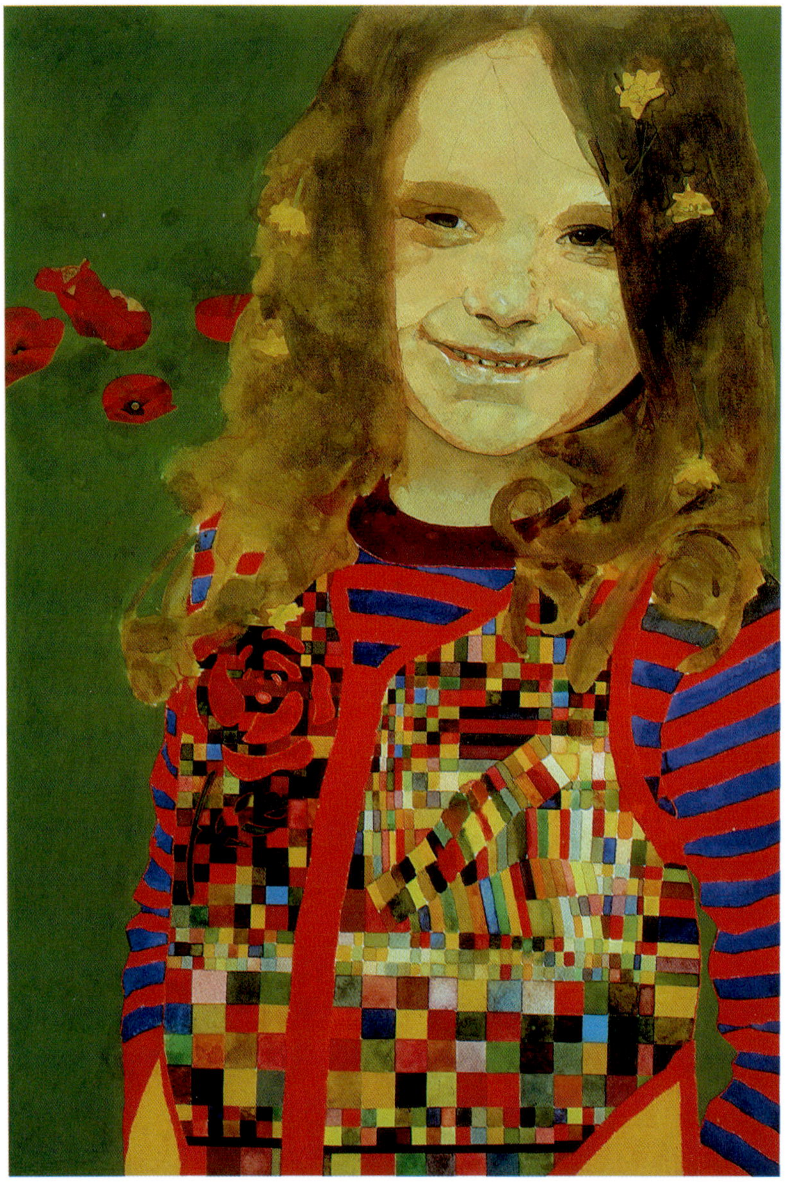

127 **Girl in a Poppy Field**, 1968–9

Plate 2, and 1956, Plate 14), portraits from life, notably *Self-Portrait with Badges* (1961, Plate 40) – in which Blake stands stiffly at attention, as he always does, self-consciously, when being photographed – and the fantasy portraits of strippers and wrestlers. It comes, therefore, as little surprise that when the imaginary figures shade into actual people, as in *Boy with Hot Dog* (1960–65, Plate 125), the same frontality and steady gaze should apply.

Although there had always been an element of portraiture even in Blake's pictures from the imagination, it was only on a very occasional basis that he had made pictures of identified individuals specifically as portraits during the 1950s or early 1960s. A small

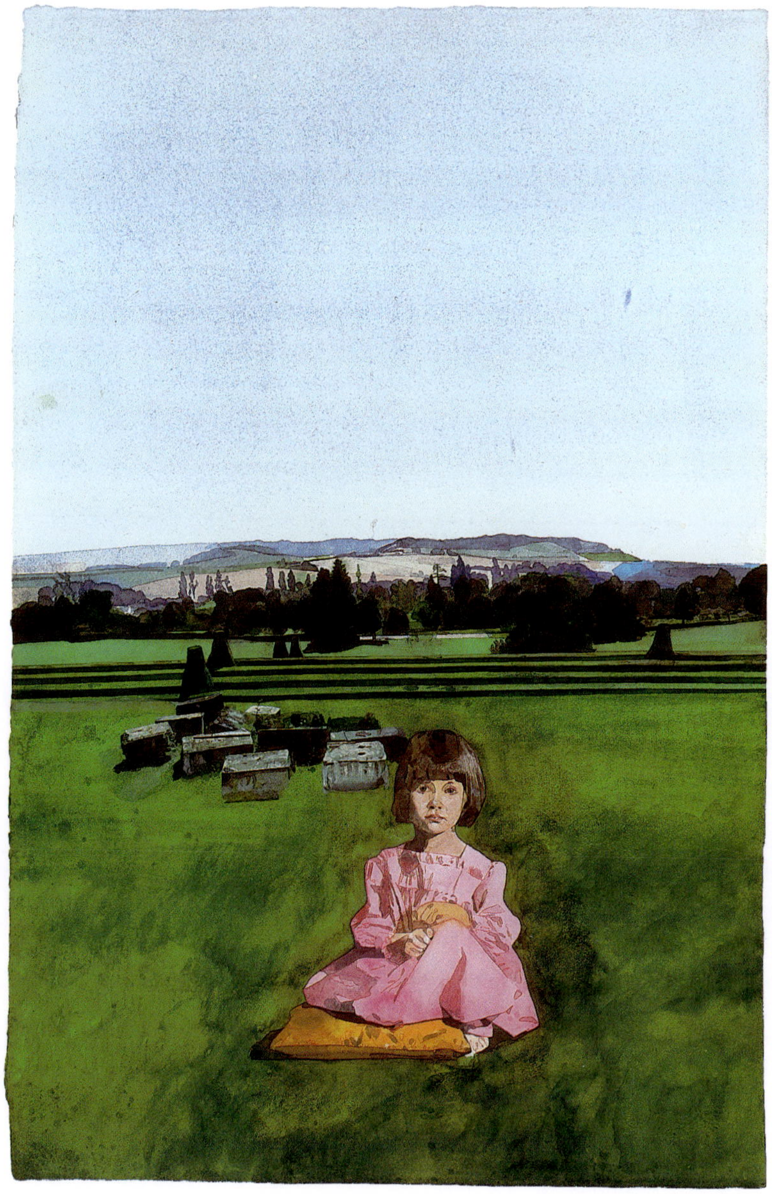

128 **Girl in a Field**, 1968–84

oil on hardboard *Self-Portrait* of 1949, showing just his head, a pen and ink and gouache *Self-Portrait in RAF Jacket* of *c.*1952–3 (Plate 11), a 1950 oil on cardboard of his sister Shirley, and a 1958 oil *Portrait of a Woman* are among the exceptions to this early rule. In 1965 he made a small and subtly detailed acrylic painting of the Italian-born Outsider artist Simon Rodia (1879–1965), the sculptor-architect of the famed Watts Towers which Blake had visited two years earlier during his first trip to Los Angeles. Blake had never met Rodia, however; the accurate rendering of his features came from a photograph he had seen in a magazine, as did the image of shards of broken pottery (typical of his much-photographed

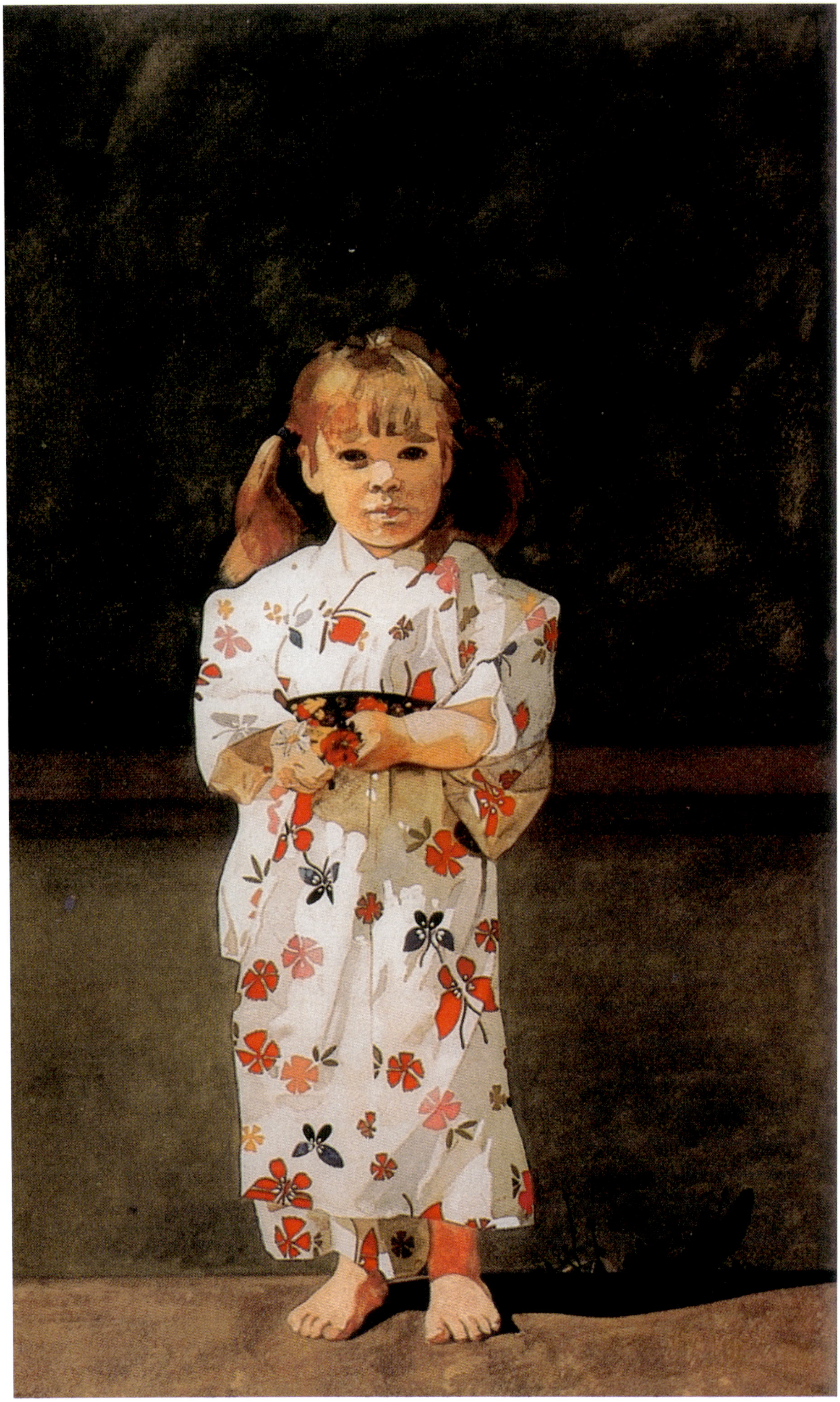

129 **Liberty Blake in a Kimono**, 1971

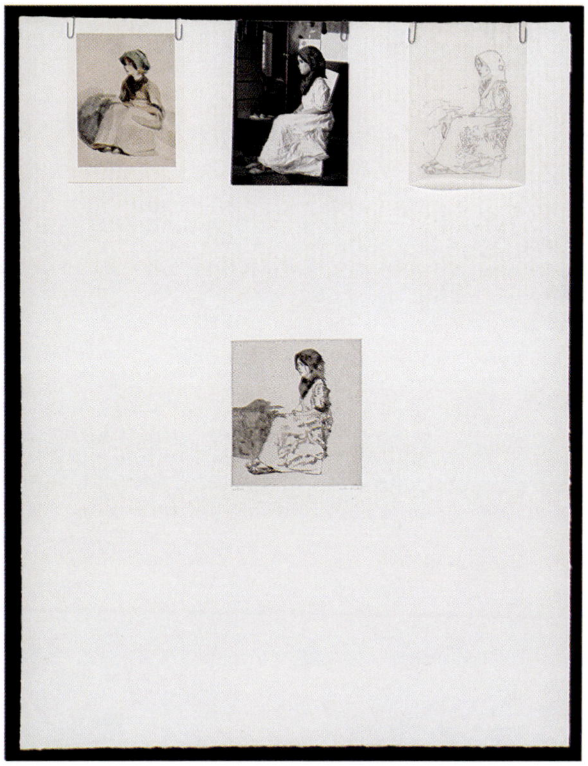

130 **Liberty as a 'Suffolk Child by John Constable R.A.'**, 1976, from the portfolio **For John Constable**

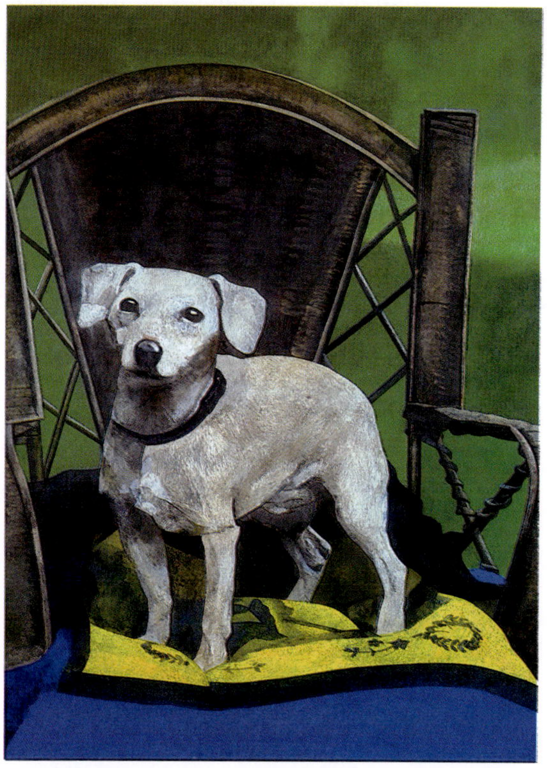

131 **Chipper 1912**, completed 1981

structure) glimpsed behind him. It was down to Blake, rather than to any of the Beatles, that Rodia's face was included among the many portraits on the cover for the *Sgt. Pepper's Lonely Hearts Club Band* album (Plate 139) two years later.

At around the same time as the Rodia portrait, Blake began work on one of his biggest canvases, *Portrait of David Hockney in a Hollywood Spanish Interior* (begun 1965, Plate 126). In it he imagines his already celebrated artist friend – by then transplanted from London to Los Angeles – seated nonchalantly in front of an attractive young man who poses suggestively, with legs spread apart, on the steps of a house in Spanish Colonial style. Although all the elements of the painting were planned from the beginning, including the colourful balloons and the shower of confetti transmitting a carefree party atmosphere, Blake was to spend nearly four decades tinkering with the picture from time to time before he finally declared it finished. Hockney, who had owned the painting since 1965 when he exchanged it with Blake for a set of his *Rake's Progress* etchings but had never taken possession of it, made it a gift to the Tate as soon as Blake told him that it was ready to be handed over. Even in its completed state it retains a half-finished look, particularly in the treatment of the two figures, even though Blake could have continued elaborating the detail as he still had in his possession the original source material – separate photographs by Michael Cooper of Hockney and the young man (printed life-size in a black-and-white

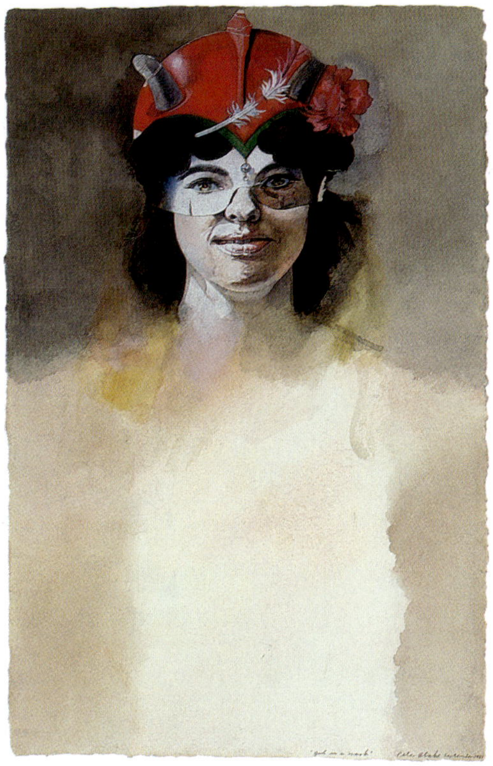

132 **Girl in a Mask**, 1981

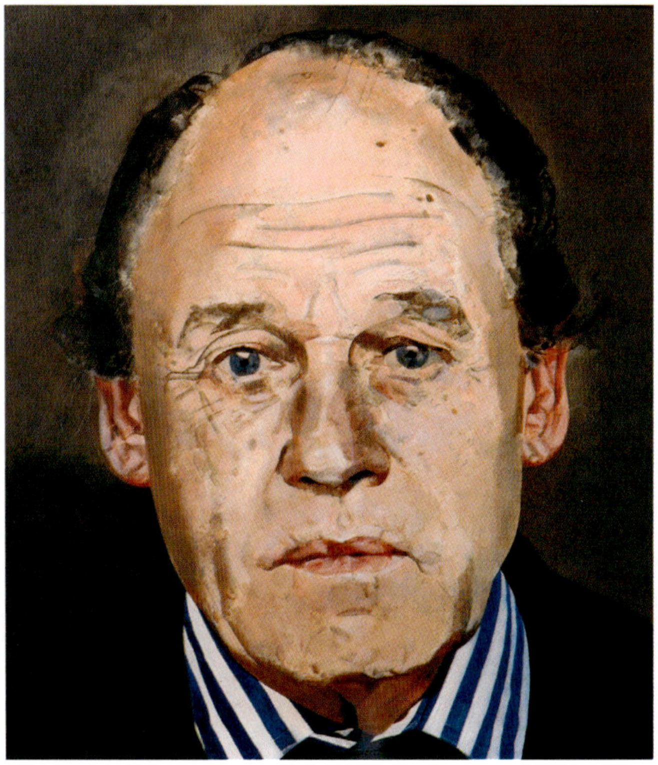

133 **Portrait of Richard Guyatt**, 1981

photograph still stored in Blake's studio). After such a long gestation period, perhaps Blake had just grown so accustomed to the painterly look of this particular picture that he was loath to sacrifice its spontaneous look simply in pursuit of a uniform finish. Whatever the reason, what one might criticise as unresolved is actually one of its great strengths as it conveys a sense of the vulnerability, tenderness and sensuality that Blake saw in his painter friend, five years his junior. With his shock of dyed blond hair and a still almost childlike fleshy face, and accompanied by the type of handsome young man to whom he was attracted, Hockney is here memorialised not so much as the *enfant terrible* of the popular press but as an eternally youthful man who experiences life in a heightened state through his eyes and all his senses.

It was in watercolours such as *Girl in a Poppy Field* (1968–9, Plate 127), *Girl in a Field* (1969–84, Plate 128) and *Liberty Blake in a Kimono* (1971, Plate 129) that Blake began to develop his most personal process for making portraits, paradoxically by basing these most delicately rendered pictures on photographs. Judging a convincing likeness to be the most important quality that characterises a painting or drawing of a person specifically as a portrait, he had no qualms about tracing from photographs (as he had seen commercial artists doing) rather than working from life. Tracing was simply a means to an end, a way of guaranteeing that the proportions and details would all look convincingly 'real'. Far from concealing his methods, he went so far as to reveal the different stages in the production of a portrait of his daughter Liberty (*Liberty as a 'Suffolk Child by John Constable R.A.'*, 1976, Plate 130), born in 1968, for a group portfolio of prints called *For John Constable*, published by Bernard Jacobson. In this case he pinned to the surface of the etched sheet a reproduction of the original by Constable, a black-and-white photo of Liberty assuming the same pose and finally the line drawing traced from that photo for transfer to the etching plate.

The process divulged in such a didactic manner in the Constable print is very similar to that he had already employed when making portraits of individuals he had not met such as Rodia or the film star Jean Harlow, whose portrait he had produced in 1964 as a commission for the *Sunday Times* magazine (Plate 75). It was, however, a different matter for him to work from photographs of people he knew personally and had scrutinised in the flesh, since this choice of method conveys the tacit admission that he has expressly chosen not to work from life. (His last such attempt, when he asked actress Helen Mirren to sit for him in about 1982, resulted in such a loss of nerve that he has never again attempted to make a portrait from life.) When painting such individuals, Blake begins by taking a series of informal photographs himself. After having the chosen photograph enlarged to the required size for the painting, so that it can be traced, or in later years by increasing the size of the snapshot on a photocopier and then tracing it onto a sheet

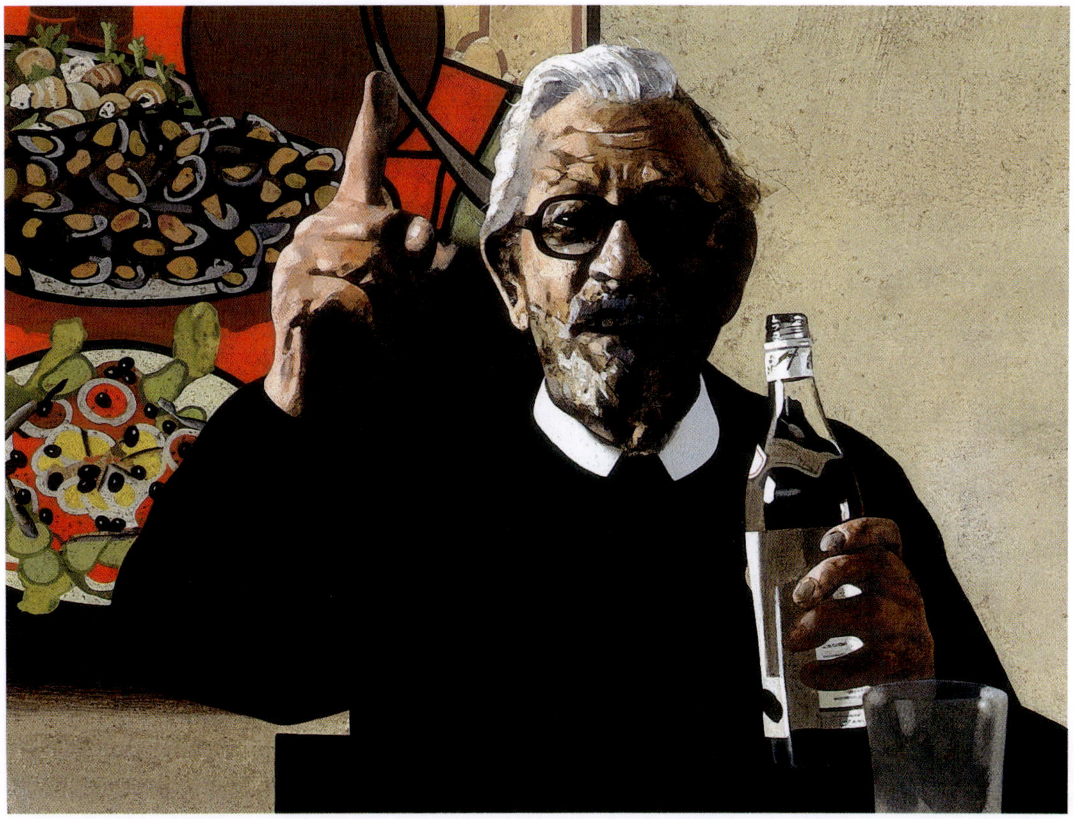

134 E.J. Power, 1987–9

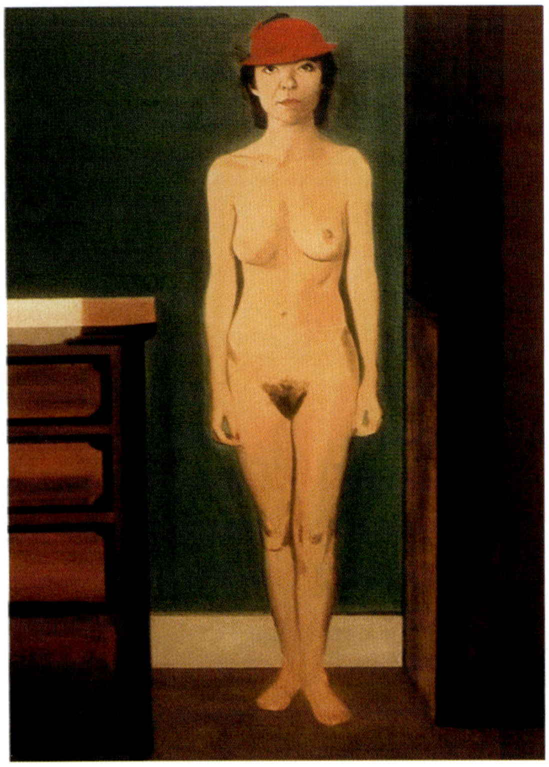

135 **The Wedding Hat**, 1981–3

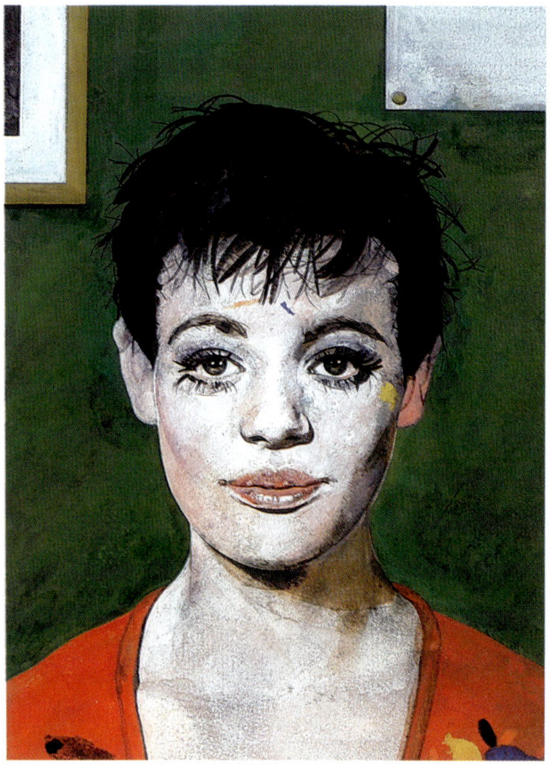

136 **Untitled (Girl in Red Sweater)**, 1989

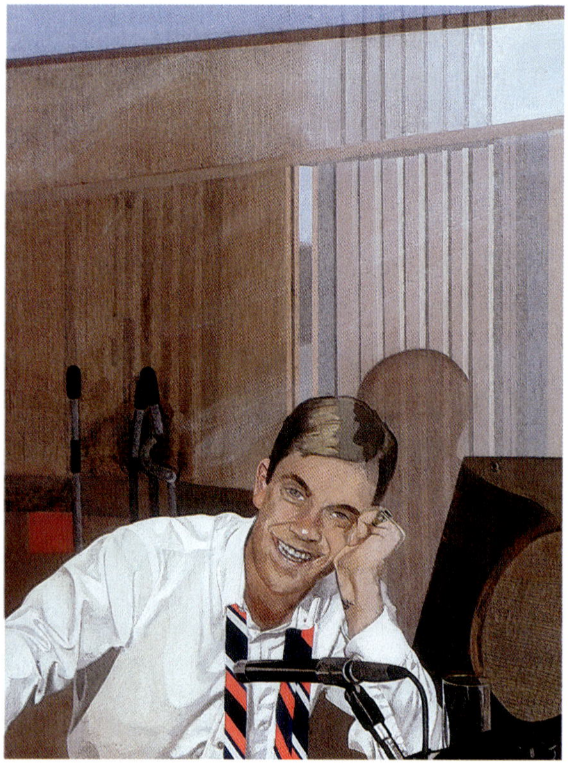

137 **Robbie Williams**, 2002

of transfer paper, so that it can be replicated exactly on the canvas or board, the colour can begin to be added. That way the photographic reference is enriched by memories of that person's appearance and character alike, and by casual observations of them during the period of slowly layering the picture with washes, all of which infiltrate both the initial choice of a suitable pose and the degree of tenderness with which the skin and facial features are slowly coaxed into life.

As a student Blake had been taught that working from photographs and, even worse, tracing from them, were not acceptable processes, and indeed some viewers of his pictures still take exception to what they regard as illustrators' shortcuts. Blake himself candidly describes his process as a means of getting the best likeness he can in the easiest way possible. What justifies the means, however, in his portrait paintings, watercolours and drawings alike is Blake's ability to conjure an uncanny and vivid likeness full of life. This is true of those he knows very well, including members of his family, colleagues (such as Richard Guyatt, the Royal College's Professor of Graphic Design and eventually its Rector, Plate 133), and collectors and patrons such as E.J. Power (Plate 134) and Simon Sainsbury (viewed with his partner, Stewart Grimshaw, in a commissioned painting of 1996). Crucially, the same applies to his portraits of those he may have met only fleetingly, as in the case of India Waters, the young daughter of musician Roger Waters of Pink Floyd fame, in a painting executed over a period of ten years (1986–96). In each instance the initial tracing itself already involves a number of decisions about what to include and what to exclude, and it also reveals – for any artist, not just for Blake – the particular qualities of the artist's hand. The process of filling in and of giving body, texture and a sense of breathing life to the linear tracing is a meticulous one, and it is not as easy as it might sound.

Within this process there are numerous decisions to be made on the way, such as where to place the shading, how to accentuate a contour while suggesting the softness of flesh and how much detail to include when painting the eyes or the hair. Far from being a mechanical procedure, it requires a delicacy of touch and a considerable degree of interpretation. Often the colour is invented. Only an artist with a lifetime of observation and experience with the figure could use such a system to produce results that convey the sensation of having been made from life. These attributes can be discerned as clearly in paintings made for his own pleasure, such the life-sized female nude of *The Wedding Hat* (1981–3, Plate 135) (painted as part of a Brotherhood of Ruralists project on 'The Definitive Nude'), as in commissioned portraits such as that of pop singer Robbie Williams in 2002 (Plate 137), originally destined for the cover of his album *Swing When You're Winning*. The 2001 portrait of pop musician Ian Dury, whom Blake had taught at Walthamstow in the early 1960s and who remained a great friend right through his years with Ian Dury and the Blockheads, was painted for a two-fold purpose soon after the singer's death from cancer. Commissioned as the cover image for an album released later that year, *Brand New Boots & Panties: Tribute to Ian Dury*, for Blake it was also a way of remembering someone for whom he had always had a soft spot, in his characteristic 'cheeky chappie' mode.

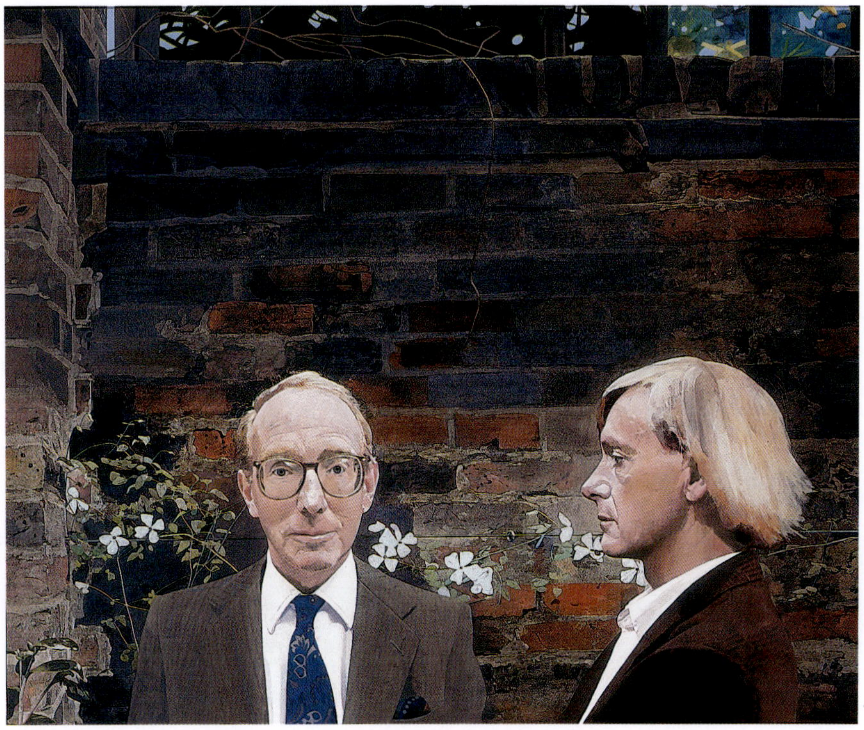

138 **Portrait of Simon Sainsbury and Stewart Grimshaw**, 1996

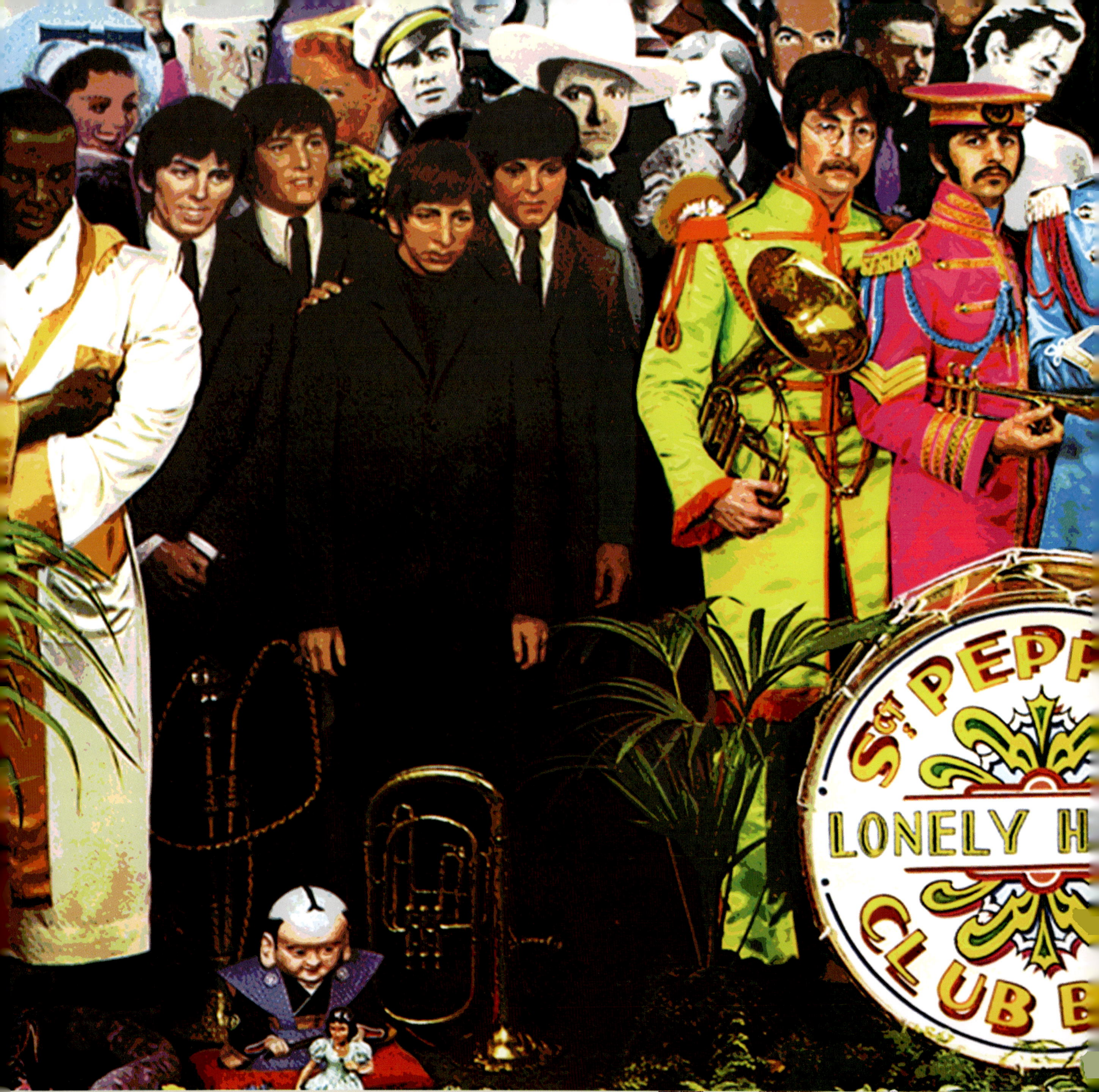

5

ART

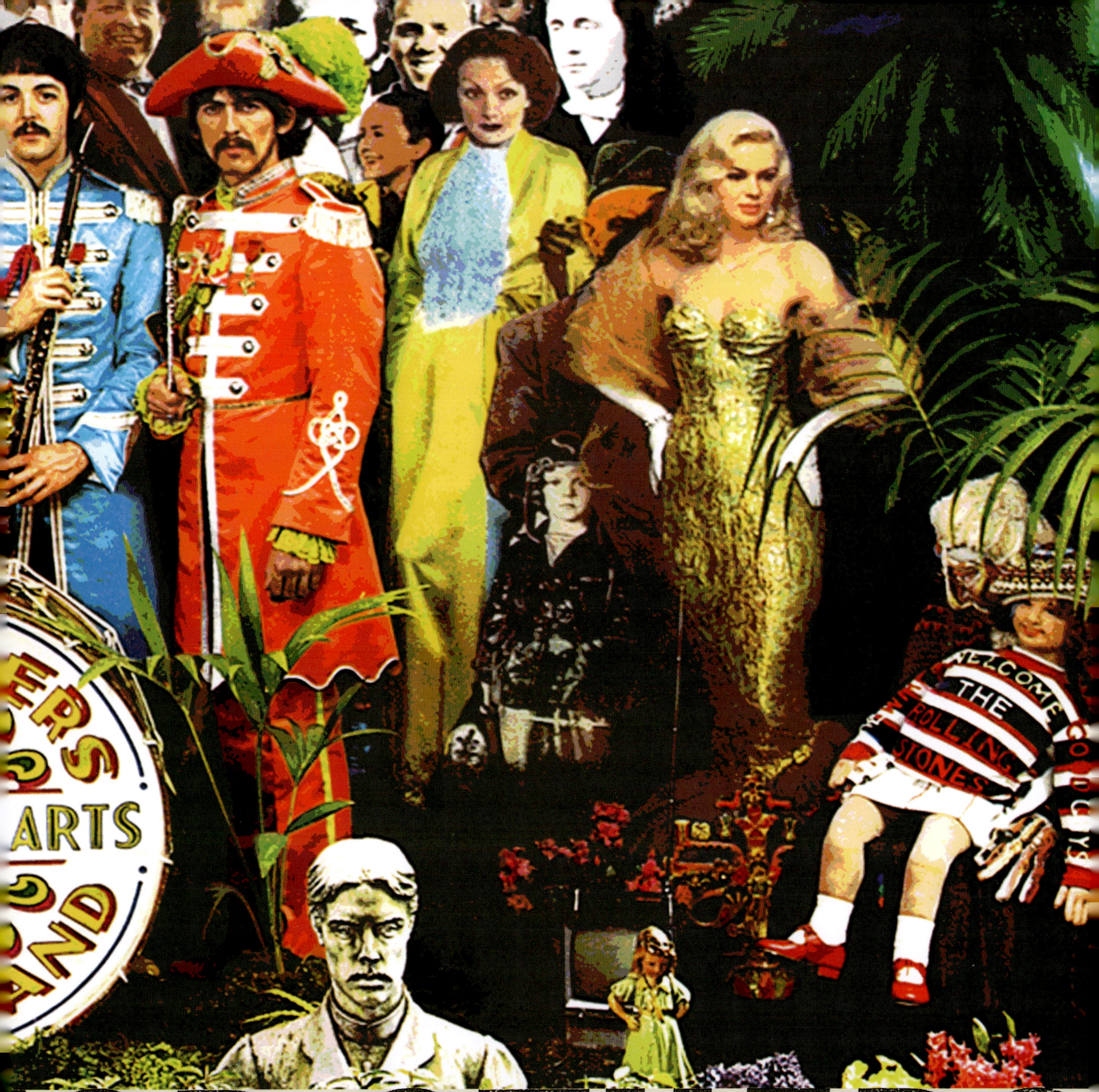

FOR OTHERS

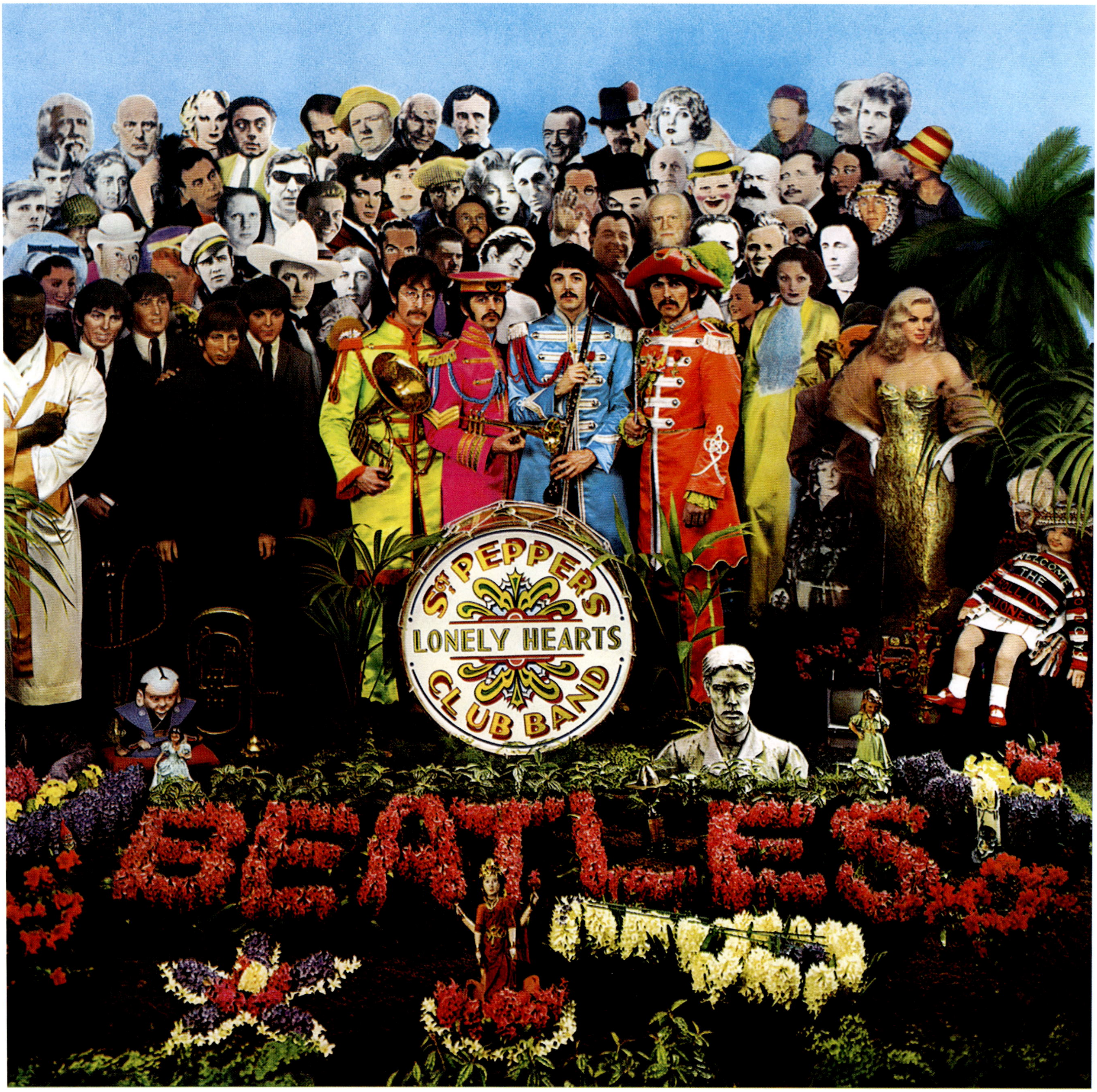

139 Cover for the Beatles' album *Sgt. Pepper's Lonely Hearts Club Band*, 1967

5 Art for Others

Commercial Art and Commissions

In 1987, six years after he was elected as a full member of the Royal Academy of Arts as a painter, Blake was admitted to the equally select band of Royal Designers for Industry in the category of Graphic Design. To be the only artist of his time to be doubly honoured in this way indicates the extent to which his work in these two very distinct worlds has been recognised. He explained to me in an unpublished interview in 1989 that he had given equal attention to painting and graphic design, with neither 'patronising' the other: 'I am almost unique in this. A lot of the painting has benefited from the graphic design, not in the sense of being illustrative but because of the skills I had learned. And some of the pictures come directly out of graphic design; for example, the wrestling pictures are virtually posters.'

Rare among his generation, Blake had a solid grounding in commercial art as a young art student and has continued throughout his life to accept commercial assignments and to view them as an integral and valued element of his activities as an artist. Magazines had provided an initial outlet for this side of his practice. The Los Angeles drawings that he made in 1963 at the request of the *Sunday Times* magazine followed on from his 'John Bull on the Brink' cover illustration and a grid of nine images created for a cover article on 'The Criminal Core' published by that same magazine on 26 August 1962 and 6 October 1963 (Plate 140) respectively. These were succeeded by other covers for the same publication, including the portrait of Jean Harlow (22 November 1964 issue, Plate 75), an immaculately rendered likeness that presaged his later paintings of celebrities, and a portrait of the poet Mary Wilson, wife of prime minister Harold Wilson (19 May 1968). Other such designs for a mass-media context followed, such as the *Morgan Le Faythful* poster created for the *Daily Telegraph* and reproduced on the cover of their 10 April 1968 magazine (Plate 141). As one of the very rare artists of his time willing to apply himself to such requests, Blake was much in demand, producing illustrations for a wide variety of publications including *The Times Literary Supplement* and *New Society*. His unerring sense of what was required for such a general audience made him a natural favourite among the art directors working for these mass-circulation newspapers and magazines.

Such requests often led the artist to extend his subject matter, to discover new imagery and to develop techniques that subsequently became familiar elements in his main body of work. That Blake gave to such projects the same seriousness of attention as all his art,

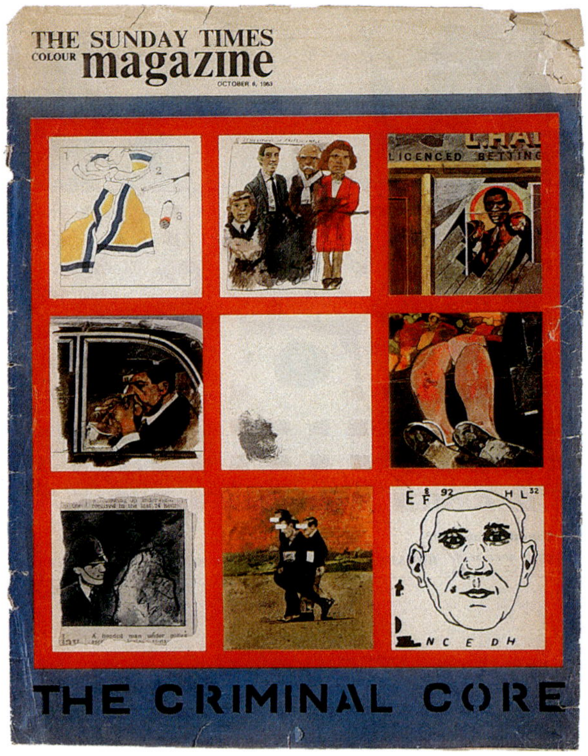

140 Cover for the *Sunday Times* magazine, 6 October 1963

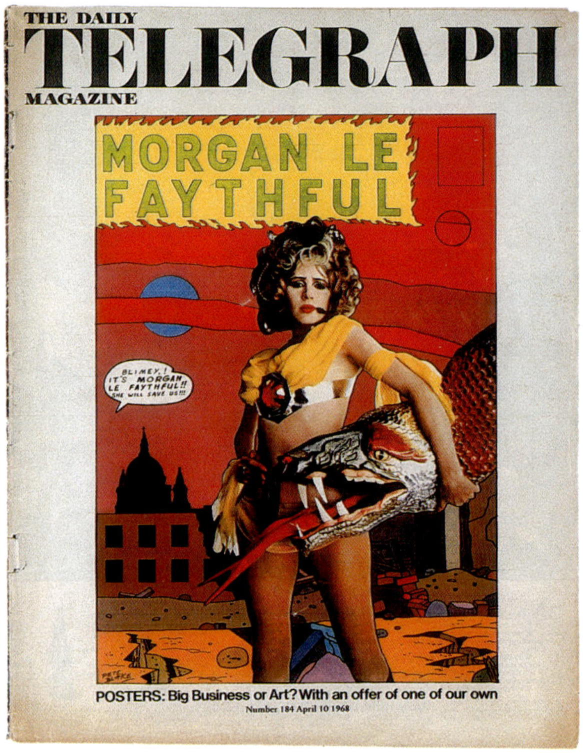

141 Cover for the *Daily Telegraph* magazine, 10 April 1968

making no distinction between works destined for mass consumption and those produced for a more select gallery audience, is evident from the fact that his portrait of Jean Harlow sits easily among his other paintings of the period – even though she was not one of his favourite stars and he would probably not have otherwise chosen to make a picture of her.

Much Pop Art concerned itself with commercial art as source material, including comic books, magazine images, movie stills and other material from the mass media. Blake, even in this context, has been very rare in his willingness to work as a commercial artist at every stage of his career. Andy Warhol, who first made his reputation in the 1950s as a commercial artist and who returned periodically to advertising in later years in a spirit of capitalist provocation, again provides the only close parallel to Blake in his production of record covers, poster designs and advertisements. With Blake, however, there is no trace of cynicism and no sense of salesmanship as a caustic aside on the art market. There is only his usual affectionate identification with traditions of commercial imagery that have long given him sustenance. With two works published in 1967 – the cover for the Beatles album, *Sgt. Pepper's Lonely Hearts Club Band* (co-designed with Jann Haworth) (Plate 139), his most widely circulated image, and *Babe Rainbow* (Plate 89), a prismatically coloured emblem of the guiltless sexuality of swinging London, printed on tin and initially sold for just £1 each – Blake made considerable inroads back into the mass culture from which his art had sprung. Once his reputation was firmly established, he even made excursions into advertising, including a painting for Daimler in 1980 (with nude and scantily clad female fairies cavorting improbably in a moonlit landscape next to a luxury sedan) and an illustration for Schweppes in 1986. In August 2007, over a period of a week, he made a 20-foot-high painted billboard for Coca-Cola – a 'magic crowd' perched on a kind of rainbow – that was displayed outdoors on London's South Bank, on the eastern corner of Jubilee Gardens on Jubilee Walk.

Works commissioned from Blake reveal the extent to which he was able to satisfy the demands of his clients while preserving his own artistic identity. These have included covers, featuring both expressly made and existing works, for the Penguin editions of various novels by Colin MacInnes including *Absolute Beginners* (1961) and *City of Spades* (1964), for the 1965 Penguin edition of George Orwell's *The Decline of the English Murder* and much later for two collections of poetry published by Enitharmon Press, *The Cat without E-mail* by Alan Brownjohn (2002) and *After the Dancing Dogs* by Michael Henry (2008). More ambitiously, he also created suites of illustrations for works of poetry and literature, including watercolours for Roger McGough's poetry collection, *Summer with Monika* (Whizzard Press/André Deutsch, 1978, Plate 142) and drawings for a limited-edition book of Michael Horovitz's poem *Midsummer Morning Jog Log* (Five Seasons Press, 1986). He also painted watercolours for the covers of four volumes in the Arden edition of the works of William Shakespeare (published by Methuen in 1979), including *Timon of Athens* (Plate 163) and *Antony and Cleopatra* (Plate 164), as part of a larger project involving artists from the Brotherhood of Ruralists (see chapter 6).

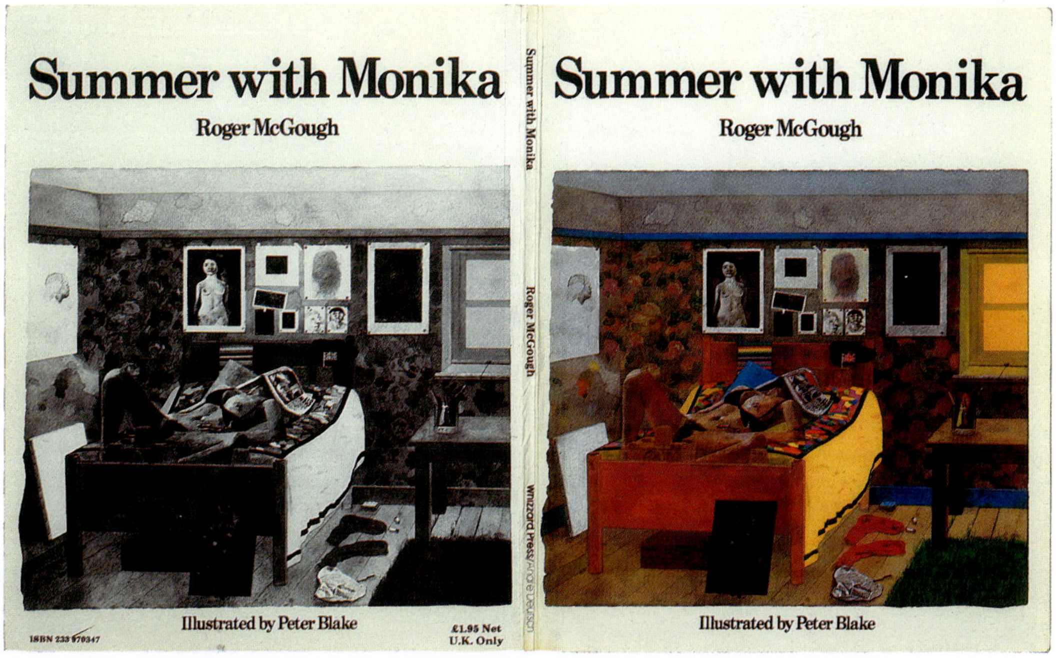

142 Front and back cover for Roger McGough's *Summer with Monika*, 1978

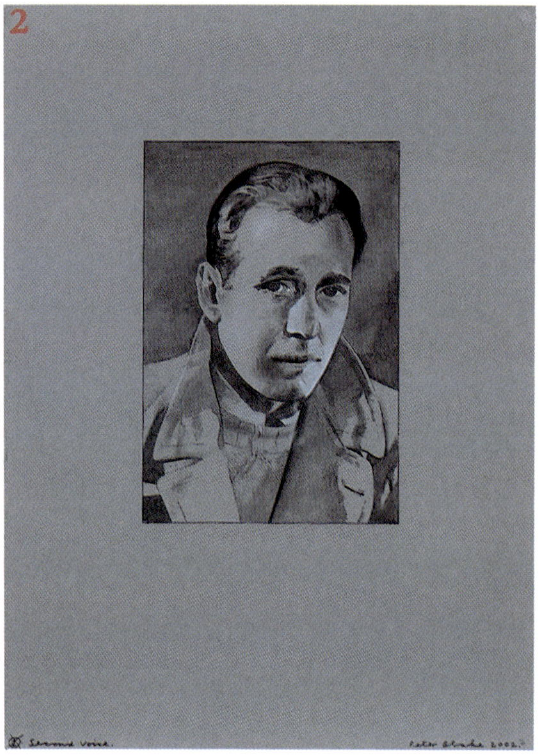

143 Illustration for Dylan Thomas's *Under Milk Wood*, 1990

More ambitious still have been plans – executed so far only as light sketches – to illustrate F. Scott Fitzgerald's novel *The Great Gatsby* (1925), perhaps in the form of linocuts, and Molly Bloom's soliloquy from the final chapter of James Joyce's *Ulysses* (first published in its entirety in 1922), possibly as erotic etchings made with cross-hatching in the manner of Giorgio Morandi or Walter Richard Sickert. The one literary project on this scale that he has already begun, a deluxe edition of Dylan Thomas's *Under Milk Wood* (Plate 143), a verse play first performed on radio in 1953, was initiated in the early 1980s but remains to be completed a quarter of a century later. Working with the typographer and printer Michael Mitchell of the Libanus Press and with the designer Brian Webb, Blake undertook to illustrate the text with a series of wood-engraved portraits to be published as one volume, with a separate volume containing a set of watercolours of the dreams. By the summer of 2008, he had completed 27 of these watercolours, 60 sheets of portraits in the form of pencil drawings and about 50 drawings of other subjects including some of a topographical nature. The wood engravings had by then been put to one side, though with the intention of returning to them.

Blake's excursions into commercial work have taken a great variety of forms, indicating his restless curiosity to try his hand at anything that comes his way. Posters for Madame Tussaud's in 1968, for the Contemporary Art Society in 1985 and for the London Transport Museum (and London Underground) in 2008, postage stamps celebrating the millennium

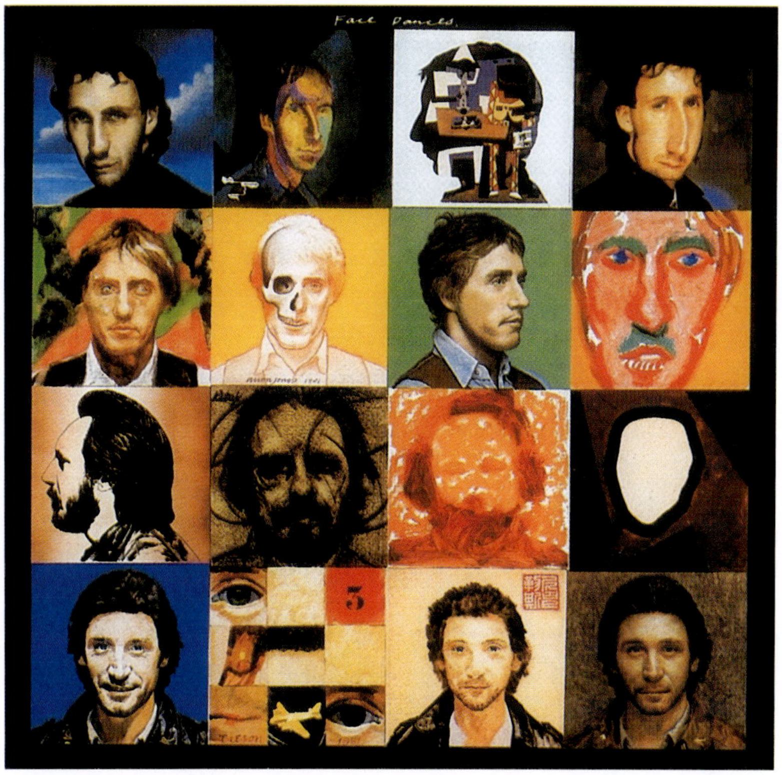

144 Cover for the Who album, *Face Dances*, 1981

for the Royal Mail, a phone card for Mercury, images for Trickett & Webb calendars (beginning in 1992), a bone-china plate with a printed design for Wedgwood, a table for Aram Designs in 1987, a Mod-inflected design for a printed bomber jacket made of paper for the ICA in 1976 (when punk rock was in the ascendancy) and a plastic wristwatch with a target image for the Royal Academy at the time of their *Pop Art* exhibition in 1990 give an indication of the range of these activities. Much more recently he designed an Alphabet tapestry for the Rug Company, produced in a limited edition of five, and carpets for the new courts of the Law Lords.

It is in the sphere of music, however, and specifically record-cover design, that Blake has excelled and to which he has most vividly brought his style and imagery to the large popular audience he had imagined as the potential public for his Pop Art paintings. Within this sphere, his cover for the 1967 album by the Beatles, *Sgt. Pepper's Lonely Hearts Club Band* (Plate 139) – arguably not just the most famous record cover of the decade but also one of the greatest pop records – stands out not only as his most celebrated piece of commercial art, and as the artefact that led to so many other commissions, but as one of the most influential and memorable such designs of the late twentieth century. Beatles fans the world over seized upon its imagery of famous and obscure personalities, animatedly discussing their identities and the possible reasons for their presence with the same earnest enthusiasm with which they were now decoding the lyrics of Lennon and McCartney

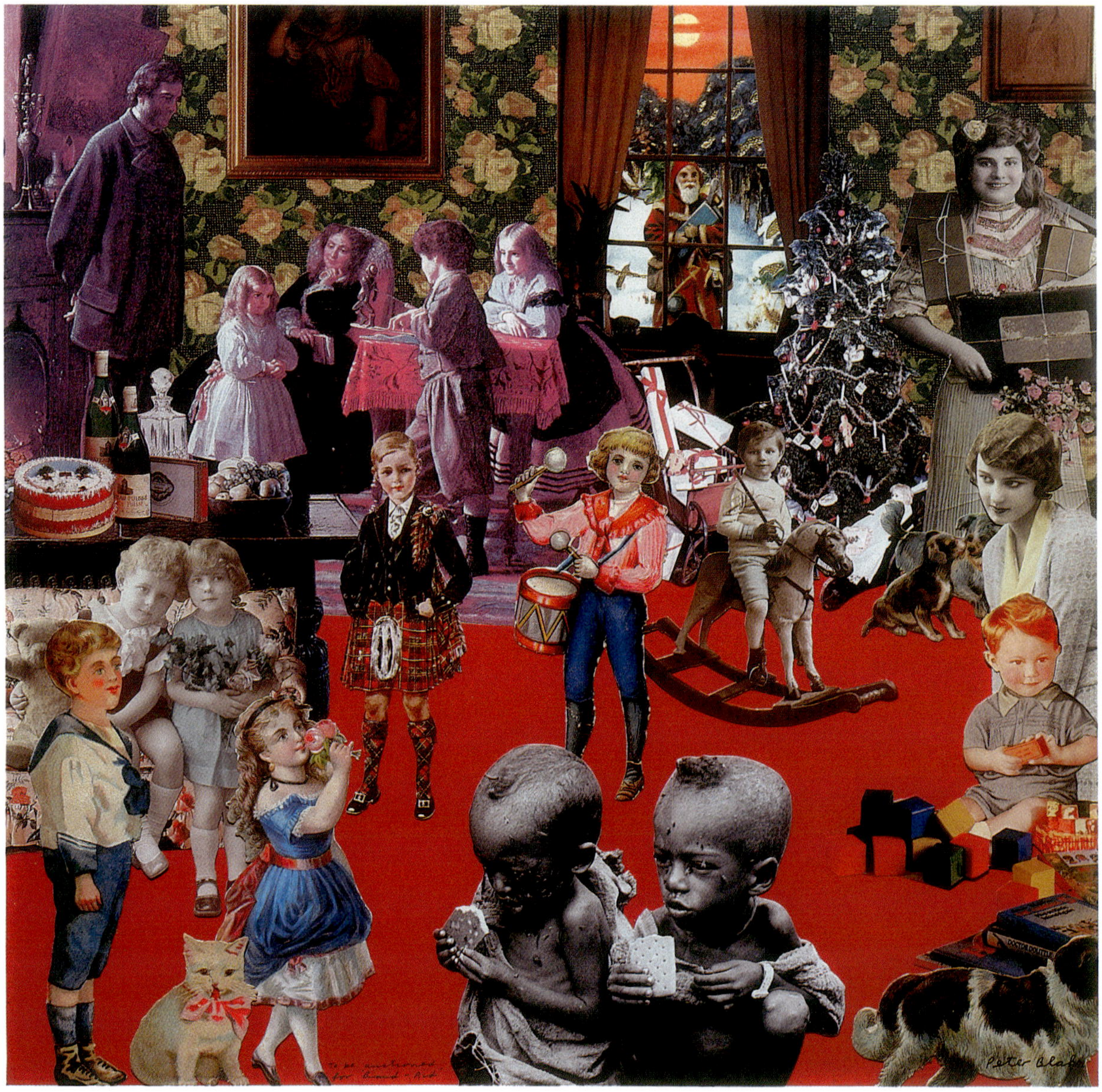

145 Original artwork for the Band Aid single 'Do They Know it's Christmas?', 1984

and the other great songwriters of the day. Had the internet existed then, blog pages would have been overloaded with comments and passionate arguments.

Blake's art dealer during the 1960s, Robert Fraser, was regarded as the hippest man in the London art world and he was friendly with some of the great pop bands of the time, including the Rolling Stones as well as the Beatles, acting as a conduit between these normally very separate worlds. While recording *Sgt. Pepper*, Paul McCartney asked Fraser to find an artist to design the cover, after Fraser had persuaded them not to use a psychedelic illustration first made for the album by a design team called The Fool. Fraser signed a contract with the Beatles and then subcontracted the commission to Blake, who in turn asked his wife to collaborate with him on it. The indirect nature of the request eventually resulted in a flat fee of £200 that Blake found deeply unsatisfactory, especially as the record became such a huge seller, but he could at least take satisfaction in the fact that his art had finally found an audience of millions. This album cover remains, if not his greatest single work, then certainly his best-known.

The idea of the crowd, within which an assortment of extraordinary strangers cross paths as if by accident, had preoccupied Blake a decade earlier in paintings such as *On the Balcony* (1955–7, Plate 39) and *The Preparation for the Entry into Jerusalem* (1955–6, Plate 37) as well as in a number of his collages using cut-out printed imagery. Perhaps the impetus for such gatherings came from the artist's sense of aloneness as a child, teenager and young man, and a desire not just for conviviality but for direct contact with his heroes. Who other than the adolescent and 20-something Peter, repeatedly suffering unrequited crushes, would have been a more suitable member of a Lonely Hearts Club? In any case, a crowd of famous personalities surrounding the four members of the Beatles – seen in the flesh in their glorious, multicoloured maturity as a marching band and as wax works in their earlier guise as the Merseybeat moptops – seemed a perfect solution to McCartney's desire for the group to be represented as if accepting a municipal award of some sort.

The regalia in which the Beatles are dressed, together with the Victorian lettering of their alter-egos' names on the drum and the floral display in the foreground, are all suggestive of a self-conscious and quintessential Englishness. Blake and Haworth asked each of the Beatles to make a list of the people, living and dead, real and imaginary, that they would like to accompany them on the cover. The artists (with some input from Fraser) added further names and then set about researching the imagery. They had life-sized photographic enlargements made of Bob Dylan, Mae West, Marlon Brando, Marilyn Monroe, Oscar Wilde, Karl Marx, Jayne Mansfield, Edgar Allen Poe, W.C. Fields and the rest, and then started arranging them in a photographic studio in the manner of a football team or schoolchildren posing for a group photo. (Mae West was at first affronted by the request, demanding to know what she would be doing in a lonely hearts club, but relented when the Beatles sent her a personal letter.) With the addition of some sculptural objects, including (at the far right) a sculpture by Haworth of a young girl welcoming the Beatles' arch-rivals, the Rolling Stones, it was left to the Beatles themselves to complete the scene.

The cover design, often assumed to be a collage, in fact came from the photograph taken by Michael Cooper of this elaborate set-up. With the original editions of the album came a sheet of Sgt. Pepper cut-outs (including the sergeant's stripes, a handlebar moustache

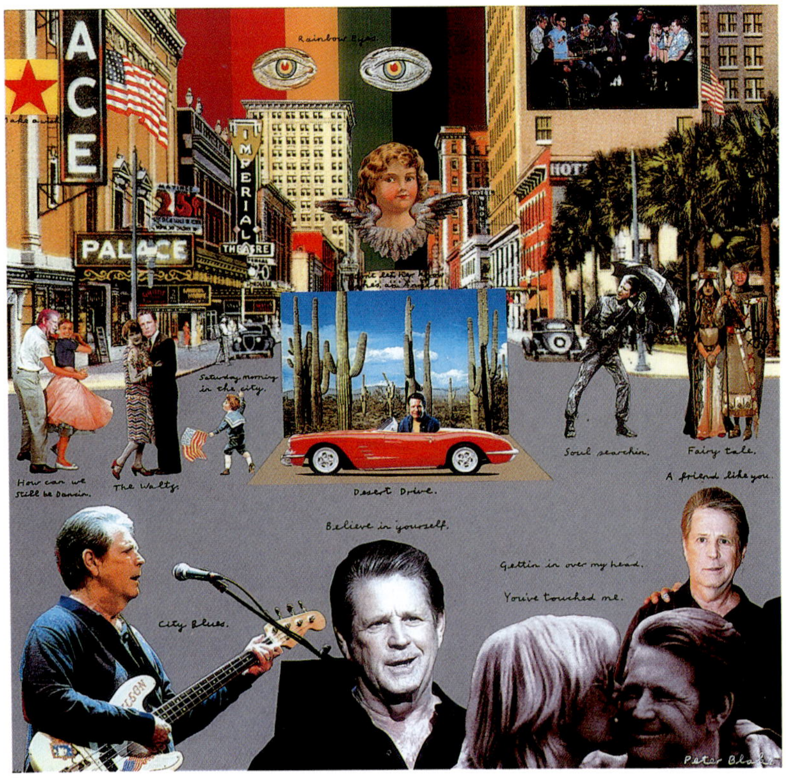

146 Original artwork for the Brian Wilson album, *Gettin' In Over My Head*, 2004

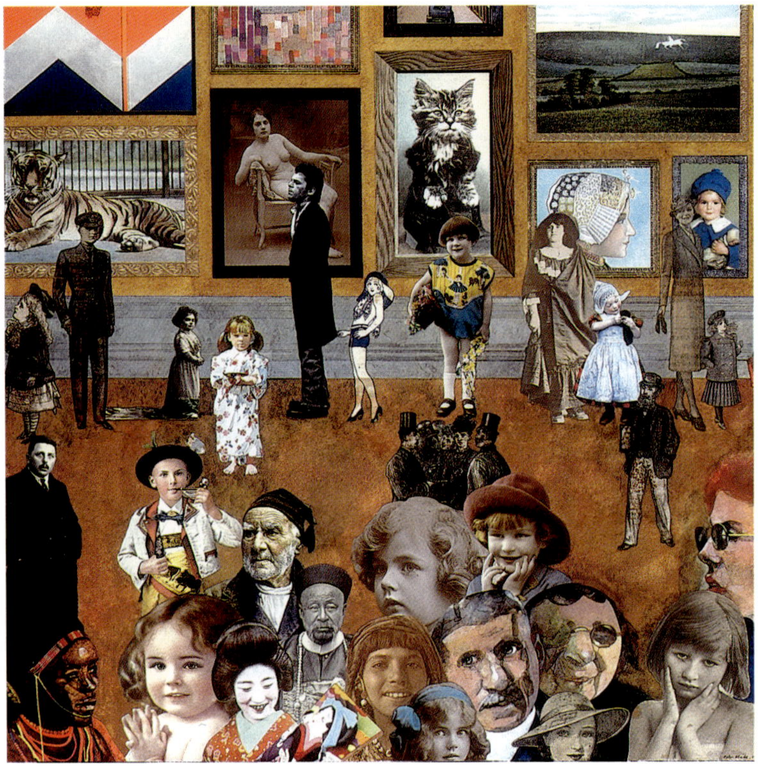

147 Academy, 1975

and two badges) conceived in the same spirit of pseudo-Victoriana. In the lower-right corner of this sheet were the printed signatures of Blake and Haworth, completing the conceit that the cover and its printed extras constituted a gift for the consumer: a work of art in a huge unlimited edition.

After the great success of *Sgt. Pepper*, Blake's love of music continued to find an outlet in record covers. One of the first of these to follow from the celebrity he had gained in this field was the gatefold sleeve for Pentangle's double album *Sweet Child* (a recording of their Royal Festival Hall concert of 29 June 1968 released later that year), for which he created a bold interlaced five-pointed star circumscribed by two concentric circles, the whole bathed in strong colours and a glittering surface. In the next decade he designed *The Adventures of Valentine Vox the Ventriloquist* (1974) by Chris Jagger (brother of Mick), followed by the more commercially successful *Face Dances* album (Plate 144) by his friends, the Who, in 1981. For this he made a small watercolour of drummer Kenney Jones but also enlisted the portraiture skills of a stellar cast of 15 fellow artists: Michael Andrews, Clive Barker, Patrick Caulfield, Richard Hamilton, David Hockney, Howard Hodgkin, David Inshaw, Bill Jacklin, Allen Jones, R.B. Kitaj, Tom Phillips, Patrick Procktor, Colin Self, Joe Tilson and David Tindle. Each of the four members of the band is portrayed four times, in a grid of sixteen squares, suggesting different aspects of their appearance and personality. Blake's rapidly designed cover for the best-selling charity single by Band Aid,

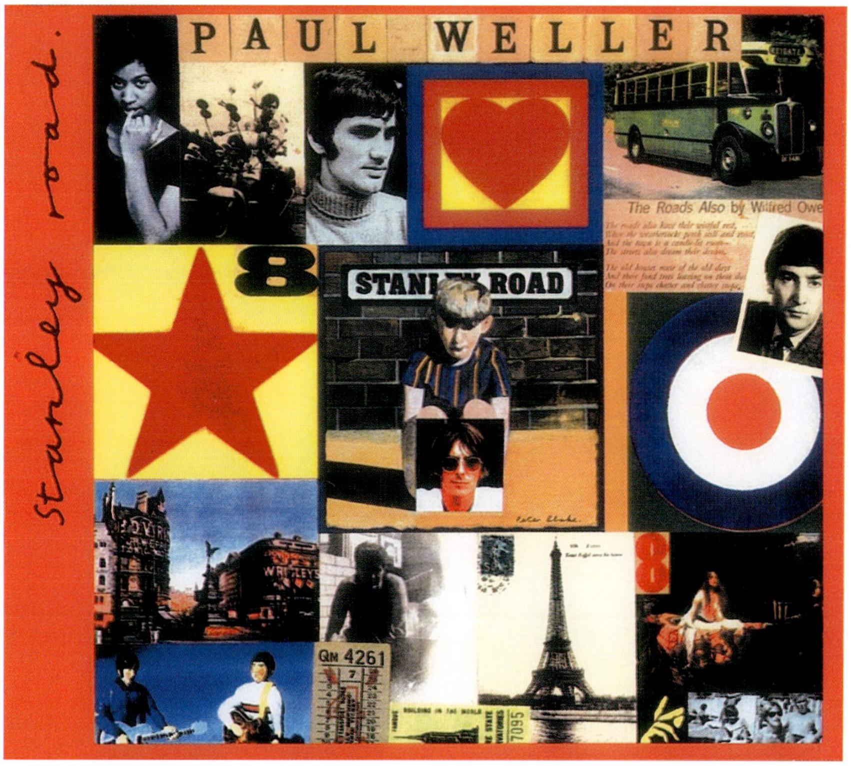

148 Cover design for Paul Weller's album, *Stanley Road*, 1995

'Do They Know It's Christmas?' (Plate 145), in aid of the Ethiopian Famine Relief Fund in November 1984, and the poster for the Live Aid concert in 1985 both consciously recalled the 'magic crowd' of *Sgt. Pepper*, as did his 1975 poster for the Royal Academy Summer Exhibition (for which he created a collage, see Plate 147).

An extravagantly packaged box set, *24 Nights: The Music of Eric Clapton. The Drawings of Peter Blake*, published by Genesis Publications Ltd in Guildford, Surrey, was marketed in 1991 in a deluxe edition of 3,500 copies signed by both Clapton and Blake. It contained facsimile reproductions of drawings the artist had made of Clapton and his band (relaxing, practising and on stage) in three sketchbooks; the box also contained a scrapbook volume into which were pasted reproductions of tickets and other ephemera relating to the 24 concerts Eric Clapton gave at the Royal Albert Hall as the climax of his 1990–91 tour.

Among Blake's later successes in the area of pop music have been record covers for Paul Weller's *Stanley Road* (1995, Plate 148), Brian Wilson's 2004 solo CD, *Gettin' In Over My Head* (Plate 146) (fulfilling a long-standing ambition to work with the Beach Boys, his favourite pop band), the Oasis greatest hits collection *Stop the Clocks* (2006) and a watercolour portrait for *John Peel – Right Time, Wrong Speed: 1977–1987*, the double album released in 2006 in memory of the recently deceased and much-loved disc jockey. Several of these works have a frankly nostalgic air and an overt self-referencing, as had been the case with the Victoriana and music-hall postcards that were featured on the Jagger cover.

There are 1960s overtones in the collaged multiple portrait of Wilson, as in *Stanley Road*, which is appropriate given Weller's sartorial and musical styles and his nickname of 'The Modfather'. Blake selected his images in this case from a list the singer had devised, at the artist's request, of his favourite things. Blake went so far as to use his 1959 *Locker* sculpture (Plates 1 and 55) as the container of imagery for the Oasis compilation. He can be excused for imposing his aesthetic and his own history on the covers in this way, since in recent years it is those associations, rather than just his redoubtable skill as a graphic designer, for which his involvement has been sought.

Souvenirs

In 1968 Blake made the first two of a series of works that he termed *Souvenirs*, intended both as homages and as gifts for fellow artists and other friends: one of the initial ones was given to David Hockney (Plate 150). When he agreed to put on a solo show at the Festival Gallery in Bath as part of the Bath Festival six years later, he opted for a thematic coherence by creating a further 30 *Souvenirs*, all reliant on collage and all on an intimate scale as gestures of friendship. Dedicatees in this new series included John Lennon, with a charmingly old-fashioned print of a circus performer commemorating the song that closed side one of *Sgt. Pepper*, 'For the Benefit of Mr Kite', the lyrics of which Lennon had lifted from a Victorian circus poster. For the most part, the *Souvenirs* focused on Blake's fellow painters and sculptors, some of whom, like Joe and Jos Tilson, were living reasonably near his new rural home at Wellow, near Bath, so he was able to see them regularly. Others he saw less frequency, including Hockney, who at that moment was living in Paris and was consequently remembered via five vintage tourist postcards of the French capital. The American painter, sculptor and printmaker Jim Dine, who had lived in London from 1967 to 1971, is brought to mind with old engraved images of hand tools, the category of objects most closely associated with Dine's art.

The material for each *Souvenir* was as thoughtfully chosen as the attributes of the saints in traditional religious pictures, but the import of this selection sometimes becomes apparent only on closer inspection. For Richard Hamilton, for instance, he pasted onto a sheet of marbled paper a photograph of a large suburban American house, the home of Bing Crosby, who is seen waving from his doorway; Crosby's portrait, based on a still from the 1954 film *White Christmas*, had recently featured in Hamilton's painting *I'm dreaming of a white Christmas* (1967–8) and in two related prints published in 1969 and 1971. For the artist team of Gilbert & George (Plate 151), then still better-known as performance artists than for the pictures they had begun making from grids of their own black-and-white

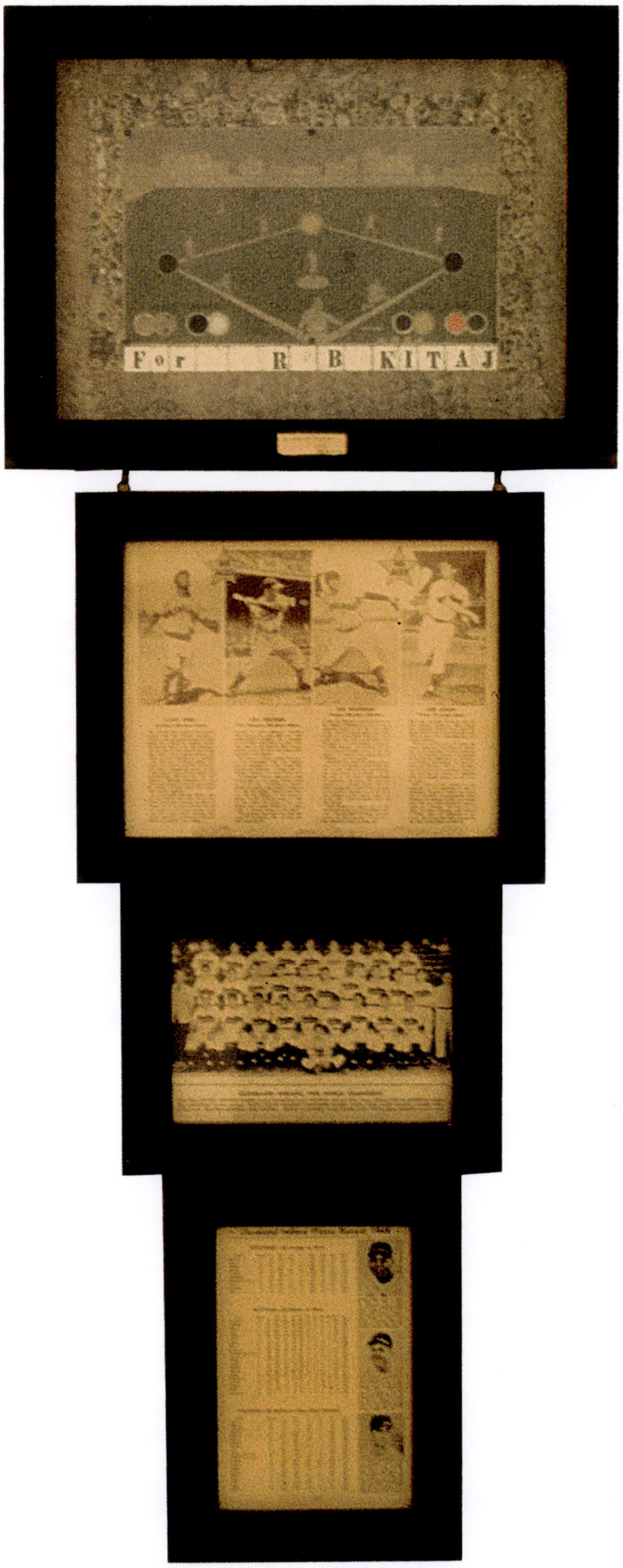

149 **Souvenir for Kitaj**, 1974

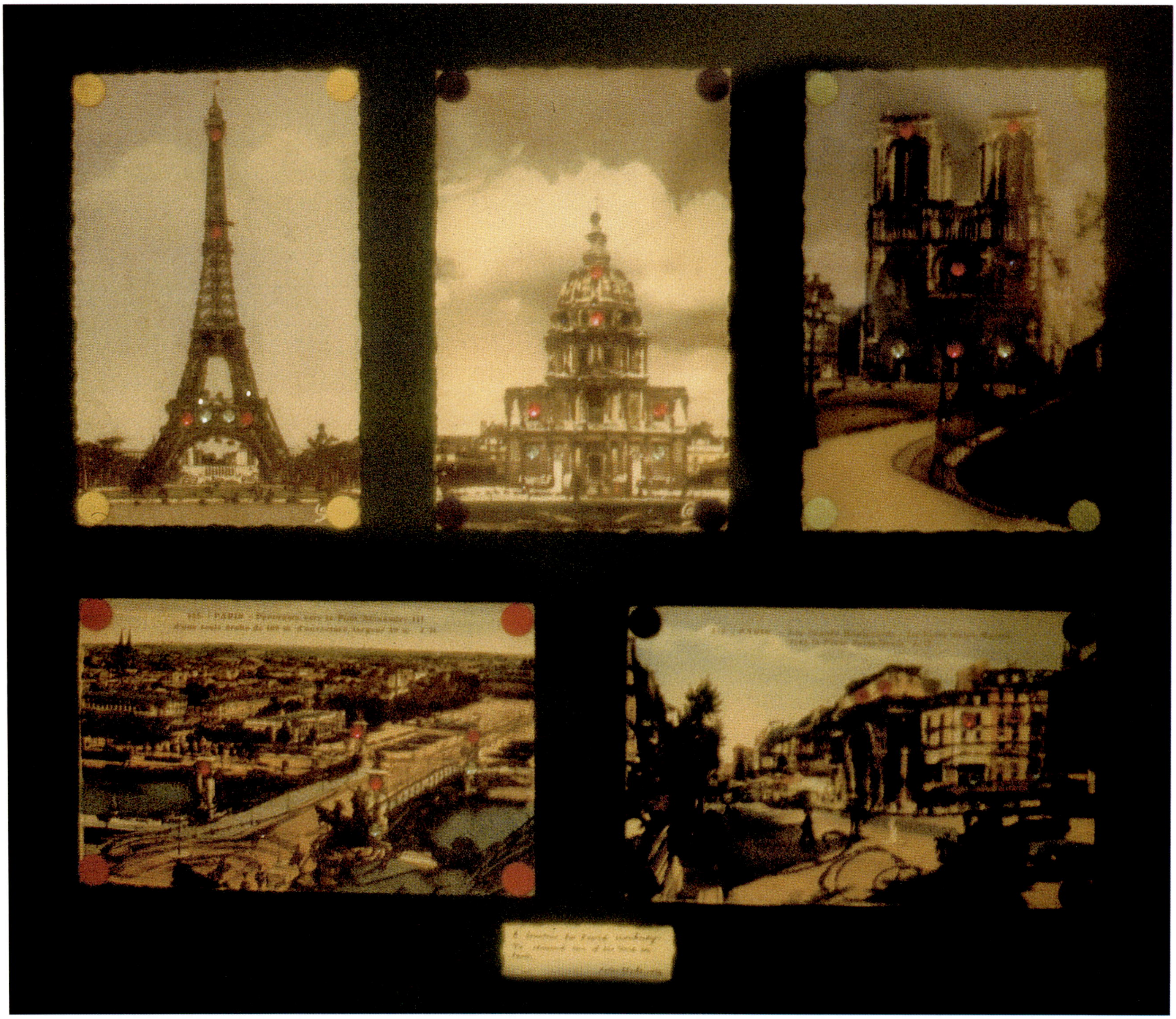

150 **Souvenir for Hockney**, 1974

photographs, Blake presented a signed photograph of the music-hall duo Bud Flanagan and Chesney Allen, whose 'Underneath the Arches' had provided the soundtrack to Gilbert & George's celebrated *Singing Sculpture*. It is accompanied by an inscription in printed letters rephrasing the greeting on the photo so that the best wishes are conveyed specifically to the younger artists by Peter Blake as well as Bud and Chesney. For Kitaj, it is the artist's American origins and particularly his passion for baseball that are the focus of attention (Plate 149).

For his *Souvenirs and Samples* solo show at Waddington and Tooth Galleries, London, from 26 April to 21 May 1977, Blake showed a selection of the 1974 *Souvenirs*, supplemented by some new works in the same mode such as *A Little Museum for Tom Phillips* (1977). In his preface to the catalogue he explained that 'They were made to be given to the person to whom each is dedicated.' In fact, many of them were in the end kept by Blake, and for good reason. Having left London in 1969 and moved to the countryside with his family, Blake had yet to become part of a new community of artists, the Brotherhood of Ruralists, and was probably feeling a certain loneliness and sense of isolation. The works he made in 1974 were ultimately not 'souvenirs' in the sense of something brought back from another place as a gift to others, but in the literal sense of memories, specifically in this case of the people whose company he missed. Thus, keeping the *Souvenirs* for himself was a way of remembering and of keeping those old friends forever by his side.

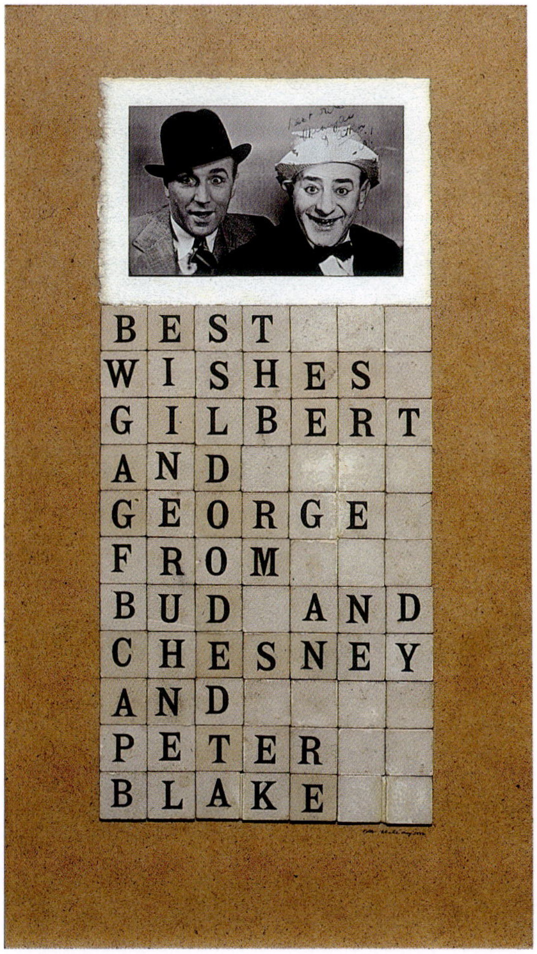

151 Souvenir for Gilbert & George, 1974

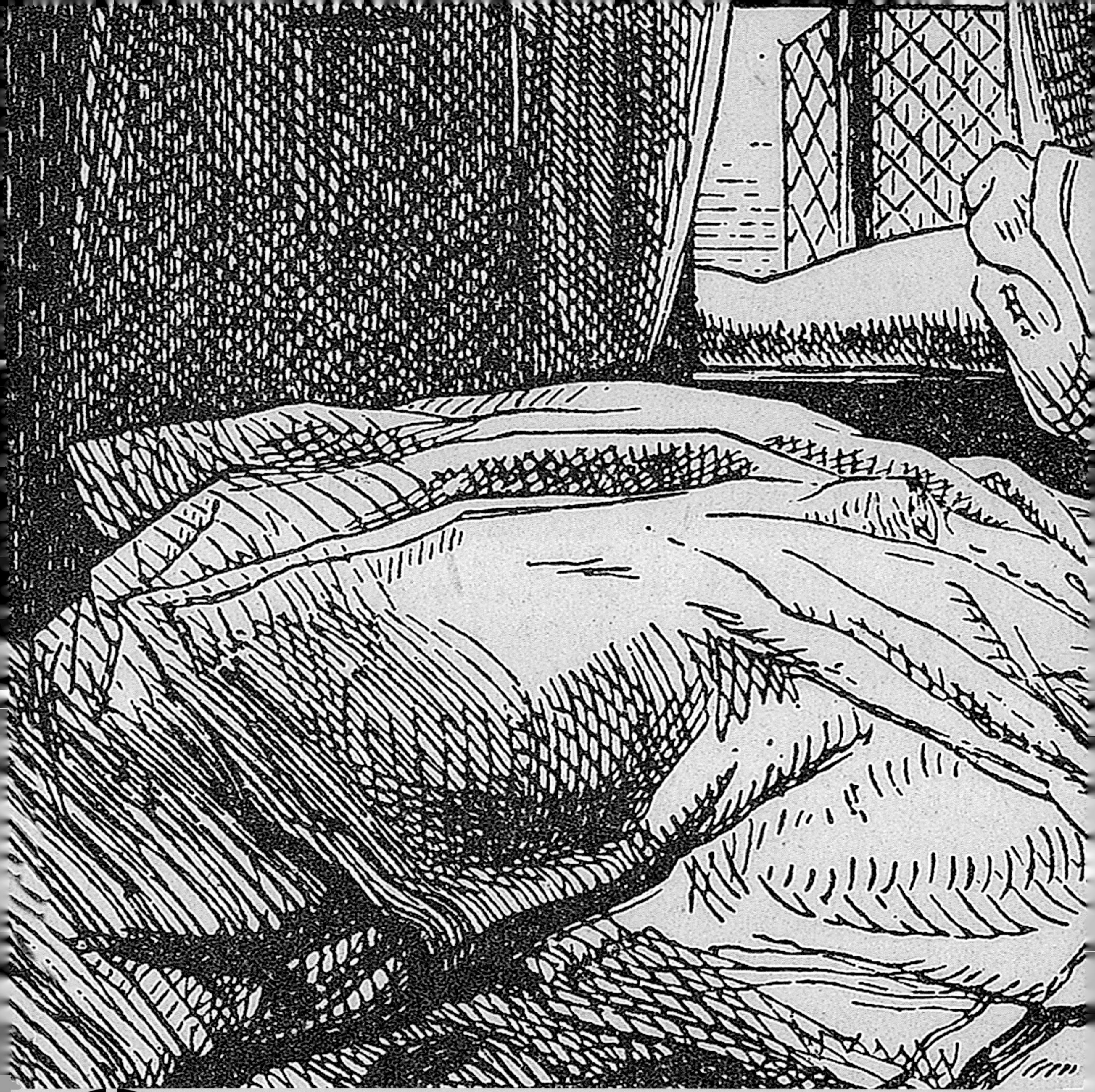

6 ESCAPIST

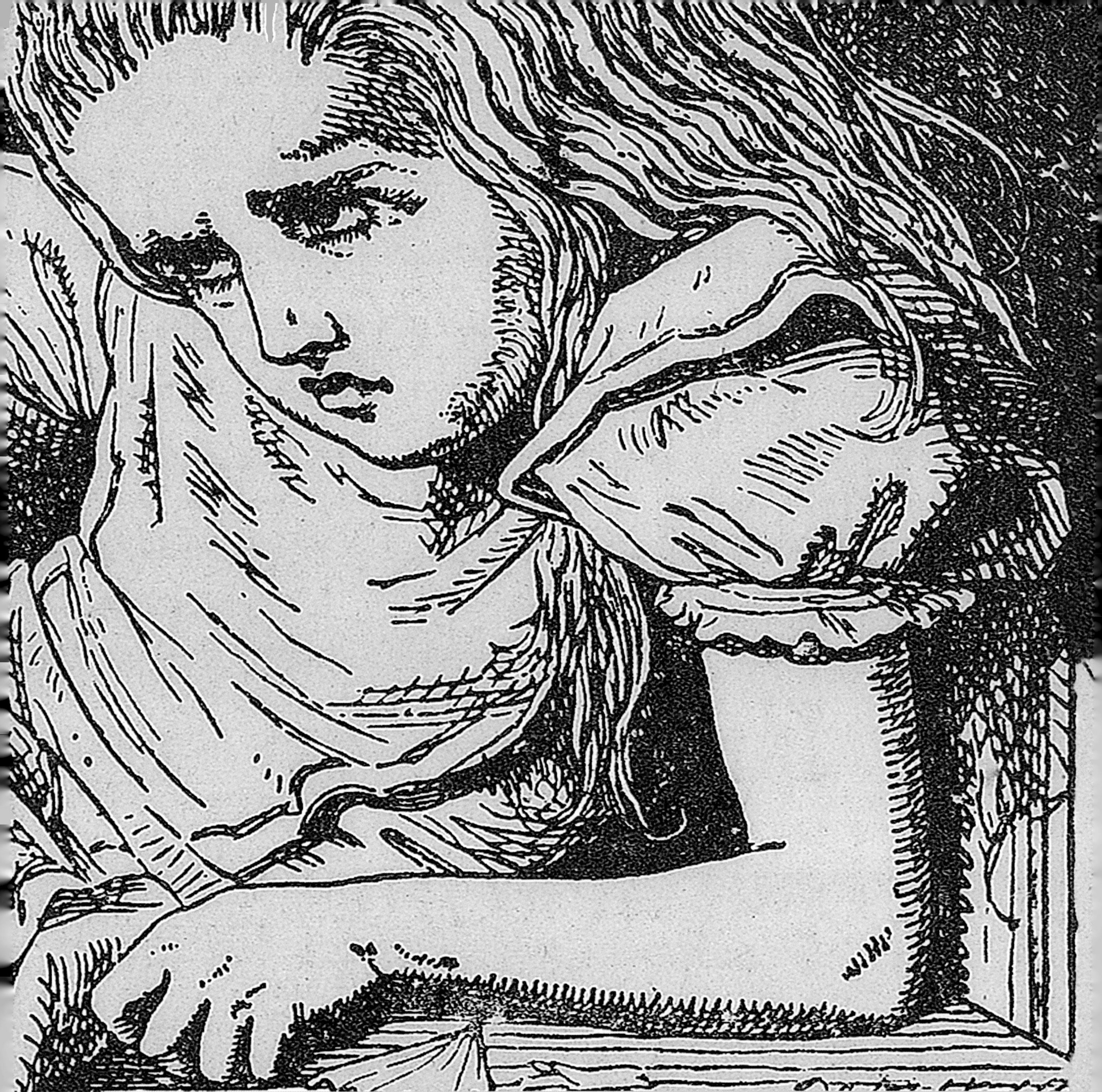

FANTASIES

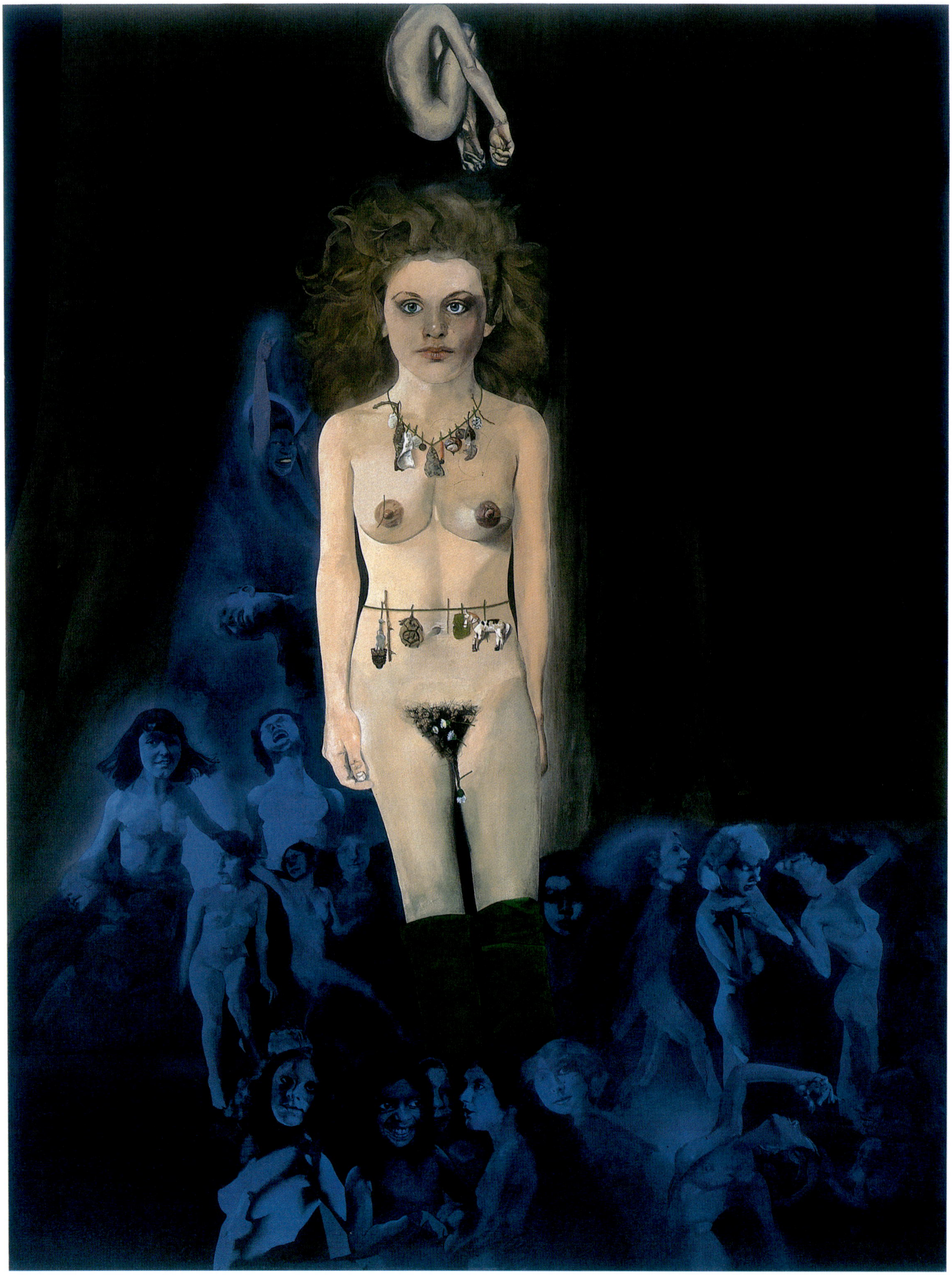

152 **Titania**, 1976–83

6 Escapist Fantasies

If nostalgia is defined as a longing for the return to an idealised past, in Peter Blake's art the frequent recourse to such moods, tinged with sadness and regret, can perhaps best be accounted for by a sense that he was robbed of half his childhood by the circumstances of World War II. Blake emerged as an artist at a time when emotion in art was considered acceptable only if it was suitably angst-ridden, as in Abstract Expressionist painting, or through the traumatic howls of despair in the work of Francis Bacon, or even in the existentialist overtones of the 'geometry of fear' sculpture of the immediate postwar period. Blake's natural preference for a quieter, even sentimental, state of feeling can be very touching in the fragility and vulnerability it exudes. Through all the changes in artistic fashions that have taken place during his lifetime, when formalism, intellectualism and cynicism have been championed as hallmarks of seriousness, he has remained faithful to this unfashionable impulse.

Nostalgia and Time Travel

Although Blake has been castigated by some critics for the expression of soft-centred sentiments deemed more appropriate to the Victorian era than to the late twentieth century, more sympathetic commentators have long understood – as the painter Gordon House succinctly wrote in his catalogue introduction to Blake's 1960 show at the ICA in London – that 'His works are stretched between a fine sense of topicality and nostalgia.' Were it not for the warm, rosy glow in which he bathes the past – whether it be in his respectful recreation of Sir Edwin Landseer's *Monarch of the Glen* (Plate 153) or in a much later watercolour of *Tommies Playing Football* (Plate 154), completed in 1984 – this constant experience of travelling back in time could seem almost like a continuous bereavement.

One often has the sensation when looking at Blake's art of things slipping away even as they happen: of youthful beauty shading into maturity and old age, of newly manufactured objects becoming tomorrow's collectables, of today's stars enjoying their moment of fame before they sink back into obscurity. It is, in fact, this feeling of being pulled in opposite directions that gives Blake's art its tension and saves it from descending into bathos: a delight on the one hand in living in the moment and finding excitement in the new, and on the other a lingering on the past as a place of comfort, familiarity and security, a kind of cultural return to the womb. Though Blake knows full well from his own experience that things were not necessarily 'better in the old days', he somehow cannot

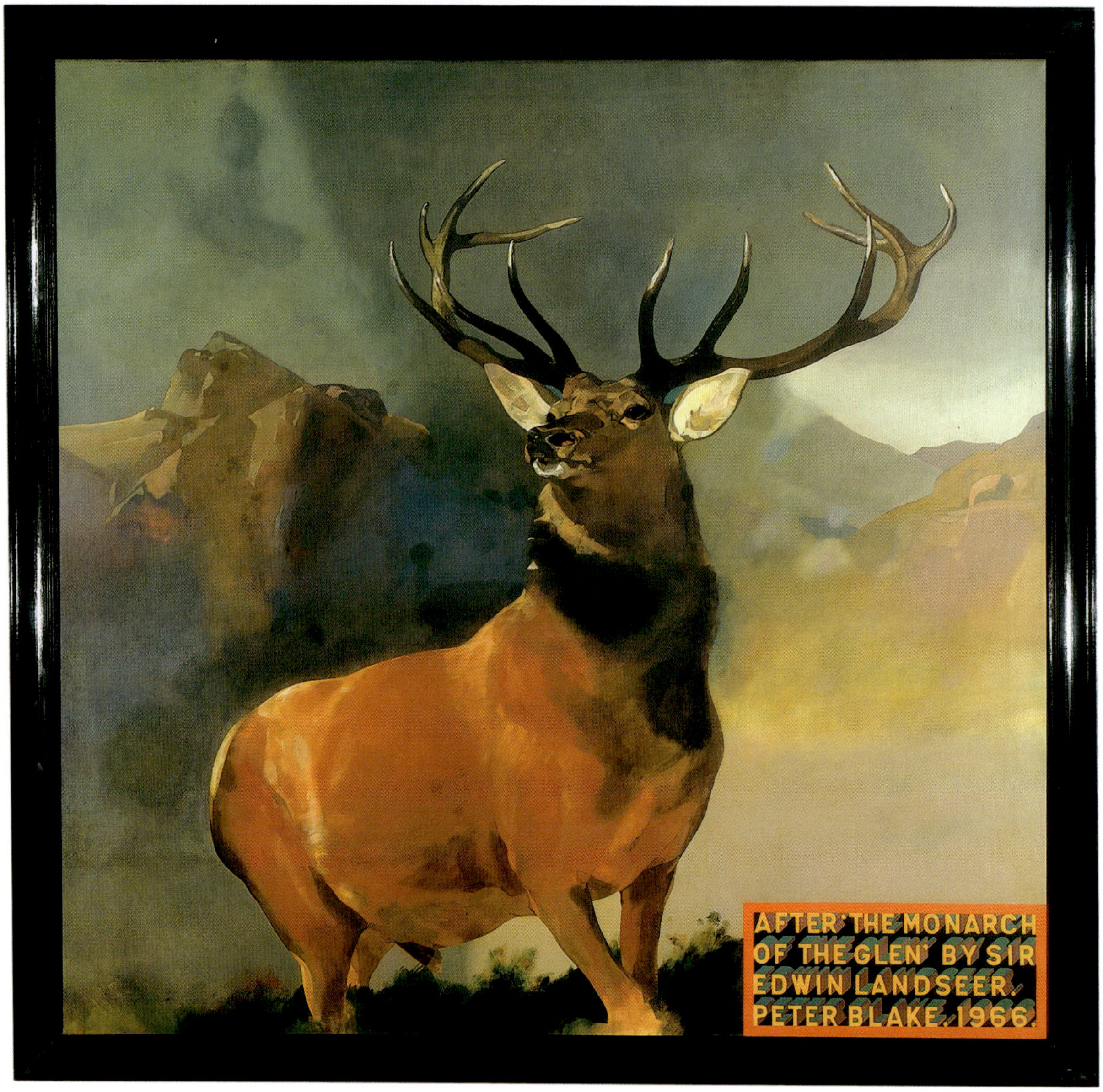

153 **Monarch of the Glen**, 1965–8

stop himself from taking backward glances, both into his personal history and more generally through his allusions to earlier periods or his creation of objects with a timeworn look. All of this is tinged with a bittersweet recognition of transience and therefore of mortality, animated by the impulses suggested by the alternative translations of the title of Marcel Proust's great seven-volume novel, *A la recherche du temps perdu*: a 'remembrance of things past' and a 'search for lost time'.

In an interview with Mervyn Levy published as 'Peter Blake: Pop art for admass' in the November 1963 issue of *Studio International*, Blake articulated this strain of nostalgia as a defining characteristic of his particular brand of Pop Art, citing one of his first boxing pictures as supporting evidence. As one of the earliest recorded declarations of his artistic intentions, it is worth quoting at length:

> I started to become a pop artist from my interest in English folk art. Especially my interest in the visual art of the fairground, and barge painting too. It all originated while I was still a student at the Royal College. Now I want to recapture and bring to life again something of this old-time popular art. For instance, I'm working at the moment on a small picture of a boxer called Kid McCoy. He was fighting around 1910. I read all the boxing and wrestling magazines, by the way. So that this picture will have an authentic old-time feel about it, I'm making the wooden surface look old. I feel that if I bore artificial woodworm holes in it, it will acquire the quality of age. This is essential to my purpose. For me, pop art is often rooted in nostalgia: the nostalgia of old, popular things. And although I'm also continually trying to establish a new pop art, one which stems directly from our own time, I'm always looking back at the sources of the idiom and trying to find the technical forms that will best recapture the authentic feel of folk pop.

The nostalgic impulses in Blake's work are most exaggeratedly in evidence in the pictures he made during the 1970s, his 'Ruralist' phase, which will be discussed in more detail later in this chapter. Such tendencies, however, have surfaced unprompted and without warning in the art he has produced throughout his life. Here is an example.

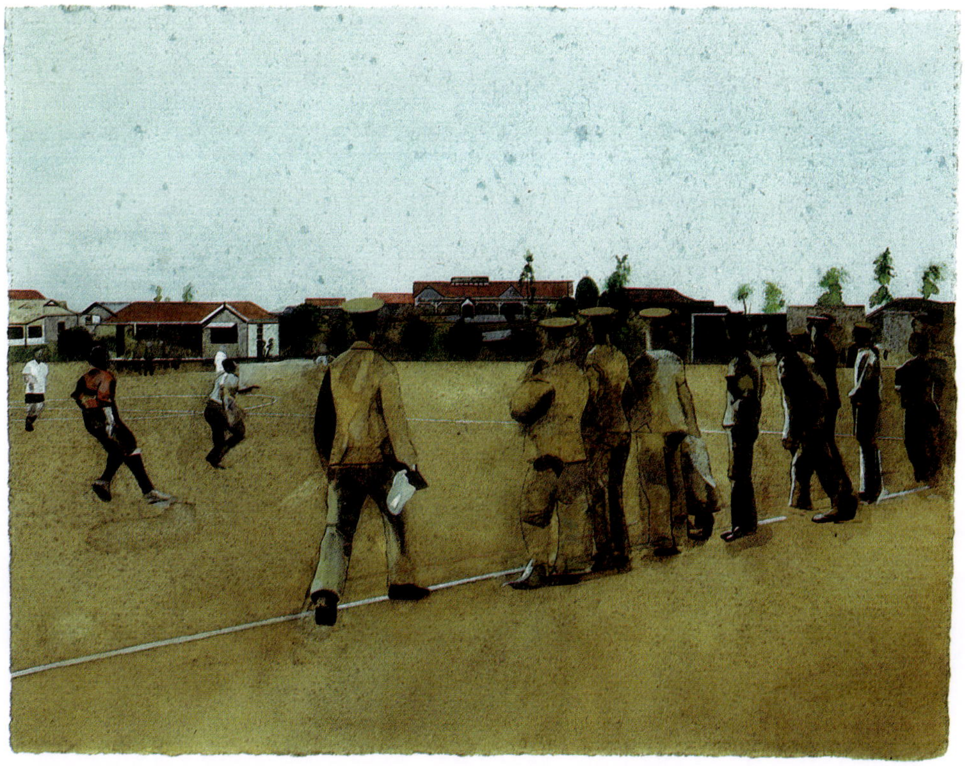

154 Tommies Playing Football, 1984

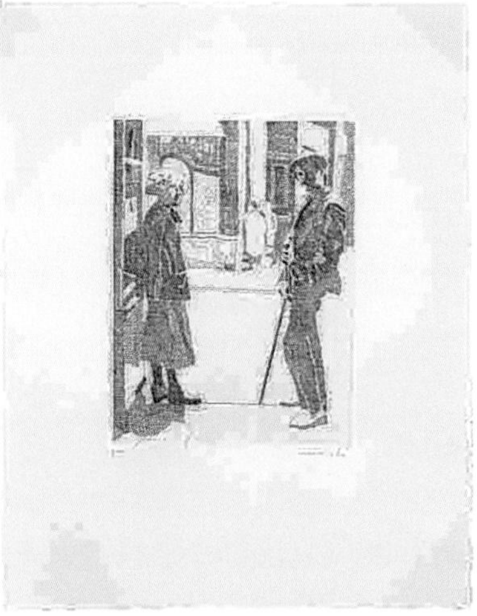

155 Sylvia Beach and James Joyce in front of her bookshop 'Shakespeare & Company', 1983–4, from the portfolio *James Joyce in Paris/Series of nine etchings 1983–1984*

In 1983 he was sent by his print publishers of the time, Waddington Graphics, to work in Paris for three weeks with the master printer Aldo Crommelynck, one of the great etching printers of the twentieth century. Crommelynck had worked with Picasso and Matisse from his late teens, and later formed important partnerships with such major artists of Blake's own generation as Jim Dine, Richard Hamilton and David Hockney. Whereas they all arrived in Paris already armed with considerable experience with etching, Blake turned up without ever having used the medium before except briefly as a student. During their first week together in the workshop, Crommelynck patiently taught Blake the rudimentary techniques. In the second week, Blake settled on *James Joyce in Paris* as the subject for a portfolio of nine etchings, making reference in part to photographs by Gisèle Freund that he found in the book she co-authored with V.B. Carleton, *James Joyce in Paris: The Final Years* (New York: Harcourt, Brace & World, 1965).

Perhaps slightly daunted by the pressure of having to take command of a new medium at such speed and needing to produce an entire suite of prints that would be commercially viable, Blake decided to avoid some of the more elaborate processes used by Crommelynck – such as sugar-lift – and to employ instead the most economical combination of outline and dense cross-hatching, sometimes with the addition of aquatint. The example of Walter Richard Sickert's sparser etchings, some of which also relied on photographic sources, seems to have been of particular relevance. One of Blake's images, *Joyce's Dance by Desmond Harmsworth*, is created with a spare and lively shorthand reminiscent of early twentieth-century drawings by such French artists as Henri Matisse and Albert Marquet, adding to the nostalgic atmosphere of these evocations of a particular period of life in Paris, of its café society and of its literary circles; in fact, it is derived from a drawing by the British artist and publisher named in the title. Crisply delineated, faithful to their photographic sources and basking in the dandyish elegance of their subject, prints such as *Sylvia Beach and James Joyce in front of her bookshop 'Shakespeare & Company'* (1983–4, Plate 155) are among Blake's most reticent but attractive prints. On completion of the series there were problems over the issue of copyright for the photographs from which the etchings drew inspiration, sadly limiting their distribution. Only on rare occasions has he since returned to etching, notably for a portfolio yet to be completed on the subject of (Sir John) *Betjeman's Women*. In general, he has preferred to make much bolder, colourful and decorative screenprints or (more recently) digital prints based on his collages or scanned from found objects and printed ephemera.

Exoticism

Blake often seems quintessentially English as an artist. This comes through in his gentle humour and love of whimsy, in his references to the great children's book illustrations of the nineteenth century and in his celebrations of native traditions of typographic and graphic design. It is evident also in his recreations of various forms of English folk and popular art (including barge painting, fairground art and circus and wrestling posters), in his depictions of animals and in his idyllic portraits of life in the countryside and the village. Paradoxically, one of the ways in which from time to time he has expressed this outlook has been through his forays into exotic subjects, tapping as they do into the strain of Romanticism that came particularly to the fore in the early nineteenth century, when British artists travelled to Egypt, the Near East and other sun-drenched locations to document the landscape and customs of an unfamiliar way of life.

As usual, Blake created his own innovative response to such themes and found his original solutions, paradoxically, by availing himself (as he has often done) of existing pictorial material created by others. The postcards he had collected over the years provided the substance of some of his earliest paintings of this sort, such as *Aparicio* (1963, Plate 63), *Le Petit Porteur* (1964–5, Plate 65) and *Bedouin* (1964–5, Plate 66), all of which are included in chapter 2 in the context of Pop Art. It was in this same spirit that he later produced such works as *An Arab Woman* (Plate 156), an oil on canvas completed in 1981,

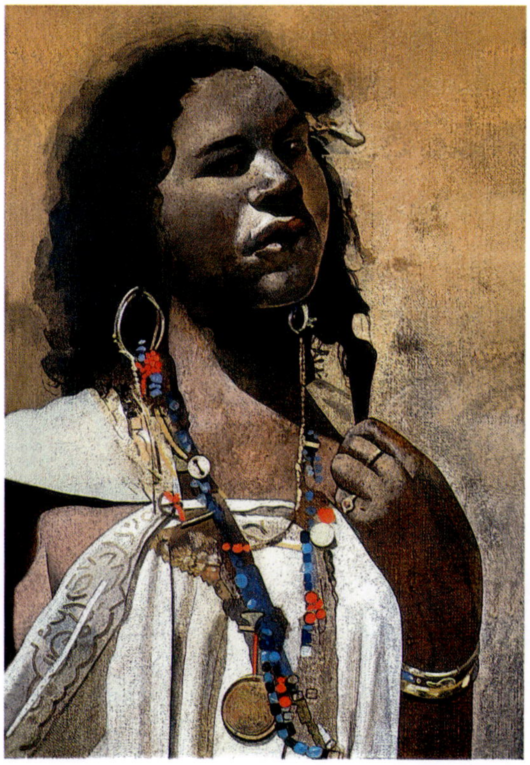

156 An Arab Woman, 1981

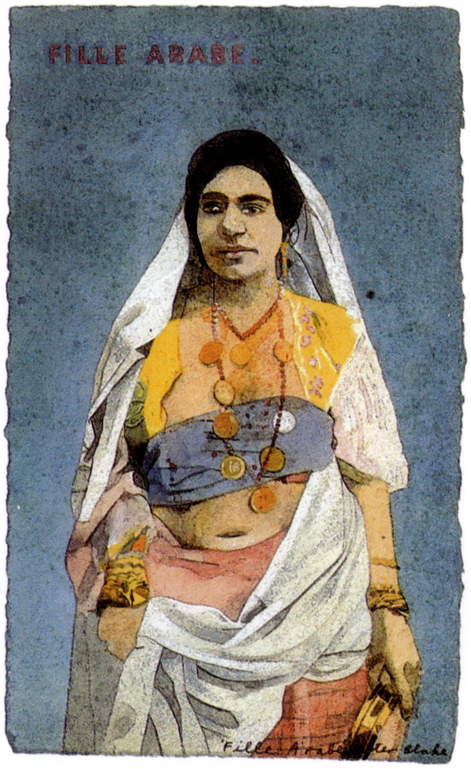

157 Fille Arabe, 1984

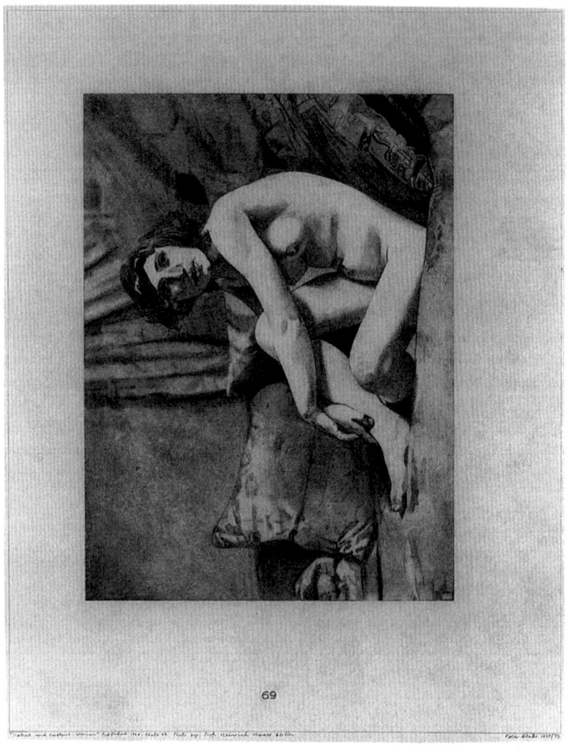

158 Plate 69, Czech Woman. Photo by Professor Heinrich Maass, Berlin, from *Nature and Culture, Woman* series, 1973–7

the 1984 watercolour *Fille Arabe* (Plate 157) and (between 1973 and 1977) a set of five softly shaded pencil drawings meticulously copied from an ethnographic volume of 120 black-and-white photographs published in 1928 as *Nature and Culture*. Each of these drawings is titled, with poker-faced matter-of-factness, with the caption accompanying the source photograph in the book. One such work, with the wonderfully anthropological-sounding title *Plate 69. Czech Woman. Photo by Professor Heinrich Maass, Berlin* (1973–7, Plate 158), is hung on its side, mimicking the orientation of the photograph in the book.

Shakespeare and Fairies: The Ruralist Period

In 1969 Blake left London with Jann Haworth and his infant daughter Liberty to settle in a former railway station in the village of Wellow, Avon, just outside of the beautiful Georgian city of Bath. Their second daughter, Daisy, was born there (in a cottage hospital in Somerset) in 1974 and Peter and Jann continued to live there until their separation in 1979. This period of retreat into the countryside, paralleling the escape from London to Wiltshire of other artist friends, notably Howard Hodgkin, Richard Smith and Joe Tilson, brought with it substantial changes in his art. That 'mass exodus' to the country was, as he later explained, part of a general exhaustion that he and some of his fellow movers and shakers felt at the end of the 1960s with London and the ever more tedious demands put

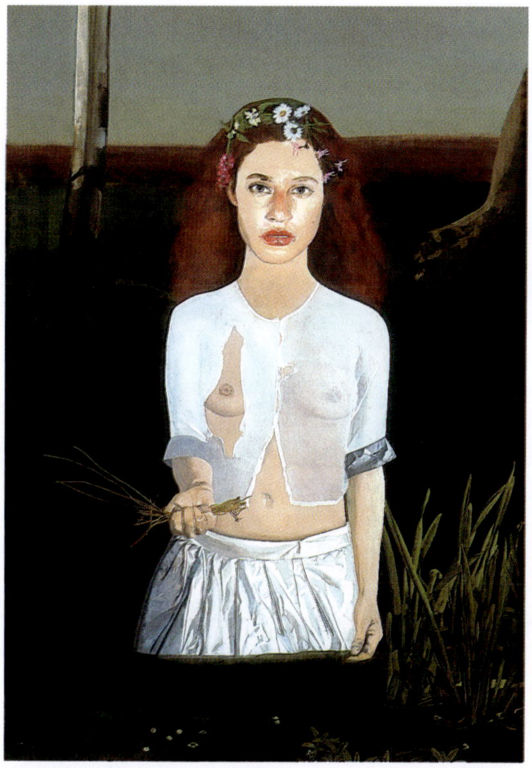

159 Ophelia, 1977–2002

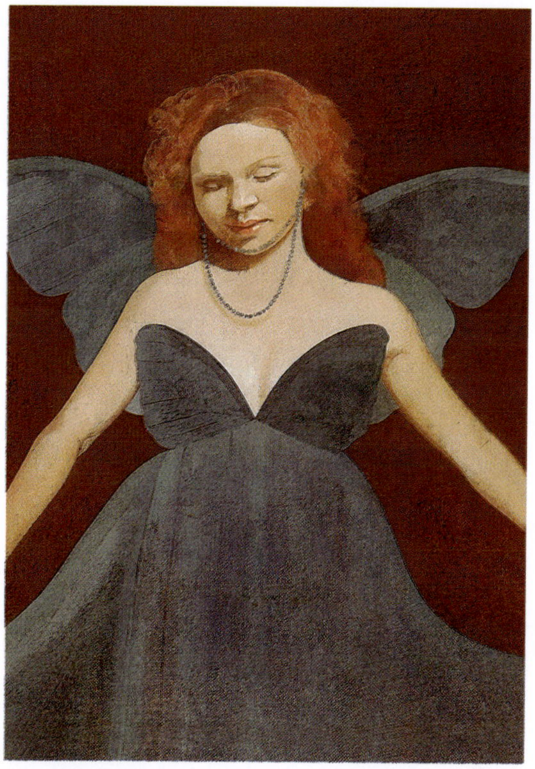

160 Firoza, 1973–4

on them by the media in search of another soundbite. However pronounced his fascination with celebrity culture, and whatever pleasure he experienced in his own growing fame, he clearly found it distasteful to be constantly drawn into the shallowness of the journalistic domain. It was in any case bad for his concentration to be repeatedly interrupted by such requests. By the end of the 1960s, he must have been at his wits' end, given the way in which he had spoken about just these issues in the Levy interview published in November 1963:

> I want to get out of the limelight. I just want to paint in peace. Too much publicity is dangerous; but the most destructive thing of all for a young painter is the premature, often inflated reputation that has already killed so many talents in recent years. This I am determined to avoid, and this means refusing to permit any particular dealer to run your life for you. So I'm just going to teach a bit and paint in seclusion. Besides, I want to re-establish the idea of myself as *a painter;* as an artist who uses *paint.*

By 1968 the Blakes had also come to the conclusion that a rural existence would be healthier for their young child, a decision hastened by the fact that the landlady of their flat in London did not like having children among her tenants. They were never exactly hippies (though Jann later came to refer self-deprecatingly to this phase of her sculpture as her 'hippie period'), and they never lived a communal existence, but they felt close to the land and sought to live a self-sufficient existence, keeping chickens and growing their own fruit and vegetables. This sense of oneness with nature, which also became an important element of Tilson's work during those years, soon became a notable feature of Blake's art, which had previously been either grittily urban or more gently suburban in its orientation.

In 1975 Blake and Haworth formed a close association with other artists – including Graham and Ann Arnold, David Inshaw and Graham and Annie Ovenden – as the Brotherhood of Ruralists, a name consciously evoking their Victorian predecessors, the Pre-Raphaelite Brotherhood. Inshaw and the Arnolds had already been part of a group known as the Broadheath Brotherhood. Blake first met Inshaw when coordinating a group exhibition for the Bath Festival, a show to which the post-Minimalist sculptor Richard Long, resident in Bristol, declined to contribute because he felt that the space was too small for presenting one of his works. Through Inshaw, Blake then met Graham Arnold, and during an after-dinner conversation on 21 March 1975 they talked about the Pre-Raphaelites and asked each other which of those mid nineteenth-century artists they would have been. Blake said that he identified with Sir John Everett Millais, for whose work he had particular enthusiasm. Out of this playful chat the idea was born to form their own society of artists. Although they lived in a variety of locations, they would meet for a big picnic for the Summer Solstice and for a feast at the Winter Solstice, and every summer for about four or five years they all decamped to a small Cornish village, Coombe, where each family

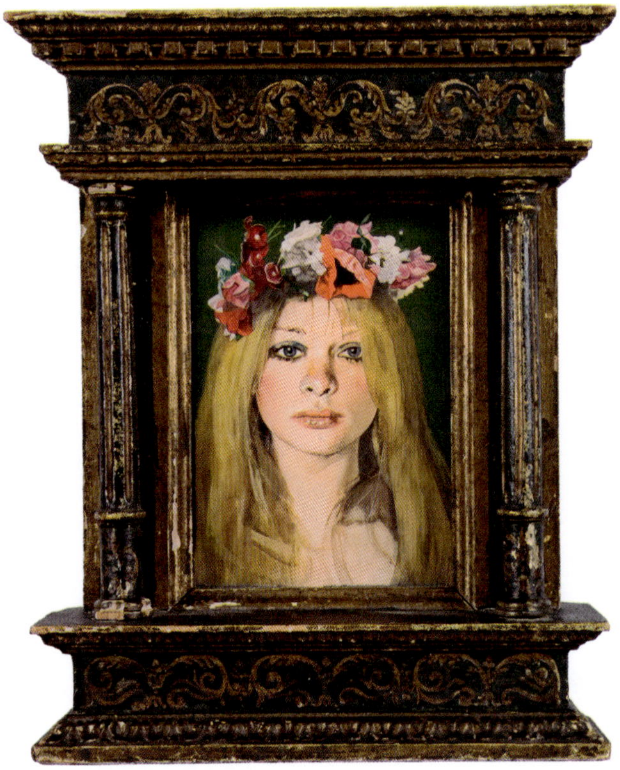

161 **Flora – Fairy Child**, 1977

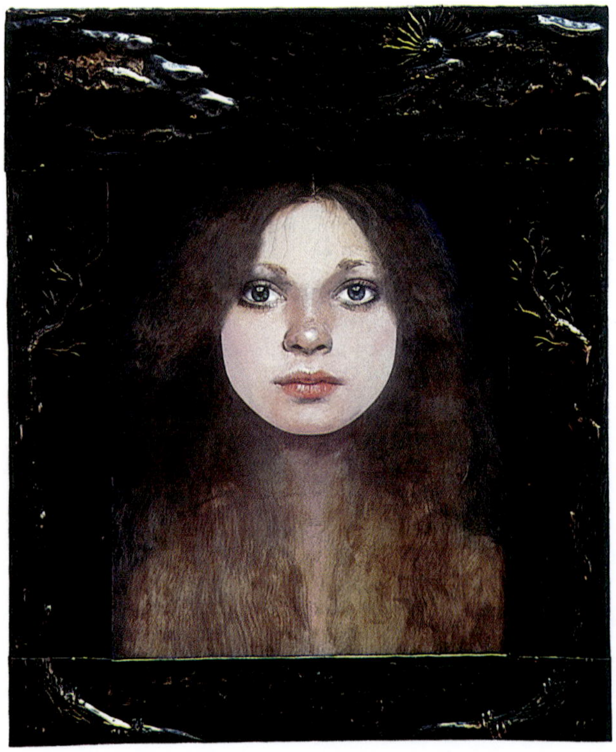

162 **Titania**, 1977

rented one of the Landmark Trust cottages. During their days there they would draw each other, go out on painting excursions and meet for dinner. Although Blake, as the best-known of the artists, was often assumed to be their leader, they were keen on an egalitarian outlook, judging each of the artists to have his or her particular strengths and areas of expertise.

The Brotherhood of Ruralists first exhibited together as part of a room selected by Blake at the *Royal Academy Summer Exhibition* in 1976. With the disappearance of the urban basis of his previous work, his Pop orientation gave way to the rich vein of fantasy and imagination that had provided a subtext for his earlier pictures. His watercolour illustrations for Lewis Carroll's *Through the Looking-Glass,* painted in 1969–71 and disseminated to a much wider audience in the form of limited-edition screenprints, heralded other literary subjects. These include a number of pictures derived from Shakespeare, including several relating to *A Midsummer Night's Dream,* such as *Titania* (1976–83, Plate 152) and various fairy subjects endowed with a similar eroticised and magical atmosphere. The 'Ruralist' interlude brought him more closely into contact with literature, with nature and with the dreamlike and often openly sentimental pictures, including of fairy subjects, by Victorian artists such as Richard Doyle, Joseph Noël Patton and, above all, the extraordinary Richard Dadd. The latter's masterpiece, *The Fairy Feller's Master-Stroke* (1855–64), in which tiny figures of Oberon and Titania appear among the many figments of his own imagination, had entered the collection of the Tate Gallery in 1963.

With no appointed leader and no firm programme of intent, the Ruralists were left to

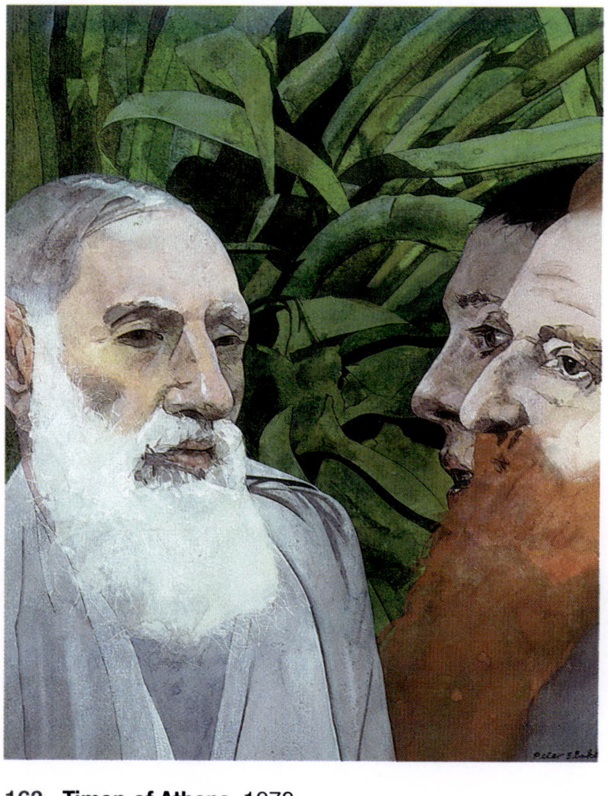

163 **Timon of Athens**, 1978

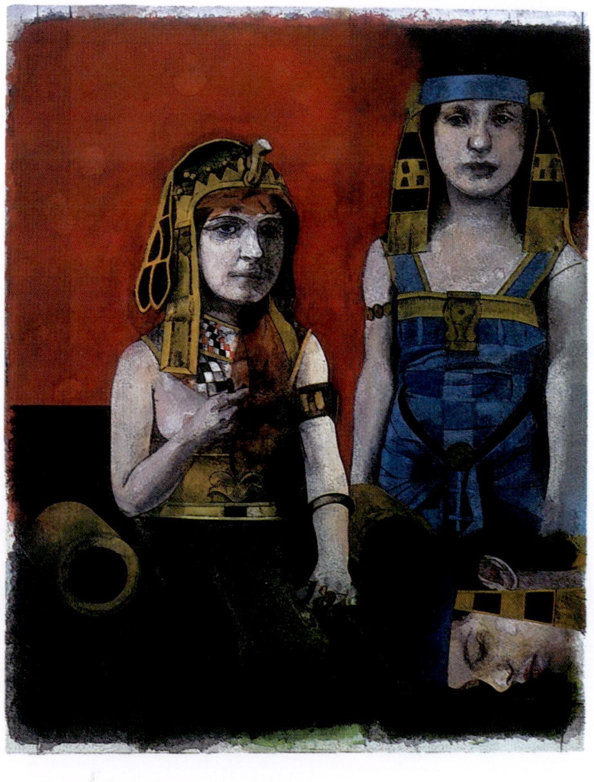

164 **Antony and Cleopatra**, 1979

explore their personal concerns in the styles that most suited them, with predominating strains of bucolic Englishness, photographically derived or more naively detailed magical realism and a sometimes titillating eroticism that helped push these already slightly fruity elements to the edge of kitsch. They never published a manifesto, and the closest that Blake himself came to a declaration of intent was in an article, 'Contrariwise', that he published in the spring 1978 issue of a quarterly journal, *Aspects*; this was written in the context of an ongoing battle with the art critics Richard Cork, Paul Overy, Caroline Tisdall and Peter Fuller, all of whom had intemperately attacked his art when it was shown in 1977 in the context of the *Hayward Annual* group exhibition. As he explained in one of the more relaxed passages included, almost as an aside, within the context of a more argumentative piece:

> Simply, our aims are the continuation of a certain kind of English painting; we admire Samuel Palmer, Stanley Spencer, Thomas Hardy, Elgar, cricket, English Landscape, the Pre-Raphaelites, etc. This is just a short list, as names come to mind, but perhaps it will give you an idea. The word 'Ruralist' means 'a person who has moved from the city to the country' – which we all have done. Our aims are to paint about love, beauty, joy, sentiment and magic. We all still believe in painting with oil paint on canvas, putting the picture in a frame and, hopefully, that someone will like it, buy it and hang it on their wall to enjoy it.

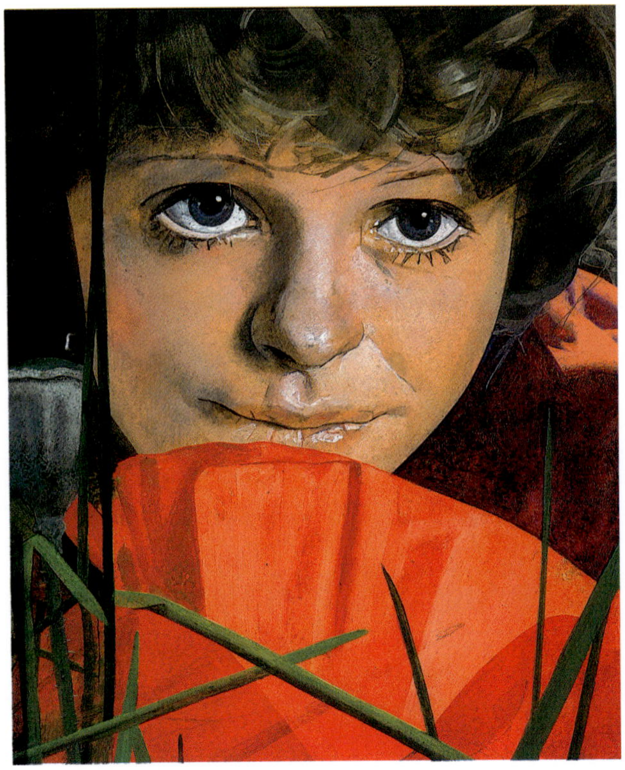

165 Poppy Fairy, 1981–2

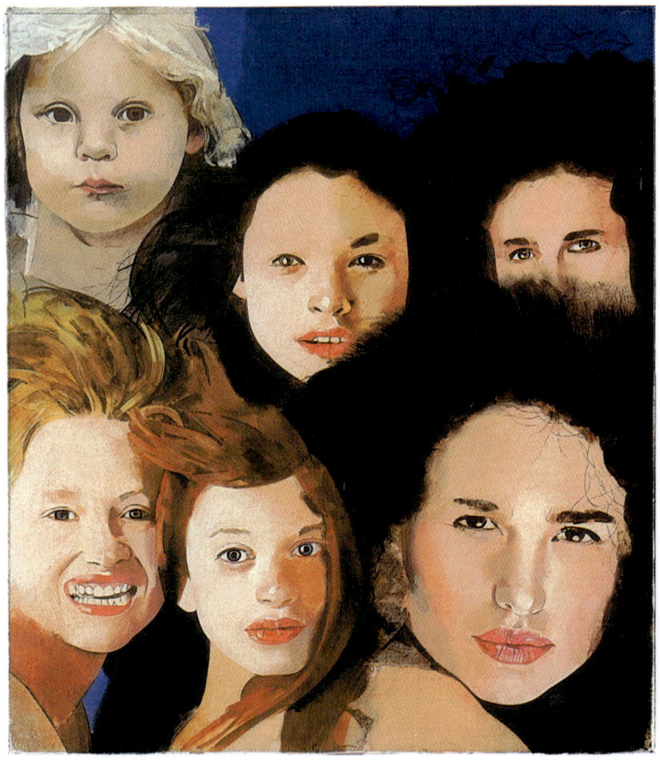

166 Titania with Attendants, 1986 (unfinished)

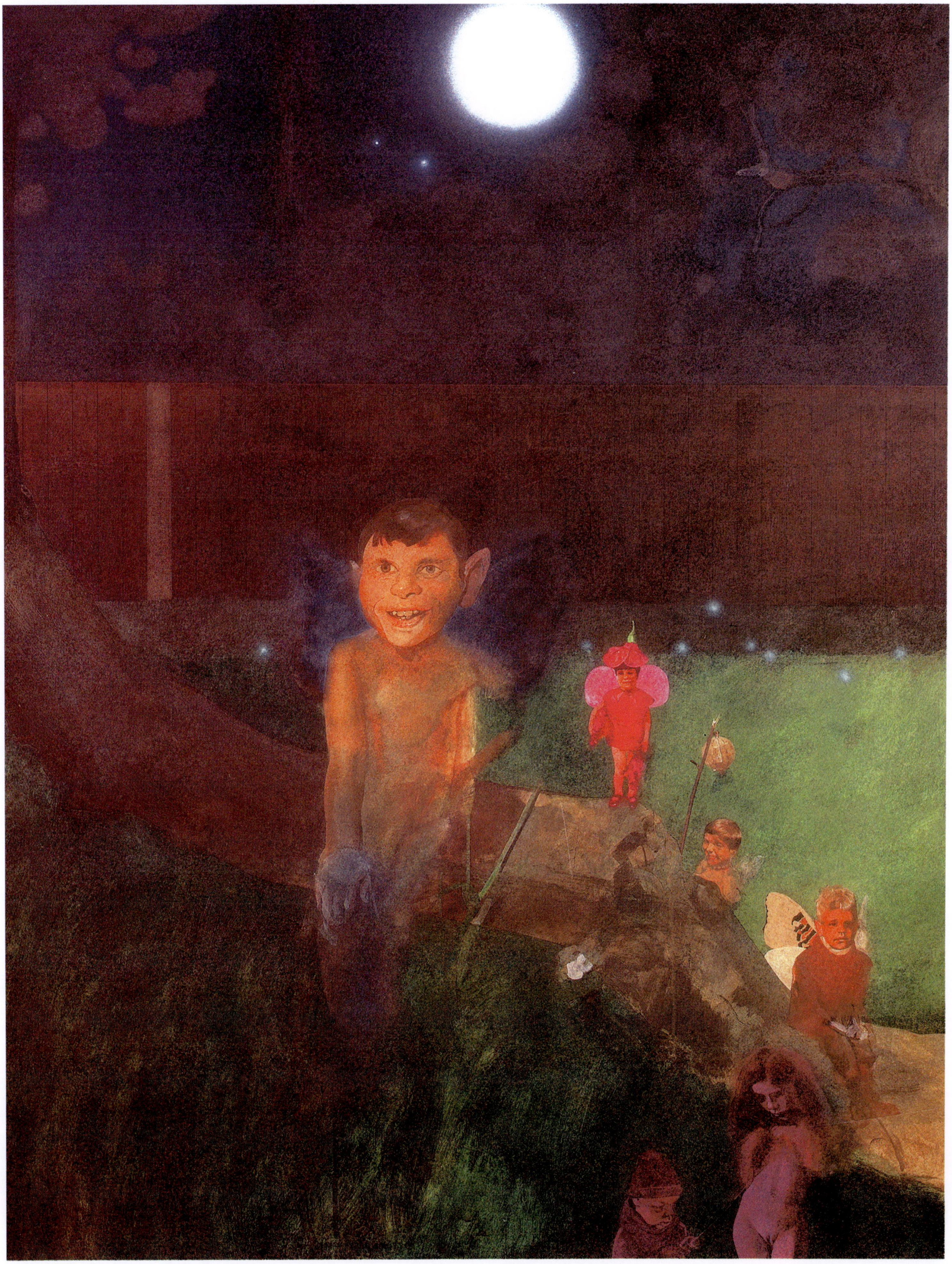

167 **Puck, Peasebottom, Cobweb, Moth and Mustardseed,** 1969–84

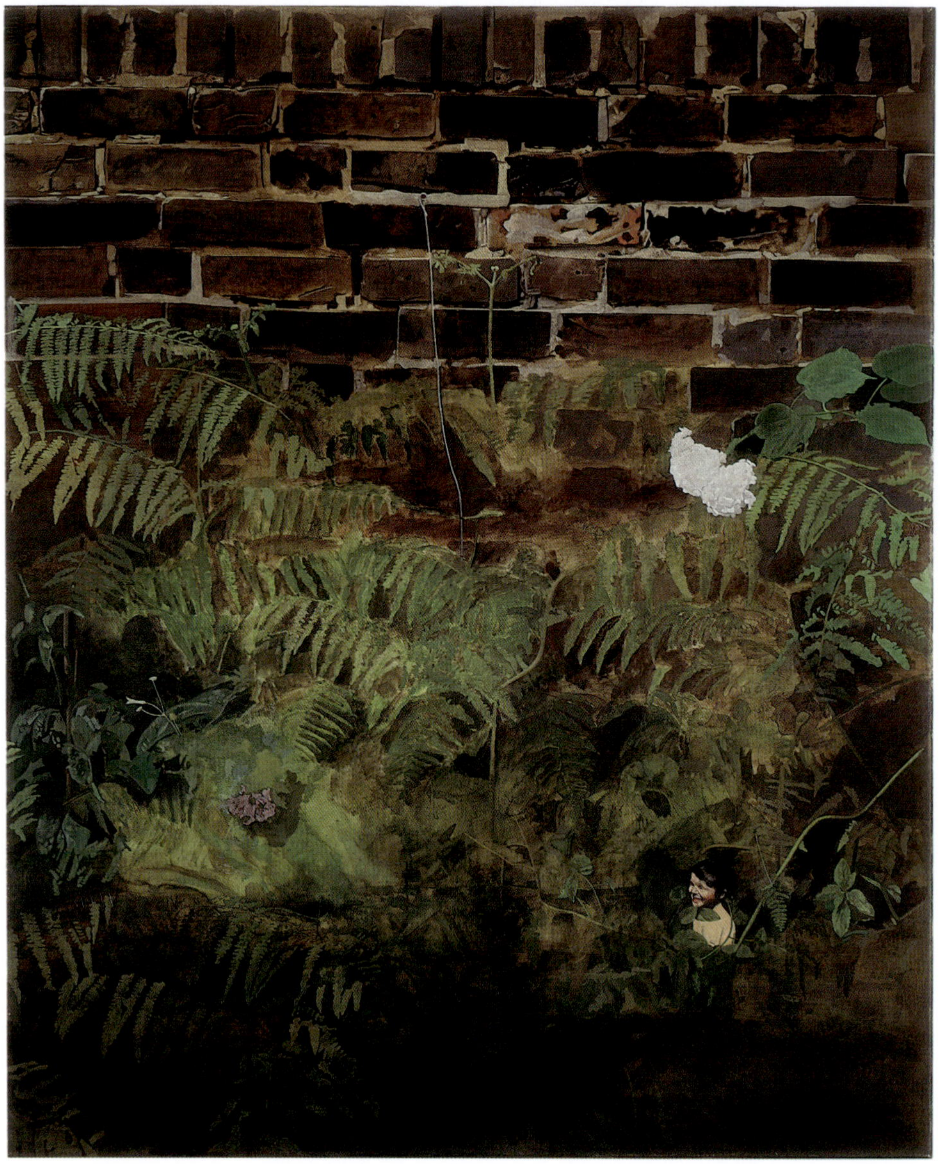

168 I may not be a Ruralist anymore, but this morning I saw a fairy in my garden in Chiswick, 1982–91

Blake made a great variety of work during his decade-long sojourn in the country, some of it still attuned to the more Pop and urban concerns expressed in his art of the 1950s and 1960s. Among these are a marvellous series of watercolours depicting imaginary wrestlers (1972), an intricately rendered set of five wood engravings on the theme of a *Side Show* (1974–8), paintings of Tarzan and his family, posters and other commercial art designs and the extensive series of collages and assemblages conceived as *Souvenirs* for artist friends. These works are all discussed separately in other chapters, contextualised within the artist's various thematic concerns. The pictures that one most closely identifies with Blake's Ruralist period, however, are those that are deeply rooted in an attachment to the English countryside as a timeless place of magic, enchantment and mystery. Referencing Victorian fairy painting and justifying the fantastical subject matter largely by reference to Shakespeare, Blake escaped for a time into a neverland of luxuriant sensuousness (even licentiousness).

There is an undoubted charm in his various portraits of Titania (Plates 152, 162) and in a large oil painting of an alluring *Ophelia* (Plate 159), begun in 1977 but not completed until 2002, which is disarmingly tinged at once with a frank eroticism and a childlike innocence and whimsy. The garlands of daisies and other flowers that crown not only Ophelia but other young women presented as vixens and temptresses, including *Flora – Fairy Child* (1977, Plate 161) and *Daisy Fairy* (1981–2), might now strike us as perhaps just a little too pretty and sentimental, the last vestiges of a hippy dream still surviving in the English countryside while punk anger raged in the cities. Depending on the viewer's own temperament and perspective, these might well seem to cross the line from the captivating to the cloying. It is undeniable, however, that in purely painterly terms these Ruralist pictures are among Blake's most successful representations of the human figure, as compelling in their realism as in their flights of fancy. Painted with fine brushes and built up with layer upon layer of thin glazes, they reveal an impressive technical command and an ambition to take on the Old Masters in a language now largely forsaken by contemporary artists. The gradations of tone and colour in the rendering of the face and body endow them with a miraculous sense of life – one can see the dewy moisture on the skin of these girls – and in the detailed observation of their facial features one finds oneself confronted also by the intense individuality of each person portrayed.

Blake set to work on the first of his fairy paintings, *Puck, Peasebottom, Cobweb, Moth and Mustardseed* (Plate 167), in 1969, the very year that he settled in Wellow, though it was to take him a further 15 years to complete to his satisfaction. Its literary source is, of course, the most spellbinding of Shakespeare's plays, *A Midsummer Night's Dream.* Blake concentrates his attention on Puck, servant to Oberon, and on the train of Titania's fairy servants. Eerily illuminated by moonlight, these pixies emerge from the undergrowth as pranksterish creatures from another world, ready to make mischief as they draw us into a land of pure reverie. Blake had never hidden the pleasure he took in escaping into make-believe, and even after his return to London – partly in response to the aforementioned brutal attacks written by a handful of art critics – he continued to express his defiant embrace of the otherworldly with an amusingly titled painting *I may not be a Ruralist anymore but this morning I saw a fairy in my garden in Chiswick* (Plate 168), begun in 1982 and completed in 1991. Like his Ruralist paintings proper, this meticulously rendered view of a small corner of an urban garden proposes a unity between microcosm and macrocosm and an unwavering belief in the power of the imagination. As a get-out clause, Blake need only quote from Puck's epilogue:

> If we shadows have offended,
> Think but this, and all is mended:
> That you have but slumber'd here,
> While these visions did appear.

Lewis Carroll and Alice

Given the love of Victoriana, the memories of childhood, the celebration of innocence, the taste for fantasy and the central role accorded to the imagination manifested in Blake's art from the time he reached adulthood in 1953, there is an air of inevitability about the choice of Lewis Carroll's tales of a young girl's adventures as a source of inspiration for one of the most intoxicating series of pictures of his maturity. Yet these eight watercolours of 1970–71, and the screenprints made from them (Plates 170–77) might never have come about had a publisher not suggested the possibility of bringing out a new edition of *Through the Looking-Glass* (on the centenary of its publication in 1872) to be illustrated by Blake, paired with a similar edition of *Alice in Wonderland* with drawings by Graham Ovenden, whose fascination with the Alice books had initially led Blake to this subject matter. These book editions were abandoned and the pictures were immediately published instead in the form of limited-edition screenprints, but the literary context remains paramount in the understanding of images intended to be 'read' visually in every sense.

Blake based his Alice pictures on black-and-white photographs he took himself during a Dutch holiday to the home of an Englishman called Peter Gatacre, whose grandmother had created gardens inspired by Alice in Wonderland. Abandoning his original plan to make a film of Alice with Gatacre's children acting out the roles, he used his host's three children as models for his illustrations: Amelia as Alice and again as one of Tweedledum and Tweedledee with her sister Sophie, with William as the Mad Hatter. For the settings he decided in the end not to photograph the garden in Holland, but to take his cue instead from the photographs he found in an Edwardian book on gardening. Blake later described the process of making these pictures and reproduced some of the source material, photographs and preparatory drawings in an illustrated edition of Carroll's book, titled in full *Alice Through the Looking-Glass and What Alice Found There*, published in London by Merrell Publishers Ltd in 2006. Thus, like so many of Blake's paintings and exhibition projects, the commission finally reached its intended resolution long after it was first proposed: in this case after a waiting period of over 35 years.

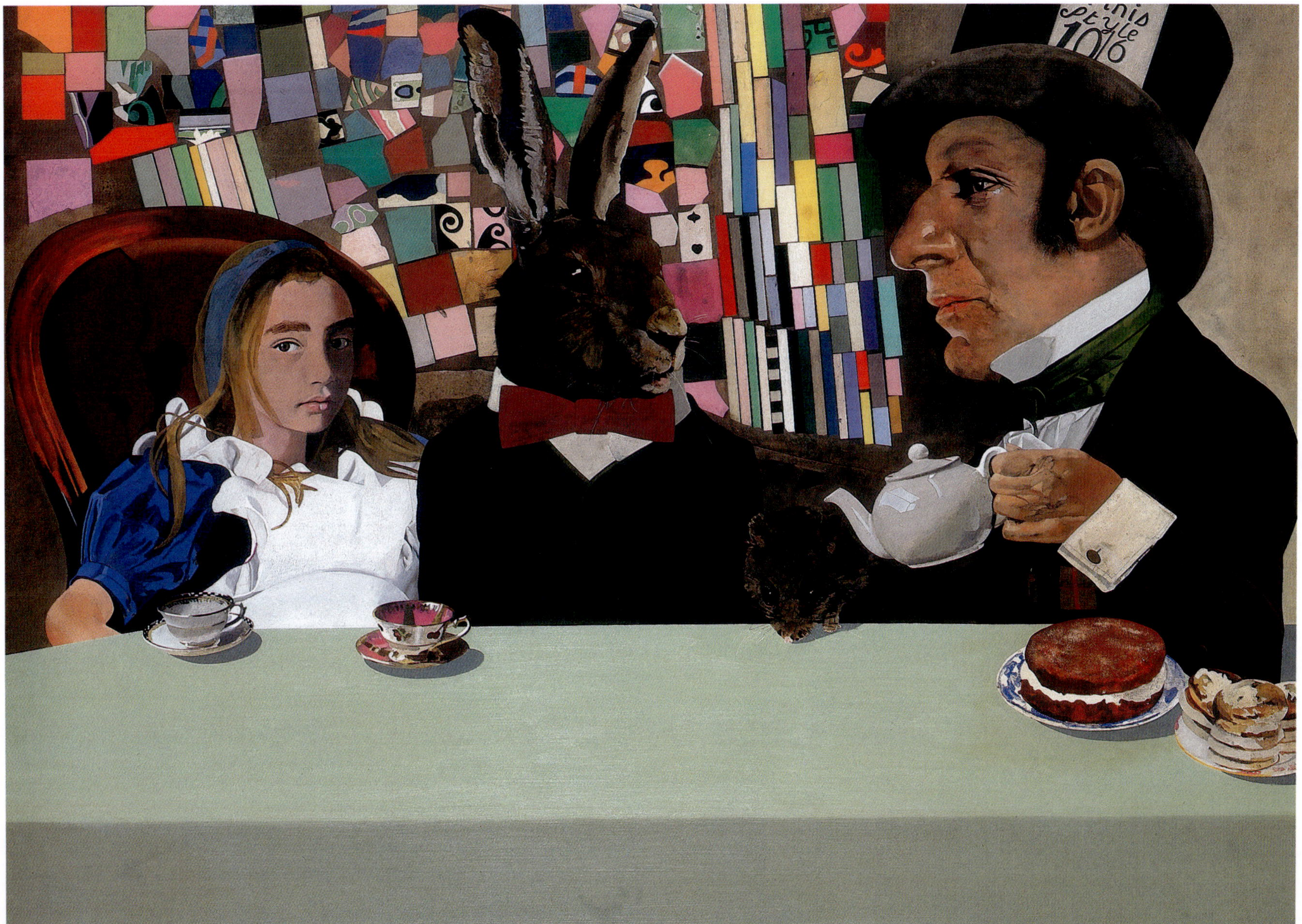

169 **A Mad Tea Party at Watts Tower**, 1968–92

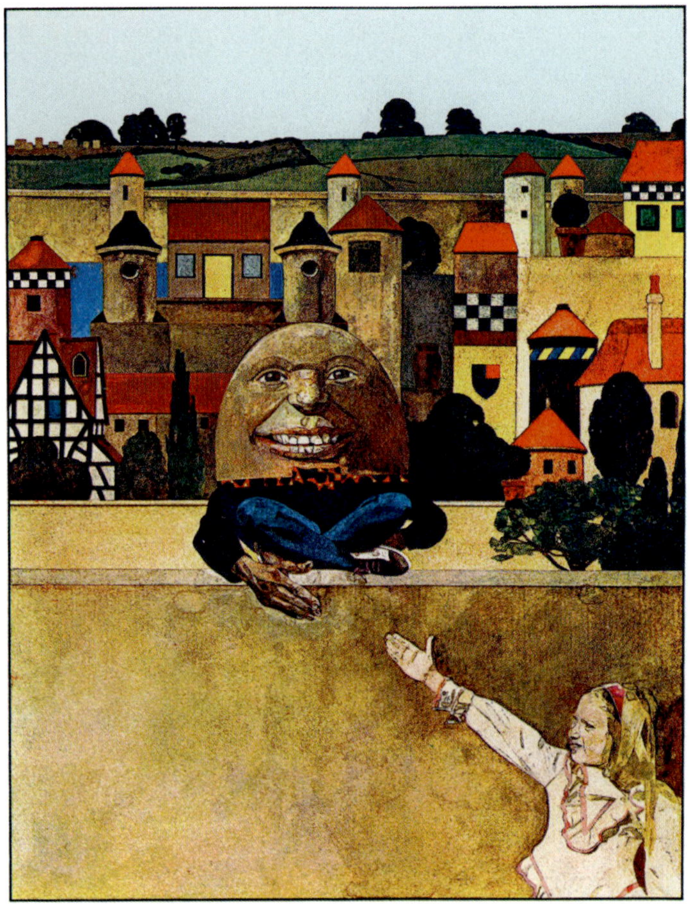

170 'And to show you I'm not proud, you may shake hands with me!'

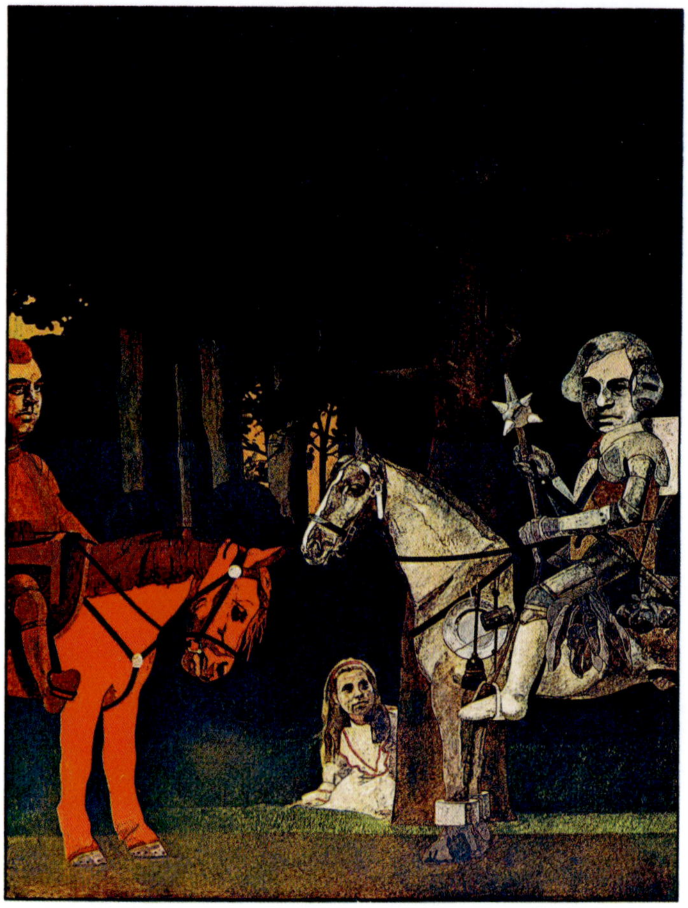

171 And the two knights sat and looked at each other for some time without speaking

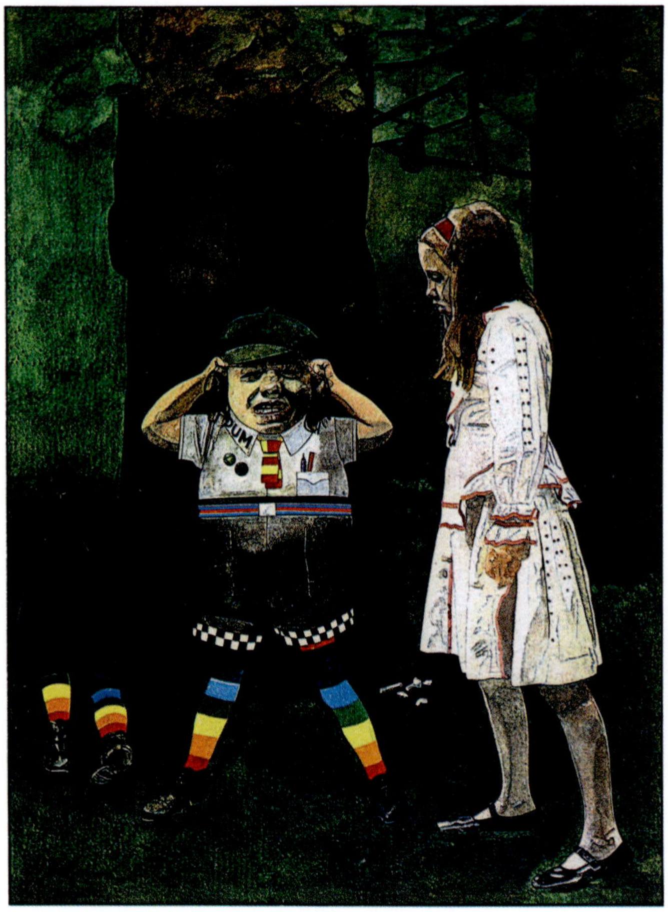

172 'But it isn't old!' Tweedledum cried

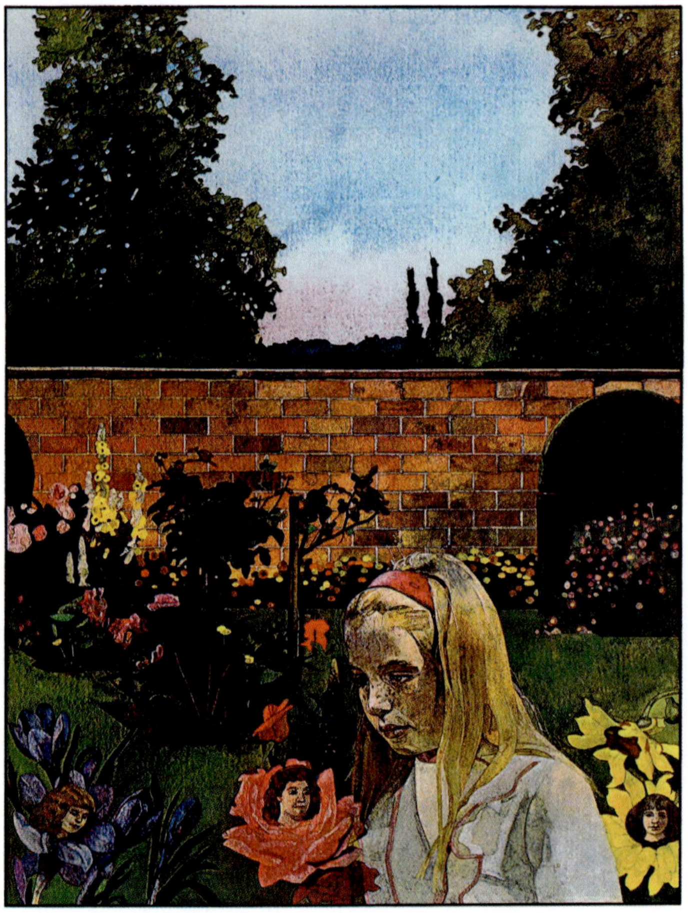

173 'It isn't manners for us to begin, you know,' said the Rose

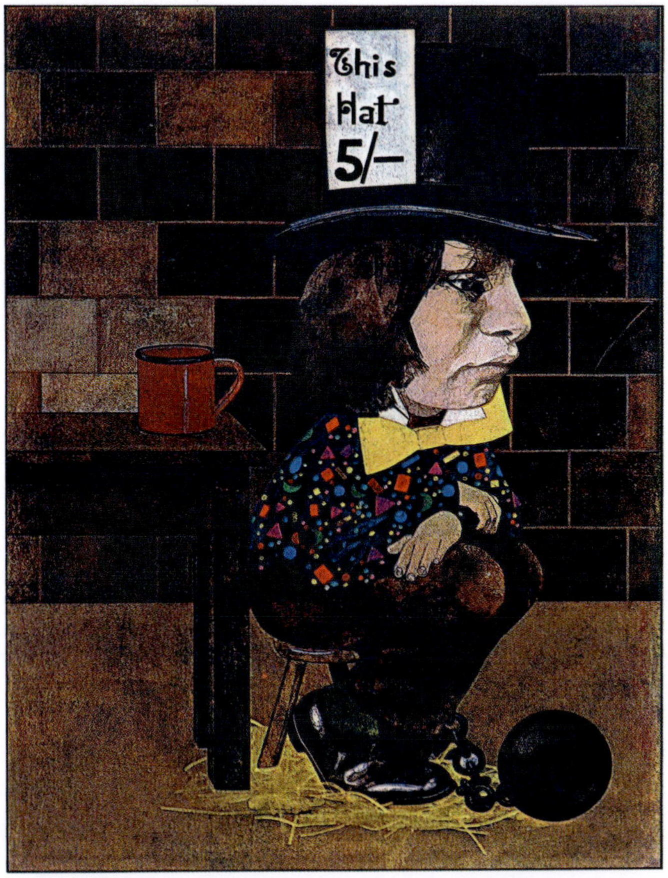

174 For instance now, there's the King's messenger

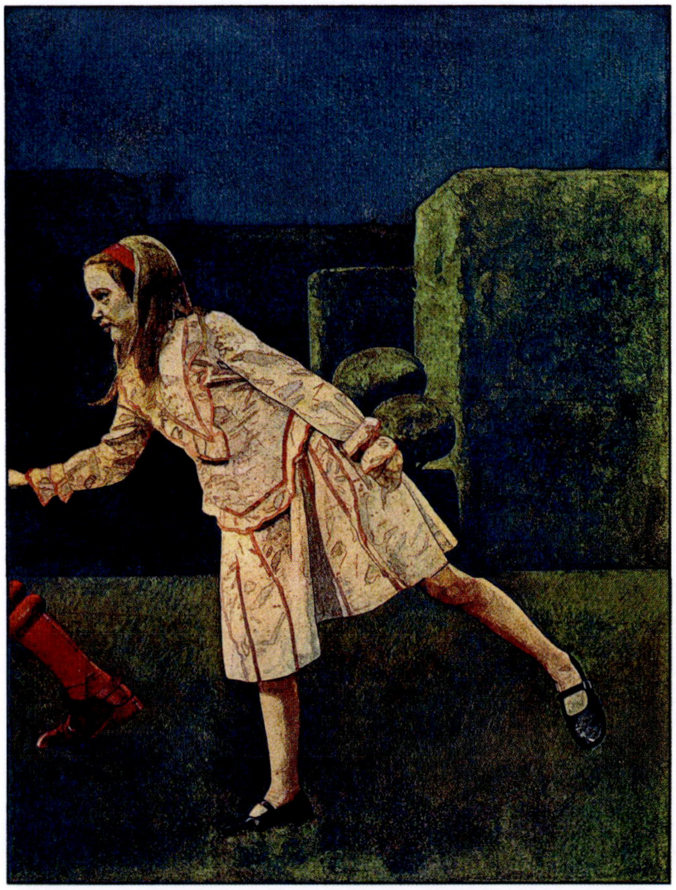

175 Just at this moment, somehow or other, they began to run

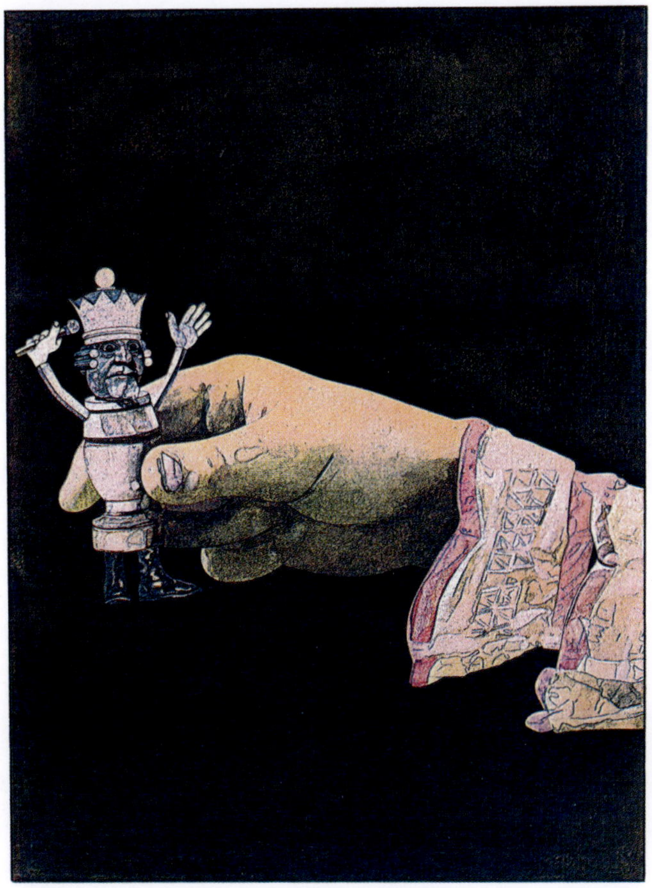

176 So Alice picked him up very gently

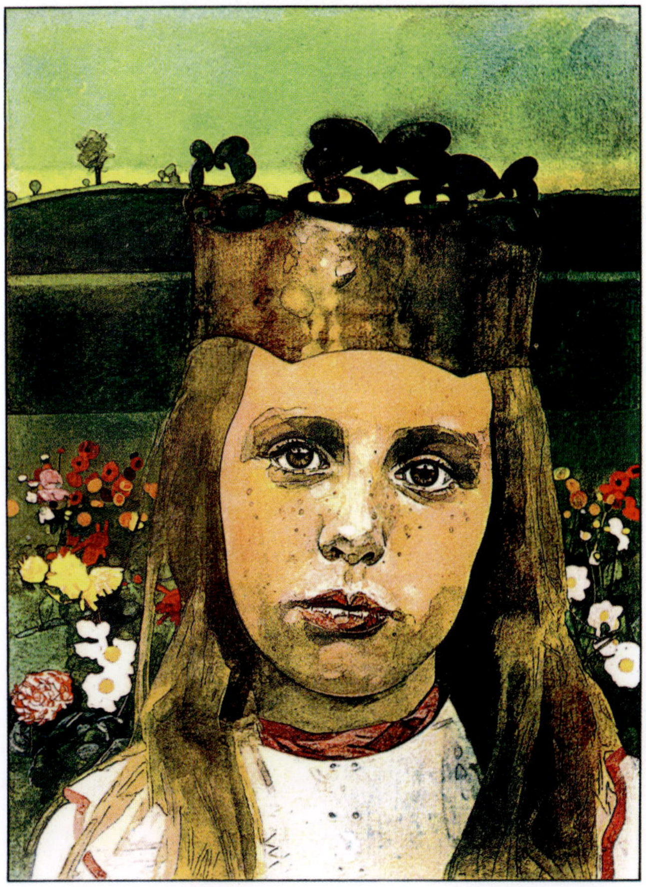

177 'Well, this is grand!' said Alice

Illustrations to Lewis Carroll's *Through the Looking Glass*, 1972

Many of the vital strands of Blake's work come together in these delicately worked yet richly layered watercolours, which render homage to earlier sources (notably John Tenniel's original illustrations for the same story) while being voiced unmistakably in a late twentieth-century idiom. However removed they might seem from the Pop Art pioneered by Blake in the late 1950s, because of their handmade quality and illustrational deference to a literary source, the familiarity of the novel's imagery to the general public nevertheless guaranteed an equivalent popular appeal. They are also unmistakably the work of a painter who, as discussed, was equally at home functioning as a fine artist or as a commercial artist responding to commissions.

These immaculately rendered pictures display a miniaturist's concern with the details of surface appearance, allied to a decorative opulence worthy of manuscript illumination and an illustrator's eye for capturing key narrative moments on which the unfolding of the narrative hinges. Painstakingly built up over tracings from photographs, they convey a fidelity to optical appearances typical of the traditional (and almost academic) naturalism that the artist himself sees as the central thread of his art. Yet they convey above all a delight in creating a parallel universe, in which – to borrow a phrase from John Lennon's 'Strawberry Fields Forever', a poignant song of remembered childhood – 'nothing is real'. Perfectly placed to take his public on a wholly believable visual journey into the realms of the unexpected, Blake created what might best be called a form of magical realism. The potent imagery and memorable characters created by Lewis Carroll could not fail to have stimulated the minds of artists, beginning notably with Tenniel himself. However, Carroll has been more than fortunate in prompting, a century later, Blake's eight illustrations which teem with information and are suffused in a dreamlike atmosphere, exerting their fascination as windows into another world.

Screenprinting, used here as an essentially photomechanical process, might seem a contrary choice of medium for disseminating such personal and resolutely handpainted pictures. As recently as 1962, when Andy Warhol and Robert Rauschenberg both began to employ the process in their paintings, screenprinting was regarded as a crude medium appropriate for advertising posters or commercial packaging, but contentious in a fine-art context. In Britain Eduardo Paolozzi, one of the most experimental of the proto-Pop artists, had engaged with it in three prints during the 1950s as a convenience for reproducing collaged found images, but even he did not at that time recognise its full potential. That all changed with the publication in 1964 of the ICA portfolio, masterminded by Richard Hamilton, to which 24 artists (including Blake, with his *The Beach Boys* print, Plate 74) contributed. Chris Prater, previously a commercial silkscreen printer, took charge. The success of the project, and the enthusiasm with which the medium was immediately embraced by many artists, enabled Prater to give up his commercial assignments and to devote his Kelpra Studio entirely to collaborations with artists. By the end of the 1960s he was indisputably the great master of screenprinting as a fine-art medium, having by that time worked with such eminent artists (and friends of Blake) as Hamilton, Patrick Caulfield, Peter Phillips, R.B. Kitaj and Joe Tilson, in each case expanding the possibilities of the medium according to their own aesthetic principles and ways of working.

It was a foregone conclusion that Prater should be entrusted with the reinterpretation of Blake's *Alice* watercolours as screenprints. What could not have been anticipated is that Prater would devise such a straightforwardly practical solution for conveying the subtle detail and range of colours and tones of Blake's paintings. Instead of creating a huge number of screens for the different colours, he worked from photographs of the watercolours that he then broke down into separate screens to be printed in the basic colours used in commercial offset lithography (for example, for colour magazines): yellow, cyan and magenta, plus black. Prater's stroke of genius was to print each sheet several times in each colour, creating a density of pigment equivalent to the watercolour washes of the originals. Given the technology available at the time, long before computers and digital imaging, the results were both subtle and visually rich.

Four of Blake's *Alice* designs were later also translated into large stained-glass panels, originally intended to be incorporated into a small chapel dedicated to Lewis Carroll in Somerset, a project formulated with Ovenden. The first of these appears to have been sold,

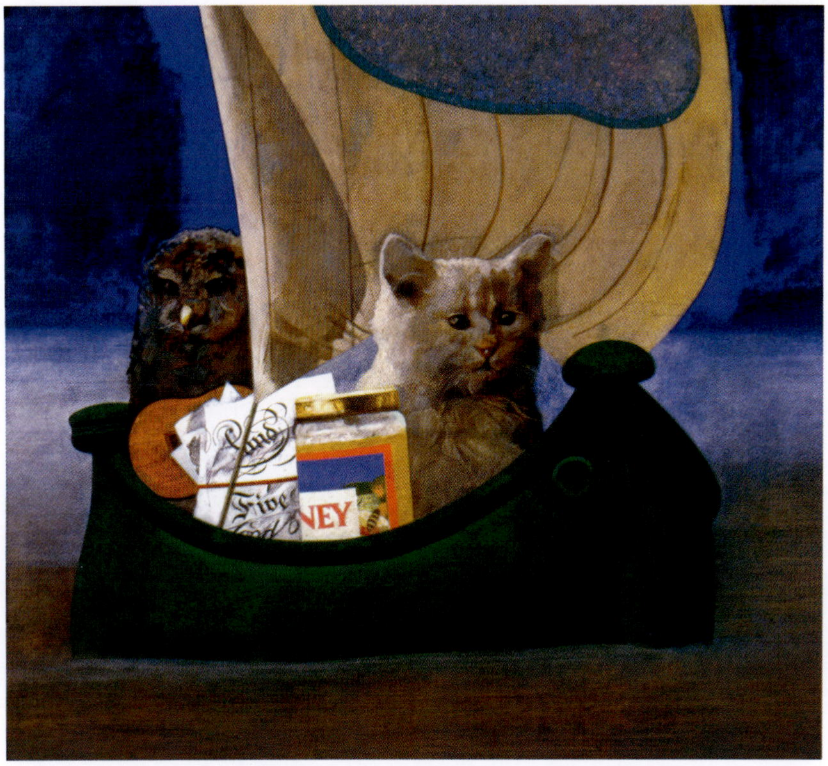

178 **The Owl and the Pussycat**, 1981–3

even though Blake's intention had been to keep it. The further three panels made subsequently, after Blake had decamped back to London, were eventually housed in the space adjoining the kitchen of his new home in Chiswick.

After Ruralism

Blake's marriage came to an abrupt, unhappy and messy end in 1979 when he discovered that Jann had been having an affair with a man whose children were attending her Looking-Glass School in Wellow. When she left Peter for the other man, taking their two young daughters with her, Blake's rural idyll fell apart, and they separated. He decided to resettle in London to rebuild his life. The single most important factor in reigniting his native optimism was meeting the young painter Chrissy Wilson, with whom he quickly formed a strong and lasting bond, in 1980; they married seven years later, the year in which she gave birth to their daughter Rose.

After resettling in London in 1979 and divorcing in 1981, Blake turned once again to a more urban art, while continuing to produce occasional works in a Ruralist spirit. Some of these, such as *The Owl and the Pussycat* (1981–3, Plate 178), a small and frankly cute painting on hardboard inspired by Edward Lear's poem, continued to cross into areas – the coy, the saccharine, the pretty and the overtly illustrative – considered unacceptable by die-hard Modernists, including some of Blake's own admirers. Often mustering his most impressive technical skills to his aid in these supposedly lightweight pictures, Blake remained unapologetic in his attachment to old values and new systems alike, declaring his freedom to move from one to the other. It is symptomatic that the large *I may not be a Ruralist anymore...* painting (1982–91, Plate 168), begun after his return to London as an ambitious reply to the realism of Lucian Freud's paintings representing the back views of domestic buildings, should have been infiltrated by an imaginary and mischievous little figure from the spirit world. Blake remained intransigent in his idiosyncratic Englishness, in his refusal to take heed of passing fashions and in his lack of concern about the degree to which his art subscribes to notions of modernity.

Blake's willingness to reveal his working methods by exhibiting pictures in various degrees of completion demonstrates not only an unusual degree of generosity towards his audience but also a remarkable faith in his own technical abilities. In their early stages, his largest paintings – the group of canvases begun in the mid-1960s that includes *A Mad Tea Party at Watts Tower* (1968–92, Plate 169) and *Portrait of David Hockney in a Hollywood Spanish Interior* (begun 1965, Plate 126) – have looked almost naked in the apparent casualness with which the first layers of colour have been loosely applied. The Shakespearean

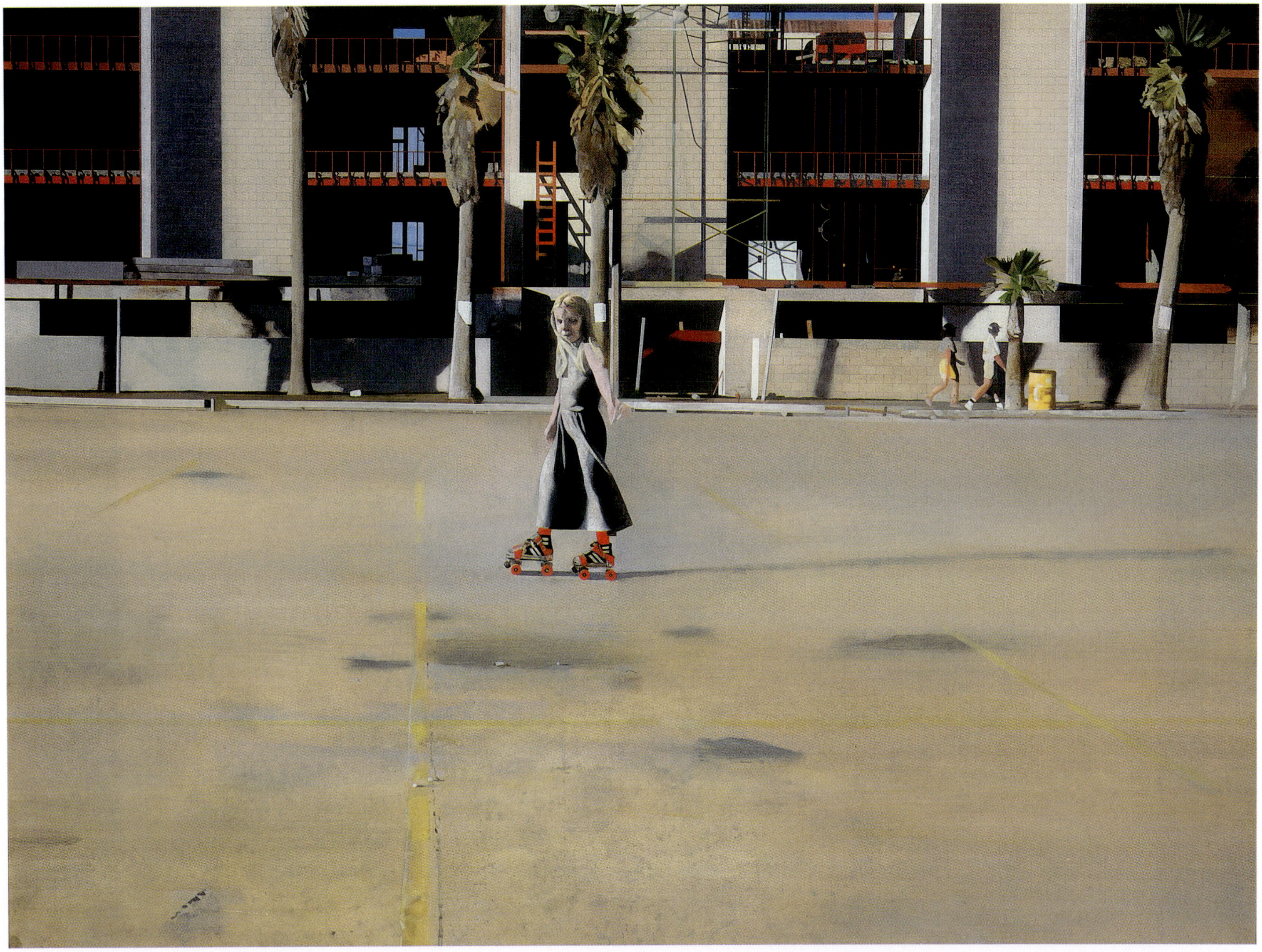

179 **A Remembered Moment in Venice, California**, 1981–3

paintings of the Ruralist period started in a similar way, but with an inbuilt ambition to achieve an overall level of precise finish. As he himself has described it, there was always a further stage to which a painting could be taken: once a face has been blocked in, the features are added as realistically as possible; to the edges of the eyes the lashes can be inserted one by one as delicate, almost invisible lines; yet even at this point, he could consider adding specks of dust to the surface of the lashes. In principle, his paintings of this sort can never reach a conclusion, since they could always be taken to an ever further level of obsessive perfection. In being thus constantly reworked, he acknowledges that the pictures are not necessarily improved in terms of quality, just taken further in terms of the degree of detail. In these situations, the paintings can be prized away from him only by external factors: the need for them to be sent off to an exhibition or sold to a dealer, private collector or institution.

In later years Blake moved away from these additive methods. Some of his more recent paintings, including the *Madonna of Venice Beach* series of the 1990s (Plates 5, 195–8) and the *Marcel Duchamp's World Tour* (Plates 111, 208–10, 212) pictures of the following decade, have started life as meticulously traced outlines that are then filled in with a patient, systematic but rather bland painting-by-numbers mentality. Only as the details of the figures and other elements are worked up, layer by layer, to the required degree of finish do the images suddenly come into focus while simultaneously giving extra weight to the paint surface. Blake's skilful manipulation of oil and acrylic paints alike, working from the general to the particular and enriching the hues with glazes as if he were working with the spontaneity of watercolour, returns us to a level of accomplishment that for centuries was taken for granted by academically trained painters but that today is virtually a lost art.

California Dreaming

In 1979, just at the moment that Blake and his wife were parting company, it was suggested to Blake that he travel to Los Angeles for the first time since his 1963 visit. The invitation was from an English art dealer, Peter Goulds, to participate in part two of a group exhibition of British painting called *This Knot of Life* (27 November – 22 December) at his recently established L.A. Louver Gallery in Venice, California. As a father of two young daughters, Blake had tended not to travel for openings, and out of habit he initially declined to make the journey; on reflection he realised that there was no longer anything to stop him. His fellow painter Howard Hodgkin, who had also recently separated from his wife, was invited too. After much vacillation they decided to travel there together in the company of the print publisher Paul Cornwall-Jones of Petersburg Press, and to stay with their old friend

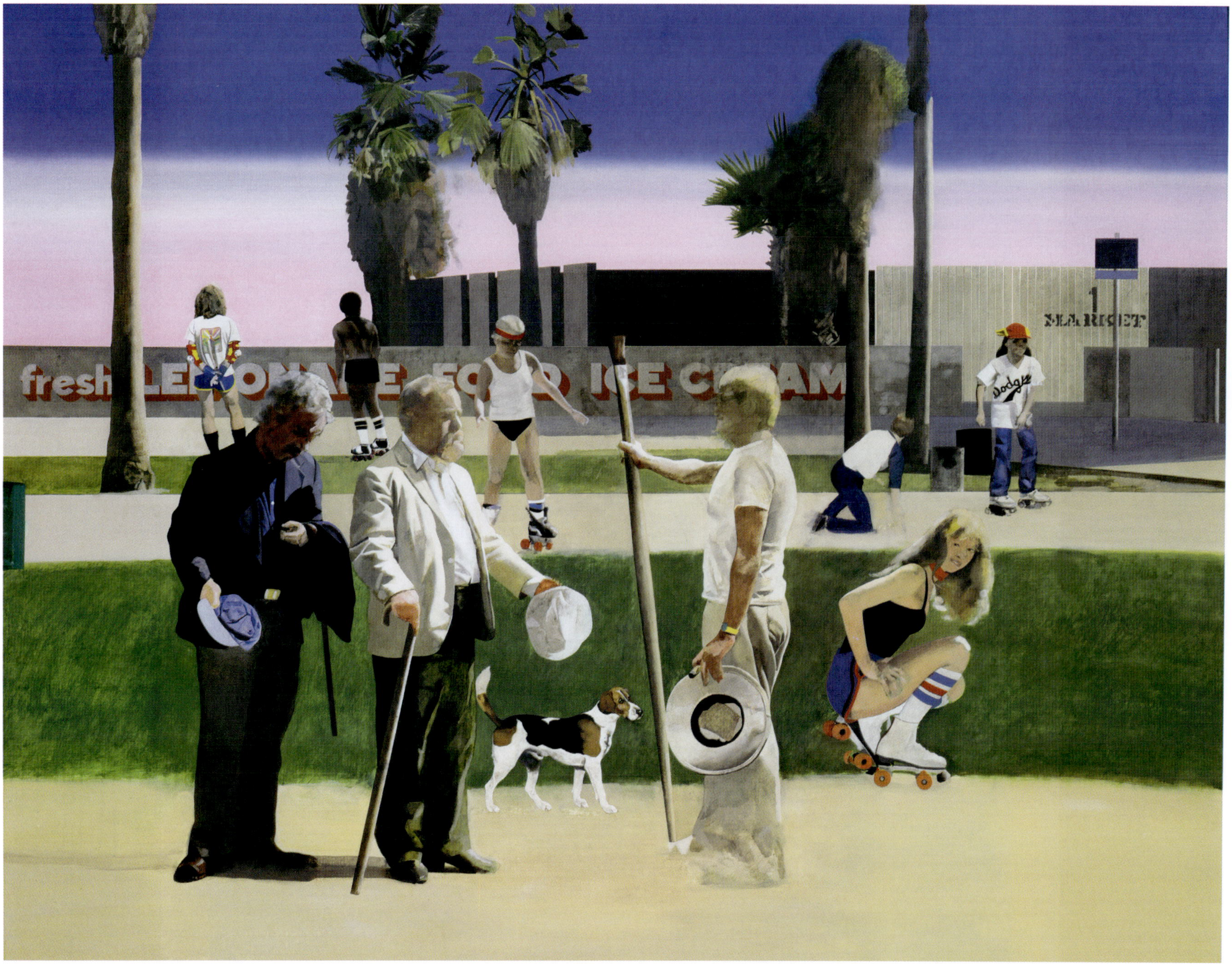

180 **'The Meeting' or 'Have a Nice Day, Mr Hockney'**, 1981–3

David Hockney, who had moved back to Los Angeles in the previous year. 'Howard was on a kind of voyage of discovery to decide if he was gay or not. I was just on my own voyage of discovery, just to start life again,' Peter recalled in a conversation with me in 2004. And Hockney, for his part, was excitedly rediscovering the city in which he had made his most exuberant and influential early paintings in the mid-1960s.

On the return flight to London, Blake proposed to Hodgkin that they each paint three pictures linked to their experiences in Los Angeles, with the idea of eventually showing them together. The plan never materialised as intended, but Blake conceived three substantial paintings: *A Remembered Moment in Venice, California* (1981–3, Plate 179), *'The Meeting' or 'Have a Nice Day, Mr Hockney'* (1981–3, Plate 180) and *Montgomery Clift was a Twin* (1981–3, Plate 181). In early 1981 he was invited by Alan Bowness to have a major retrospective of his art at the Tate Gallery in London; the opening date of 9 February 1983 gave him a final deadline for the L.A. works, which he did his best to meet, but Hodgkin produced only one of his paintings in time as well as one work on paper. Blake's three works were shown in varying stages of completion and the most elaborate of the three – '*The Meeting*', which he had begun a couple of months prior to the other two – was sold soon afterwards to the Tate and handed over to them in a state that Blake considered unfinished. A parody of Gustave Courbet's *'The Meeting', or 'Bonjour Monsieur Courbet'*, it is the most playful of the three paintings and the one that deals most overtly with the circumstances of Blake's visit to Hockney in the company of Hodgkin. Hockney assumes the role of the master allotted by Courbet to himself in the nineteenth-century picture, while Hodgkin is shown rather mischievously as the humble and obsequious servant. Blake presents himself as Hockney's equal, but one who has come to pay him homage.

At Easter 1980, shortly after his visit to Hockney, Blake met Chrissy Wilson, who left her husband to live with him in the London house that Peter had bought with Jann and in which Jann's mother was also still living. To ease themselves out of those very awkward circumstances, they bought a large but run-down house in Chiswick, the leafy area of West London in which Blake had lived as a young man, and had it extensively renovated, with a spacious studio designed by the architect M.J. Long. In the following year he asked Chrissy to accompany him on another trip to Los Angeles, travelling there on his 59th birthday.

A Remembered Moment relates to an incident seen by Blake when walking along Venice Beach in Hodgkin's company. On a big parking lot opposite L.A. Louver, at the end of working hours as dusk was falling, was a young teenage girl roller-skating, doing figures of eight in a dreamlike state. The image lingered in his mind, but when he returned to the site a year later he found that a building had been constructed on one side of the former

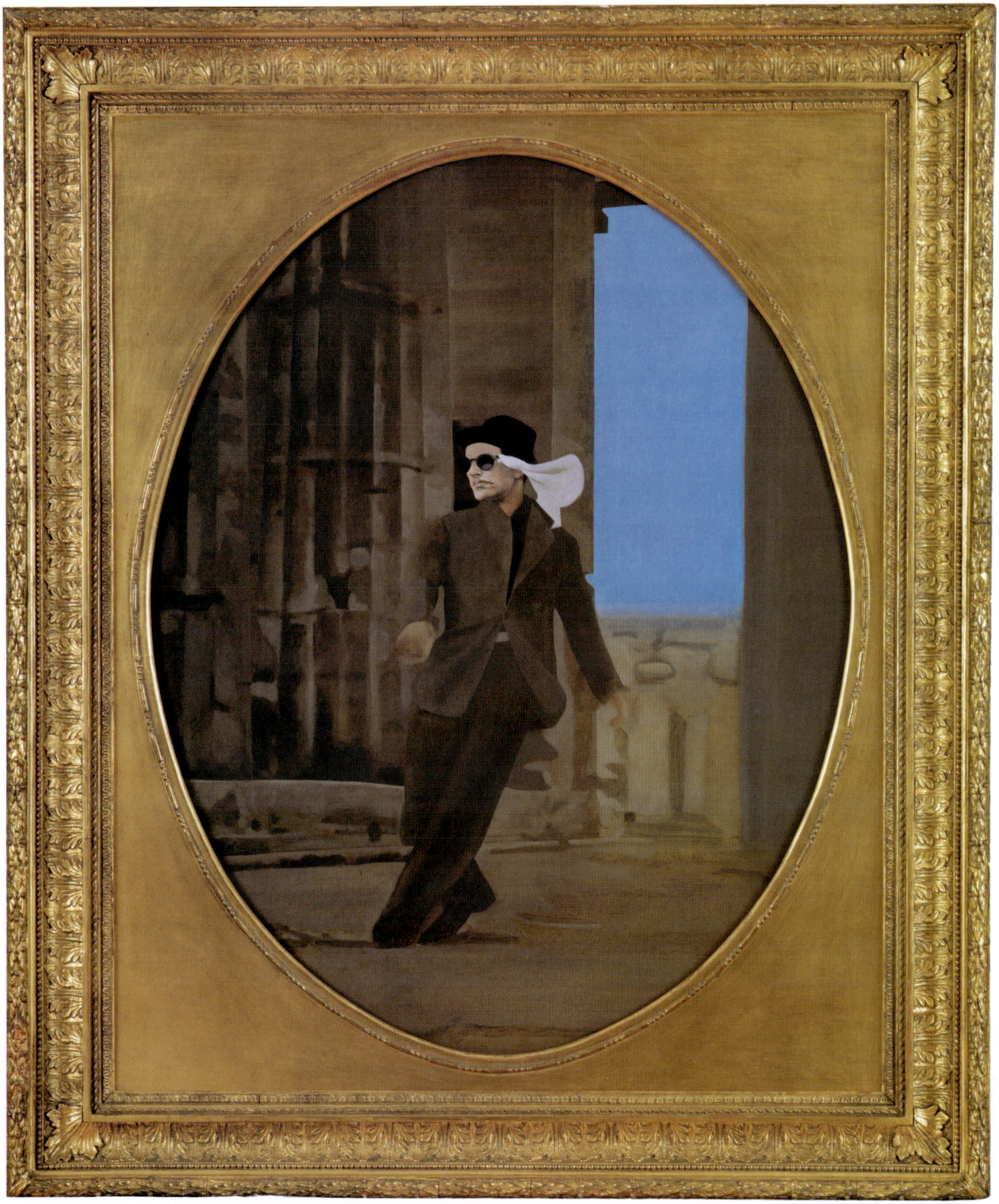

181 **Montgomery Clift was a Twin**, 1981–3

parking lot, so he changed the prospect and incorporated this sense of a city in constant flux into his conception of the painting. For the girl he now used photographs of his daughter Daisy.

Blake's portrayal of Montgomery Clift (1920–66), which places the American screen idol centre stage, dancing in a kind of daydreaming, gliding moment, becomes (almost certainly subconsciously) a kind of surrogate for himself at an important crossroads in his life. Blake had been interested in Clift more as a person than as an actor, and had identified with him because they had both suffered road accidents that left them partly disfigured facially: Clift, at the height of his acting career, nearly died in a car crash in May 1956 when he was drunk at the wheel, leaving a section of the left side of his astonishingly handsome face permanently paralysed. Wanting something to read on the outward trip to L.A. in 1979, Blake had taken with him a recently published biography of Clift by Patricia Bosworth which he found particularly intriguing on the subject of the actor's confused sexuality. Blake had long had a passing interest in the subject of homosexuality as a theme for his paintings, for example as a subtext of some of his wrestling pictures. After witnessing so much of the gay subculture of Los Angeles in the company of Hodgkin and especially Hockney, who had made it a point of honour to be open about his sexuality since his early twenties in both his life and his art, the idea formed of making a portrait of Clift that would address, tangentially, the question of the actor's sexual orientation. Bosworth recounts that Clift, his much plainer twin sister and their older brother Brooks, two years their senior, were all brought up in the same way and dressed in a unisex manner. Such details informed the making of the painting, which projects a sense of the actor as elusive, mercurial, troubled and ambiguous.

The painting of Clift was based by Blake entirely on a grainy black-and-white photograph of the actor on holiday in Paestum, 'an old Greek colony, south of Naples', which featured in the Bosworth biography. There is so little information in the reproduction that Blake, in effect, had to invent the details for himself, while remaining faithful to the hazy and indistinct atmosphere of his source. Like its companion paintings, it was made to fit exactly into an old and battered gilt frame intended to exaggerate the 'academic' look of the finished work, as if it belonged in the atmosphere of one of the great nineteenth-century Salons. (The deliberate use of battered frames in the California pictures was also a nod to the use of painted frames in Hodgkin's work, alongside which they were originally intended to be exhibited.) The only adjustments to the composition were made for the sake of fitting the picture into the existing frame, and specifically into its oval format. The association with Victorian photographs, frequently made in that oval 'vignette' shape, is confirmed by the sepia tones adopted for most of the scene; only the limpid blue sky and

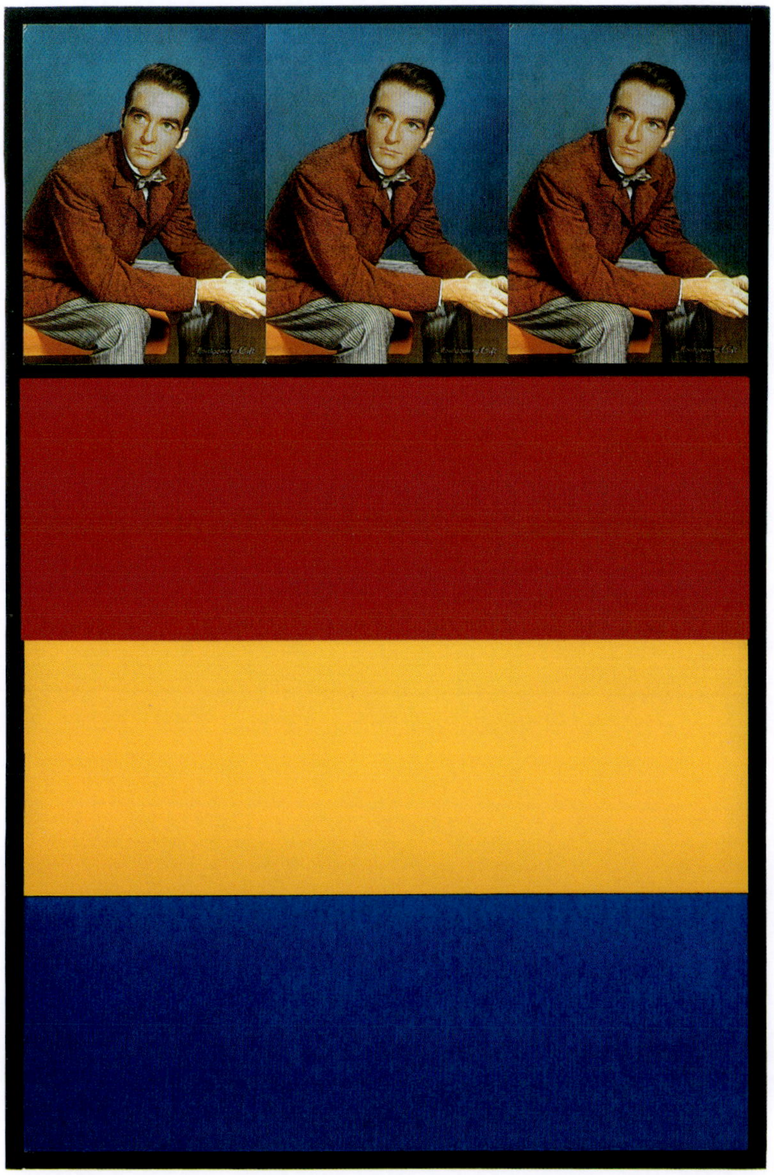

182 **Montgomery Clift**, 1987

the actor's flesh-coloured face are picked out in brighter colours.

Blake concedes that *Portrait of David Hockney in a Hollywood Spanish Interior* (begun 1965, Plate 126) must have been on his mind when he was staying with Hockney in 1979, and that it may have reinforced his decision to produce new Los Angeles pictures in a closely related style. There are similarities not only in the paint application and technique, but also in the reliance on photographic sources. As he himself points out, however, these are all characteristics of part of his painting practice throughout his career. As in so many other aspects of his art, the sense of continuity here and the links with earlier works suggests Blake's characteristic ability – even when embarking on a new direction, or when deliberately exploring unfamiliar territory – to begin the journey in a sure-footed way by placing himself on the firm ground of his own past.

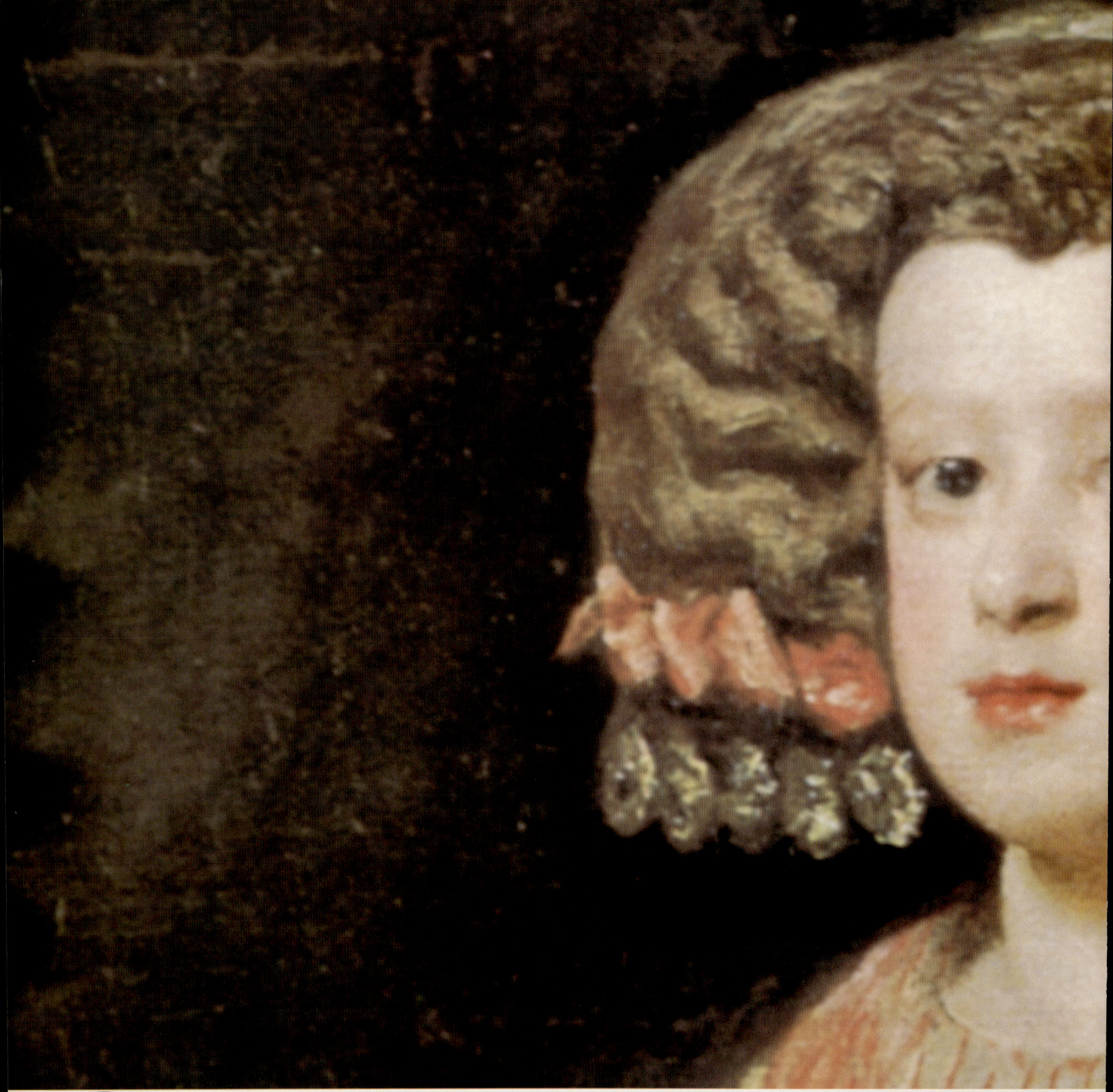

7 REVISITING

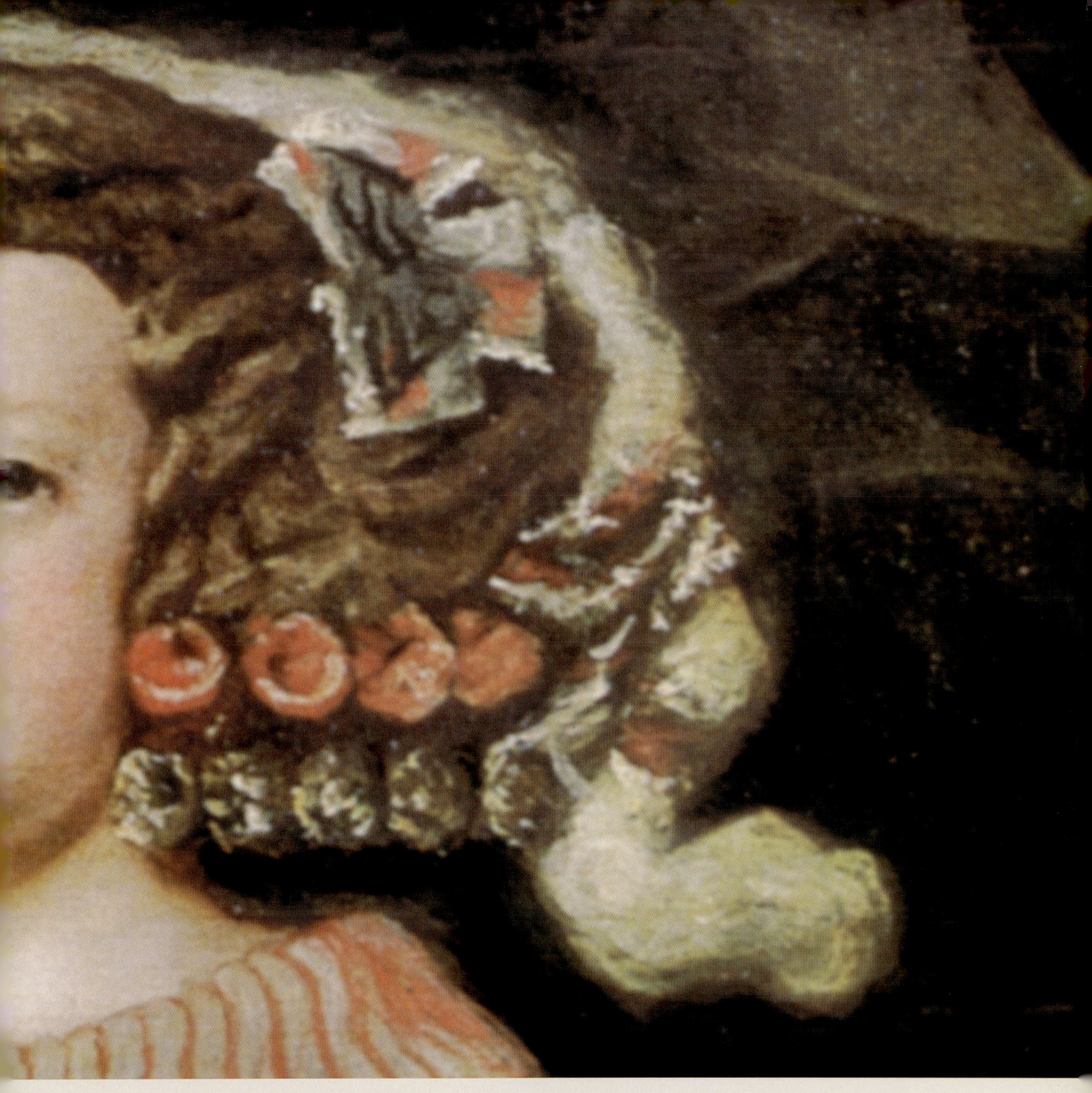

ART HISTORY

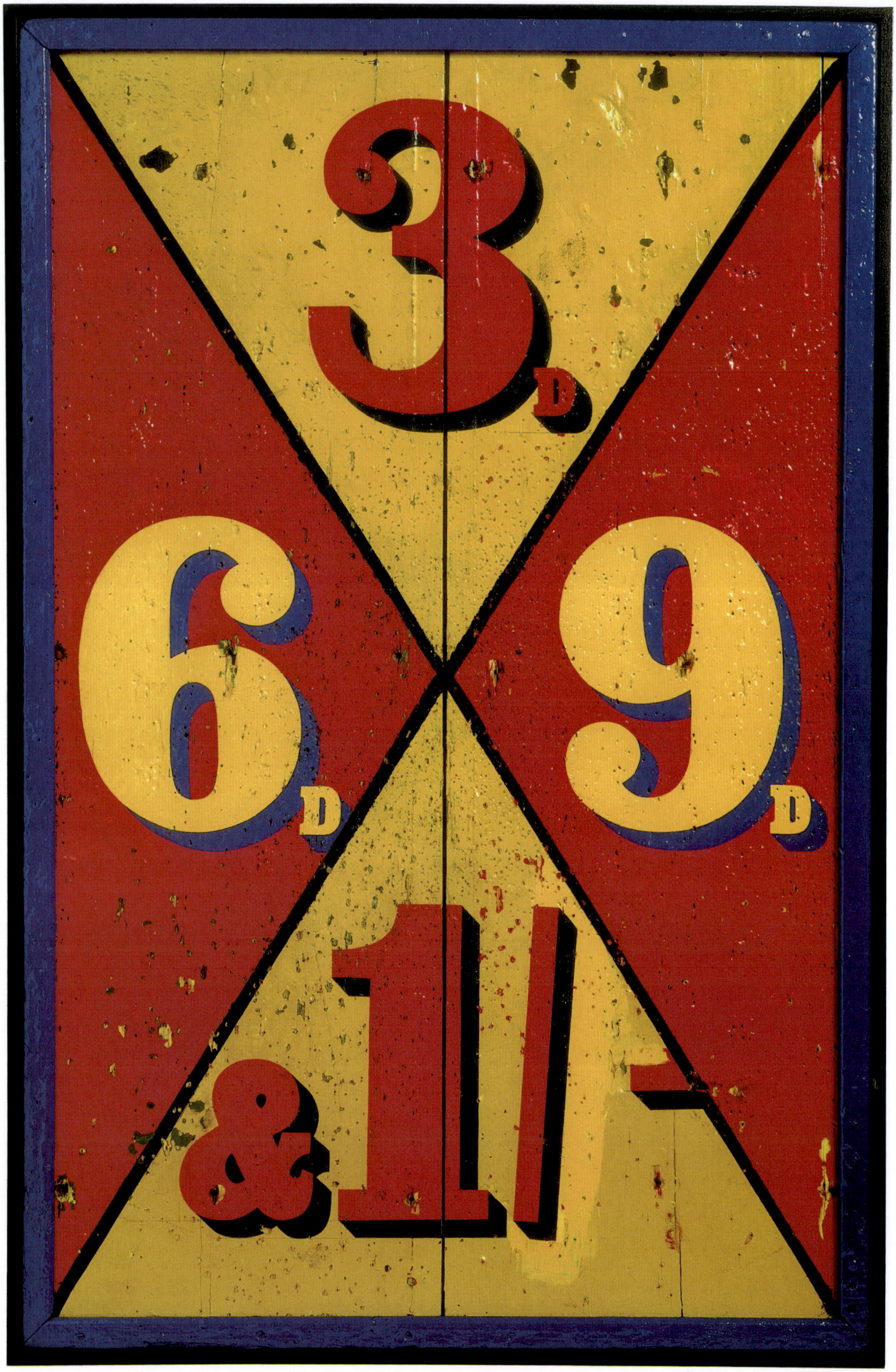

183 **3D 6D 9D & 1/–**, 1986

7 Revisiting Art History

'Homage' is a recurring word in the works made by Blake in his sixties and seventies, a mark of respect to his artistic forebears and contemporaries alike. In these years Blake took some backward glances at his own history, too, tying up loose ends, seeing connections, presenting long imagined exhibition projects and revisiting his past as a source of inspiration for new departures. For someone who made a very public (if mischievously misleading) announcement of his retirement in his mid-sixties, these have been extraordinarily productive years. Many people fantasise about the creative urges in which they will be able to indulge once they have given up the drudgery of their work routine: to take up painting, perhaps. For Blake, art-making has always been a source of pleasure, never a penance or a duty. Having achieved so much, he could, however, set aside any lingering career ambitions and pursue his painting – and all his other art-making – with a vengeance and a renewed energy.

Déjà Vu

Déjà vu was the title given by Blake, in a spirit of defiance tinged with self-mockery, to a one-man exhibition of new works held at the Nishimura Gallery in Tokyo, 9–31 May 1988. Explaining in the catalogue introduction that he wanted to give himself the excuse to rework some ideas from his earlier Pop paintings, he noted that these self-appropriations formed a kind of reply to the Postmodernist inclinations of certain artists to rely on styles and images invented by others. The idea was further pursued on a more precise theme, *In Homage to Marilyn Monroe* (Plates 189–91), for exhibitions of new works in 1990 at Waddington Galleries in London and at the Wetterling Gallery in Gothenburg, Sweden. It was at this time that he also began work on an exhibition dedicated to Elvis Presley, the centrepiece of which was meant to be a garden shed containing an elaborate shrine to the king of rock'n'roll, though he set this aside after a number of younger British artists, notably Tracey Emin, had presented sculptural installations using the very same architectural form.

With these and later works, the most extravagant examples of his return in middle age to a Pop idiom, Blake cast a retrospective look on his own career, rephrasing his earlier art – much of it itself based on found images and ready-made styles – and presenting it as a conceptual gesture that brought to the fore the unity of thought that had guided him for nearly half a century. It was, as he recalled later, a very self-conscious gesture, but one

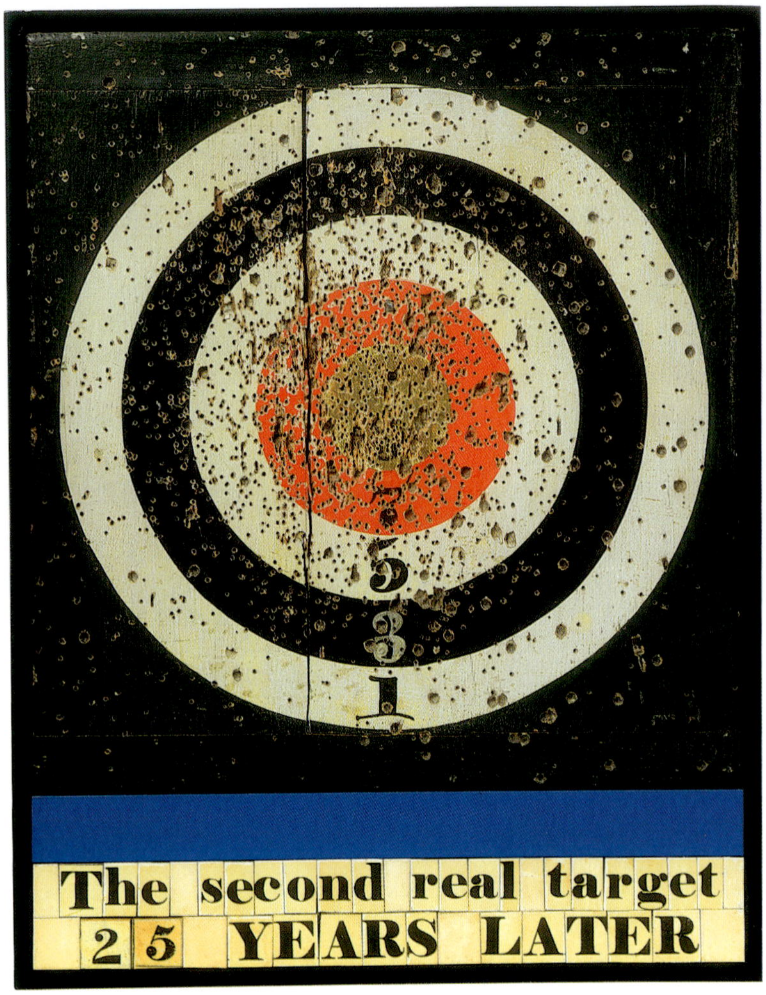

184 **The Second Real Target 25 yrs later**, 1986

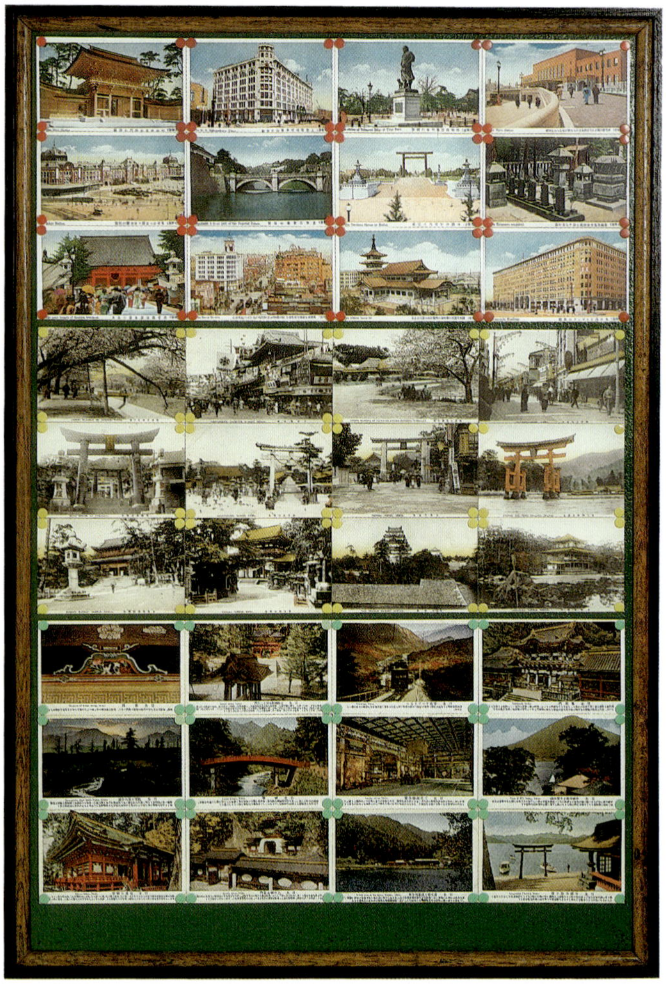

185 **Noticeboard with Japanese Postcards**, 1987

that offered him the opportunity both to recreate works from his youth and to make entirely new ones in a similar spirit. With other artists endlessly repeating themselves, he gave himself permission to dig into this back catalogue of his early hits, as his pop musician friends had long been allowed to do. The fashion that became particularly visible during the 1980s for 'appropriating' the work of other artists – Elaine Sturtevant, Sherrie Levine and Mike Bidlo being among the most notable examples – also helped persuade Blake that, as he explained in his catalogue introduction, it was 'Better to have ripped myself off than to have been "ripped off".' He added: 'Part of the reasoning behind the exhibition was that I felt that some of the American Pop-artists had only one idea in the early 1960's, then repeated that idea over and over again, mainly for commercial reasons, whereas

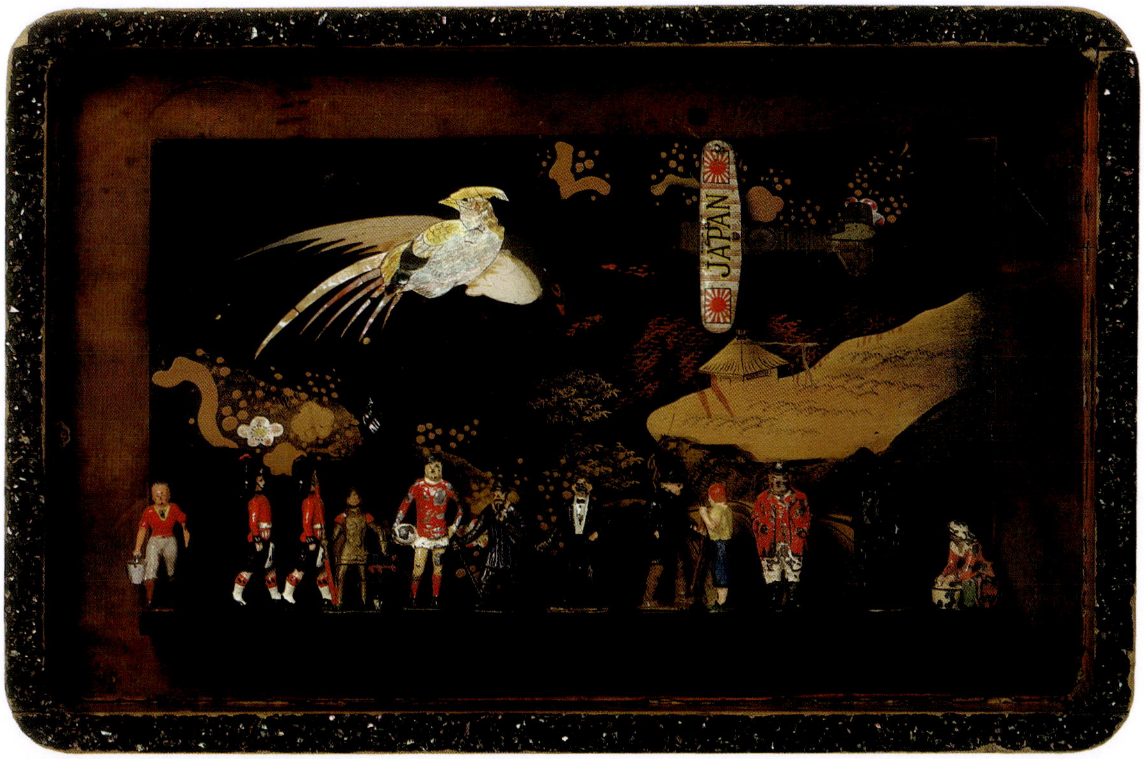

186 **British Tourists in Japan**, 1988

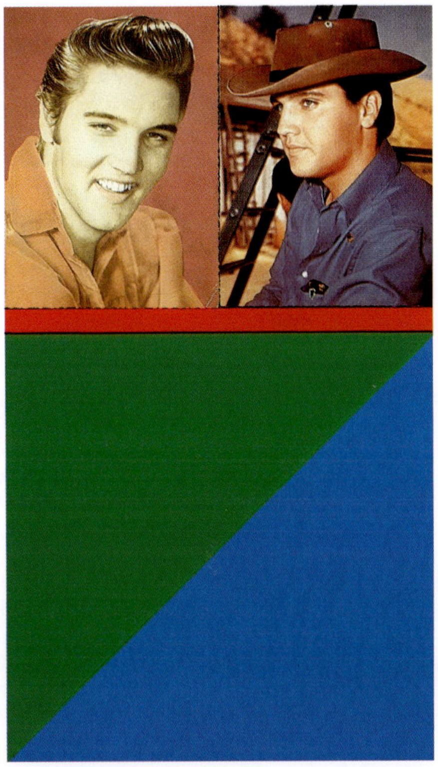

187 **Elvis Presley**, 1987

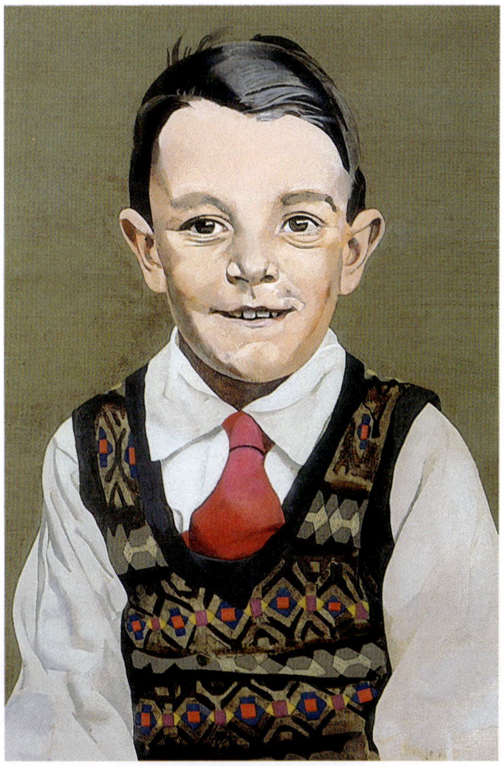

188 **Déjà vu – 'A Boy'**, 1987–8

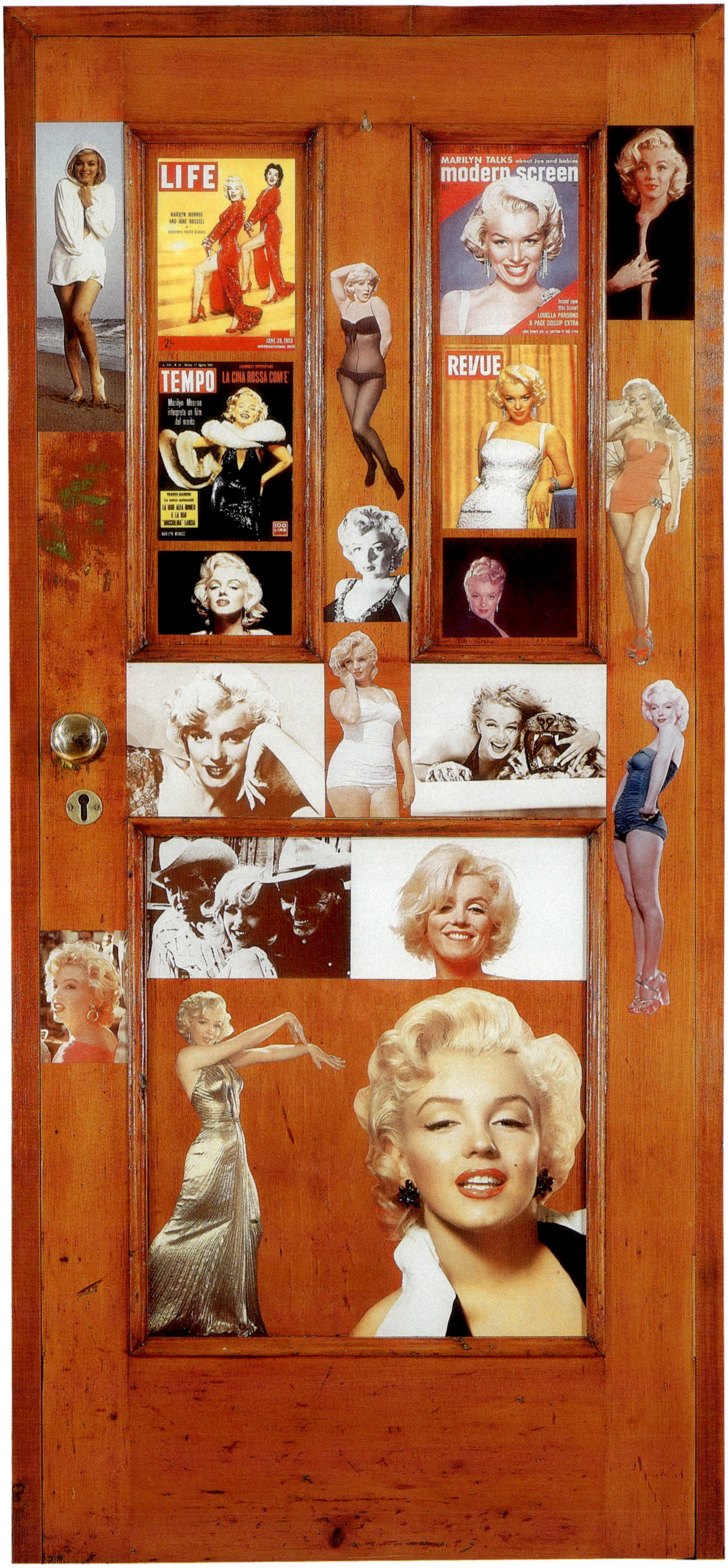

189 **Marilyn Monroe, Door (Miniature)**, 1990

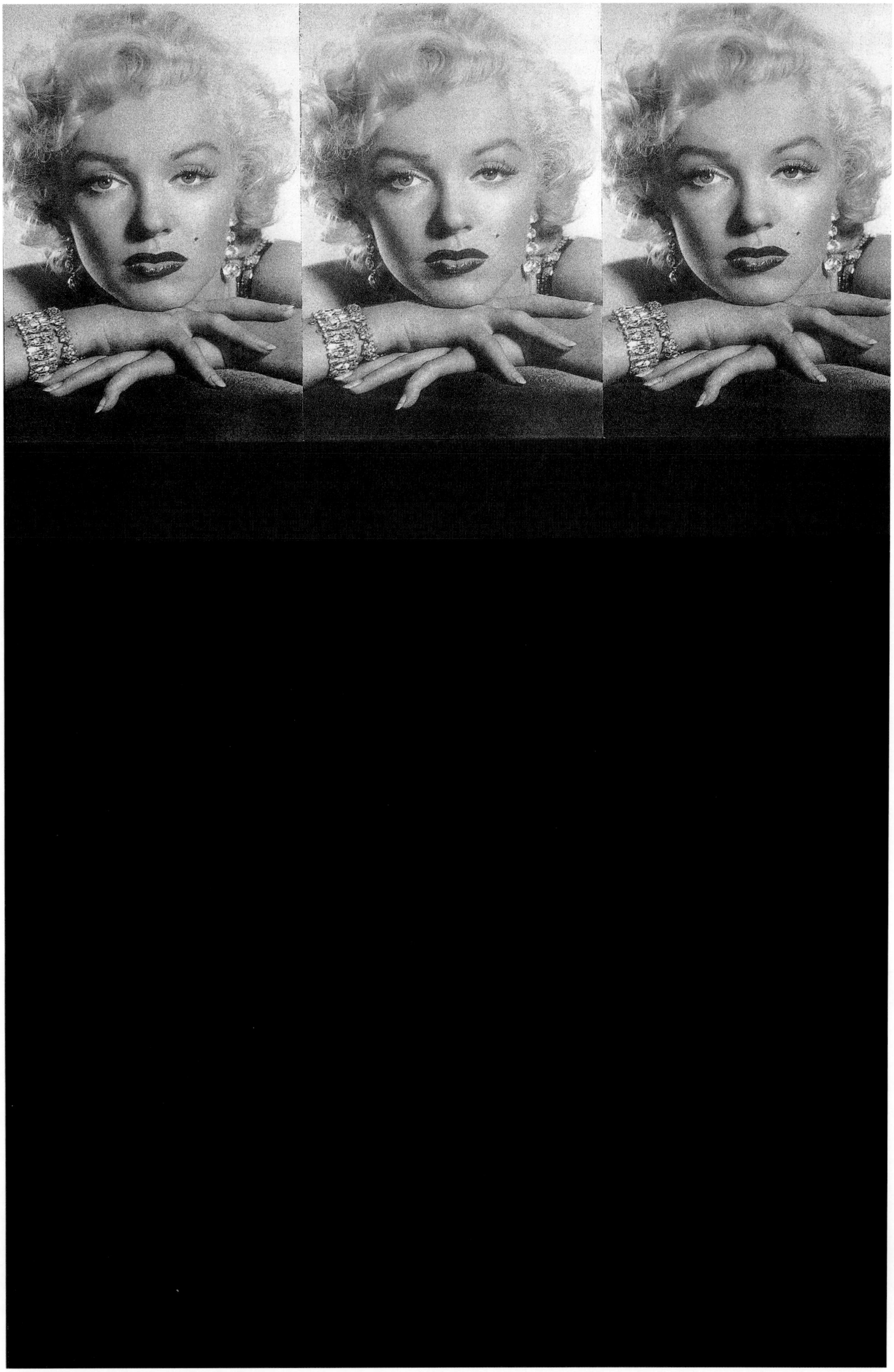

190 **Marilyn Monroe, Black**, 1990

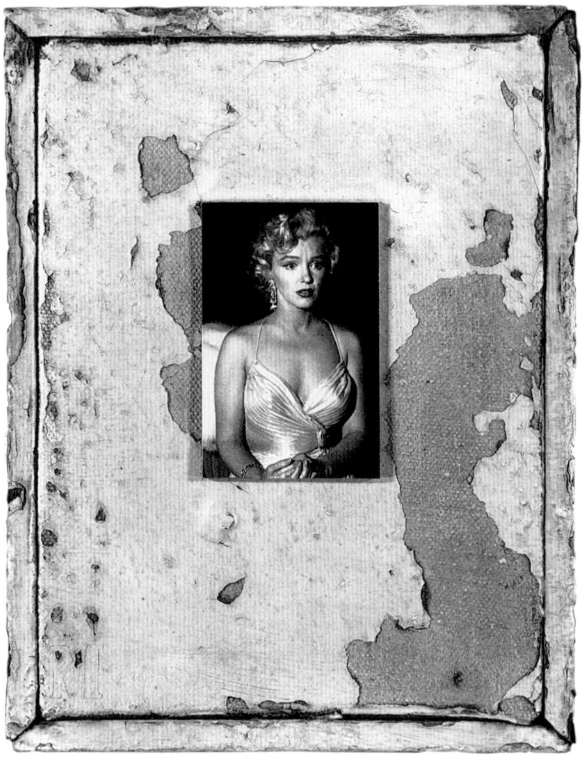

191 **Marilyn Monroe, White No. 1**, 1990

I had often only painted one picture from an idea, and it would sometimes have been worth further paintings.' With his tongue more than slightly in his cheek, but also with a surprising sincerity, this was another way of remaining true to his maxim about 'staying ahead of the avant-garde'.

At the National Gallery

Like the artistic equivalent to Superman, Batman and other comic-book heroes, but without the muscular body armour or superhuman strength, Blake remains a man of multiple identities. By the time he took up his two-year post as Associate Artist at the National Gallery in London in September 1994, he had presented himself, with equal conviction, as Pop artist, folk artist, (faux-)naive painter, collagist, painter in the naturalist tradition, portraitist, watercolourist, Ruralist, heir to the Victorian fairy painters, Realist and commercial artist. Those who knew or understood him in only one of these guises were in for a surprise when confronted by the new body of work from that two-year tenure, especially as his tendency to explore an idea through many variations can lead to a substantial production that seems like nothing less than a reinvention of himself or even like a rejection of his previous selves. No sooner does he persuade us that he is confronting us with his real identity than he slips out of it again to don another disguise, changing his stripes

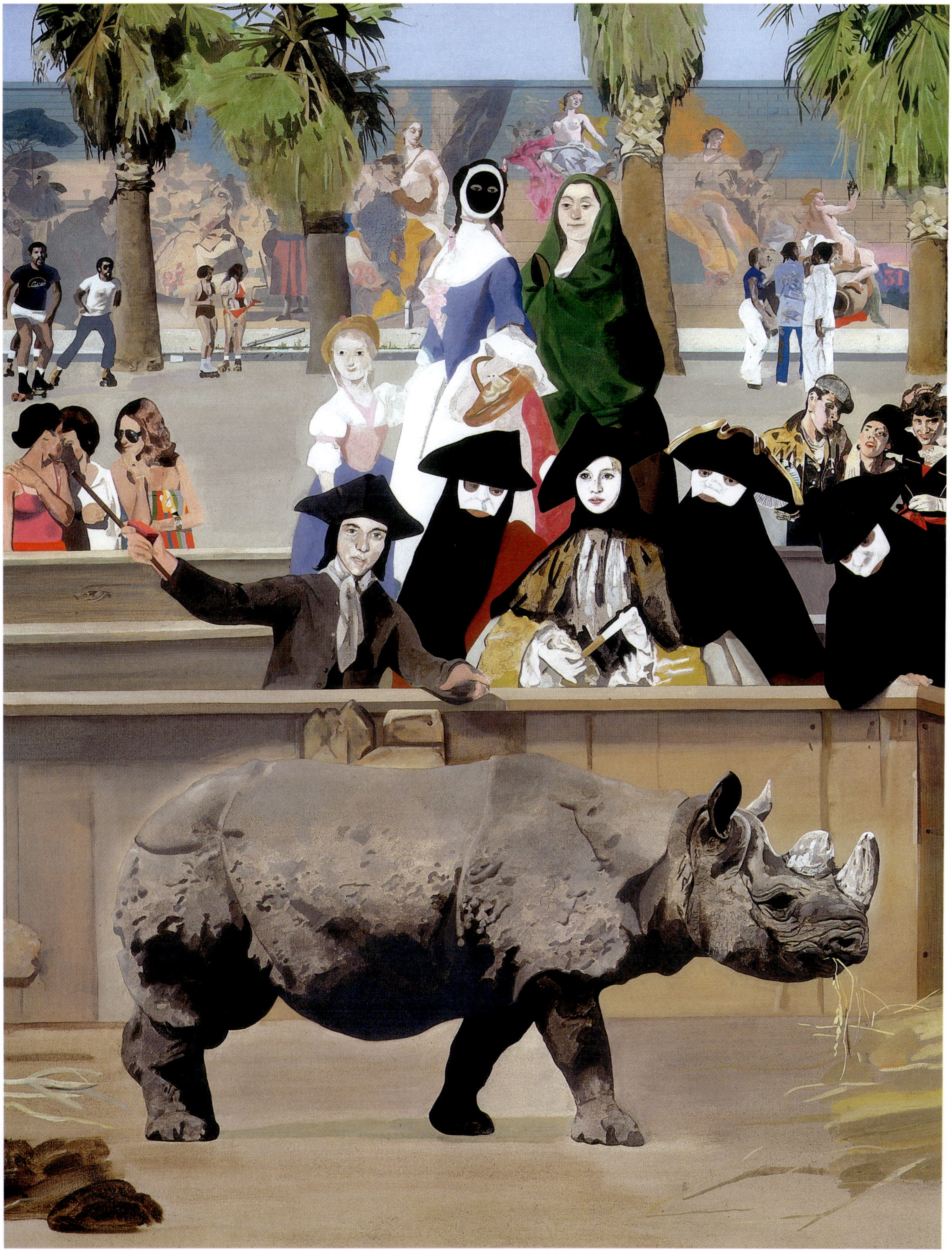

192 **Exhibition of a Rhinoceros in Venice**, 1996

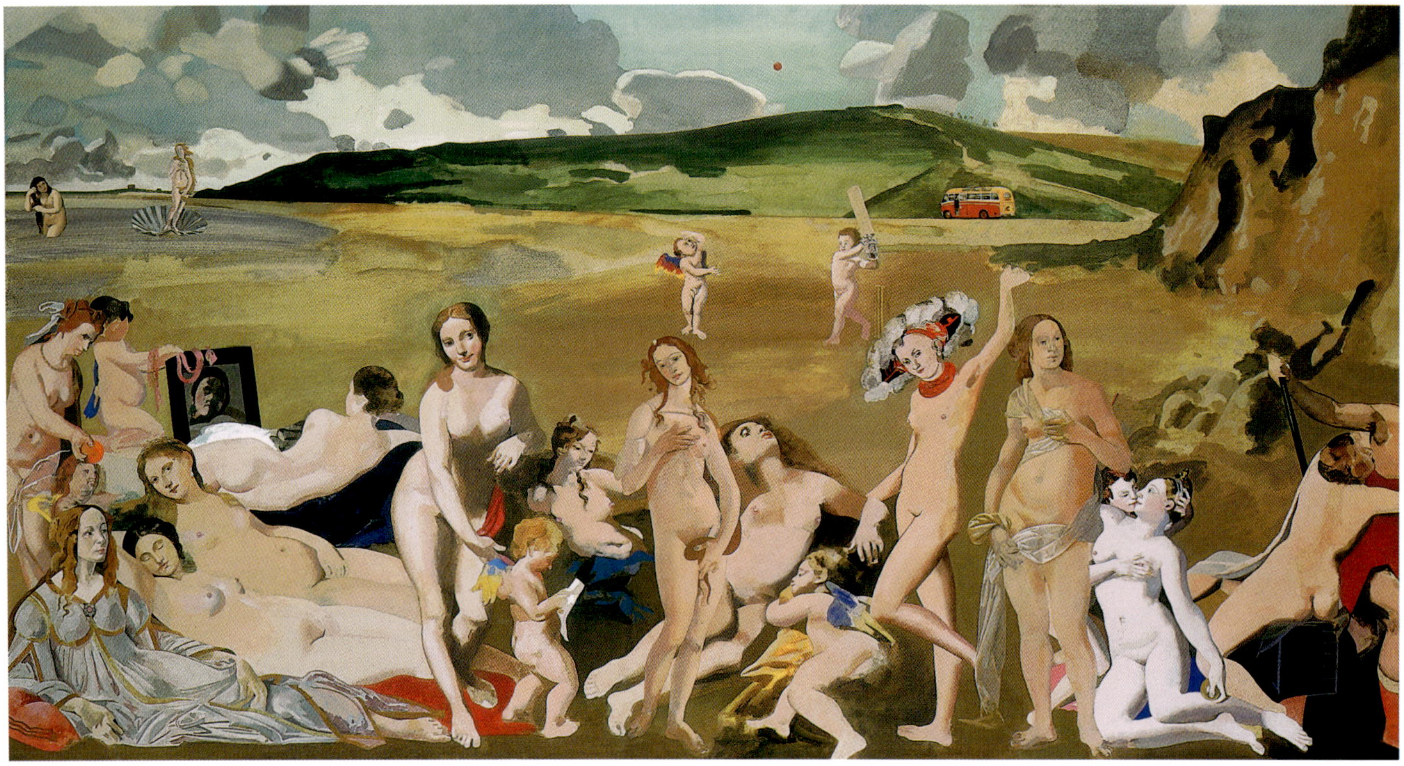

193 **The Venuses' Outing to Weymouth**, 1994–2004

for a pretty girl's face or hanging up his entertainer's uniform in favour of some sensible walking shoes with which to take a brisk hike into the fresh country air. It is little wonder that some of his most memorable portraits have been of masked figures, like the real and imaginary wrestlers who have enchanted him since his childhood, whose public lives take the form of a prolonged and good-natured game of hide-and-seek.

Though Blake had always enjoyed visiting museums and learning from looking closely at historical paintings, he had not had such an intense relationship with Old Master paintings since his year of travelling on a Leverhulme Research Award in 1956–7. He was aware that, as for any artist, as he got older his eyes were changing and he was also looking at different aspects of such pictures, taking more care, for example, to examine how Diego Velásquez used black or how he conjured up a fleshy face or embroidered finery in hugely confident, broad strokes. As he later explained to his interviewer on the Artists' Lives projects, 'You never stop learning *how* to paint, and what you learn changes all the time.'

During his time at the National Gallery, Blake set himself the task of producing several groups of pictures based directly on works in the collection. Shown together, they might suggest that he had undergone another of his characteristic transformations, not into an Old Master – his humility before the great achievements of the past, and his recognition of the lack of imagination that mere imitation would entail, would preclude such bland ambition – but into a kind of Postmodernist raider of the past. Seen in the wider context

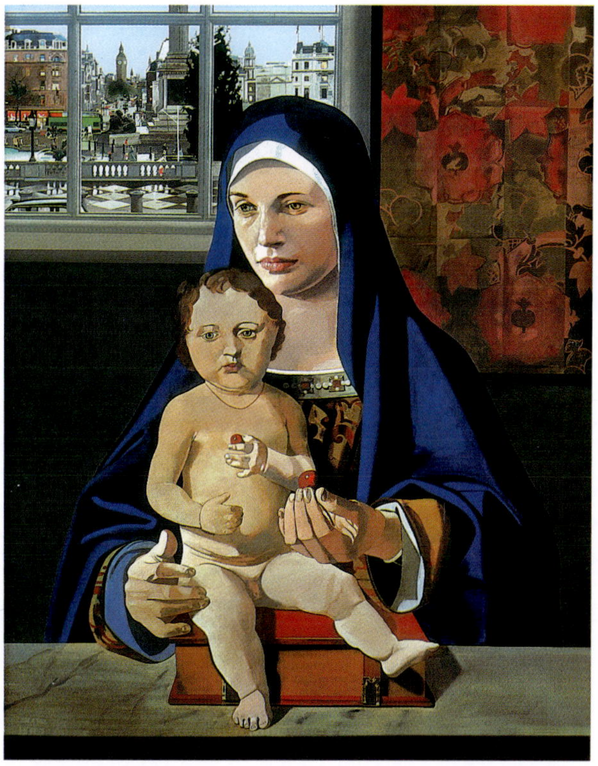

194 The National Gallery Madonna, 1994–2000

of his life's work, however, these pictures form part of a lifelong dialogue with the art of the past, stretching back at least as far as the mid-1950s when as a postgraduate student he was set the challenge of responding to set subjects and of transcribing paintings by earlier artists into a modern idiom. His aim, even then, was not simply to replicate an admired work by imitating its style or copying its composition or imagery, but to transform it into something of his own that encompassed his subjective responses, his sense of nostalgia and his own way of looking at the world. Although at the National Gallery he exploited the ample opportunities to study the actual paintings, out of convenience he worked mainly from reproductions, preferring the solitude of the studio and more concerned with reinventing the pictures for himself than with mimicking their paint application with the fidelity of a copyist.

Much as he loves Old Master paintings, Blake has never treated them with sanctimonious reverence, judging the art of the past to be robust enough to withstand a little teasing or good-natured humour. As early as 1959, in the slightly sarcastically titled *The Fine Art Bit* (Plate 41), he positioned a row of postcard reproductions of works by Fra Angelico, Hans Memling, Paulus Potter and others, collected on his travels around European museums, along a narrow shelf surmounting a hardboard surface painted in brightly coloured stripes of household gloss paint; the conjunction of high art (in its cheapest and most accessible form) and everyday decoration ambiguously suggests an equivalence between the two but

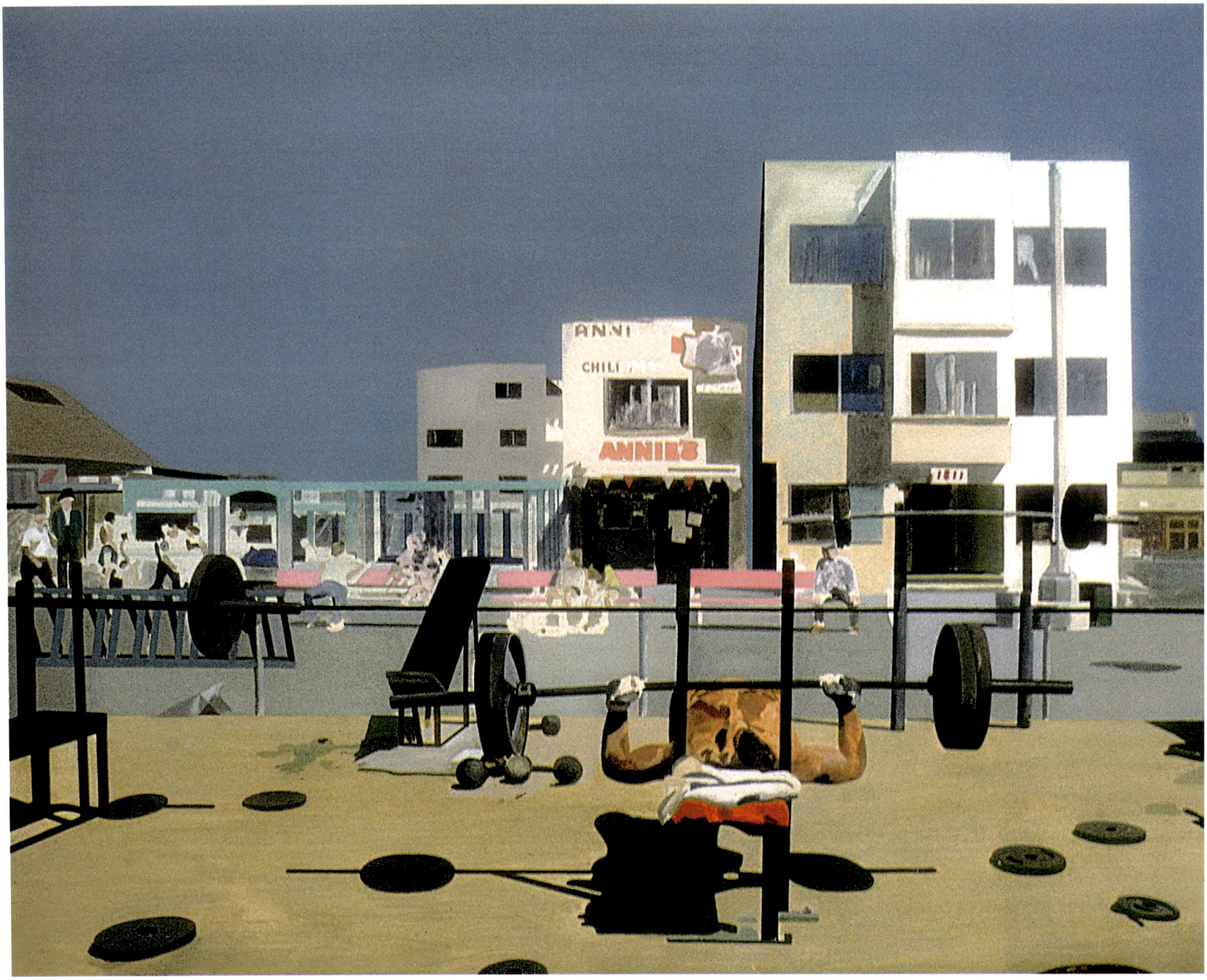

195 **Madonna of Venice Beach, No. 4**, 1995

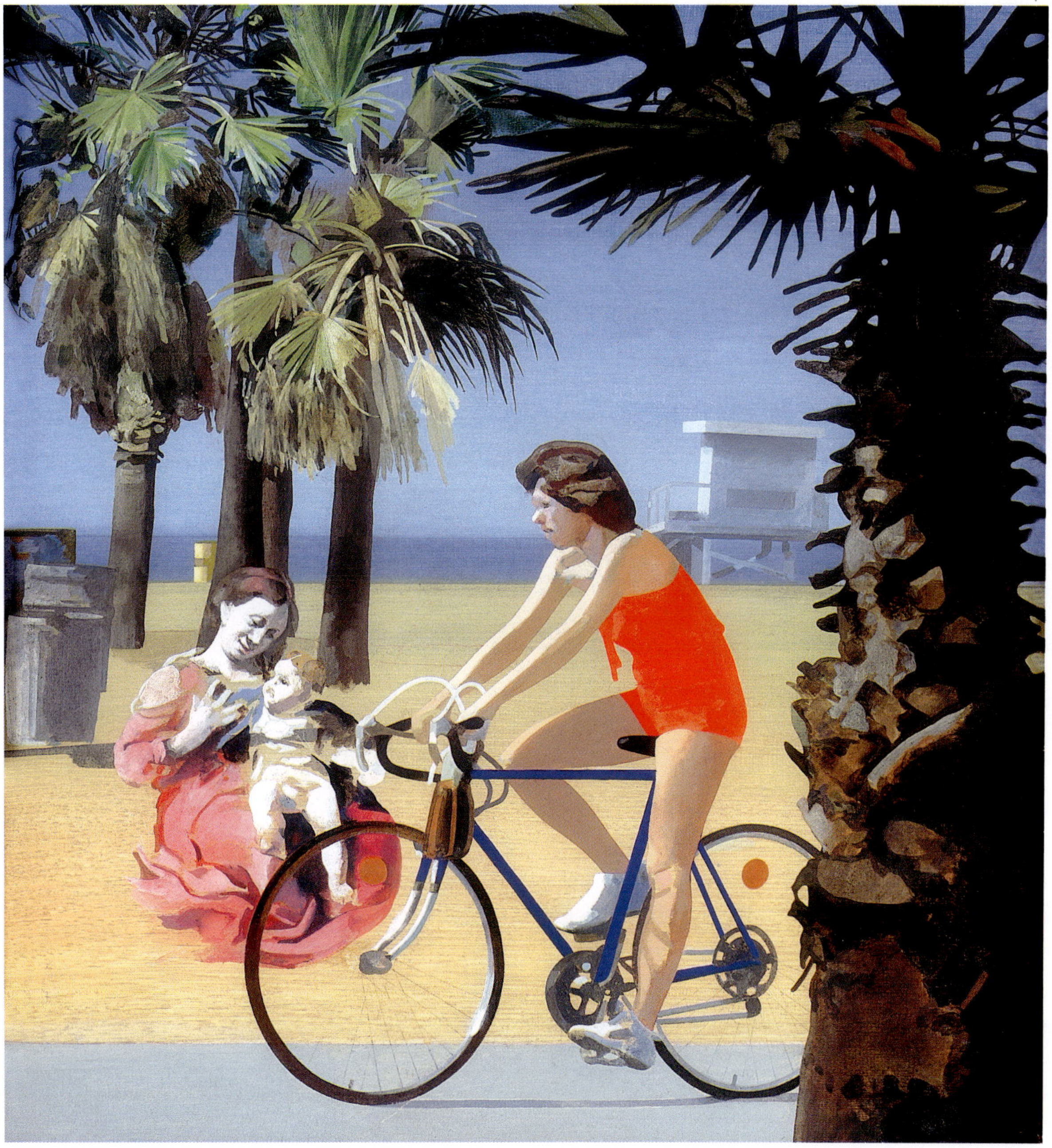

196 **Madonna of Venice Beach, No. 2**, 1995

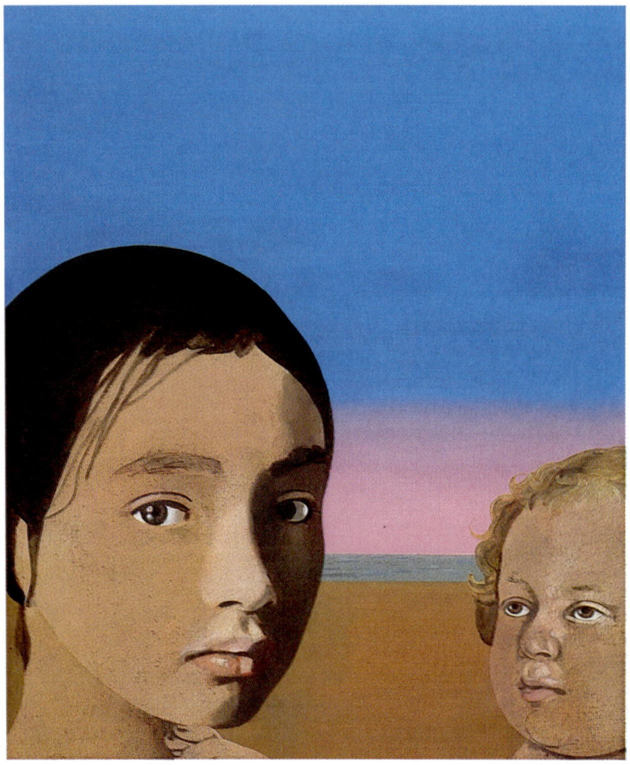

197 **Madonna of Venice Beach, No. 3**, 1995

at the same time affords an elevated position to 'the fine art bit' of the equation. Even earlier, in circus-derived paintings such as *Siriol, She-Devil of Naked Madness* (1957, Plate 20), he used garish paste jewellery collaged to the rough wooden surface to pay his respects simultaneously to the rough-and-ready beauty of old-fashioned advertising and to the richly encrusted and embossed surfaces of panel paintings from the Italian pre-Renaissance.

This intermingling of the past and present, by way of humour and an inspired recognition of visual characteristics shared by artefacts devised for radically different purposes, continued to exercise Blake's imagination in later decades. It lies behind such otherwise different works as a straight-faced rendering in 1965–8 of Landseer's *Monarch of the Glen* (Plate 153), by then demoted from Victorian favourite to an icon of kitsch taste, and his rephrasing in the 1980s of Courbet's *'Bonjour Monsieur Courbet'* as the cheery Californian scene of *'The Meeting' or 'Have a Nice Day, Mr Hockney'* (1981–3, Plate 180).

A magpie both in his appropriations of images made by others and in his habits as a collector, Blake clearly was in his element, like a child in a particularly well-stocked sweet shop, when he found the whole of the National Gallery's riches at his disposal. Even before setting himself up in the Gallery's handsome basement studio, he had begun to map out the various projects that would give him the excuse to raid his favourite paintings for images. These included *Exhibition of a Rhinoceros in Venice* (1996, Plate 192), a transposition, suspended between the eighteenth century and our own time, of Pietro Longhi's unfor-

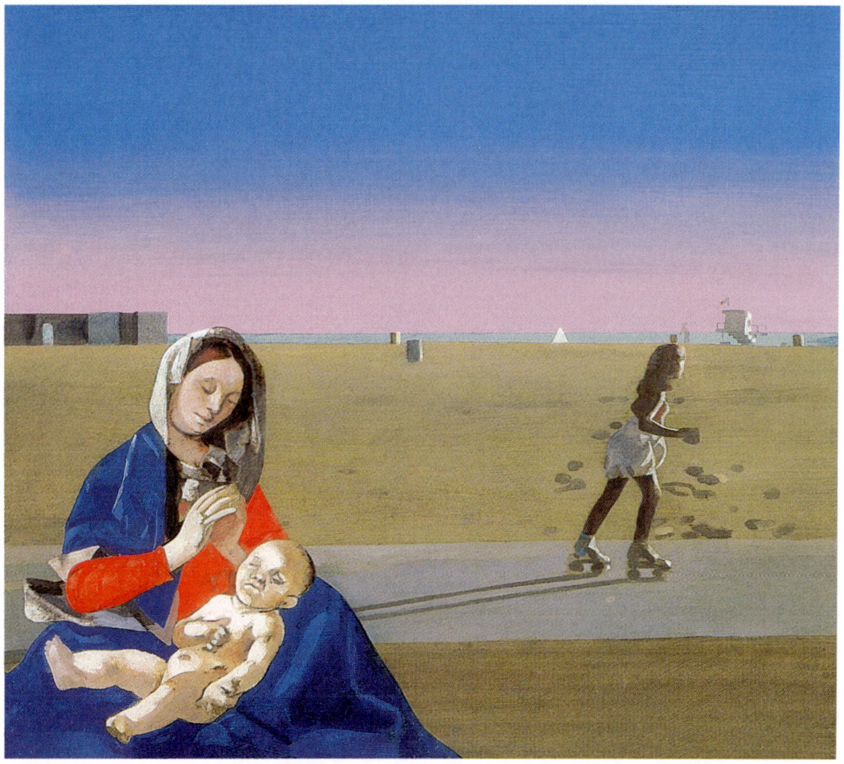

198 Madonna of Venice Beach, No. 5, 1995

gettable image of Venetian spectators marvelling at a rhinoceros on display, and a painting called *The Venuses' Outing to Weymouth* (Plate 193), begun in 1994 but not completed until 2004, in which representations of Venus and Cupid by Velásquez, Cranach, Giorgione, Botticelli, Correggio, Bronzino, Titian and others frolic improbably together in scenery derived from a landscape by Constable. Having previously shied away from religious themes, the proximity of so many devotional Christian images led him to create a group of Madonna and Child images. One of the most imposing of these, closely based on Bartolomeo Montagna's *The Virgin and Child* of *c.*1485–7, was named *The National Gallery Madonna* (1994–2000, Plate 194) in deference to this derivation but also because the view through the window has been altered to that of Trafalgar Square as seen from the windows at the front of the building in which he painted it. An entire series of Madonna and Child images was based on the concept of transplanting figures from fifteenth-century Flanders (Dieric Bouts) or Renaissance Italy (Raphael, Bellini, Cima da Conegliano, Correggio) to the southern California playground of Venice Beach. In this *Madonna of Venice Beach* series (Plates 5, 195–8), prefigured by a picture begun in 1981, *A Remembered Moment in Venice, California* (Plate 179), Blake turned his attention to unlikely events: apparitions of the Madonna and Child in the most prosaic of circumstances. These are not conventional religious pictures, but images of communion, emblems of the bonds between a mother and her child and between an artist and his forebears.

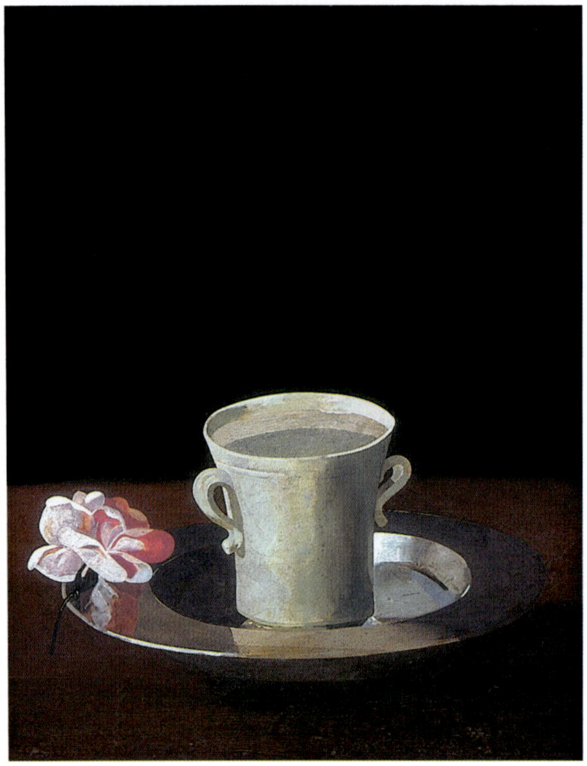

199 **After 'Cup of Water and a Rose on a Plate' by Francisco de Zurbaran**, 1995–9

Among the other paintings begun by Blake at the National Gallery were a series of female portrait heads, *In Homage to Woman*, derived from Holbein, Rembrandt, Vermeer, Piero della Francesca and others, and five heads of dwarves after paintings by Velásquez in the Prado. In a rather sober mood he produced a set of mainly very small-scale still-life paintings conceived as slice-of-life details from such masters as Chardin, Courbet and Velásquez. At the risk of offending more serious sensibilities, he also made a group of *The Nine Prettiest Bottoms in the National Gallery*, in which he calls our attention, without fear of indelicacy, to the little pink mounds of flesh by Boucher, Rubens and Renoir, as well as by less predictable connoisseurs of feminine posteriors, that afford visitors to the collection illicit pleasures under the guise of culture. Often assumed to be a painfully slow worker, Blake certainly could not be accused on this occasion of being anally retentive. His residency at the National Gallery proved to be an enormously productive period.

In every one of these cases, Blake selected his subjects or interpreted his chosen images in such a way as to suit his own purposes. The portrait heads, in their concentration on the character suggested by the faces to the exclusion of signs of a particular place or time, extend the family of images that include such paintings as *Titania* (1972–4) as well as more recent commissioned portraits of real people painted from life or from photographs. The Velásquez dwarves, similarly, are both the art-historical antecedents for, and the heirs to, the wrestlers, side-show freaks and circus performers that have been the objects of Blake's

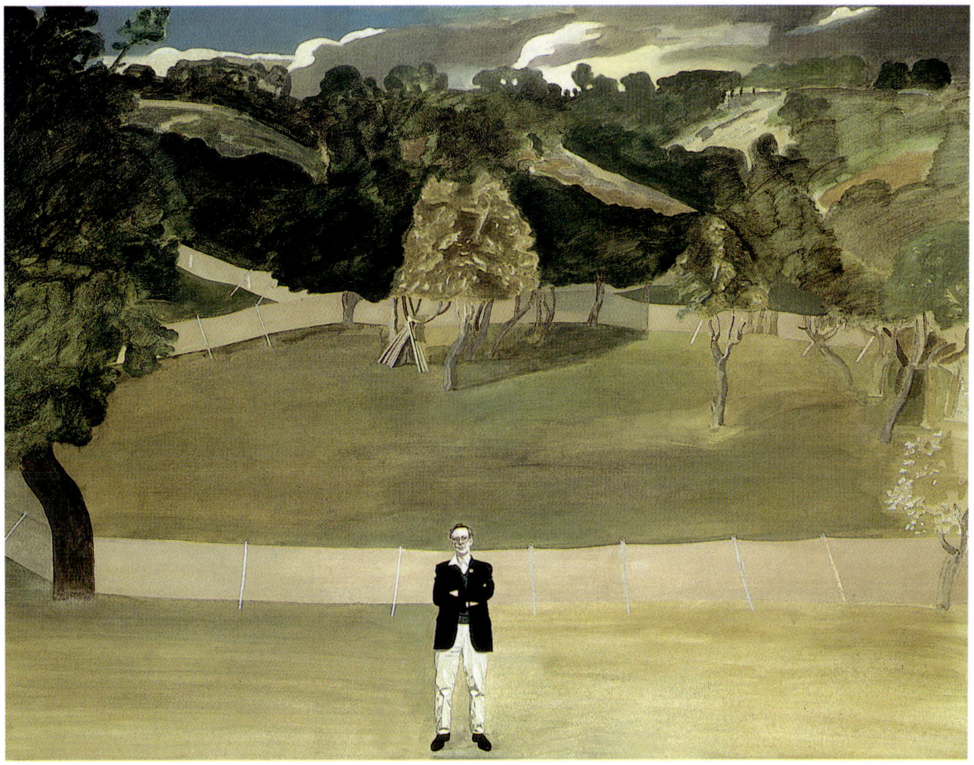

200 **The Deer Park (After Velásquez' *The Boar Hunt*). In Memory of Michael Andrews 1928–1995**, 1996

affectionate and sympathetic portrayals since the mid-1950s. The still lifes, culminating in a full-scale copy of a Francisco de Zurbarán painting borrowed for the National Gallery's recent exhibition of Spanish still-life painting (*After 'Cup of Water and a Rose on a Plate' by Francisco de Zurbaran*, 1995–9, Plate 199), were chosen to fit into the interesting and elaborate frames that he had been collecting for years, and which had been sitting empty in patient expectation of the paintings that would fulfil their purpose. As he himself noted, they thus pay as much heed to the frames as to the art on which they are based; the Zurbarán can be said to have selected itself, since Blake made his copy as the most appropriate way of using the frame that had been constructed for the borrowed original.

In other works that have emerged from his residency, Blake has taken an even more subjective stance, as in his huge paraphrase of a tiny Cranach, *The Close of the Age of Silver* from the mid-1990s, for which he employed a very loose, painterly idiom in deference to two painters he admired from his own time, Francis Bacon and Lucian Freud. There is also a personal agenda behind *The Deer Park (After Velásquez'* The Boar Hunt*). In Memory of Michael Andrews 1928–1995* (1996, Plate 200), conceived in a spirit of remembrance in honour of the painter Michael Andrews, who had died in 1995: by alluding both to Andrews's painting of that name, now in the Tate, and to the National Gallery's *Philip IV hunting Wild Boar* by Velásquez, which is depicted in the centre of Andrews's large canvas, Blake aligns himself with both artists as mentors and fellow travellers and dignifies his departed friend as an artist who had proved himself a legitimate heir to the great tradition in painting.

Elsewhere, Blake made it clear that while he recognised a hierarchy of importance in art history, he was prepared to make his own evaluations and to trust his instincts when looking at earlier art, just as he was when faced with the work of his contemporaries, rather than enslaving himself to received opinion. During the period of his residency he produced a sensuous painting after an early copy of Michelangelo's *Leda and the Swan*, and, more touchingly still, to my eyes, a number of tiny painted notations of fragments from paintings by Piero della Francesca, Puvis de Chavannes and Velásquez. It is in these intimate and spontaneous renderings that one recognises most powerfully the whisperings of artists to each other across the centuries.

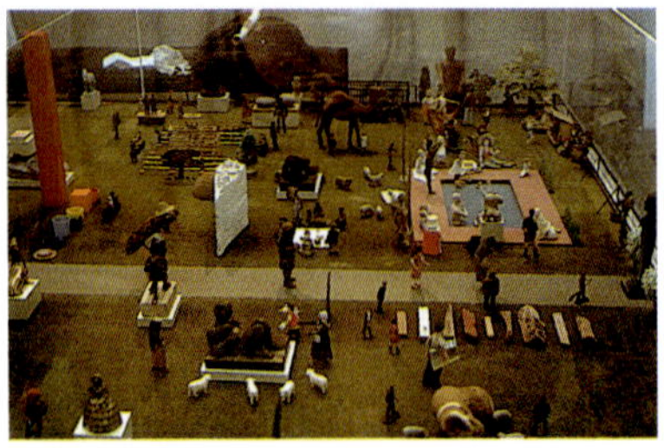

201 **Sculpture Park**, 1981–3

Collage and Sculpture

In January 2004 two specially commissioned sculptures, by far the largest in scale that Blake had ever made, were installed on the South Shore Promenade as part of an extension of the Golden Mile in Blackpool. The fact that the city had a permanent indoor circus gave him license to turn again to circus themes for these monumental bronzes, scaled up from

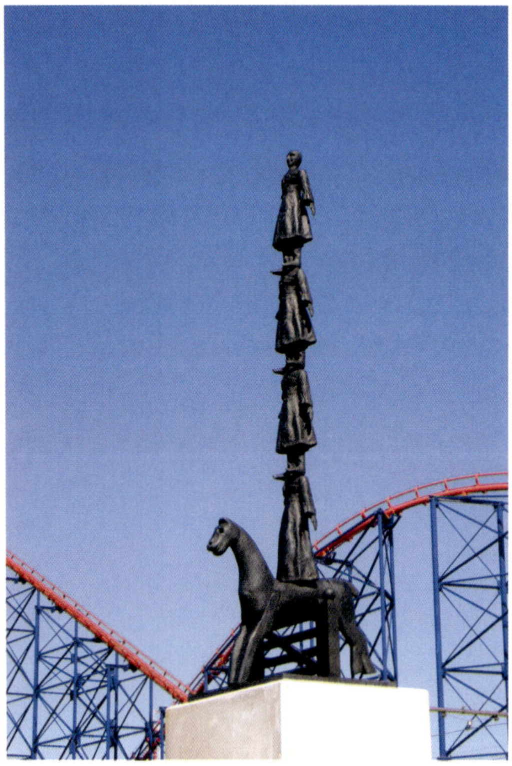

202 **Equestrian Act**, 2003–4

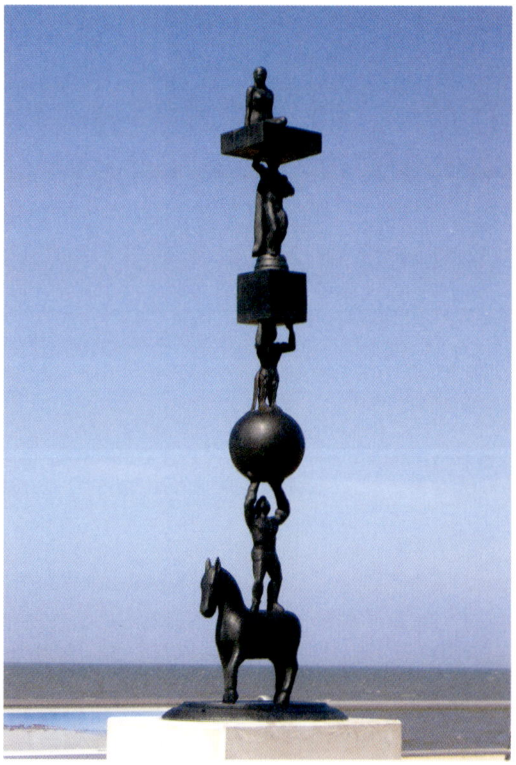

203 **Four Man Up**, 2003–4

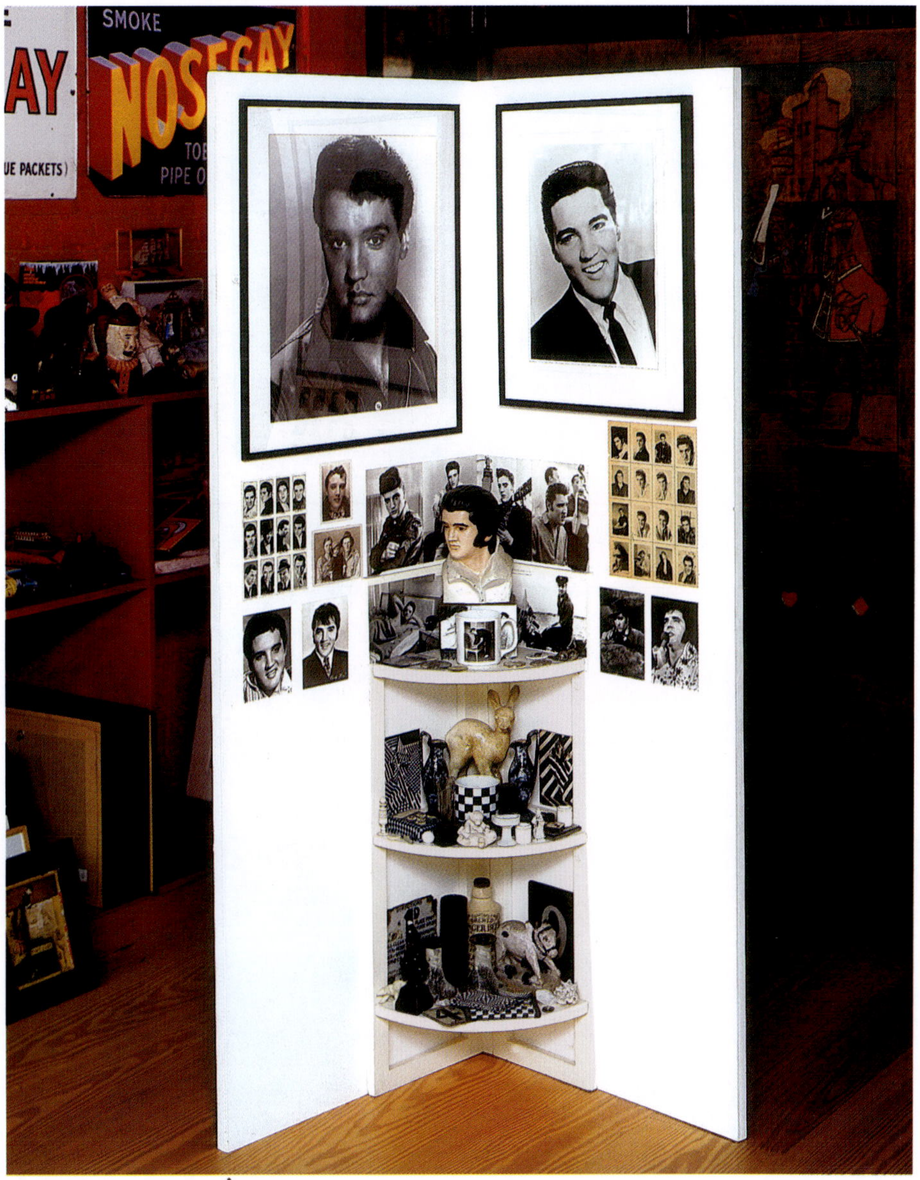

204 **Shrine for Elvis (Black & White)**, 2003

found objects. *Four Man Up* (Plate 203) relates to themes first seen in his art nearly four decades earlier, while *Equestrian Act* (Plate 202) extends the playful response to Constantin Brancusi he had created in his *Endless Column* of 2003 (Plate 206), this time reconfigured as an acrobatic feat of four stiffly posed Cossacks standing on each other's shoulders, all balanced on the back of a horse leaping over a wooden gate.

In their replication of manufactured objects these works are not only of a piece with Blake's arrangements of toys and other found objects since the late 1950s, but also relate to the methods employed by the English Pop sculptor Clive Barker, who was an old friend

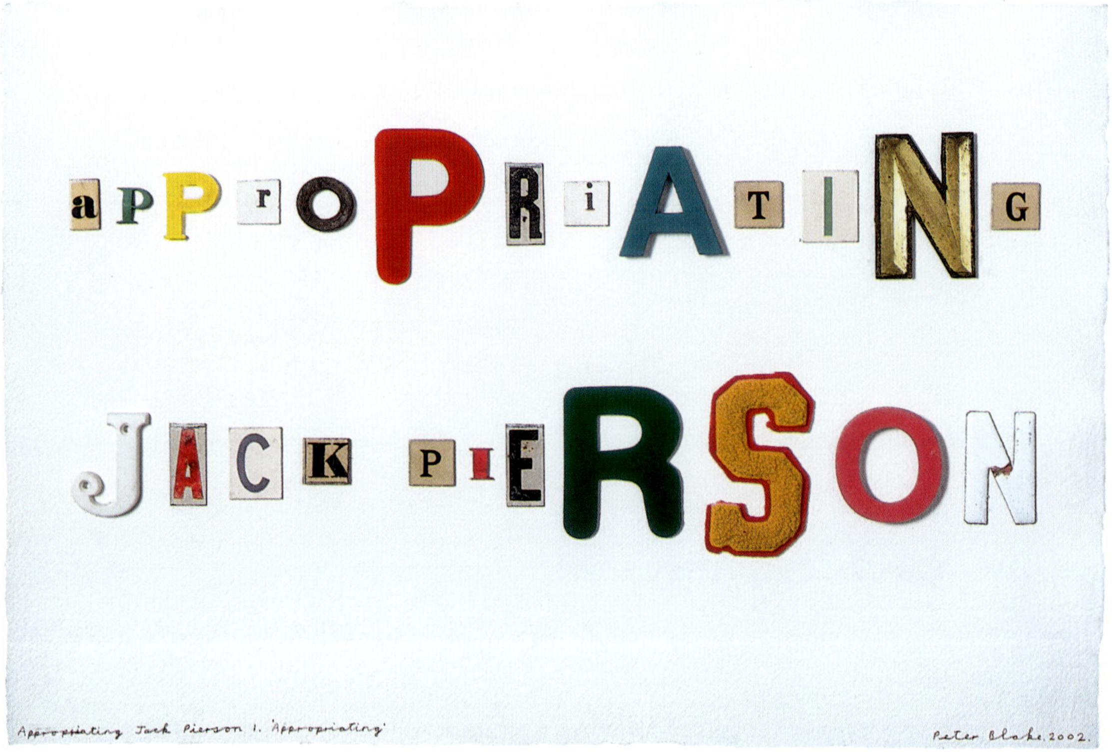

205 Appropriating Jack Pierson 1. 'Appropriating', 2002

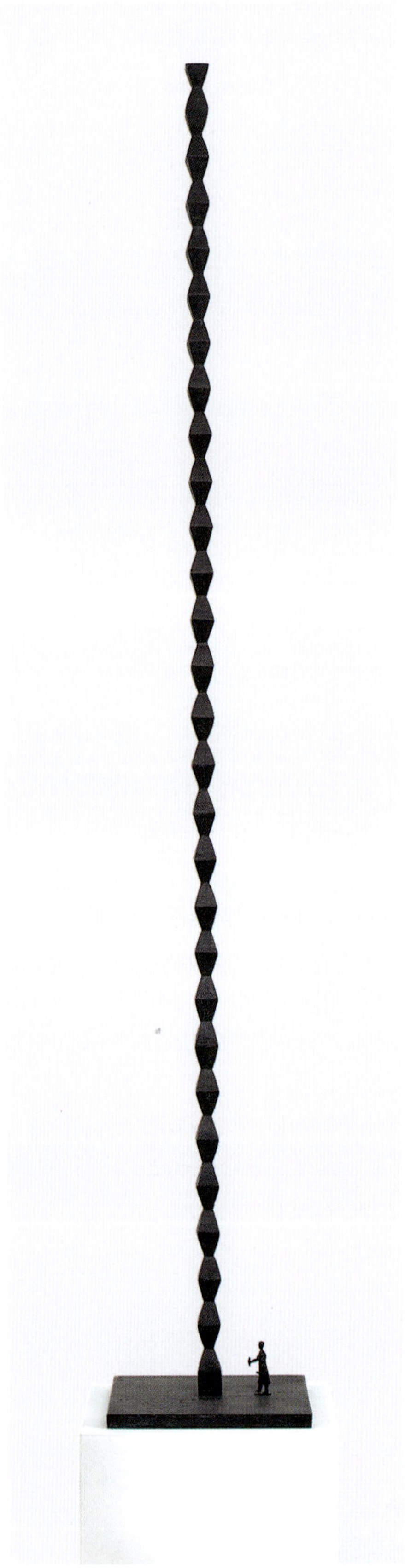

206 Endless Column, edition of 8 plus 1 artist's cast, 2003

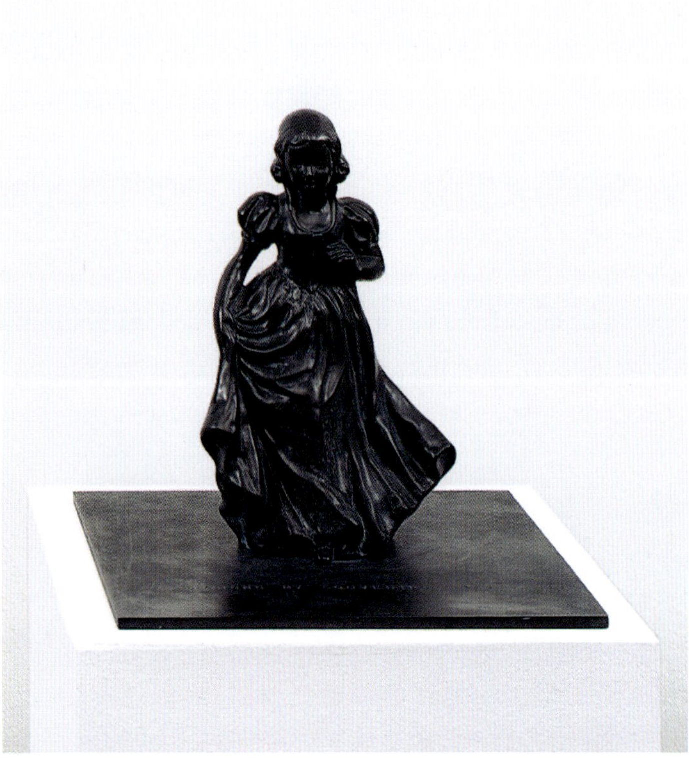

207 Among my Souvenirs 1: Snow White from Sgt. Pepper's Lonely Hearts Club Band, edition of 8 plus 1 artist's cast, 2003

and whose work Blake had been collecting for many years. During much of 2003, in preparation for a survey exhibition of his sculpture, much of Blake's energy was directed towards the making of sculpture by such methods, including the casting of objects that were part of his collection of curiosities (such as Tom Thumb's boots and Max Miller's shoes) or that already played a part in his art (as with the Snow White figure, Plate 207) from the *Sgt. Pepper* cover, Plate 139). The Blackpool bronzes (Plates 202, 203), the most ambitious in size to have been created by Blake, were cast at AB Foundry in East London, where other sculptors from the Waddington Galleries stable, including Barry Flanagan and William Turnbull, had long been working.

Marcel Duchamp's World Tour

Blake whimsically declared his retirement at the age of 65, just after his tenure as Associate Artist at the National Gallery had drawn to a close. It was, however, not a retirement from the making of art, but a distancing of himself from the fray, a decision to set aside petty squabbles, disappointments and competitiveness with other artists and to take a more relaxed view of life. He realised that his ambitions had either already been met, were no longer of importance to him or would now be unlikely to happen, though two very significant honours were to follow that surely pleased him and that marked his final acceptance by the Establishment: the awarding of an honorary doctorate by the Royal College of Art in 1998 and being knighted four years later (along with Mick Jagger, Jonathan Miller and Trevor Nunn), in the same month in which he turned 70.

On completing his tenure at the National Gallery, Blake had quickly thrown himself into numerous projects – some of which had been conceived years earlier – which, with his characteristic wit, he labelled 'encores'. These encores included some long-standing projects, such as the *About Collage* exhibition that he curated for Tate Liverpool in 2000, but which he had referred to by name in his preface to his 1988 Nishimura Gallery catalogue as one of the projects on which he had been working 'for some time'. Tying up loose ends, he curated or co-curated a series of exhibitions during this period that reflected on aspects of his interests other than painting: one focused on his collecting (*A Cabinet of Curiosities from the Collections of Peter Blake* at Morley Gallery, London, 8 October – 11 November 1999), another on his commercial art (at the London Institute Gallery, 4 August – 11 September 2003) and a third on sculpture (both his and that of others, from 10 November – 19 December 2003, again at the London Institute Gallery). He also worked with more urgency on the task of bringing to a close some major works begun as far back as the 1960s; this, too, was something that had been on his mind for many years, and which he referred to in the same Nishimura Gallery essay as destined to result in an exhibition called *Works in progress finished*, to consist of 'about ten pictures which have been exhibited at intervals in various stages of completion'.

In addition to these essentially retrospective activities, Blake was engaged in the production of a great variety of new works. Among these are some major series that stand alongside anything from earlier years, including the paintings grouped together under the banner *Marcel Duchamp's World Tour* (Plates 111, 208–10, 212), in which the long deceased great Modernist hero (1887–1968) finds himself in a variety of surprising situations. They were first shown as a group as half of a solo exhibition at Waddington Galleries held on 19 October–12 November 2005.

The other section of this exhibition was devoted to a series called *1–10 (Collages, Constructions, Drawings & Sculpture)*, which included samples from a number of separate aspects of his past work. Never one to waste anything, Blake intended in part to make use of a series of small, still unfinished paintings he had begun while at the National Gallery on the theme *In Homage to Woman*, though in the end these did not feature here, either. He certainly had plenty of material from which to choose for the *1–10* series. Work number *1* was represented by *Museum of the Colour White* (*c.*1995), an assemblage of objects laid out simply in rows, of the sort he had been producing as long ago as the early 1960s. For *2* (*M.M,.* 1990), he paired two paintings with photographic collage in the idiom he had first devised in 1959 and more recently in his *Déjà vu* and *Homage to Marilyn Monroe* exhibitions; each of these paintings contains, in its upper register, two copies of the same photographic portrait of Marilyn, with a diagonally bisected square in two primary colours below. The *About Collage* exhibition that he had curated for Tate Liverpool in 2000 is recalled in work number *3*, *In Homage to Collagists* (2000, Plate 211), a set of witty pastiches of the styles associated with three great Dadaists, Max Ernst, Kurt Schwitters and Hannah Höch. Proceeding through to *10*, each time creating a composite work from the relevant number of elements, Blake once again demonstrated his versatility and the diversity of his artistic practice. For *9*, for instance, he presented a grid of nine framed, individually signed and dated *Tracings* made as part of his working process right through his career.

It is fitting that Blake, in his notional retirement, should have chosen to pay tribute to Duchamp, who in mid-career had famously announced his withdrawal from art to devote himself to playing chess at a very high level. Duchamp, as it turned out, had in fact never given up making art and had devoted the last 20 years of his life to working secretly on his last major sculptural project, *Etant donnés: 1. La chute d'eau 2. Le gaz d'éclairage*, now in the Philadelphia Museum of Art. Blake's fellow artist and Pop Art pioneer Richard Hamilton had played an important part in resuscitating Duchamp's reputation from the late 1950s

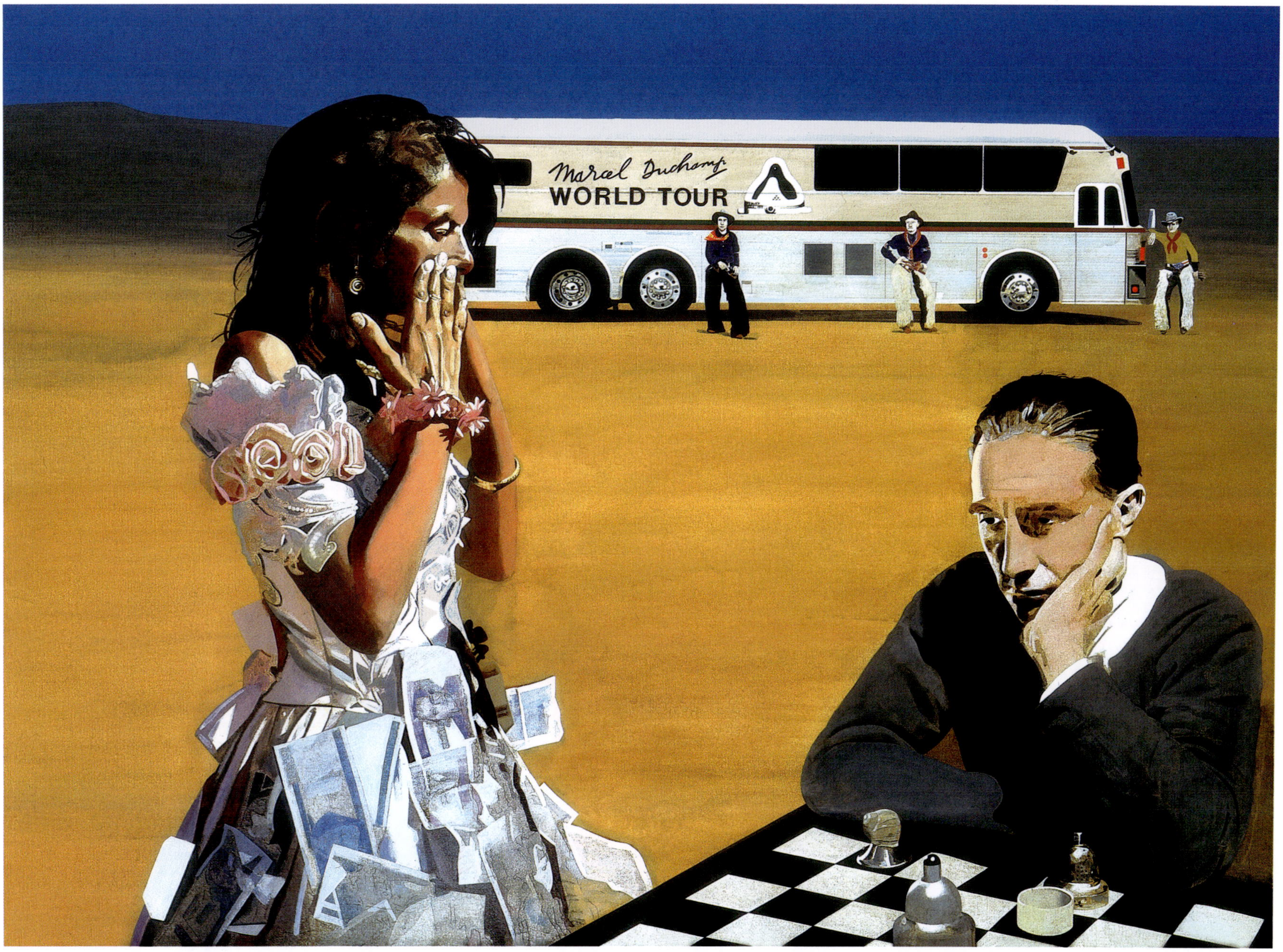

208 **Marcel Duchamp's World Tour: Playing Chess with Tracey**, 2003–5

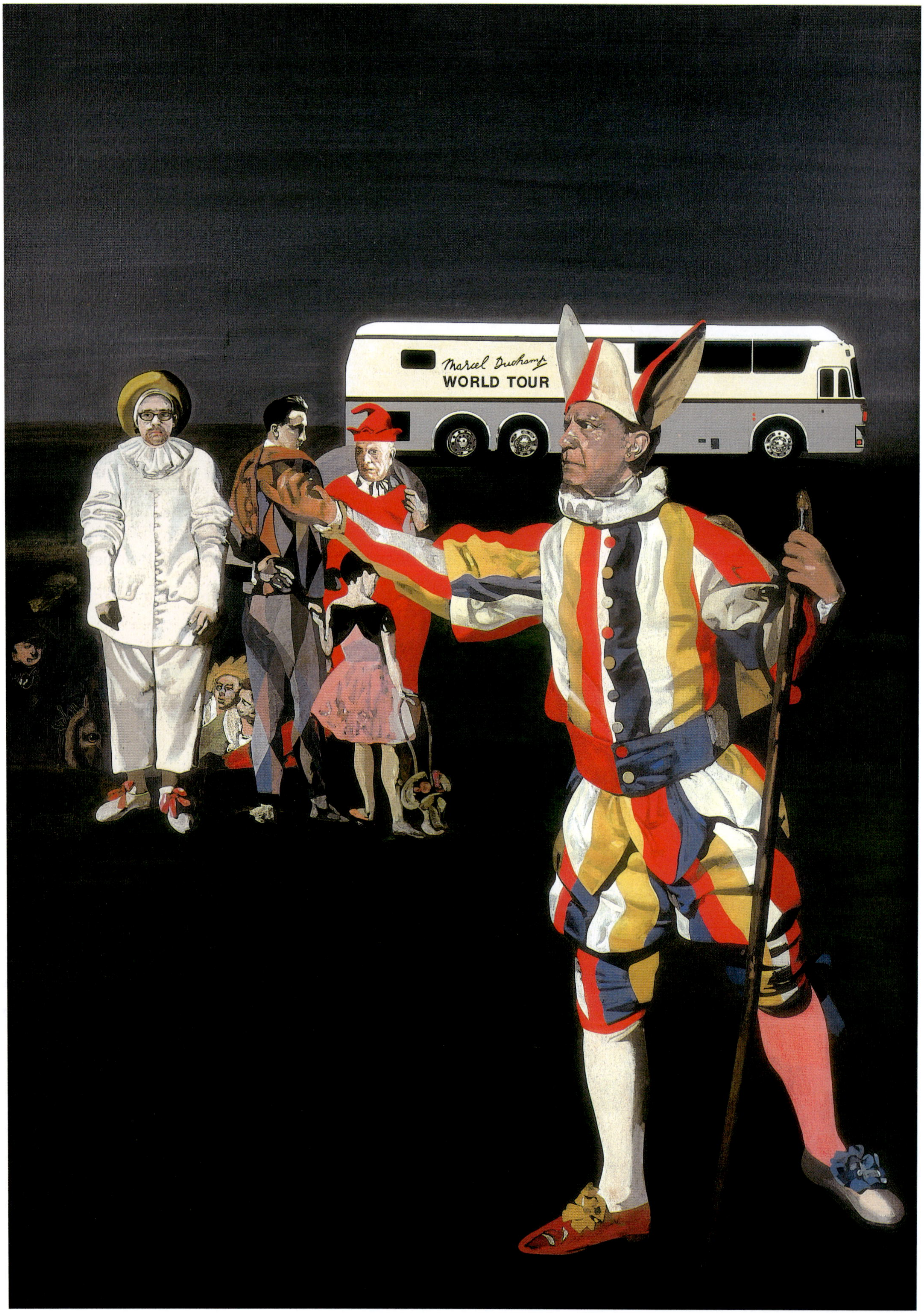

209 **Marcel Duchamp's World Tour: The Artists' Fancy Dress Ball**, 2004

and had curated Duchamp's important Tate Gallery retrospective of 1966, for which Hamilton made a life-size replica of the Dadaist's most celebrated work, *The Bride stripped by her Bachelors, Even*, also known as *The Large Glass*. By the end of the twentieth century, it was apparent that the work of this most cerebral of modern artists, inventor of the ready-made (by which a manufactured object is redesignated and recontextualised as a work of art) and grandfather of conceptual art, had decisively influenced the course of late Modernism and Postmodernism and was continuing to seep into the practice of succeeding generations.

Duchamp's impact in particular on the 'Young British Artists' who emerged in the 1990s, including Damien Hirst, Tracey Emin, Gavin Turk and Marc Quinn – all of whom were to become great friends of Blake – may have been an important factor in Blake's decision to honour him. For Blake, though, it was also a way of expressing gratitude to an artist who opened so many doors to others. Kinetic art, installation art and Pop Art (especially in its dependence on found imagery and manufactured objects) are among the many developments that can be traced back at least in part to Duchamp's example. The overriding principle, as expressed simply by Blake, was that anything an artist did could be art. This freedom of movement was one that Blake had long since exemplified in his own art, in his apparently abrupt (but in fact always conceptually and thematically consistent) ruptures of style, method and medium.

Duchamp began his career as a painter and had produced one of the most arresting experimental post-Cubist paintings, *Nude descending a Staircase No. 2* (Philadelphia Museum of Art) in 1912, creating a furore with it at the *Armory Show* in New York a year later, but he soon came to reject easel painting as outmoded and limiting. There is more than a touch of irony, therefore, in Blake's decision to express his respect for him through that very medium, and to do so in a painstaking and essentially Realist style. In the previous decade Blake had sewn the seeds for the *World Tour* paintings in a series of small collages which featured a single image of the back of Duchamp's head, sporting a tonsured star shape in his haircut. The *World Tour* paintings are also all photographically derived, but this time from a variety of sources, assembled in the spirit of collage but entirely handpainted. Conforming to his established practice of working from tracings of photographic images, he had each motif enlarged to the requisite size on a photocopier and then traced it onto transfer paper so that the outlines could be imprinted on the surface of the canvas and then slowly elaborated in layers of thin paint. The resulting paintings have what some might term an illustrator's eye for detail, but they have a finesse, a delicacy of touch and an astonishing degree of control that place them within a tradition stretching back to Renaissance miniatures.

In each of the paintings a huge aluminium tour bus, of the sort used by rock musicians when travelling around the United States, is seen either in its entirety in profile or

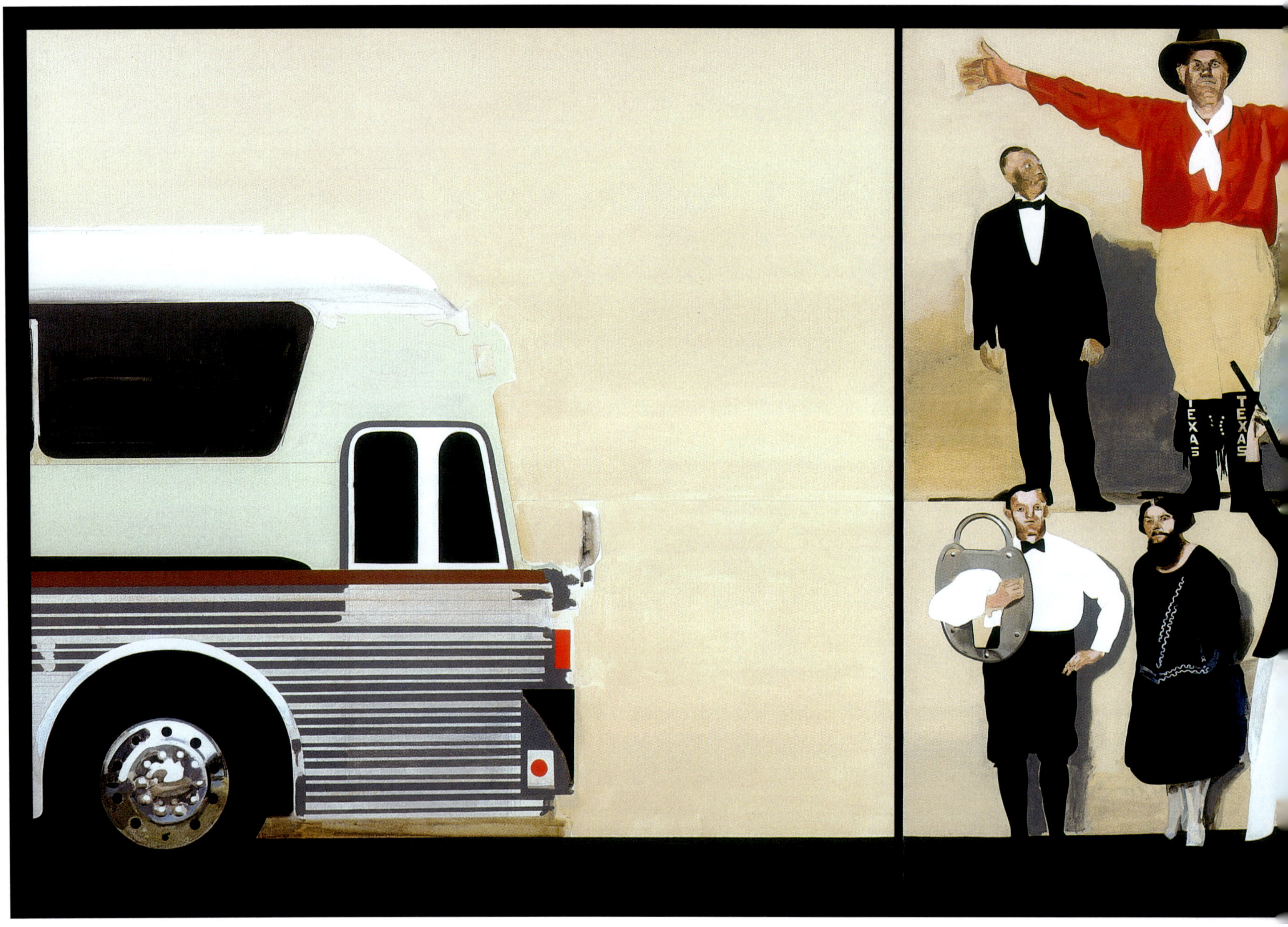

210 **Marcel Duchamp's World Tour: He Meets the Congress of Unusual People with the Ringling Brothers and Barnum and Bailey (Combined) Circus Season – 1929**, 2004–5

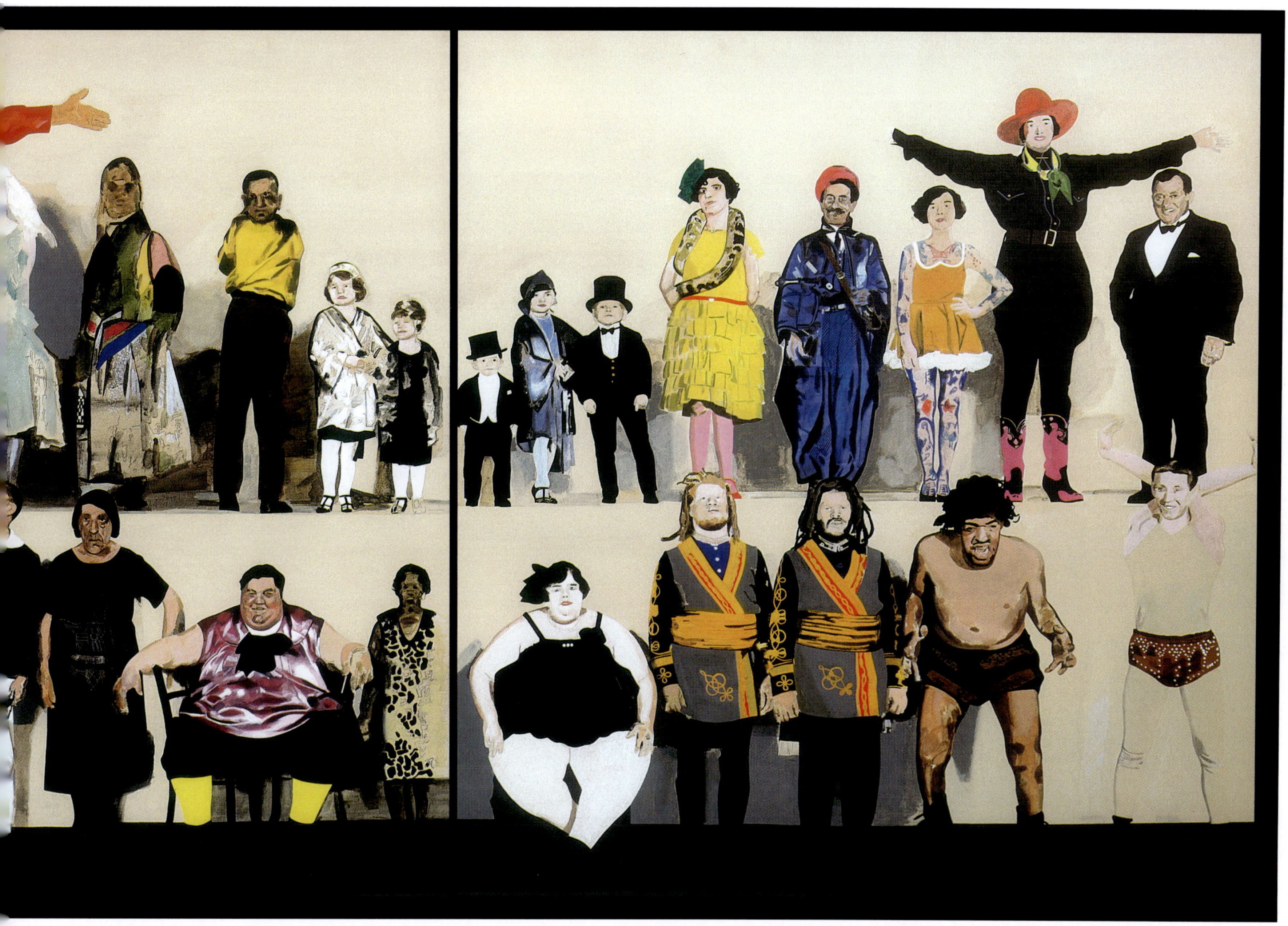

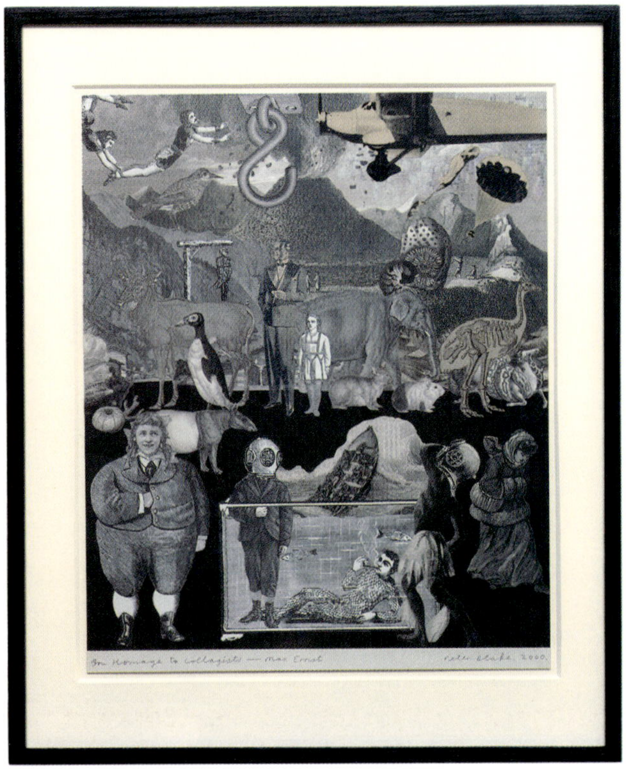

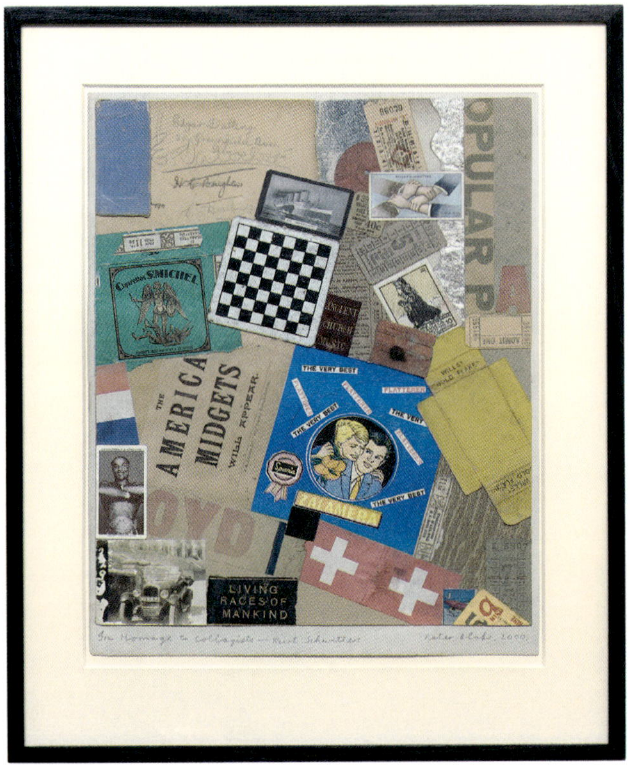

in a close-up detail. With 'The Marcel Duchamp WORLD TOUR' emblazoned in giant lettering on its upper flank, it proudly suggests a major rock band's gruelling itinerary to the hinterlands or a champion's valedictory lap. Blake had travelled occasionally with Ian Dury (to whom he had taught painting in the 1960s) and the Blockheads, and more pertinently had once been driven in the tour bus used by the Everly Brothers, whom he also knew as friends (and in Don's case, as godfather to Blake's daughter Rose). Now it is Blake who imagines himself offering a lift to his artist hero, taking him on something of a magical mystery tour across space and time, one that he likens to two of his favourite works of fiction from childhood: *Alice in Wonderland* and the Judy Garland film of *The Wizard of Oz*. The adventures that he offers to Duchamp, who of course also appears in each picture, are as entertaining as they are incongruous. Each picture is an excuse to make reference to and copy motifs Blake has seen and liked, on the pretext that it is for his forebear's sake that he is recreating these things.

In *The Artists' Fancy Dress Ball* (2004, Plate 209), Duchamp, wearing a harlequin costume borrowed from a celebrated rose-period Picasso (*Family of Santimbanques*, National Gallery of Art, Washington D.C.), stands with his back to the viewer between the great American Realist painter Edward Hopper, also dressed as a clown (from the same 1905 picture), and Damien Hirst in the guise of Watteau's *Gilles* (Louvre, Paris). The choice of Watteau was also predicated on Blake's understanding that Picasso's early work owed debts

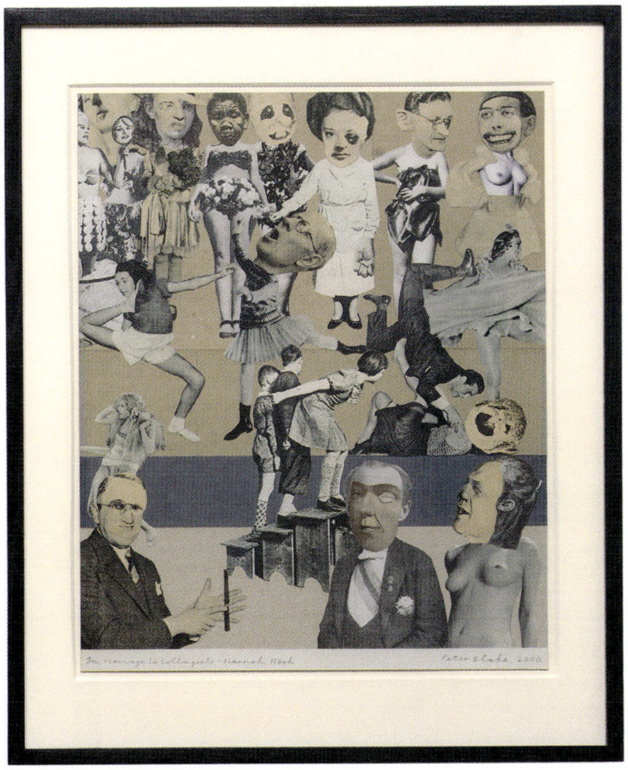

211 In Homage to Collagists: Max Ernst, Kurt Schwitters, Hannah Höch, 2000

to that very artist. Striking a pose in the foreground is that other titan of twentieth-century art, Picasso himself, his lugubrious expression undiminished by the theatrical stance and jester's outfit copied verbatim from a painting by the eighteenth-century English artist Johann Zoffany representing *Thomas King (Playing the role of Touchstone in 'As you like it')* (in the collection of the Garrick Club, London). Since in Blake's view to paint even a single clown had become tainted as a subject for a modern artist – with connotations of the corny, sentimental and clichéd – his solution was that to make it work it would be a question of the more clowns the better. So it is that he arrived at this idea of a convention or informal gathering of clowns with a rather superior pedigree.

Like his exact contemporary and friend R.B. Kitaj, the London-based American painter whom he had known since the early 1960s, Blake in these pictures ransacks art history to his own ends, piecing together his compositions from fragments of some of his favourite earlier art. As with Kitaj, too, there is a sense of meanings accruing through the juxtapositions and through the layering of images. Whereas Kitaj often favoured esoteric sources conjoined in mysterious ways, Blake proposes a more playful game of spotting the source and of enjoying the gentle humour of the transformations. There is a congruence between the clarity of the pictorial language and the familiarity (whether generic or art-historically specific) of the sources. In *Playing Chess with Tracey* (2003–5, Plate 208), for instance, Tracey Emin is pictured exactly as seen in her photographic inkjet self-portrait, *Sometimes the Dress is worth more Money than the Money* (2000), which Blake had found in a recent issue of the magazine *Parkett*; the gesture of her hands held to her face now connotes astonishment at being faced with the daunting task of outwitting that most intelligent of chess-players, seen pondering his next move exactly as in the cover photograph on *The Chess Biography of Marcel Duchamp*, volume one (Moravian Chess, 2002), by Vlastimil Fiala. In *He Meets the Spice Girls and Elvis* (2000–05, Plate 212), Duchamp appears in the bus window as his female alter ego Rrose Sélavy, while the girl band, formed long after the death of both Duchamp and Elvis, poses outside with the raven-haired giant of rock'n'roll in his youthful incarnation.

The notion of the magical crowd, which had intrigued Blake since the 1950s in pictures such as *The Preparation for the Entry into Jerusalem* (Plate 37) and which was most famously enshrined in the improbable encounters featured on his cover for the Beatles' *Sgt. Pepper* album (Plate 139) in 1967, continues to recur in his art and in particular in some of the Duchamp pictures. Among his first ideas for the series, but begun only after the others were completed, was *He Meets Robin Hood and his Merry Men and Is Particularly Taken with Maid Marian* (2008). An equally elaborately titled example from the *World Tour* paintings is also the most densely populated in its cast of characters: *He Meets the Congress of Unusual People with the Ringling Brothers and Barnum and Bailey (Combined) Circus Season – 1929* (2004–5, Plate 210). Its frieze-like display is faithful to the extraordinary photograph, labelled with rather less political correctness 'Congress of Freaks', on which this painting in triptych format is based. As always, however, the artist has made aesthetic choices in making his transcription, in this case replacing the tarpaulin backdrop of the original photograph with subtly gradated grey walls against which the figures' shadows create an eerie secondary crowd of ghost-like presences and establish a defined if airless and claustrophobic space. The master of ceremonies dressed in black tie in the centre panel, looking up at the giant with outstretched arms, is now, of course, none other than Duchamp.

With a loving attention to detail, Blake here ropes Duchamp into his own lifelong project of celebrating the outsider, the misfit, the eccentric and the less than beautiful: the very types that had populated his art since the fairground paintings of the mid-1950s, such as *Loelia, World's Most Tattooed Lady* (1955, Plate 21), and at intervals in such tender and affectionate works as the *Side Show* wood engravings of 1974–8. Perhaps the only surprising omission from the *Congress of Unusual People* is Blake's own image, though in the bearded lady just below Duchamp one might detect just a hint of a self-mocking self-portrait. (By curious coincidence, at a dinner following the opening in 1995 of Blake's solo show at Galerie Claude Bernard in Paris his then eight-year-old daughter, Rose, made a drawing of her bearded Dad wearing a skirt, which she sold to me for the princely sum of 50p.)

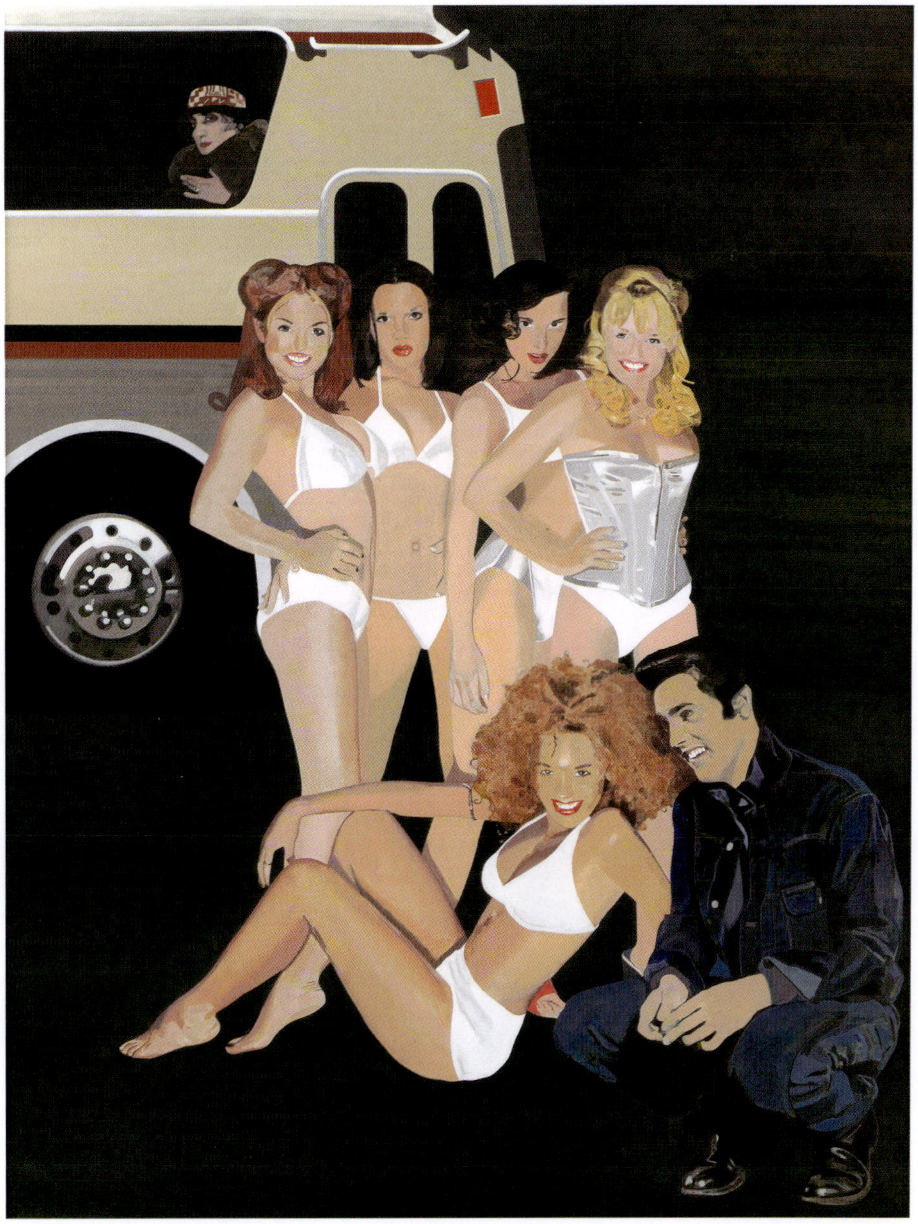

212 **Marcel Duchamp's World Tour: He Meets the Spice Girls and Elvis**, 2000–05

With *The Tarzan Family* (1995–2005, Plate 111), the most beautifully rendered of all the *World Tour* paintings, Blake cleverly finds a way of bringing to a close a picture on which he had commenced work long before the *World Tour* series had formed in his mind. Tarzan, Jane, Boy and Cheeta each stare back at us, their eyes full of curiosity, while Duchamp, calmly smoking a cigar, takes their naked presence in his stride. Boy's face is a marvel of intense observation, down to the last eyelash: encouraged to come close to the surface and gaze into his eyes, one somehow feels under his spell.

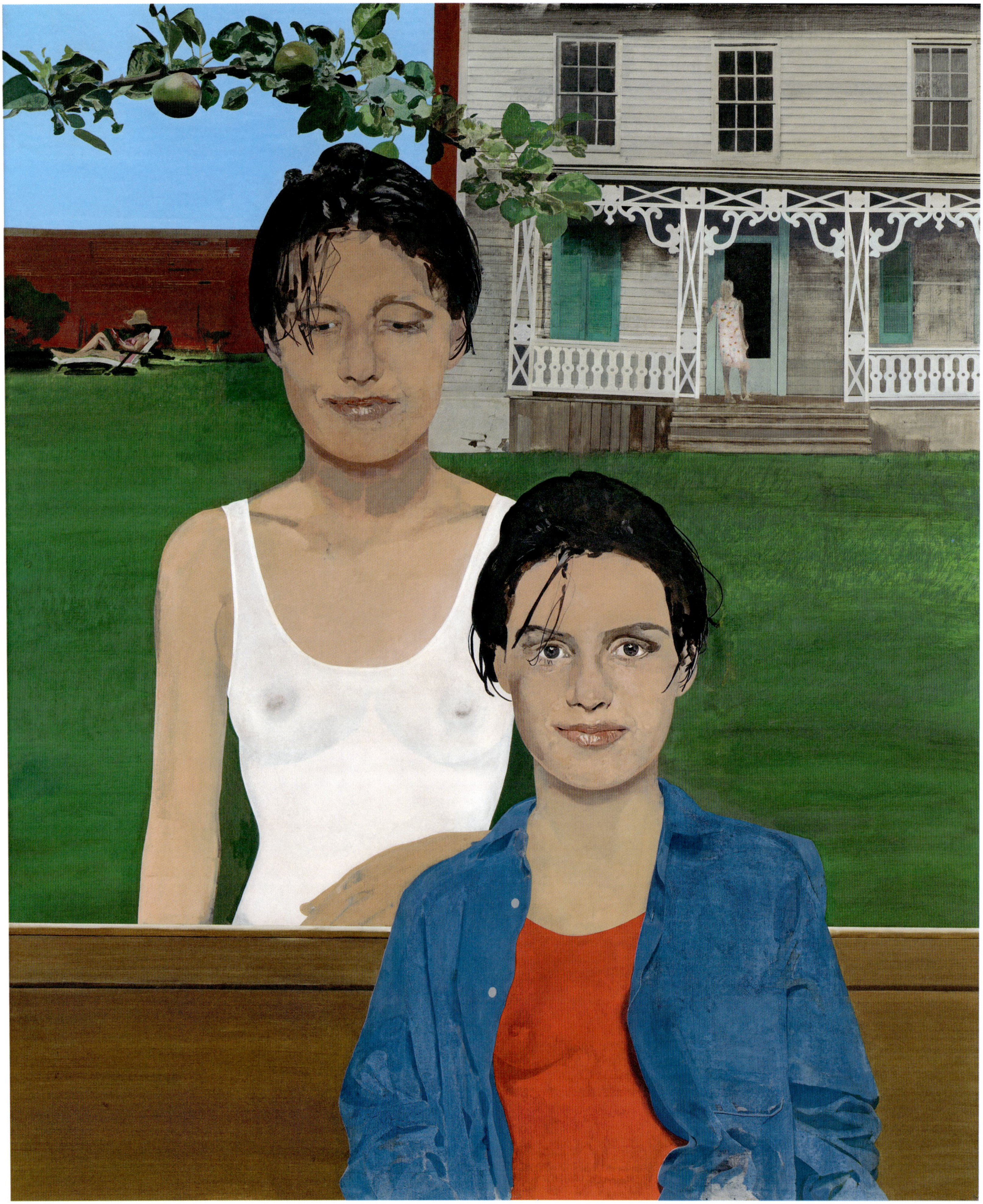

213 **The Twins in their Tea Garden**, 1991

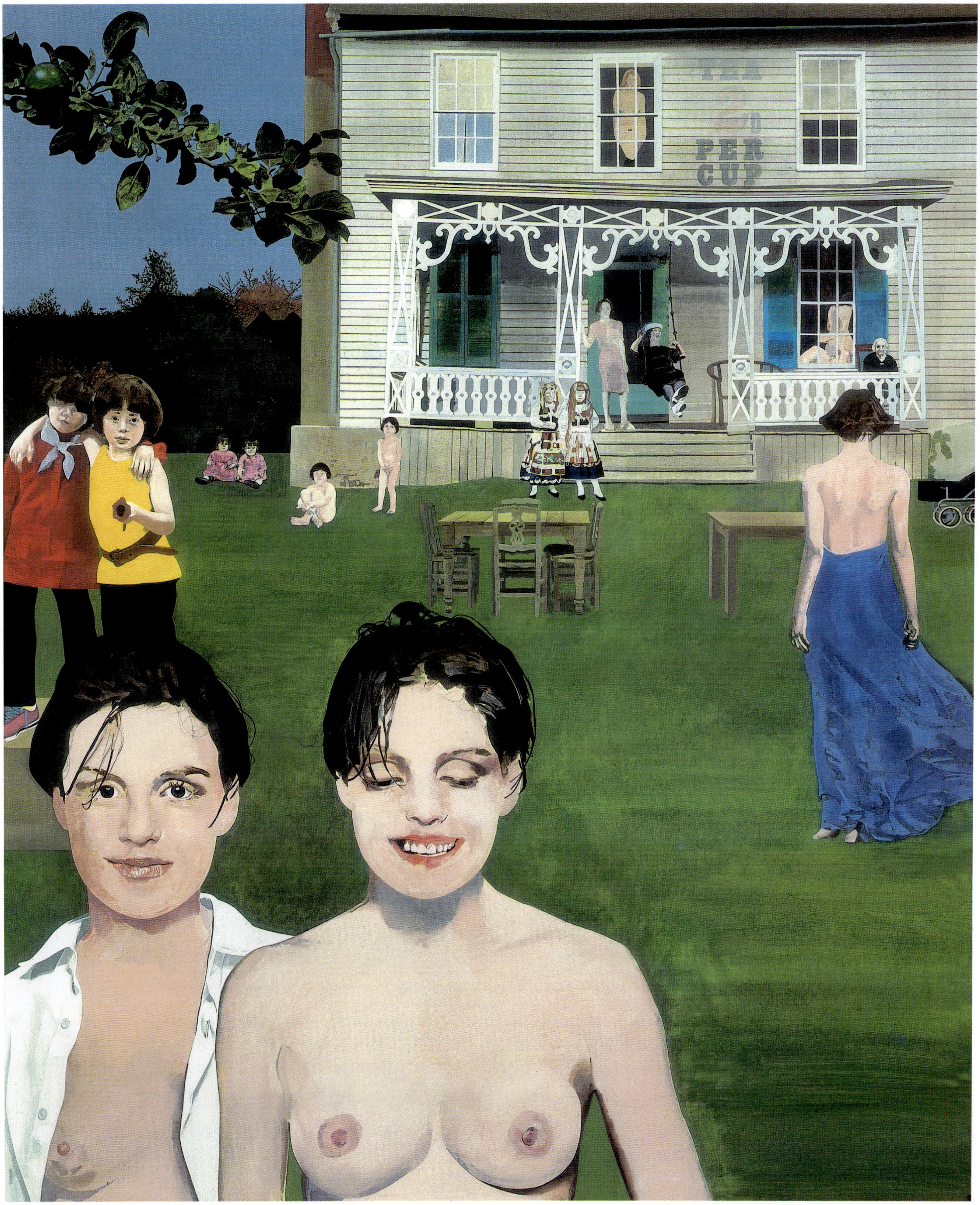

214 **The Twins in their Tea Garden** (2nd version), 1995–9

Further Fantasies

Any visitor to Blake's studio will encounter works in various stages of completion, some of them dating back decades, and interviewers will have a dizzying number of future plans patiently spelt out to them. So it should come as no surprise that within larger groups of works, such as the National Gallery pictures or the *World Tour* paintings, Blake has continued to imagine other subjects that could yet fan out into more extensive series. A case in point is *The Twins in their Tea Garden* (Plates 213, 214), depicting a pair of dark-haired and attractive young women in front of their clapboard house, which exists in two versions, from 1991 and 1995–9 respectively, which immediately precede and postdate his time at the National Gallery.

The owners of the Nishimura Gallery in Tokyo, where Blake had shown periodically, had seen the first of these double portraits at an early stage in his studio and in promising to buy it had asked him when it would be ready for collection. Having been told that it would take a year to complete, they phoned him a year to the day later and asked him about taking possession of it. So it was that he found himself having to bring the picture as it stood to a satisfactory level of technical finish, but without the additional elements that he had intended to include. In a resourceful reworking of the classical subject of the Seven Ages of Man, and conflating numerous time frames within a single coherent space (as in pre-Renaissance narrative paintings), in the second version Blake pictures the same two women at vital stages of their life, from early infancy (as represented by their unseen presence in the pram), as toddlers, through pre-pubescence and sexual maturity (caught *in flagrante* in the uncurtained window) and finally in old age. It is not too fanciful to think of this definitive rendering of the subject as another permutation in Blake's disguised self-portraits, one which enables him to reflect, in his own advancing years, on prized moments of happiness in his own eventful life.

In 2002 Blake turned 70, an age he was happy to reach after suffering a couple of health scares. Judging that he has now experienced his expected 'ration' of three score and ten years, he has cheerfully enjoyed every subsequent day, and every new opportunity to make more art, as a bonus. In his usual jovial spirit and with a love of paradox, he has taken it upon himself to announce what is normally left for posterity to judge retrospectively: that he has now embarked upon his 'late period'. One thing that the humour of the Duchamp paintings and other septuagenarian works such as *Gender Benders* (2002–3, Plate 104) makes abundantly clear is that he is no more likely now than ever to lose the childlike sense of fun, spirit of play and adventure, gentle subversiveness and devil-may-care whimsicality that have guided his art-making for more than 60 years.

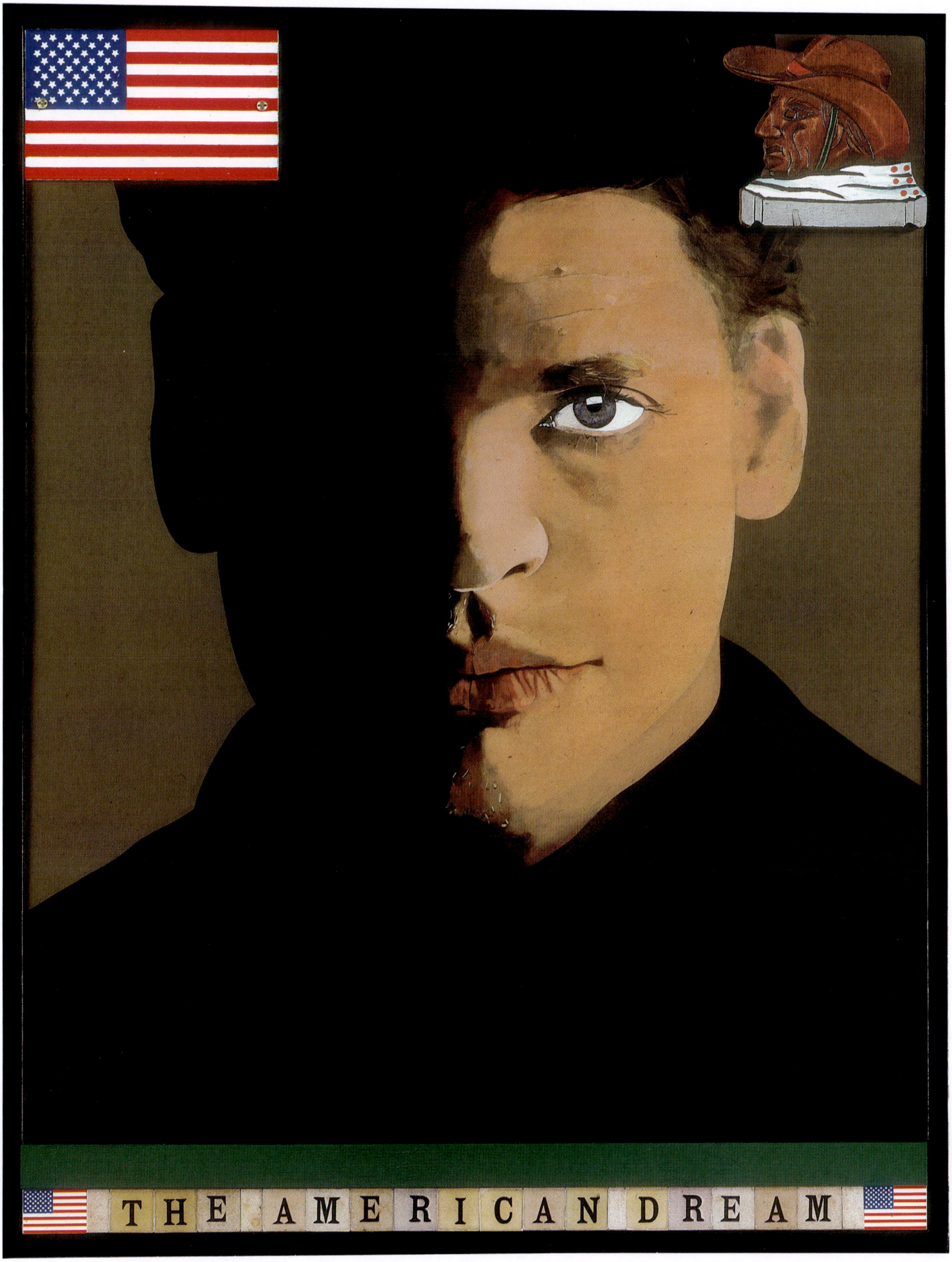

215 **The American Dream**, 1997–2003

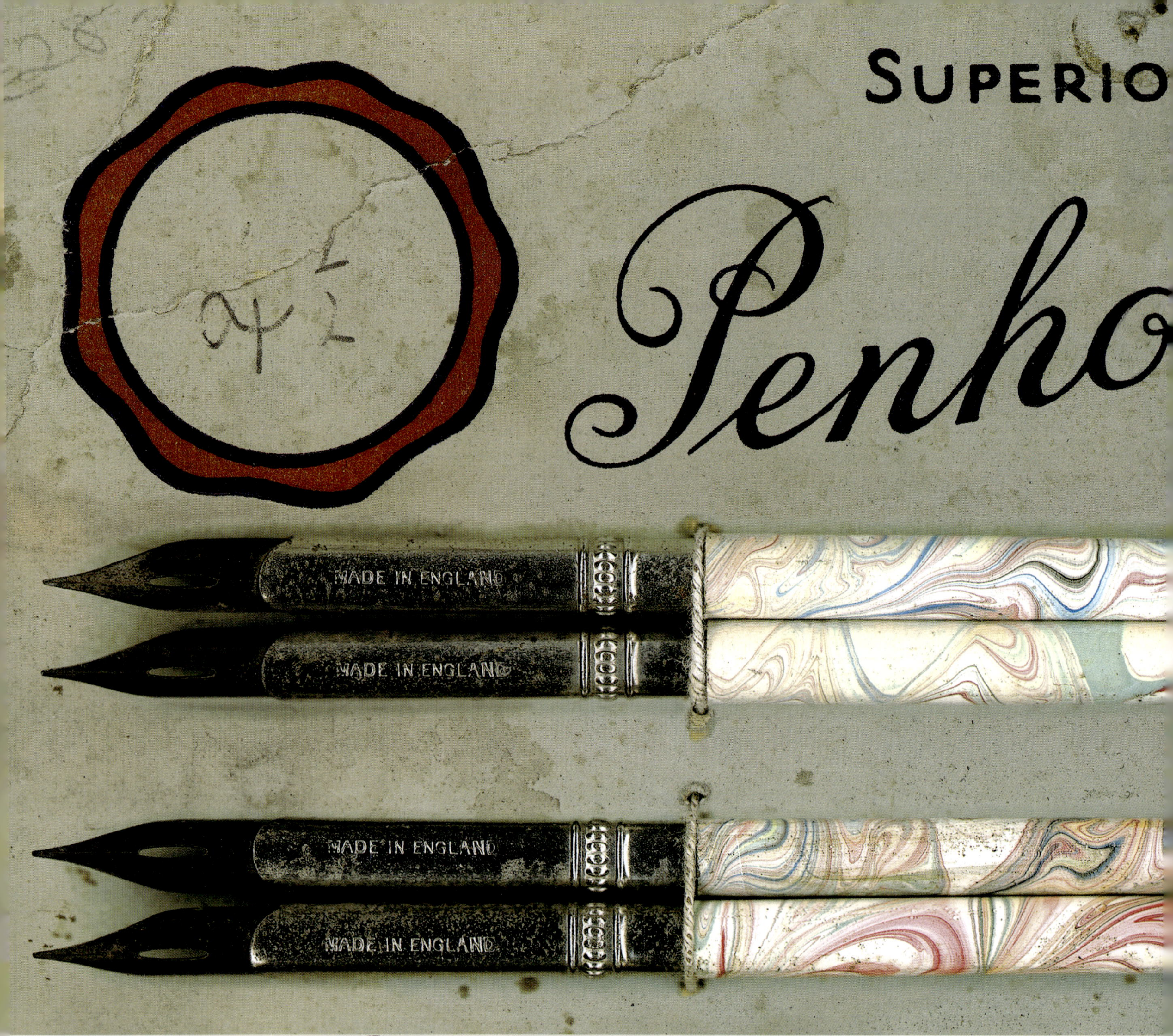

POSTSC
COLLECTIN

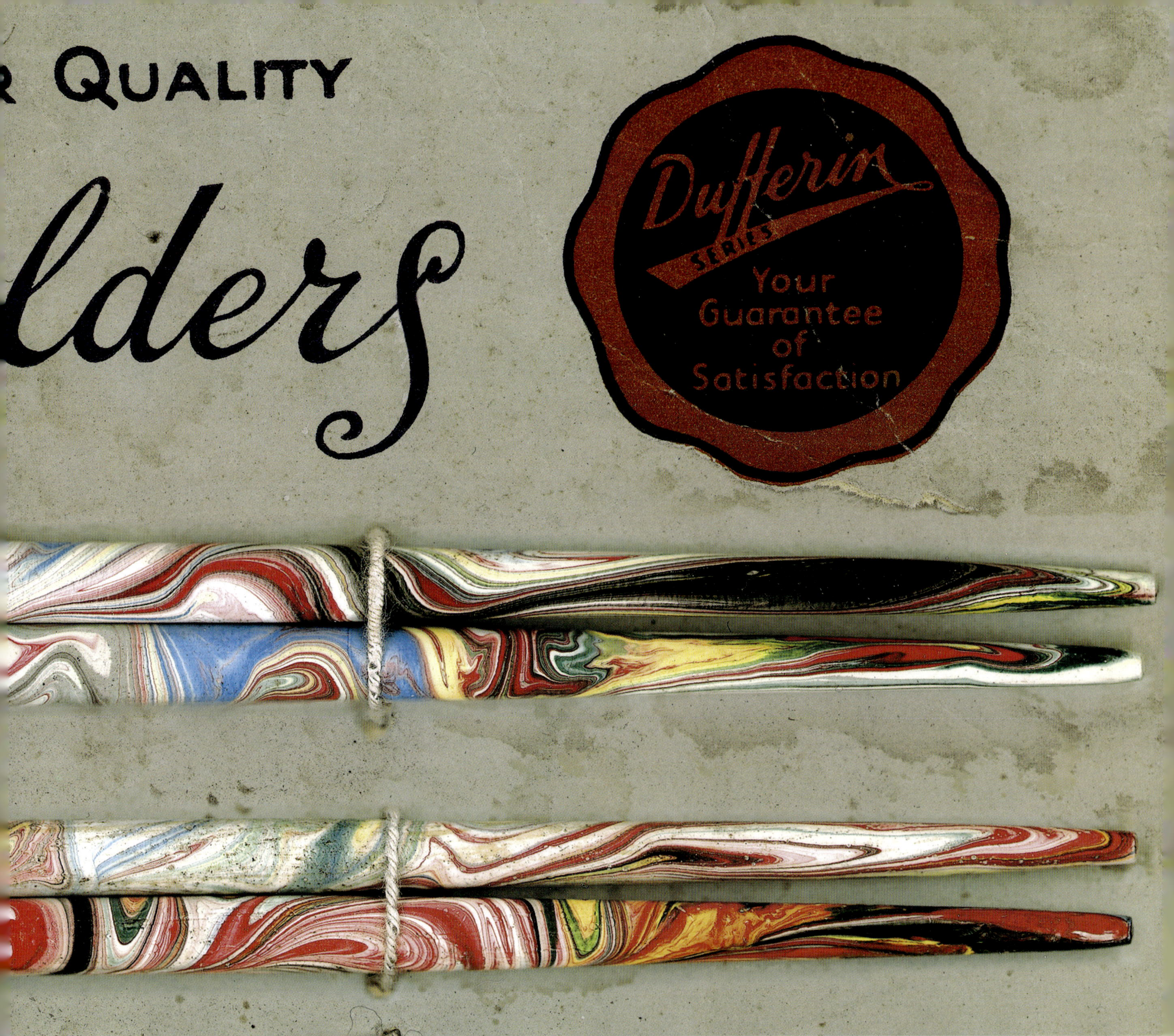

CRIPT:
G AS AN ART

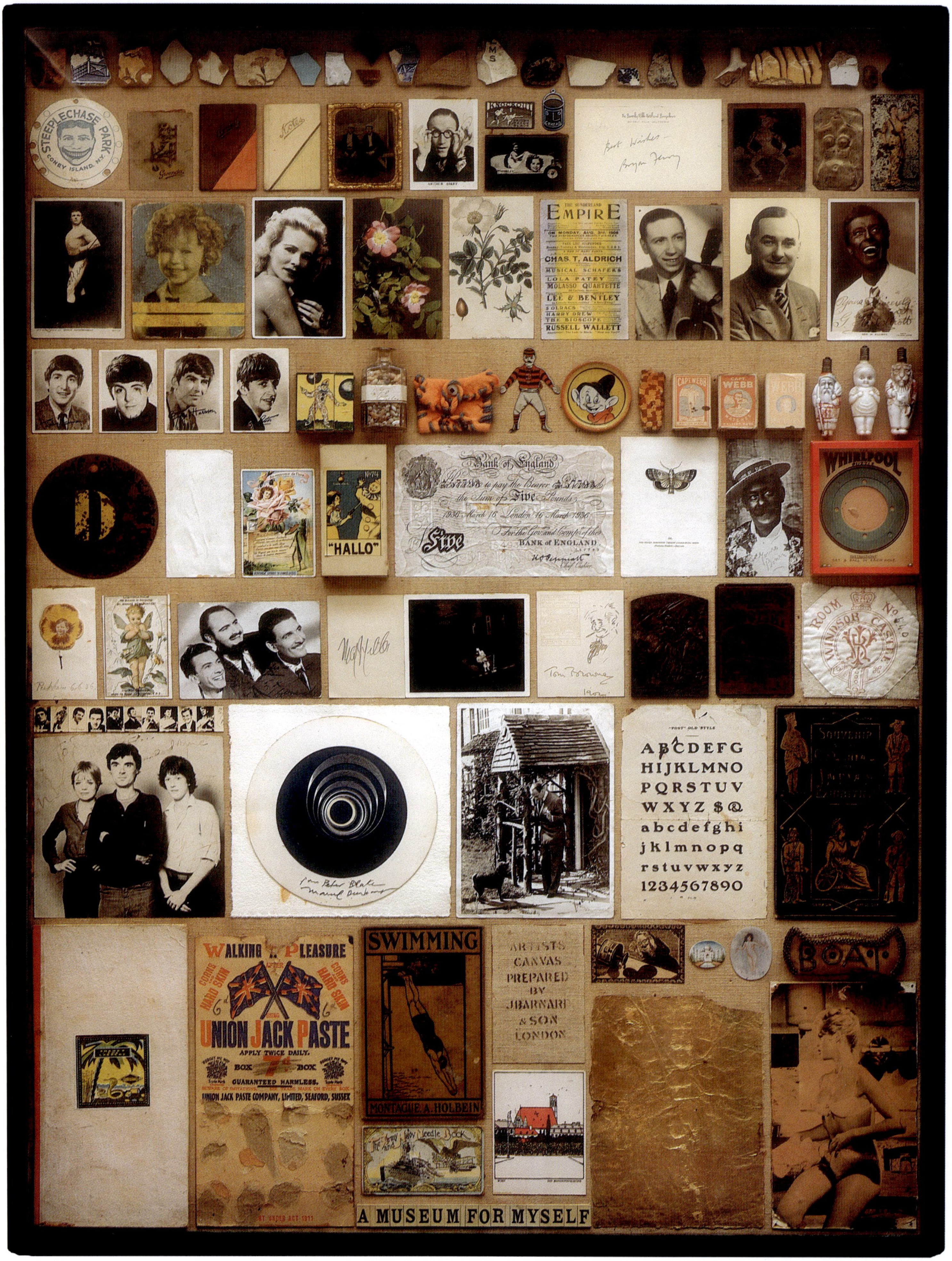

216 **A Museum for Myself**, 1982

Postscript: Collecting as an Art

Peter Blake's compulsive and for many years rather secretive parallel life as a voracious collector, not only of other art but of all kinds of artefacts, can be seen as another manifestation of the concerns behind much of his Pop work of the early 1960s: a desire to preserve, to classify and to document. His father had collected 0-gauge locomotives, but Blake's voracious accumulations of all kinds of objects, from ephemera through to valuable works of art, was on another scale of obsession altogether. Perhaps, as in the case of Andy Warhol, another Pop artist of blue-collar origin who accumulated a vast array of possessions, Blake never got over the relative deprivations of his childhood and the consequent excitement of being able to possess things that he would once never have dreamt of being able to afford. In focusing in particular on artefacts generally regarded as too marginal in importance to be worthy of special attention, but recognised by him as deeply imbued with traces of humanity through their previous use and existence, Blake accords even the humblest of objects a touching status as part of our shared past and collective memory.

Parts of Blake's house and studio alike resemble cabinets of curiosities, a spectacle alluded to also in some of his more sculptural works, including the *The Toy Shop* (1962, Plate 61), the assemblages of certain wrestling paintings of the mid-1960s and *Tarzan Box* of 1965 (Plate 106). His instincts as a collagist have likewise found form not only in his work – in his use of the medium and of a *trompe-l'oeil* painted version of it since the 1950s – but also in his intelligent appraisal of the history of collage in the hands of other artists, the subject for an exhibition first mooted in the mid-1980s and held at Tate Liverpool in 2000. The most vivid and consistent expression of these impulses in his own art can be found in the *Souvenirs* (Plates 149–51) that he began making for friends, including other artists, from 1968, which have been discussed in chapter 5. Like much of Blake's art, these carefully presented fragments – each selection, in its way, a portrait of the personality to whom it is dedicated – are presented in a generous spirit as celebrations of friendship and shared interests.

Closely connected to this collecting instinct is the surprisingly large body of sculpture produced by Blake throughout his career, much of it in the form of three-dimensional collages using found objects and more specifically manufactured items denoted by Marcel Duchamp as 'ready-mades'. Conceived in the same spirit with which he had brought together printed images, cheaply produced toys and other items in his collage paintings since the late 1950s, works such as the miniturised *Sculpture Park* of 1981–3 (Plate 201) extend his playful language into real space.

The meticulous nature of Blake's paintings, watercolours, drawings, collages and prints is the necessary by-product of his love of order, a motivating force evident also in his tendency to conceive of his works in a number of set categories that he has devised for himself. This habit of systematising his versatile production has been manifested with particular clarity in exhibitions. Each of the 142 works presented in 1977 at the Waddington and Tooth Galleries in London, under the title *Souvenirs and Samples*, was placed in one of 31 sections, sometimes simply according to medium, occasionally by style, often by subject or by following the purpose for which the work had been made; but in order to remain faithful to this system, certain works had to be accommodated in categories of their own. His Tate Gallery retrospective in 1983 followed similar lines, helping the visitor to make sense of his extremely varied offerings by placing the works in such groups as 'The Circus', 'Pop Art', 'Musicians', 'Wrestlers', 'Strippers', 'Fairies and Ruralist Works' and 'Paintings in Progress'. In planning a show at the Galerie Claude Bernard in 1984, as he explained in his preface to the catalogue, he again grouped the works, though the concept changed in response to circumstances. For his solo show at Waddington Galleries in 2005, discussed in chapter 7, he went further still, devoting half the exhibition to a sequence of ten numbered works, each of which embodied the relevant number in its very format.

The tidiness of mind betrayed by such principles of organisation has more than a little in common with the mentality of a collector or accumulator in its need both to make sense of what might otherwise appear to be random evidence and also to take possession of the material by naming it and then bringing it together with similar objects. It should come as no surprise that Blake's living quarters and studio space have always accommodated, in part, an ever-growing private museum. The scale of this largely secret hoard of treasures has expanded further since 1997, when he moved his studio out of his house in Chiswick and into a large dedicated space in Hammersmith, where visitors are offered glimpses of this Aladdin's Cave. Subdividing the warehouse-like space into sections devoted to particular activities – painting, sculpture, wood engraving and collage – Blake also made full use of the opportunity to create a kind of gallery or museum both for storage and for a constantly evolving display of his favourite items.

In the Hammersmith studio, on any given occasion, one might see drawings by George Grosz and Stanley Spencer, a collage by Joseph Cornell, engravings by Paul Nash, paintings by Derek Boshier and Richard Smith, and drawings by Patrick Caulfield (including one large one made on a paper tablecloth after a meal with the Blakes). There are also examples of the circus, funfair and wrestling memorabilia that he has collected all his life, Punch and Judy puppets, mass-produced packaging and other ephemera redolent of the Victorian and Edwardian periods. There are fragments, of course, of sculptural assemblages made from toys and other manufactured objects, as well as Elvis memorabilia, postcards and other material waiting for a possible use in new work: the dividing line between collecting and art-making, when viewed in these circumstances, can seem very thin indeed. More recently he has added to such oddities as Victorian collage screens, junk-shop paintings, collages by self-taught artists and furniture encrusted with shells yet more eccentric objects, including narrative anthropomorphic dioramas of taxidermy animals purchased in September 2003 from an auction of the contents of the recently closed Mr Potter's Museum of Curiosities.

Blake lent some of his collection of collages – mostly anonymous works by Outsider artists that had caught his eye – to the exhibition *About Collage*, which he curated for Tate Liverpool in 2000. Only on one occasion, however, for the *A Cabinet of Curiosities from the Collections of Peter Blake* exhibition at Morley Gallery, London, from 8 October to 11 November 1999, has he made a broader cross-section of his accumulated possessions available to the public at large. There, he displayed not only groups of works by artist friends that he has collected in depth, such as Colin Self and Clive Barker, but also talismanic objects such as a pair of hand-stitched leather boots once worn by General Tom Thumb, the life-sized waxwork portrait of the heavyweight boxing champion Sonny Liston (as featured on the *Sgt. Pepper* cover, Plate 139) and a signed and dedicated sheet by Damien Hirst of fake Beatles autographs. However, as a collector of RMS *Titanic* memorabilia once inadvertently remarked of the objects he proudly displayed on the BBC television programme *The Antiques Roadshow*: this was only the tip of the iceberg.

As a lifelong project, Blake's collecting has been pursued to such an obsessive degree as to suggest almost a second creative life parallel to his art-making. One day, when he is no longer with us, all this might end up as the core of a Peter Blake museum. Or, as he has remarked nonchalantly, it might all simply be sent off for sale at the auction of a lifetime – an occasion that he would be particularly keen to attend as a buyer were he able to return from the dead and start his collecting, and his creative life as an artist, all over again.

Chronology

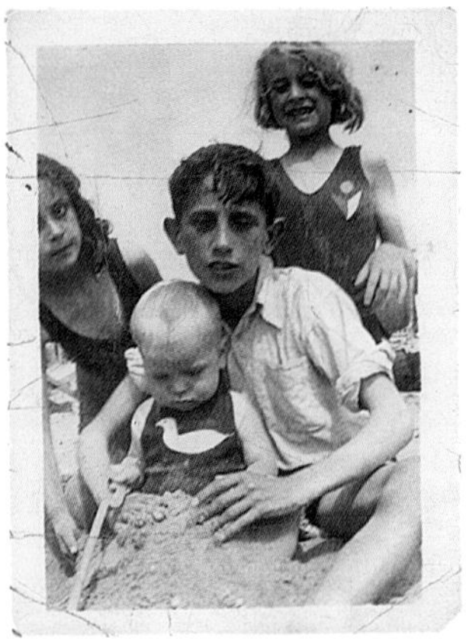
Peter on the beach 1933

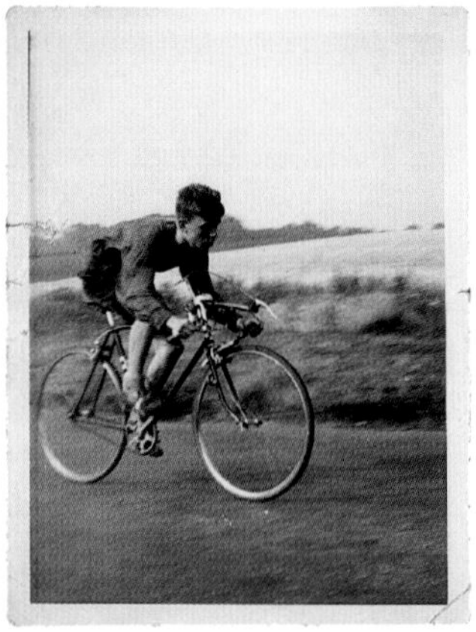
Peter cycling 1947

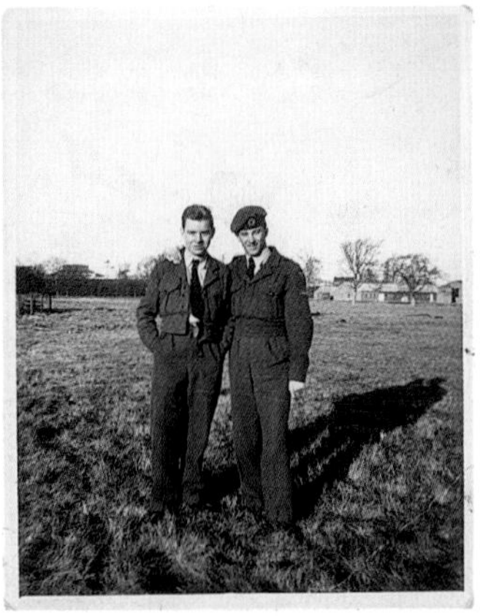
Peter and friend doing National Service RAF 1952

1932 Born 25 June, Dartford, Kent

1946–9
Gravesend Technical College and School of Art; Junior Art Department

1949–51
Gravesend School of Art

1950
Accepted by the Royal College of Art, London

1951–3
National Service in the Royal Air Force

1953–6
Royal College of Art, London – First Class Diploma (1956)

1956–7
Leverhulme Research Award to study popular art; travelled to Holland, Belgium, France, Italy and Spain

1958
Guggenheim Painting Award, Whitechapel Art Gallery, London

1960–62
Taught at St Martin's School of Art, London

1960–63
Taught at Harrow School of Art

1961–4
Taught at Walthamstow School of Art

1961
First Prize Junior Section, John Moores Liverpool Exhibition

1962
Featured in Ken Russell's film *Pop goes the Easel*, 'Monitor', BBC
Appeared in first *Sunday Times* colour supplement (4 February)
First one-man exhibition, Portal Gallery, London

1963
Married Jann Haworth
Visited Los Angeles to complete a portfolio of drawings for the *Sunday Times*

1964–76
Taught at Royal College of Art, London

1968
Daughter, Juliette Liberty Blake, born

1969
Moved to Wellow, Avon
Retrospective exhibition at City Art Gallery, Bristol

1973–4
Retrospective exhibition in Amsterdam, touring to Hamburg, Brussels and Arnhem

1974
Daughter, Daisy Blake, born
Elected Associate Member of the Royal Academy of Arts, London

1975
Founding member of the Brotherhood of Ruralists, with Jann Haworth, Ann and Graham Arnold, David Inshaw, and Annie and Graham Ovenden; first exhibited as a group in Royal Academy Summer Exhibition, 1976; major group exhibition at Arnolfini Gallery, Bristol, 1981, touring to Birmingham, Glasgow and London (Camden Arts Centre)

1979
Separated from Jann Haworth; returned to London

1980
Began relationship with Chrissy Wilson

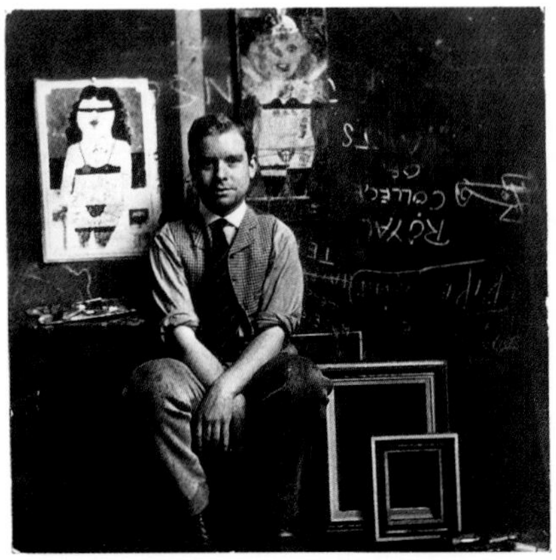
Peter at the Royal College of Art 1955. Photo: Robert Buhler

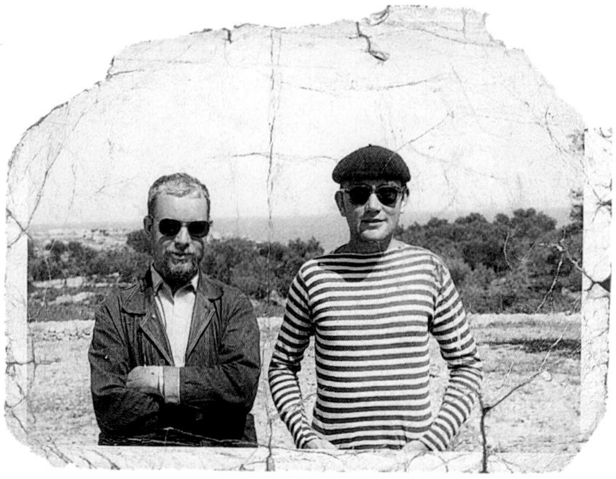
Peter with Joe Tilson, Spain 1957

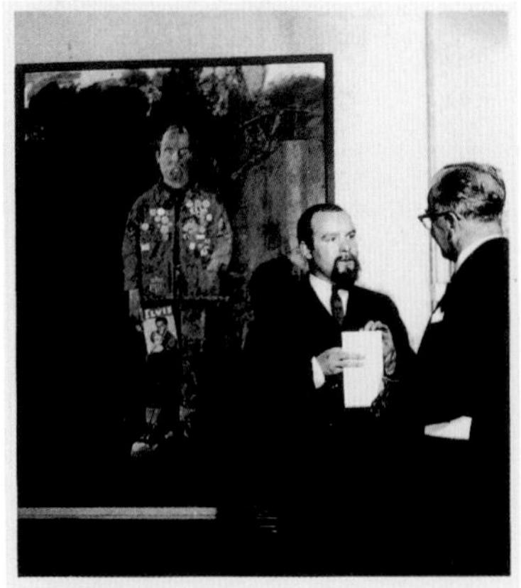
24th John Moores Exhibition opening 1961

Robert Fraser opening 1965

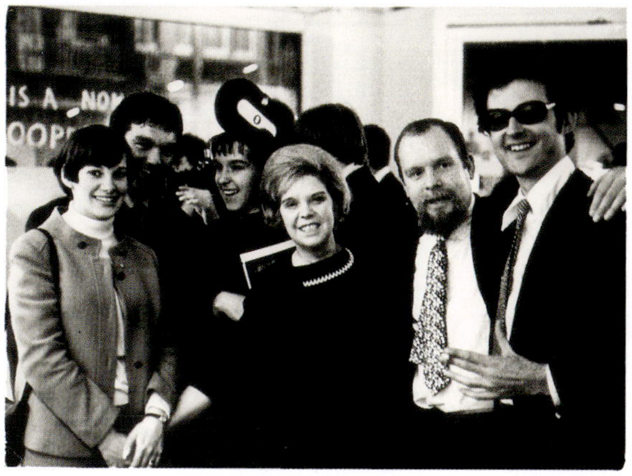

Brotherhood of Ruralists 1978

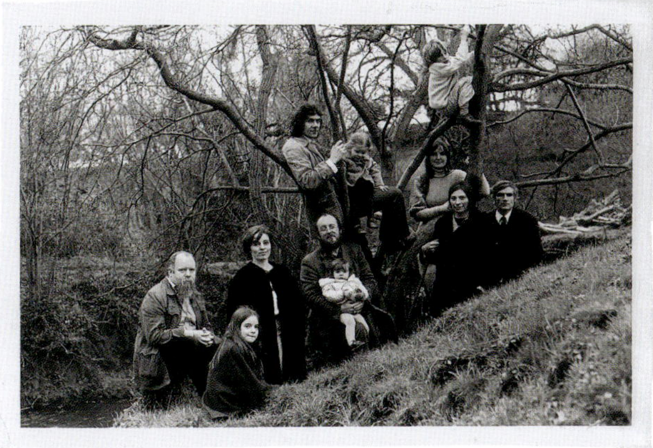

Trip to Ohio State University, Columbus 1973

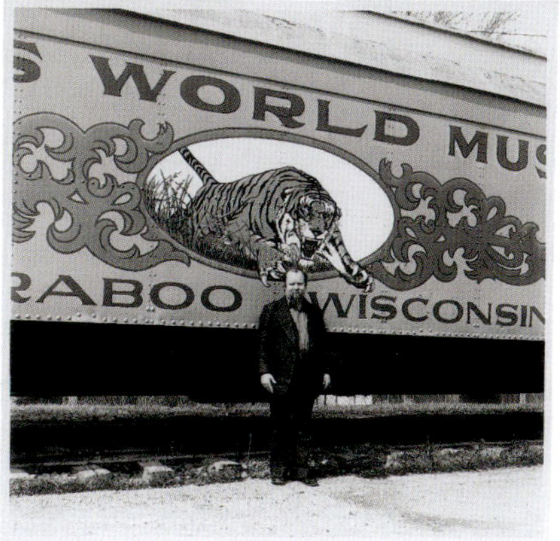

1981
Elected Member of the Royal Academy of Arts, London

1983
Featured in John Read's film *Peter Blake: Work in Progress,* BBC2, 21 February
Retrospective exhibition at Tate Gallery, London, touring to Hannover
Awarded CBE

1985
Designed poster for Live Aid, world's largest ever multi-national pop concert on 13 July, in aid of African famine relief

1986
Publication of Marina Vaizey's monograph, *Peter Blake*

1987
Married Chrissy Wilson
Daughter, Rose Blake, born
Elected Member of the Royal Designers for Industry in the category of Graphic Design

1988
Featured in LWT Arts Festival programme, 31 July
1990 One of three judges for Arts Festival, London
Featured in LWT Arts Festival programme, 25 March
Featured in *Channel 4 Daily* programme directed by David Roper for Channel 4 Television, 21 March

1994–6
Third Associate Artist of the National Gallery

1997
Moved to new studio in Hammersmith, West London

1998
Made Honorary Doctor, Royal College of Art, London

2002
Received Knighthood

2003
Publication of Natalie Rudd's monograph, *Peter Blake*

2004
Creates a new two-part bronze sculpture entitled *Four Man Up* and *Equestrian Act*, for Blackpool Borough Council's 'Great Promenade Show'

2005
Designed poster for the Live 8 concert, 2 July
Resigned from the Royal Academy of Arts, London
Produces 'Peter Blake's Mystery Tour' for BBC Radio 3's programme *Between the Ears*, based on a fictional account of a day spent with Marcel Duchamp

2006
Invited to judge the John Moores contemporary painting competition, *John Moores 24*, along with Tracey Emin, Jason Brooks, Ann Bukantas and Andrea Rose
The *South Bank Show* programme 'Peter the Painter', presented by Melvyn Bragg, aired on ITV on 19 November

2007
Peter Blake: A Retrospective opens at Tate Liverpool in June, touring in 2008 to Museo de Bellas Artes de Bilbao

2009
Publication of Marco Livingstone's monograph, *Peter Blake: One Man Show*

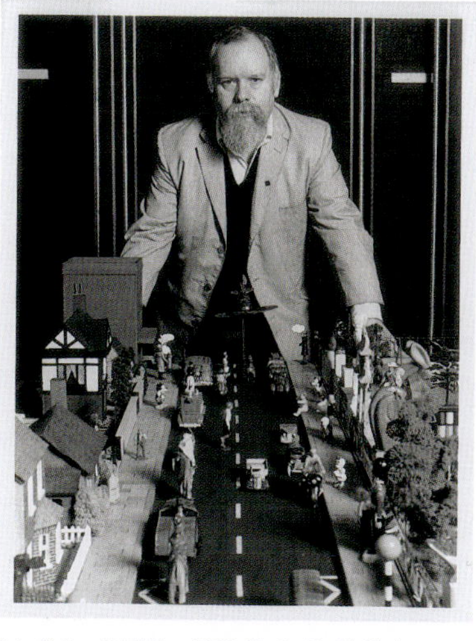

Tate Gallery Exhibition 1983. Photo: David Clarke

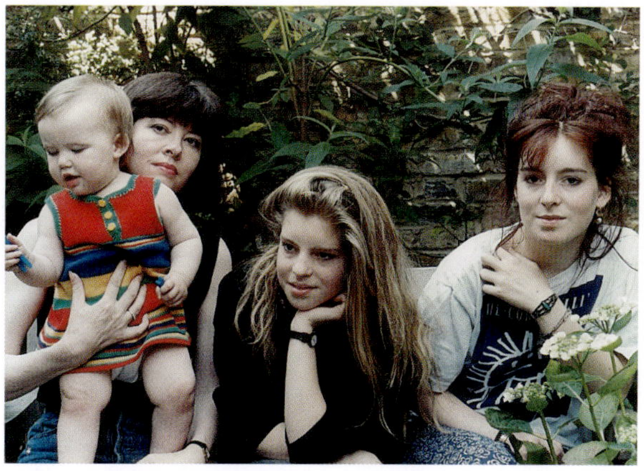

Rose, Chrissy, Daisy and Liberty 1988

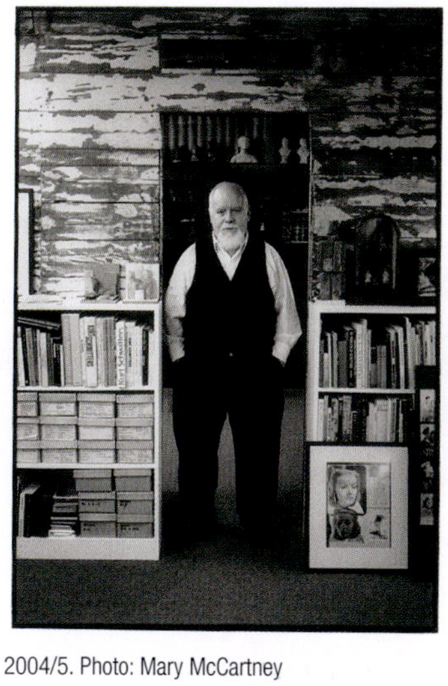

2004/5. Photo: Mary McCartney

Solo Exhibitions

1962
Portal Gallery, London

1965
Robert Fraser Gallery, London

1969
Leslie Waddington Prints, London
Robert Fraser Gallery, London
City Art Gallery, Bristol

1970
Ashgate Gallery, Farnham

1972
Waddington Galleries, London (watercolours and drawings)

1973–4
Stedelijk Museum, Amsterdam; touring to Kunstverein, Hamburg; Gemeentemuseum, Arnhem; Palais des Beaux-Arts, Brussels

1974
Natalie Stern Gallery, London (print retrospective)

1977
Waddington and Tooth Galleries, London

1978
Waddington Graphics, London

1979
Bohun Gallery, Henley-on-Thames (drawings and prints)

1980
Galleria Documenta, Turin (drawings and prints)

1983
Tate Gallery, London (retrospective); touring to Kestner Gesellschaft, Hannover

1984
Galerie Claude Bernard, Paris

1986–7
Watermans Art Centre, Brentford, Middlesex; touring to Turnpike Gallery, Leigh

1988
Nishimura Gallery, Tokyo

1990
Waddington Galleries, London
Wetterling Gallery, Gothenburg

1992
Govinda Gallery, Washington DC (Eric Clapton sketches)

1993
Tabernacle Cultural Centre, Machynlleth (silkscreen prints)

1995
Galerie Claude Bernard, Paris

1996–7
Now We Are 64: Peter Blake at the National Gallery, National Gallery, London; touring to Whitworth Art Gallery, Manchester

1999
A Cabinet of Curiosities from the Collections of Peter Blake, Morley Gallery, London

2000
Peter Blake: About Collage, Tate Liverpool

2001–9
Alphabet, York College of Further and Higher Education and extensive tour around the UK organised by Hayward Touring

2002
Over the Rainbow, Harley Gallery, Welbeck
Sir Peter Blake/And Now We Are 70, Paul Morris Gallery, New York

2003
Peter Blake, Artiscope (Zaira Mis), Brussels
Peter Blake: Commercial Art, London Institute Gallery, London (graphic design)
Peter Blake: Sculpture, London Institute Gallery, London (sculpture)

2005
Peter Blake: 1–10 (Collages, Constructions, Drawings & Sculpture) & The Marcel Duchamp Paintings, Waddington Galleries, London
New Prints by Peter Blake, Charing X Gallery, London
Peter Blake: Love, Paul Stolper, London (prints)

2006
With a Little Help, Spring Fine Art, Design & Antiques Fair, London
Peter Blake: 1975–2005, Bjorn Wetterling Gallery, Stockholm
Peter Blake Prints and Sculpture, Harley Gallery, Welbeck

2007
Peter Blake: A Retrospective, Tate Liverpool, Liverpool; touring to Museo de Bellas Artes de Bilbao, 2008
An Alphabet by Peter Blake, Paul Stolper, London (prints)

2008
Galerie Thomas Levy, Hamburg; touring to Lorenzelli Arte, Milan in 2009

Public Collections

Albright-Knox Art Gallery, Buffalo
Art Gallery of New South Wales, Sydney
Arts Council Collection, Hayward Gallery, South Bank Centre, London
Astrup Fearnley Collection, Oslo
Baltimore Museum of Art
Bristol City Art Gallery
British Council, London
Cecil Higgins Art Gallery, Bedford
Colecção Berado, Centro Cultural de Belém, Lisbon
David and Alfred Smart Museum of Art, The University of Chicago
Ferens Art Gallery: Hull Museums & Art Gallery
Fundaçao Calouste Gulbenkian, Lisbon
Government Art Collection, UK
Leeds Museums and Galleries (City Art Gallery)
Los Angeles County Museum of Art
Museo de Bellas Artes de Bilbao
Museum Boymans-Van Beuningen, Rotterdam
Museum Ludwig, Cologne
Museum Moderner Kunst, Vienna
Museum of Modern Art, New York
National Museums Wales
Pallant House Gallery, Chichester (Wilson Gift through the National Art Collections Fund)
Royal College of Art, London
Sheffield City Art Galleries
Tate, London
Tullie House Museum and Art Gallery, Carlisle
University of Lethbridge Art Collections, Alberta
Victoria and Albert Museum, London
Whitworth Art Gallery, University of Manchester
Wolverhampton Art Gallery

Selected Bibliography

1956

Roger Coleman, 'A Romantic Naturalist – Some Notes on the Paintings of Peter Blake', *Ark* (Journal of the Royal College of Art), 18 November, pp 60–61

1962

Robert Melville, 'The Durable Expendables of Peter Blake', *Motif*, no.10, pp 15–29

1963

Mervyn Levy, 'Peter Blake: Pop art for admass', *Studio International*, November, vol.166, no.847, pp 184–9

1965

Mario Amaya, *Pop as Art: A Survey of the New Superrealism*, London: Studio Vista

Bryan Robertson, John Russell and Lord Snowdon, *Private View*, London: Thomas Nelson and Sons Ltd

London: The New Scene, exh.cat., Minneapolis: Walker Art Center. Essays by Martin Friedman and Alan Bowness, biographies by Jasia Reichardt

1966

Lucy R. Lippard, *Pop Art*, London: Thames and Hudson. With essay by Lawrence Alloway, 'The Development of British Pop'

1969

Christopher Finch, 'Image as Language', *Aspects of British Art 1950–1968*, Harmondsworth, Middlesex: Penguin

John Russell and Suzi Gablik, *Pop Art Redefined*, London: Thames and Hudson

Peter Blake, exh.cat., Bristol: City Art Gallery. Introduction by Roger Coleman

1970

The Tate Gallery 1968–70, biennial report, London: Tate Gallery, pp 72–4

1973

Peter Blake, exh.cat., Amsterdam: Stedelijk Museum. Essay by Rainer Crone

Peter Blake, exh.cat., Hamburg: Kunstverein, Hamburg. Introduction by Uwe Schneede

1977

Souvenirs and Samples, exh.cat., London: Waddington and Tooth Galleries. Introduction by Peter Blake

1978

Peter Blake, 'Contrariwise', *Aspects*, no.3, pp 1–2

1980

The Tate Gallery 1978–80, illustrated biennial report, London: Tate Gallery, pp 41–2

1981

The Tate Gallery 1978–80, illustrated catalogue of acquisitions, London: Tate Gallery, pp 66–8

1982

Stephen Hackney, 'Peter Blake: The Masked Zebra Kid', *Completing the picture: materials and techniques of twenty-six paintings in the Tate Gallery*, London: Tate Gallery, pp 104–17

1983

Peter Blake, exh.cat., London: Tate Gallery. Essay and catalogue notes by Michael Compton, essay by Nicholas Usherwood and reprint of 1962 article by Robert Melville

Nicholas Usherwood, *The Brotherhood of Ruralists*, London: Lund Humphries

1984

Peter Blake: peintures, aquarelles, dessins et gravures, exh.cat., Paris: Galerie Claude Bernard. Introduction by Leslie Waddington and essay by Peter Blake

1986

Marina Vaizey, *Peter Blake (Royal Academy Painters and Sculptors)*, London: Weidenfeld & Nicholson

1987

Pop Art U.S.A. – U.K.: American and British artists of the '60s in the '80s, exh.cat., Tokyo: Odakyu Grand Gallery. Texts by Marco Livingstone and Lawrence Alloway

1988

Peter Blake: Déjà vu, exh.cat., Tokyo: Nishimura Gallery. Preface by Peter Blake in English and Japanese, essay by Michael Compton in Japanese only

1989

Tilman Osterwold, *Pop Art*, Cologne: Taschen

1990

Marco Livingstone, *Pop Art: A Continuing History*, London: Thames and Hudson

Peter Blake in homage to Marilyn Monroe, exh.cat., Gothenburg: Wetterling Gallery. Preface by Peter Blake

1991

'The Ruralists', *Art and Design*, no.23. Edited by Christopher Martin

Pop Art, exh.cat., London: Royal Academy of Arts. Edited by Marco Livingstone

1992

'Pop Art', *Art and Design*, no.24

1993
David Mellor, *The Sixties Art Scene in London*, London: Phaidon
1995
Peter Blake: peintures et acquarelles, exh.cat., Galerie Claude Bernard, Paris. Introduction by Marco Livingstone
1996
Now We Are 64: Peter Blake at the National Gallery, exh.cat., London: National Gallery Publications. Foreword by Neil McGregor, essays by Marco Livingstone and Colin Wiggins, texts by David Hockney and R.B. Kitaj
1997
The Pop '60s: Transatlantic Crossing, exh.cat., Lisbon: Centro Cultural de Belém. Edited by Marco Livingstone
1999
A Cabinet of Curiosities from the Collection of Peter Blake, exh.cat., London: Morley Gallery. Introduction and interview by Andrew Lambirth
Pop Impressions Europe/USA, exh.cat., New York: Museum of Modern Art. Text by Wendy Weitman
Signature Pieces: Contemporary British Prints and Multiples, exh.cat., London: Alan Cristea Gallery. Text by Marco Livingstone
2000
Peter Blake: About Collage, exh.cat., Liverpool: Tate Liverpool. Texts by Peter Blake, Dawn Ades and Natalie Rudd
2001
Pop Art: U.S./U.K. Connections, 1956–1996, exh.cat., Houston: Menil Collection. Texts by David E. Brauer, Jim Edwards, Christopher Finch and Walter Hopps
2002
Martin Harrison, *Transition: The London Art Scene in the Fifties*, London: Merrell
2003
Natalie Rudd, *Peter Blake*, London: Tate Publishing
Peter Blake Commercial Art, exh.cat., London: London Institute Gallery. Text by Alan Powers
Peter Blake Sculpture, exh.cat., London: London Institute Gallery. Essay by Michael Benson
2004
Pop Art UK: British Pop Art, exh.cat., Modena: Palazzo Santa Margherita and Palazzina dei Giardini. Edited by Marco Livingstone and Walter Guadagnini
Art & the 60s: This was Tomorrow, exh.cat., London: Tate Britain. Edited by Chris Stephens and Katharine Stout
2005
British Pop, exh.cat., Bilbao: Museo de Bellas Artes. Catalogue by Marco Livingstone
Peter Blake: 1–10 (Collages, Constructions, Drawings & Sculpture) & The Marcel Duchamp Paintings, exh.cat., London: Waddington Galleries. Essay by Lewis Biggs
Mark Francis and Hal Foster (eds), *Pop*. London: Phaidon
2006
Marco Livingstone, 'Montgomery Clift, through the eyes of Peter Blake', *B'05 Bulletina Boletín Bulletin*, February, Bilbao: Museo de Bellas Artes, pp 111–38
Lewis Carroll, illustrated by Peter Blake, *Alice Through the Looking-Glass and What Alice Found There*, London: Merrell. Preface by Marco Livingstone
2007
Peter Blake: 1975–2005, exh.cat., Stockholm: Wetterling Gallery. Essay by Bo Nilsson
Pop Art Portraits, exh.cat., London: National Portrait Gallery. Catalogue by Paul Moorhouse
Peter Blake: a retrospective, exh.cat., Liverpool: Tate Liverpool. Essays by Simon Faulkner, Marco Livingstone, Christoph Grunenberg and Laurence Sillars. Repackaged in Spanish for the exhibition at the Museo de Bellas Artes, Bilbao, 2008
Pop Art 1956–1968, exh.cat., Rome: Scuderie del Quirinale. Edited by Walter Guadagnini
An Alphabet by Peter Blake, exh.cat., London: Paul Stolper. Preface by Gavin Turk and essay by Mel Gooding
2008
Peter Blake Collages and Works on Paper 1956–2008, exh.cat., Bielefeld/Leipzig: Kaber Verlag. Essay by Walter Guadagnini and conversation between Peter Blake and Belinda Grace Gardner
2009
Marco Livingstone, *Peter Blake: One Man Show*, Farnham, Surrey: Lund Humphries

List of illustrated works

Prelims and Chapter 1

1 **Locker**, 1959
Mixed media
152.4 × 76.2 × 76.2 cm
(60¼ × 30 × 30 in)
Collection Peter Blake

2 **Children Reading Comics**, 1954
Oil on hardboard
36.9 × 47 cm (14½ × 18½ in)
Tullie House Museum and Art Gallery, Carlisle

3 **Everly Wall**, 1959
Oil on hardboard
91.4 × 61 cm (36 × 24 in)
Collection Terry Blake

4 **The Lettermen**, 1963
Oil on board
124.5 × 185.4 cm (49 × 73 in)
Ferens Art Gallery, Hull City Museums and Art Galleries

5 **Madonna of Venice Beach, No. 1**, 1994–6
Oil on canvas
137 × 84 cm (53⅞ × 33 in)
Private Collection

6 **ABC Minors**, 1955
Oil on hardboard
76 × 49 cm (29⅞ × 19¼ in)
Museum Ludwig, Cologne

7 **Conversation**, *c.*1948
Lithograph
17.8 × 15.2 cm (7 × 6 in)
Collection Peter Blake

8 **Fairground Boxing Booth**, 1948
Lithograph, printed in black ink from one stone
image 24.2 × 28.4 cm
(9½ × 11⅛ in)
sheet 25.5 × 30 cm (10 × 12 in)
National Gallery of Australia, Canberra

9 **Circus Poster**, 1949
Gouache
48.2 × 30.5 cm (19 × 12 in)
Collection Peter Blake

10 **Landscape**, 1950
Gouache
49.5 × 39.4 cm (19½ × 15½ in)
Collection Peter Blake

11 **Self-Portrait in RAF Jacket**, *c.*1952–3
Pen and ink and gouache on paper
34.2 × 23.5 cm (13½ × 9¼ in)
Private Collection

12 **Adam and Eve**, 1954–5
Oil on hardboard
45.7 × 26.7 cm (18 × 10½ in)
Private Collection

13 **Footsteps**, 1955
Oil on board
34.3 × 24 cm (13½ × 9½ in)
Museums Sheffield

14 **Children Reading Comics**, 1956
Oil on board
39.4 × 29.2 cm (15½ × 11½ in)
Royal College of Art Collection

15 **Boy with Paintings**, 1957–9
Oil and enamels on wood
30.5 × 26.4 cm (12 × 10 in)

16 **Little Vigorous Daunt**, 1958 (unfinished)
Oil on hardboard
106.7 × 88.9 cm (42 × 35 in)
Collection Shirley Blake

17 **Only Sixteen**
Comic strip, published in the Royal College of Art magazine, *Ark*, no. 25, Spring 1960, p.29

18 **Tattooed Lady I**, 1955
Pen, ink, gold paint and collage on paper
53.2 × 35.5 cm (21 × 14 in)
Franco Castelli

19 **Knife Thrower's Board**, 1957
Oil and collage on hardboard
170.5 × 49.9 cm (67⅛ × 19⅝ in)
Collection of Irma and Norman Braman, Miami, Florida

20 **Siriol, She-Devil of Naked Madness**, 1957
Mixed media on board
76.2 × 21.6 cm (30 × 8½ in)
Pallant House Gallery, Chichester (Wilson Loan)

21 **Loelia, World's Most Tattooed Lady**, 1955
Oil and collage on panel
74.9 × 26.7 cm (29½ × 10½ in)
Collection Fleur Cowles

22 **Dixie, Darling of the Midway**, 1955–8
Oil and collage on panel
31.7 × 23.5 cm (12½ × 9¼ in)
Private Collection, courtesy Offer Waterman & Co

23 **Cherie, Only Bearded Tattooed Lady with Collage**, 1957
Oil on panel
30.5 × 17.8 cm (12 × 7 in)

24 **Tattooed Lady with Collage**, 1958
Gouache and collage
68.6 × 53.3 cm (27 × 21 in)
Victoria & Albert Museum, London

25 **Drum Majorette**, 1957
Oil and collage on hardboard
86 × 65.5 cm (33⅞ × 25¾ in)
Private Collection

26 **Bird Act**, 1957
Collage
24.5 × 36.2 cm (9⅝ × 14¼ in)

27 **Untitled Collage with Horse**, 1957
Collage
28 × 20.3 cm (11 × 8 in)
Collection Shirley Blake

28 **Medals**, 1960
Oil and collage on board
34.3 × 26.7 cm (13½ × 10½ in)

29 **Jockey Act**, 1957
Collage
72.4 × 87.6 cm (28.5 × 34.5 in)
Private Collection

30 **Wrestling at the Albert Hall**, 1961
Pencil on paper
19 × 12.1 cm (7½ × 4¾ in)
Private Collection

31 **Bearded Lady** from *Side Show Series*, 1974–8
Original engraving on box wood printed on Japanese 'Tonosawa' paper, with individual wrappers in a

cloth-covered portfolio with leather ties
Image 15.2 × 12.7 cm (6 × 5 in), sheet 26.7 × 21 cm (10½ × 8¼ in)

32 **Tattooed Man** from *Side Show Series*, 1974–8
Original engraving on box wood printed on Japanese 'Tonosawa' paper, with individual wrappers in a cloth-covered portfolio with leather ties
Image 15.2 × 12.7 cm (6 × 5 in), sheet 26.7 × 21 cm (10½ × 8¼ in)

33 **Sacre Coeur, Paris**, 1956
Pencil on paper
22.8 × 14.6 cm (8⅞ × 5⅞ in)

34 **Shoe on the Beach at Nice**, 1957
Oil on hardboard
18.4 × 15.2 cm (7¼ × 6 in)
Private Collection, London

35 **Guardia Civil**, 1957
Oil on board
28.5 × 21 cm (11⅜ × 8¼ in)
Waddington Galleries, London

36 **Goldfish**, 1957
Oil on board
22.9 × 18.4 cm (9 × 7¼ in)
Private Collection

37 **The Preparation for the Entry into Jerusalem**, 1955–6
Oil on hardboard
127 × 102 cm (50 × 40⅛ in)
Royal College of Art Collection

38 **Looking at Painting**, *c.*1955
Oil on canvas
35.5 × 46 cm (14 × 18⅛ in)

39 **On the Balcony**, 1955–7
Oil on canvas
121.3 × 90.8 cm (47¾ × 35¾ in)
Tate. Presented by the Contemporary Art Society 1963

40 **Self-Portrait with Badges**, 1961
Oil on board, support 174.3 × 121.9 cm (68⅝ × 48 in)
Tate. Presented by the Moores Family Charitable Foundation to celebrate the John Moores Liverpool Exhibition 1979

Chapter 2

41 **The Fine Art Bit**, 1959
Enamel paint, wood relief and collage on board
91.5 × 61 × 2.5 cm (36 × 24 × 1 in)
Tate. Purchased from the artist (Knapping Fund) 1970

42 **Elvis and Cliff**, 1959
Enamel paint and T-shirt transfer on board
78.1 × 47.6 cm (30¾ × 18¾ in)

43 **Couples**, 1959
Collage on notice board
89 × 59.7 cm (35 × 23½ in)
Collection Peter Blake

44 **Girlie Door**, 1959
Collage and objects on hardboard
121.9 × 60.3 cm (48 × 23¾ in)
Private Collection, courtesy MaxmArt, Mendrisio

45 **Got a Girl**, 1960–61
Oil, wood, photo-collage and record on hardboard
94 × 154.9 × 4.2 cm (37 × 61 × 1⅝ in)
Whitworth Art Gallery, The University of Manchester

46 **EL**, 1961
Lipstick and collage on panel
29.5 × 21 cm (11⅝ × 8¼ in)

47 **Tuesday**, 1961
Enamel, wood relief and collage on board
47.6 × 25.7 × 3.9 cm (18¾ × 10⅛ × 1½ in)
Tate. Presented by E.J. Power through the Friends of the Tate Gallery 1974

48 **Valentine**, *c.*1959–60
Collage on hardboard
62.9 × 47 cm (24¾ × 18½ in)
Bryan Morrison

49 **Love Wall**, 1961
Collage construction
125.7 × 205.7 cm (49½ × 81 in)
CAMJAP/Fundaçao Calouste Gulbenkian, Lisbon

50 **Bodhisattva Sculpture**, 1959–60
Found pieces of wood and gilt, painted
43.1 × 12 × 7.6 cm (17 × 4¾ × 3 in)

51 **Crazy Said Snow White**, 1959 (detail)
Bust
Dimenions unknown

52 **Studio Tack-Board**, 1972
Screenprint on paper
97.2 × 136.8 cm (38¼ × 53⅞ in)
Tate. Presented by Robert Simon 1975

53 **Wall**, 1962–87
Photographs and flag
104.4 × 175 cm (41⅛ × 69 in)

54 **Drum Majorette**, 1959
Oil and collage on dressmaker's dummy
88.9 × 58.4 × 101.6 cm (35 × 23 × 40 in)
Mr and Mrs Michael Chow

55 **Locker**, 1959
Mixed media
152.4 × 76.2 × 76.2 cm (60¼ × 30 × 30 in)
Collection Peter Blake

56 **Untitled Gold Painting**, 1959
Gold leaf on hardboard
50.8 × 25.4 cm (20 × 10 in)
Collection Shirley Blake

57 **Gold Painting (Piece of a Japanese Screen)**, 1959
Gold leaf on canvas
93.4 × 63.2 cm (36¾ × 24⅞ in)
Collection Peter Blake

58 **Captain Webb Matchbox**, 1961–2
Gouache and pencil on wood box
40 × 29 × 11 cm (15¾ × 11½ × 4¼ in)
Colecção Berardo, Centro Cultural de Belém, Lisbon

59 **The First Real Target?**, 1961
Enamel on canvas and collage on board support
53.7 × 49.3 cm (2¼ × 19⅜ in)
Tate. Purchased 1982

60 **Girl in a Window**, 1962
Collage construction
112.5 × 123.9 × 34 cm (44¼ × 48¾ × 13⅜ in)
Leeds City Art Gallery

61 **The Toy Shop**, 1962
Mixed media, glass and painted wood
156.8 × 194 × 24 cm (61¾ × 76⅜ × 9½ in)
Tate. Purchased 1970

62 **Postcard**, 1962
Oil on hardboard
122 × 76.5 cm (48 × 30 in)
Private Collection

63 **Aparicio**, 1963
Oil, string and metal on hardboard
122 × 76.2 cm (48 × 30 in)

64 **3765**, from *Six French Postcards*, 1969
Screenprint on paper
42.5 × 27.2 cm (16¾ × 10¾ in)
Tate. Presented by Waddington Galleries through the institute of Contemporary Prints 1975

65 **Le Petit Porteur**, 1964–5
Acrylic on board
76 × 46 cm (30 × 18 in)

66 **Bedouin**, 1964–5
Acrylic
77.4 × 47.7 cm (30½ × 18¾ in)

67 **La Favorite**, 1967
Painted photograph
124 × 80 cm (48¾ × 31½ in)

68 **Girls and their Hero (Girls with their Hero)**, 1959–62
Oil on hardboard
134 × 125 cm (52¾ × 49¼ in)
Pallant House Gallery, Chichester. Wilson Gift through The Art Fund

69 **Portrait of Sammy Davis Jr**, 1957–60
Oil on hardboard
36.8 × 31.7 cm (14½ × 12½in)
Magda Archer and Harry Hill

70 **La Vern Baker**, 1961–2
Oil and collage on panel
52.1 × 87 cm (20½ × 34½ in)
Pallant House Gallery, Chichester (Wilson Loan)

71 **Come, Stanley!**, 1962
Enamel paint on hardboard
80.6 × 92.1 cm (31¾ × 36¼in)

72 **Bo Diddley**, 1963
Acrylic on hardboard
122.6 × 78.4 cm (48¼× 30⅞ in)
Museum Ludwig, Cologne

73 **The 1962 Beatles**, 1963–8
Acrylic on hardboard
121.9 × 91.4 cm (48 × 36 in)
Pallant House, Chichester. Wilson Gift through The Art Fund

74 **The Beach Boys**, 1964
Screenprint on paper
53 × 30.8 cm (20⅞ × 12⅛ in)
Tate. Presented by Rose and Chris Prater through the Institue of Contemporary Prints 1975

75 **Jean Harlow**, 1964
Cryla on hardboard
44.5 × 36.8 cm (17½ × 14½ in)
Collection Mr and Mrs Terry Blake

Chapter 3

76 **Kamikaze**, 1965
Cryla and collage on hardboard
78.7 × 47.6 cm (31 × 18¾ in)
Amgueddfa Cymru – National Museums Wales. Purchased 2006 with the assistance of The Art Fund and the Derek Williams Trust

77 **Pin-up Girl**, 1962
Oil on hardboard
48.3 × 34.6 cm (19 × 13⅝ in)
University of Lethbridge Art Collections, Alberta

78 **Pin-up Girl**, 1965
Cryla on board
29.3 × 24.2 cm (11½ × 9½in)

79 **Zorine, Queen of the Nudists and her TV Gorilla**, 1961–5
Cryla and collage on hardboard
115.5 × 52 cm (45½ × 20½ in)

80 **Kid McCoy**, 1961–5
Cryla and collage on hardboard
58.4 × 29 × 5.7 cm (23 × 11⅜ × 2¼ in)
Zabludowicz Collection

81 **Baron Adolf Kaiser**, 1961–3
Oil on panel
61 × 51 cm (24 × 20⅛ in)
Arts Council Collection, Hayward Gallery, South Bank Centre, London

82 **Irish Lord X**, 1963
Oil and collage on panel
52.7 × 37.5 cm (20¾ × 14¾ in)
Pallant House, Chichester. Wilson Gift through The Art Fund

83 **Da Vinci Brothers**, 1963
Oil and collage on panel
87 × 37 cm (34¼ × 14½ in)

84 **Doktor K. Tortur**, 1965
Cryla and collage on hardboard
61 × 25.4 cm (24 × 10 in)
Mr and Mrs Michael Chow

85 **Masked Zebra Kid**, 1965
Acrylic, enamel, collage and assemblage on wood
55.2 × 26.7 × 3.8 cm (21¾ × 10½ × 1½ in)
Tate. Purchased 1974

86 **Little Lady Luck**, 1965
Cryla and collage on hardboard
72.4 × 34.9 cm (28½ × 13¾ in)
Private Collection

87 **Roxy Roxy**, 1965–83
Cryla, enamel and collage on hardboard
66 × 55.1 cm (26 × 20⅛ in)
Pallant House Gallery, Chichester (Wilson Loan)

88 **Franck and Jesse, The James Brothers**, 1966–83
Cryla and collage on hardboard
45.7 × 41.3 cm (18 × 16¼ in)
Private Collection

89 **Babe Rainbow**, 1967
Silkscreen on tin
66 × 44 cm (26 × 17⅜ in)
Private Collection

90 **Pretty Boy Michael Angelo**, 1972
Watercolour
45.7 × 29.8 cm (18 × 11 ¾ in)

91 **The Tuareg**, 1972
Watercolour
45.7 × 29.8 cm (18 × 11¾ in)
Mr and Mrs Michael Chow

92 **Demolition Squad, Birmingham Drizzle and the Lady Doctor Versus the Nice Girls**, 1977
Watercolour and collage
6.3 × 31.1 cm (2½ × 12¼ in)

93 **Hollywood Blondes Versus the Gilded Sluts**, 1977–84
Watercolour
13.7 × 46.4 cm (5⅜ × 18¼ in
Private Collection

94 **Pretty Penny**, 1977
Watercolour
12.7 × 24.1 cm (5 × 9½ in)
Private Collection, courtesy Waddington Galleries

95 **Ms Super**, 1987
Watercolour and mixed media
45 × 29.8 cm (17¾ × 11¾ in)
Galerie Claude Bernard, Paris

96 **Blakes Boxing Academy**, 1988
Oil and enamel on board
124.1 × 63.2 cm (48⅞ × 24⅞ in)

97 **L.A. Phil Mozart**, 1987
Watercolour and mixed media
45 × 29.8 cm (17¾ × 11¾ in)
Private Collection, Devon

98 **The African Queen**, 1987
Watercolour and mixed media
45 × 29.8 cm (17¾ × 11¾ in)
Private Collection

99 **Foxy Yoko Koko**, 1987
Watercolour and mixed media
45 × 29.8 cm (17¾ × 11¾ in)
Private Collection, Greece

100 **Blanche Neige and Bet Noir**, 1976–81
Oil on board with collage
52.1 × 33.7 cm (20½ × 13¼ in)
Private Collection, London

101 **Ratatac**, 1997–2003
Oil on hardboard
94 × 69.2 cm (37 × 27¼ in)
Magda Archer and Harry Hill

102 **Joe Louis, Brown Bomber**, 1975–99
Acrylic, enamel and collage on board
88 × 49.5 cm (34½ × 19½ in
Jonathan Clark

103 **Kendo Nagasaki**, 1992
Oil on panel
32.4 × 27.3 cm (12¾ × 10¾ in)
Private Collection, UK

104 **Gender Benders**, 2002–3
Oil and acrylic on board
43 × 35 cm (17 × 13¾ in)
Private Collection, Sweden

105 **Baby Ruth**, 1972–89
Oil on hardboard
21.3 × 15.9 cm (8⅜ × 6¼ in)

106 **Tarzan Box – 'Big Iron Bird She Come'**, 1965
Mixed media
36.8 × 57.1 × 30.5 cm (14½ × 22½ × 12 in)
Collection Peter Blake

107 **Tarzan and his Family at the Roxy Cinema, New York**, 1964–2002
Cryla on canvas
182.9 × 152.4 cm (72 × 60 in)
Private Collection

108 **Cheeta with Confetti Falling on Him – A Tribute to Lawson Wood**, 1969
Watercolour
63.5 × 41.6 cm (25 × 16⅜ in)

109 **Jane and Boy at Watts Tower**, 1969–76
Watercolour
49.5 × 38.4 cm (19½ × 15⅛ in)
Private Collection

110 **Tarzan, Jane, Boy and Cheeta**, 1966–75
Cryla on canvas
121.9 × 91.4 cm (48 × 36 in)
Private Collection

111 **Marcel Duchamp's World Tour: The Tarzan Family**, 1995–2005
Acrylic on canvas
69 × 124.8 cm (27⅛ × 49⅛ in)
Private Collection

112 **Tarzan Meets the Jungle Goddess**, 1970s–94
Oil on canvas
92.1 × 121.9 cm (36¼ × 48 in)
Private Collection

Chapter 4

113 **Big Do-Nut Drive-in, Los Angeles**, 1963
Pencil and watercolour
31.4 × 25.1 cm (12⅜ × 9⅞ in)
Private Collection

114 **Pacific Ocean Park**, 1963
Coloured pencil
25 × 30.5 cm (10 × 12 in)

115 **Outside Grauman's Chinese Theater, Hollywood**, 1963
Watercolour
33 × 25.1 cm (13 × 9⅞ in)

116 **Mabel Stark, an 80 Year Old Lion Tamer at Los Angeles**, 1963
Pencil, watercolour and bodycolour, coloured pencil on paper
27.3 × 20.3 cm (10¾ × 8 in)
Cecil Higgins Art Gallery, Bedford

117 **Bertram Mills Circus, Season 1966–67, no. 1**, 1966–7
Pencil and coloured pencil
31.8 × 24.8 cm (12½ × 9¾ in)

118 **Roses**, 1969
Pen and ink on paper
57.8 × 45.7 cm (22¾ × 18 in)

119 **Bristol Bicycle Race**, early 1980s
32.7 × 45.1 cm (12⅞ × 17¾ in)
Private Collection, Japan

120 **Robin**, 1984
Watercolour
15.9 × 11.8 cm (6¼ × 4⅝ in)
Collection Peter Blake

121 **Baby Rabbits**, 1984
Oil on canvas board
25.5 × 20.3 cm (10 × 8 in)
Private Collection

122 **Girl Looking at Sculpture**, completed 1984
Watercolour
Private Collection

123 **Ford Cottage, Coombe**, 1976
Watercolour
42 × 26 cm (16½ × 10¼ in)

124 **Girl in a White Chair**, 1986
Oil on board
27 × 26.7 cm (10⅝ × 10½ in)
Private Collection

125 **Boy with Hot Dog**, 1960–65
Acrylic on board
36.5 × 40.7 cm (14⅜ × 16 in)
Arts Council Collection, Hayward Gallery, Southbank Centre, London

126 **Portrait of David Hockney in a Hollywood Spanish Interior**, begun 1965
Acrylic on canvas
97 × 167.4 × 3.1 cm (72 × 60 × 1¼ in)
Tate. Presented by David Hockney, 2002

127 **Girl in a Poppy Field**, 1968–9
Watercolour on paper
40.6 × 29.2 cm (16 × 11 in)

128 **Girl in a Field**, 1968–84
Watercolour
68.5 × 43.8 cm (27 × 17¼in)
Private Collection

129 **Liberty Blake in a Kimono**, 1971
Watercolour on paper
50.1 × 30.5 cm (19¾ × 12 in)
Private Collection, London

130 **Liberty as a 'Suffolk Child by John Constable R.A.'**, 1976, from the portfolio For John Constable
Etching, collage and mixed media on paper support
66.4 × 49.8 cm (26⅛ × 19⅝ in)
Tate. Presented by Bernard Jacobson Gallery 1976

131 **Chipper 1912**, completed 1981
Oil on board
29.2 × 21.6 cm (11½ × 8⅛ in)
Private Collection

132 **Girl in a Mask**, 1981
Watercolour
40.6 × 26 cm (16 × 10¼ in)
Private Collection

133 **Portrait of Richard Guyatt**, 1981
Oil on board
21.6 × 19 cm (8½ × 7½ in)
Royal College of Art Collection

134 **E.J. Power**, 1987–9
Oil on hardboard
15.2 × 19 cm (6 × 7½ in)
Leslie Waddington

135 **The Wedding Hat**, 1981–3
Oil on canvas
174 × 121.9 cm (68½ × 48 in)
Collection Peter Blake

136 **Untitled (Girl in Red Sweater)**, 1989
Gouache and watercolour on paper
20.3 × 15.2 cm (8 × 6 in)
Galerie Michael Haas

137 **Robbie Williams**, 2002
Acrylic on board
42.5 × 31.6 cm (16¾ × 12½ in)
Collection Robbie Williams

138 **Portrait of Simon Sainsbury and Stewart Grimshaw**, 1996
Oil on canvas
68.9 × 81.6 cm (27⅛ × 32⅛ in)
Private Collection, London

Chapter 5

139 Cover for the Beatles album *Sgt. Pepper's Lonely Hearts Club Band*, 1967

140 Cover for the *Sunday Times* magazine, 6 October 1963

141 Cover for the *Daily Telegraph* magazine, 10 April 1968
Collection Peter Blake

142 Front and back cover for Roger McGough's *Summer with Monika*, 1978

143 Illustration for Dylan Thomas's *Under Milk Wood*, 1990
Pencil on paper
29.5 × 21 (11¾ × 8¾ in)
Collection Peter Blake

144 Cover for the Who album, *Face Dances*, 1981
Tate. Presented by Simon Wilson 1981

145 Original artwork for the Band Aid single 'Do They Know it's Christmas?', 1984
Paper collage
31.4 × 31.4 cm (12⅜ × 12⅜ in)
Collection Peter Blake

146 Original artwork for the Brian Wilson album, *Gettin' in Over My Head*, 2004
Collage
41.6 × 41.9 cm (16⅜ × 16½ in)
Brian Wilson

147 **Academy**, 1975
Collage
45 × 45 cm (17¾ × 17¾ in)

148 Cover design for Paul Weller's album, *Stanley Road*, 1995
Paper collage
44.5 × 43 cm (17½ × 16⅞ in)

149 **Souvenir for Kitaj**, 1974
Collage
118.8 × 46.4 cm (46¾ × 18¼ in)

150 **Souvenir for Hockney**, 1974
Collage
29.8 × 35.2 cm (11⅜ × 13⅞ in)
Collection Peter Blake

151 **Souvenir for Gilbert & George**, 1974
Collage
45.1 × 24.7 cm (17¾ × 9¾ in)
Collection Peter Blake

Chapter 6

152 **Titania**, 1976–83
Oil on canvas
121.9 × 91.4 cm (48 × 36 in)
Courtesy of Michel Soskine Inc., New York

153 **Monarch of the Glen**, 1965–8
Acrylic on canvas
121.9 × 121.9 cm (48 × 48 in)
Collection Paul McCartney

154 **Tommies Playing Football**, 1984
Watercolour
16.2 × 20.3 cm (6⅜ × 8 in)
Private Collection

155 **Sylvia Beach and James Joyce in front of her bookshop 'Shakespeare & Company'**, 1983–4, from the portfolio *James Joyce in Paris/Series of nine etchings* 1983–1984
Etching on paper
Plate 18 × 13 cm (7 1/16 × 5⅛ in) on sheet 33 × 25 cm (13 × 9⅞ in)

156 **An Arab Woman**, 1981
Oil on canvas
16.5 × 11.4 cm (6½ × 4½ in)
Galerie Michael Haas

157 **Fille Arabe**, 1984
Watercolour
14 × 8.9 cm (5½ × 3½ in)
Private Collection

158 **Plate 69, Czech Woman. Photo by Professor Heinrich Maass, Berlin**, from *Nature and Culture, Woman* series, 1973–7
Pencil drawing
58.4 × 45.7 cm (23 × 18 in)

159 **Ophelia**, 1977–2002
Oil on board
139.1 × 96.8 cm (54¾ × 38⅛ in)
Private Collection

160 **Firoza**, 1973–4
Oil on canvas
13.7 × 10.2 cm (5⅜ × 4 in)

161 **Flora – Fairy Child**, 1977
Oil on hardboard
15.9 × 11.4 cm (6¼ × 4½ in)
Private Collection

162 **Titania**, 1977
Oil on board
32.4 × 26.7 cm (12¾ × 10½ in)

163 **Timon of Athens**, 1978, for Arden edition of the works of William Shakespeare, London: Methuen, 1979
Watercolour
23.3 × 18.4 cm (9⅛ × 7¼ in)

164 **Antony and Cleopatra**, 1979, for Arden edition of the works of William Shakespeare, London: Methuen, 1979
Watercolour
23.2 × 18.5 cm (9⅛ × 7¼ in)

165 **Poppy Fairy**, 1981–2
Oil on gold board
15.9 × 13.3 cm (6¼ × 5¼ in)

166 **Titania with Attendants**, 1986(unfinished)
Oil on canvas
36 × 31 cm (14⅛ × 12¼ in)
Private Collection, Japan

167 **Puck, Peasebottom, Cobweb, Moth and Mustardseed**, 1969–84
Acrylic on hardboard
100.3 × 77.8 cm (39½ × 30⅝ in)
Galerie Claude Bernard, Paris

168 **I may not be a Ruralist anymore, but this morning I saw a fairy in my garden in Chiswick**, 1982–91
Oil on canvas
126.4 × 100.3 cm (49⅜ × 39½ in)
Private Collection

169 **A Mad Tea Party at Watts Tower**, 1968–92
Oil on canvas
91.4 × 121.9 cm (36 × 48 in)
Private Collection

Illustrations to Lewis Carroll's *Through the Looking Glass*, 1972. Eight screenprints on paper:

170 **'And to show you I'm not proud, you may shake hands with me!'**
24.2 × 18 cm (9½ × 7 1/16 in)

171 **And the two knights sat and looked at each other for some time without speaking**
24.3 × 18.1 cm (9 9/16 × 7⅛ in)

172 **'But it isn't old!' Tweedledum cried**
24.2 × 18.1 cm (9⅜ × 7⅛ in)

173 **'It isn't manners for us to begin you know,' said the Rose**
24.1 × 17.8 cm (9½ × 7 in)

174 **For instance now, there's the King's messenger**
24.1 × 17.8 cm (9½ × 7 in)

175 **Just at this moment, somehow or other, they began to run**
24.3 × 18 cm (9 9/16 × 7 1/16 in)

176 **So Alice picked him up very gently**
24.5 × 18.1 cm (9⅝ × 7⅛ in)

177 **'Well, this is grand!' said Alice**
24.2 × 17.9 cm (9½ × 7 1/16 in)

178 **The Owl and the Pussycat**, 1981–3
Oil on hardboard
27.3 × 31.8 cm (10¾ × 12½ in)
Bristol City Museum and Art Gallery

179 **A Remembered Moment in Venice, California**, 1981–3
Oil on canvas
79.4 × 105.4 cm (31¼ × 41½ in)
Galerie Claude Bernard, Paris

180 **'The Meeting' or 'Have a Nice Day, Mr Hockney'**, 1981–3
Oil on canvas
99.2 × 124.4 cm (39 1/16 × 49 in)
Tate. Presented by the Friends of the Tate Gallery out of funds bequeathed by Miss Helen Arbuthnot 1983

181 **Montgomery Clift was a Twin**, 1981–3
Oil on canvas
88.9 × 68 cm (35 × 26 in)
Museo de Bellas Artes de Bilbao

182 **Montgomery Clift**, 1987
Postcards and enamel paint on wood
57.8 × 37.5 cm (22 3/4 × 14 3/4 in)

Chapter 7

183 **3D 6D 9D & 1/–**, 1986
Enamel paint on found wooden board
93 × 59.7 cm (36 5/8 × 23 1/2 in)
Jonathan Clark Fine Art

184 **The Second Real Target 25 yrs later**, 1986
Real wooden target with letters
41.9 × 32.1 cm (16 1/2 × 12 5/8 in)

185 **Noticeboard with Japanese Postcards**, 1987
Real noticeboard, postcards and drawing
93.2 × 62.9 cm (36 11/16 × 24 3/4 in)
Collection Peter Blake

186 **British Tourists in Japan**, 1988
Japanese tray, lead figures and tin aeroplane
30.2 × 45.6 cm (11 7/8 × 17 7/8 in)
Collection Peter Blake

187 **Elvis Presley**, 1987
Postcards and enamel on wood
37.5 × 21.9 cm (14 3/4 × 8 5/8 in)
Private Collection

188 **Déjà vu – 'A Boy'**, 1987–8
Oil on board
35.5 × 24.1 cm (14 × 9 1/2 in)
Private Collection, London

189 **Marilyn Monroe, Door (Miniature)**, 1990
Photographic collage on wooden door panel with brass fixtures
115.3 × 53 × 7.6 cm (45 3/8 × 21 1/8 × 3 in)

190 **Marilyn Monroe, Black**, 1990
Photographs and enamel paint on wood
55 × 36 cm (21 5/8 × 14 1/8 in)
Collection Muller-Goldberg

191 **Marilyn Monroe, White No. 1**, 1990
Oil, photograph, pencil on canvas over wood
29.2 × 22.2 cm (11 1/2 × 8 3/4 in)

192 **Exhibition of a Rhinoceros in Venice**, 1996
Oil on canvas
91.4 × 71.1 cm (36 × 28 in)
Collection of Elaine and Melvin Merians

193 **The Venuses' Outing to Weymouth**, 1994–2004
Oil on canvas
68.7 × 124.5 cm (27 × 49 in)
Collection Mr and Mrs Theodore B. Baum

194 **The National Gallery Madonna**, 1994–2000
Oil on canvas
121.9 × 91.4 cm (48 × 36 in)
Private Collection, courtesy Waddington Galleries

195 **Madonna of Venice Beach, No. 4**, 1995
Oil on panel
28 × 34 cm (11 × 13 3/8 in)
Private Collection

196 **Madonna of Venice Beach, No. 2**, 1995
Oil on board
25.5 × 23 cm (10 × 9 1/8 in)

197 **Madonna of Venice Beach, No. 3**, 1995
Oil on board
30 × 25 cm (11 7/8 × 9 7/8 in)

198 **Madonna of Venice Beach, No. 5**, 1995
Oil on board
15 × 14 cm (5 7/8 × 5 1/2 in)
Private Collection

199 **After 'Cup of Water and a Rose on a Plate' by Francisco de Zurbaran**, 1995–9
Oil on board
24.8 × 19.7 cm (9 3/4 × 7 3/4 in)

200 **The Deer Park (After Velásquez' *The Boar Hunt*). In Memory of Michael Andrews 1928–1995**, 1996
Oil on canvas
101.6 × 126.5 cm (40 × 49 3/4 in)
Waddington Galleries, London

201 **Sculpture Park**, 1981–3
Mixed media, with models by Chrissy Wilson
365.8 × 243.8 cm (144 × 96 in)
Private Collection

202 **Equestrian Act**, from *Life as a Circus*, 2003–4
Bronze
274.3 cm (108 in) high
Commissioned by Blackpool Council as part of The Great Promenade Show

203 **Four Man Up**, from *Life as a Circus*, 2003–4
Bronze
274.3 cm (108 in) high
Commissioned by Blackpool Council as part of The Great Promenade Show

204 **Shrine for Elvis (Black & White)**, 2003
Mementoes, postcards and mixed media on board
42 × 78 × 10.8 cm (16 1/2 × 30 3/4 × 4 1/4 in)
Collection Peter Blake

205 **Appropriating Jack Pierson 1. 'Appropriating'**, 2002
Collage
35.6 × 50.8 cm (14 × 20 in)
Collection Peter Blake

206 **Endless Column**, 2003
Bronze
Edition of 8 plus 1 artist's cast
146.7 × 21.3 × 21.3 cm (57 3/4 × 8 3/8 × 8 3/8 in)

207 **Among my Souvenirs: Snow White from Sgt. Pepper's Lonely Hearts Club Band**, 2003
Bronze
Edition of 8 plus 1 artist's cast
26 × 26.5 × 26.5 cm (10¼ × 10⅓ × 10⅓ in)

208 **Marcel Duchamp's World Tour: Playing Chess with Tracey**, 2003–5
Acrylic on canvas
91.4 × 121.9 cm (36 × 48 in)
Waddington Galleries, London

209 **Marcel Duchamp's World Tour: The Artists' Fancy Dress Ball**, 2004
Oil on canvas
127 × 96.5 cm (50 × 38 in)
Private Collection

210 **Marcel Duchamp's World Tour: He Meets the Congress of Unusual People with the Ringling Brothers and Barnum and Bailey (Combined) Circus Season – 1929**, 2004–5
Acrylic on canvas
3 panels of 102 cm × 102 cm (40⅛ × 40⅛ in)
David Roberts Collection

211 **In Homage to Collagists: Max Ernst**, 2000
Collage
41.3 × 33 cm (16¼ × 13 in)
Collection Peter Blake

In Homage to Collagists: Kurt Schwitters, 2000
Collage
40.3 × 31.8 cm (15⅞ × 12½ in)
Private Collection, Switzerland

In Homage to Collagists: Hannah Höch, 2000
Collage
41.3 × 33 cm (16¼ × 13 in)
Collection Peter Blake

212 **Marcel Duchamp's World Tour: He Meets the Spice Girls and Elvis**, 2000–05
Acrylic on canvas
121 × 91.4 cm (48 × 36 in)
Collection Peter Blake, courtesy Waddington Galleries, London

213 **The Twins in their Tea Garden**, 1991
Oil on board
127 × 101.6 cm (50 × 40 in)
Waddington Galleries, London

214 **The Twins in their Tea Garden (2nd version)**, 1995–9
Acrylic on canvas
132 × 106.7 cm (52 × 42 in)
Waddington Galleries, London

215 **The American Dream**, 1997–2003
Oil on hardboard with objects
63.5 × 48 cm (25 × 18⅞ in)
Laurence Graff

Postscript

216 **A Museum for Myself**, 1982
Mixed media
115.3 × 86 cm (45⅜ × 33⅞ in
Collection Peter Blake

Photo credits

Reproduced with kind permission of:

Peter Blake: plates 5, 7, 11, 17, 21, 25, 37, 39, 51, 60, 65–7, 73–4, 76, 81, 84–5, 88–9, 94, 118, 127, 129, 137, 139–43, 145, 147, 151, 153, 204, 216

Peter Blake/John Webb Photography: plates: 79, 117

Peter Blake/Prudence Cuming Associates Ltd: plate 15

The Bridgeman Art Library: plates 4, 45, 68, 77, 87, 125, 178

Trustees, Cecil Higgins Art Gallery, Bedford: plate 116

Christie's Images/Corbis: plate 38

Christie's Images Limited: plate 78

Courtauld Colour Slide Scheme, Courtauld Institute of Art, London: plates 46, 48–9, 63, 92, 152

Mike Fear: plates 16, 27, 30, 56, 161

Galerie Claude Bernard, Paris 29, 36, 62, 120–1, 152, 168

Steve Gorton: plates 10, 75

Independent Gallery, London: plates 31–2, 170–177

Marco Livingstone: plates 12, 13, 23, 28, 34, 42, 50, 54, 71, 82–3, 135, 149, 150, 155, 162, 195, 201

Jonathan Lynch: plates 202–3

Mary McCartney: frontispiece

Museo de Bellas Artes de Bilbao: plate 181

National Gallery of Australia, Canberra: plate 8

Prudence Cuming Associates Ltd, London: plate 22

Rheinisches Bildarchiv, Cologne: plates 6, 72

Royal College of Art Collection, London: plate 14, 133

Tate, London: plates 40–41, 47, 52, 59, 61, 64, 74, 126, 130, 180

Tullie House Museum and Art Gallery, Carlisle: plate 2

V&A images, Victoria and Albert Museum, London: plate 24

Waddington Galleries, London: plates 1, 18, 20, 26, 33, 53, 55, 57, 62, 69, 80, 86, 90, 93, 95-100, 104–105, 109–10, 114–5, 122, 124, 128, 131, 134, 138, 154, 157, 160, 163, 165, 169, 183, 185–6, 188–90, 192, 194, 197–99, 206, 207, 211, 213

Waddington Galleries/ Prudence Cuming Associates Ltd, London: plates 19, 35, 43–4, 70, 91, 101–3, 106–7, 111–2, 119, 136, 146, 156, 158–9, 166–7, 179, 182, 184, 187, 191, 193, 196, 200, 205, 208–10, 212, 214–5

Waddington Galleries/Rodney Todd White & Son, London: plates 108, 113, 123, 132, 164

Webb & Webb Design Ltd: plate 58

Whitworth Art Gallery, University of Manchester: plate 45

Index

Page numbers in italics refer to illustrations. Works by Peter Blake discussed and/or illustrated in the text follow in the Index of works.

Index of works

Note the titles are for works by Blake only. Titles of works by other artists, book and film titles are not included in this index. Page numbers in italics refer to illustrations.

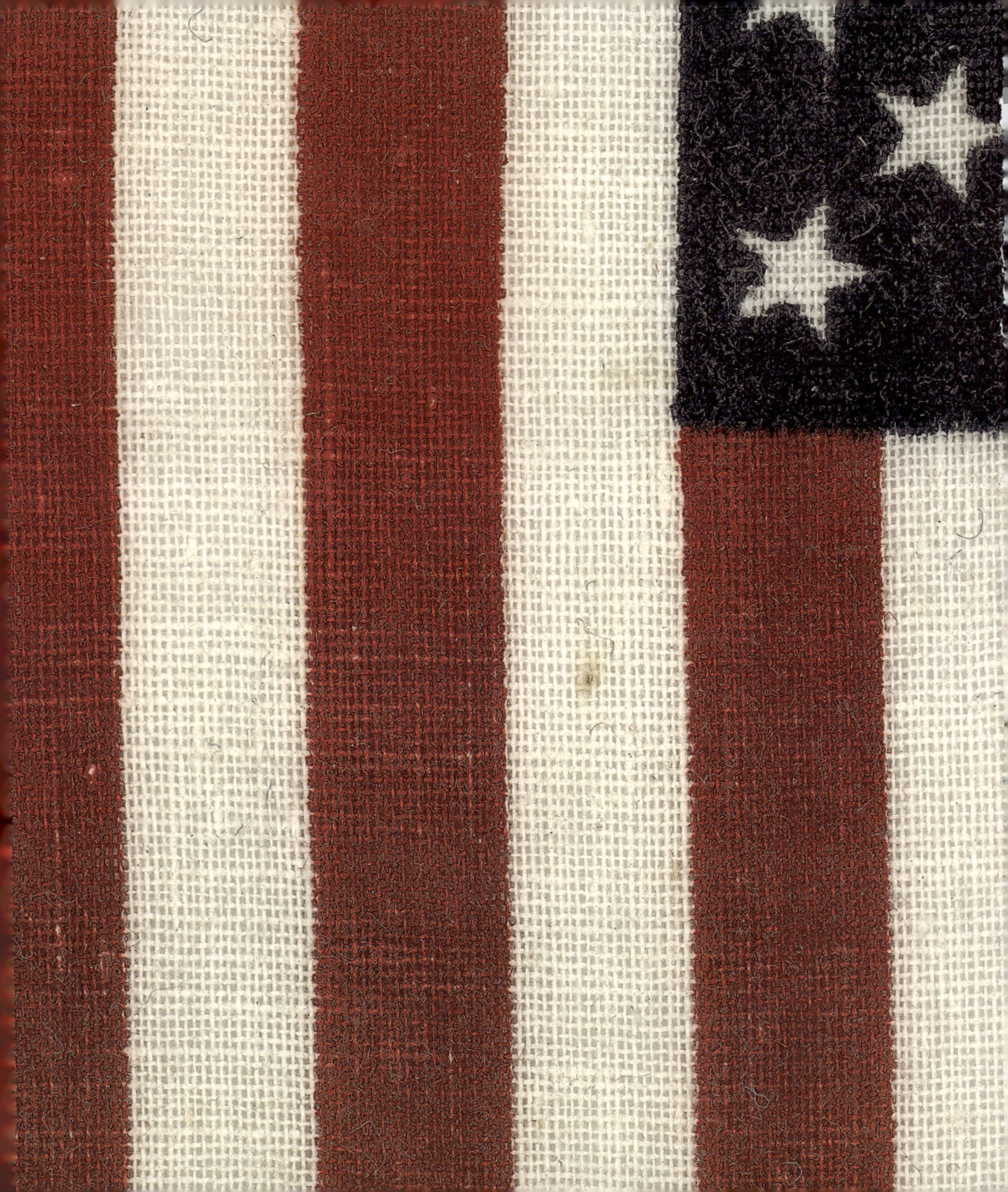